Unified IP Internetworking

Springer

Berlin
Heidelberg
New York
Barcelona
Hong Kong
London
Milan
Paris
Singapore
Tokyo

Dhiman D. Chowdhury

Unified
IP Internetworking

With 276 Figures and 61 Tables

 Springer

Dhiman D. Chowdhury
376 Kincora Ct.
San José, CA 95136
USA

Library of Congress Cataloging-in-Publication Data

Chowdhury, Dhiman Deb.
Unified IP internetworking / Dhiman Deb Chowdhury.
p. cm.
Includes bibliographical references and index.
ISBN 3540673709 (softcover)
1. Internetworking (Telecommunication) 2. TCP/IP (Computer network protocol)

TK5105.5 .C4878 2001
621.382–dc21   2001018347

ISBN 3-540-67370-9 Springer-Verlag Berlin Heidelberg New York

© Springer-Verlag Berlin Heidelberg New York
a member of BertelsmannSpringer Science+Business Media GmbH

http://www.springer.de

Springer-Verlag Berlin Heidelberg 2001
Printed in Germany

Typesetting: medio Technologies AG, Berlin
Cover design: KünkelLopka, Heidelberg

Printed on acid-free paper   SPIN: 10762882   33/3142 GF – 5 4 3 2 1 0

Dedicated to my family:

Alak, Santosh, Dipu, Goutam, Mukta, Shukla,
Shathi, Mitu, Moon, Mimi, Trisha, Shakkar, Tanya, Dristy, Mithila and Dhiraj

Preface

Earlier, in my *High-Speed LAN Technology Handbook*, I mentioned that the merger mania of data and the telecom industry had given birth to a new kind of network system, "converged networking". This new networking technique, although including multiservice features such as voice, video and data as the transport payload, is adapting a number of new technologies to meet the quality of service criteria that are the norm in the traditional telephone system. Voice transport in the traditional telephone network was acceptable to the user for its clarity of hearing perception as well as its reliability. While encapsulating the same real-time payload in the converged network, network managers and designers face the challenge of delivering quality, reliability and performance in comparison with the traditional telephone network. Although difficult, this is surely not absurd. The Voice over Internet Protocol (VoIP) transport mechanism has addressed it through the use of PSQM (Perpetual Speech Quality Measurement) and MOS (Mean Opinon Score). With these it is possible to imagine and realize the hearing and network perception of voice transport. Slowly, users are adapting the defined quality of a converged network rather than the quality of telecoms. For example, while a 100 ms "network delay" in a telephone network was not acceptable for voice transport, users now have accepted a 150 ms one-way network delay in the converged network so that hearing perception of the voice is not degraded.

The main protocol that guarantees real-time transport is the Internet Protocol, its quality of service (QoS) mechanism and other associated services; consequently, the converged network is termed the unified IP network. One perhaps can now understand that a simple IP header has more to offer, even with its 8-bit type of service field, a quite complex technology which was developed and became known as DiffServ. With this new technique, assured QoS is possible for various classes of traffic whether in real time or non-real time. Also, it has been proven that a defined policy can significantly improve the performance, reliability and management of a network with policy enable networking or PEN. The heart of PEN is the COPS (Common Open Policy Service) Protocol and its object carries all policy information to the network devices to ensure that the network is behaving in accordance with the rules defined.

Things may get quite complex when various routing protocols and techniques are concatenated in an intranet. Therefore, this book will serve as an ideal companion when dealing with the challenges posed by unified IP inter-networking. In the first chapter, you will learn about the realm of IP and its addressing techniques, IPv4 and IPv6, along with associated counterparts. While the text of Chap. 1 provides a solid understanding of IP and its service capability, Chap. 2 enhances your routing know-how by providing an in-depth discussion and practical examples of various routing techniques. This chapter can be considered as an entire routing handbook. It will firmly enhance your understanding and hands-on acuity of routing techniques, MPLS (Multi-Protocol Label Switching) and routing protocols such as RIP (Routing Information Protocol), OSPF (Open Short Path First) and BGP (Border Gateway Protocol). The design and careful approach of Chaps. 1 and 2 will certainly broaden your confidence about deploying a unified IP network. Chapter 3 then builds on this confidence to cover QoS, queuing and policy mechanisms and thereby enhance your skill. Now you will be able to deploy PEN in your own unified IP network. Finally, in Chap. 4 we consider real-time traffic, how to reduce the expanse of your telephony system, and bring voice transport to your already deployed intranet, as well as how to analyze real-time traffic behavior and choose a QoS/policy schema that fits your needs.

This book is unique; you will find it not only extremely useful, but also the best networking guide and companion.

Contents

1 IP Internetworking

1.1 Introduction

Networks are changing and growing more complex than the data networks of the 1990s. The Internet Protocol (IP) is shaping the future of unified network systems. With end-to-end QoS (Quality of Service) and policy based management mechanisms, today's networks are more intelligent and sophisticated. Now, more than ever before, the means of data and telecom transport unified into a single, more efficient, network infrastructure. Such a unified network has so far been extensively adaptable with IP internet working techniques. Building such a state-of-the-art intermediator requires an in-depth understanding of IP as well as the behaviour and constraints of various traffic. Another and most important aspect of such a complex network is how to manage it. In this regard, policy enable networking (PEN) provides significant enhancement, automation and intelligence than that of an SNMP-based network. Now traffic can be controlled and managed according to the requirements of the users.

While network administrators and engineers may be overwhelmed in obtaining an understanding of the protocols, services and traffic characteristics of IPv4 (Internet Protocol version 4) networks, and the necessity of IPv6 (Internet Protocol version 6) is adding even more complexity to the network infrastructure. As for any technology, the approach is quite clumsy given the fact that not many are well acquainted with it. The transition from IPv4 to IPv6, the coexistence of IPv6 and IPv4 networks, and the addressing and routing techniques of IPv6 all perhaps add more confusion to the user. On the one hand, there is a transition in the technology, and on the other hand there are various protocols alloyed in the network. Such an alloying is unavoidable and would be the norm for future unified network. Therefore, the stingiest methodology could be revamped to accommodate what the future network has to offer and be flexible. Technology is there to augment the network, which is driven by various business needs. Hence, some theoretical and practical considerations of unified internetworking, its protocol combinations and transport aggregates will make the reader more comfortable in facing this reality. In this chapter, you will begin studying IPv4, addressing techniques, NAT/PAT, VLSM, CIDR and IPv4 headers. Your in-depth understanding of IPv4 will help you to proceed further to IPv6, network transitioning, addressing and other details of this version. Understanding IP flavors is very important in successfully deploying multiservice transport in the intranet since IP is the most competent protocol yet to support unified internetworking.

So, let's get started ...

1.2 Internet Engineering Task Force (IETF)

It would perhaps be difficult to build today's Internet without the efforts of IETF and the people who contributed generously to such an organization. IETF is a large, open, international community of network designers, operators, vendors and researchers. It is open to any interested individual. IETF was formed officially by the IAB (Internet Advisory Board) in 1986 with Phill Gross as the first Chair, and has continuously supported the development of new protocols/technologies through RFC (Request For Comment). Engineers, scientists and vendors throughout the world participate in various IETF working groups, either by contributing to the development of new technology or by submitting a predefined protocol/technology for standardization. Although IETF does not enforce a protocol/technology as the requirement of NPI (New Product Introduction), RFC may be use to help develop a PRD (Product Requirement Document) which supports implementation of a protocol/technology that will interoperate with different vendors. Today, the RFC is considered a mandatory requirement for a product to implement a protocol/technology for which it is written.

The actual technical work is done in the IETF working groups. These working groups are organized by topic into several areas (e.g., routing, transport, security, etc.). Most of the work is handled via mailing lists, details of which are available at http://www.IETF.org/maillist.html. To discuss technology and protocol specifications etc., IETF holds meetings three times a year. A guide for new attendees at IETF meetings is available at http://www.IETF.org/tao.html.

The IETF working groups cover areas that are managed by area directors, or ADs. These ADs are members of the Internet Engineering Steering Group (IESG). Providing architectural oversight is the Internet Architecture Board (IAB). The IAB also adjudicates appeals when someone complains that the IESG has failed. The IAB and IESG are chartered by the Internet Society (ISOC) for these purposes. The General Area Director also serves as the Chair of the IESG and of the IETF, and is an ex-officio member of the IAB.

The Internet Assigned Numbers Authority (IANA) is the central coordinator for the assignment of unique parameter values for IPs. The IANA is chartered by the ISOC to act as the clearinghouse to assign and coordinate the use of numerous IP parameters.

1.3 Layer 3 Switch

LAN switches have evolved a great deal since their inception. They have become a fundamental building block of modern networks. The overwhelming demands for bandwidth, security, administration, complexity and microsegmentation have challenged the traditional approach of intranet infrastructure. To cope with such needs, layer 2 switches emerged in the early 1990s. The first use of the switch was as an alternative to a bridge, for interconnecting hubs. This is still a useful role for LAN switches, although they are now often replacing hubs, rather than interconnecting them.

Gradually enterprise networks became more complex and used a hierarchical concept in which multiple LANs are interconnected in a flexible arrangement. Therefore, to extend flexibility from one end of the intranet to the other, the need for the layer 3 switch became important. Since layer 3 (L3) switches are very significant in IP internetworking, providing an overview of the L3 switch will augment our perception of internetworking. This section does not detail the know-how but is written as a prelude for readers.

There are a number of very important features to consider on the L3 switch. They are:

- higher cost of router ports
- lower throughput, and
- higher latency.

Routers tend to be very complex to configure and manage. This is natural, given the power that they provide and the number of protocols that they need to support. A LAN switch, on the other hand, is very simple; in some cases all that the network manager needs to do is to plug it in. So in a smaller network it is often quite reasonable for a LAN switch alone to handle the movement of data between hubs. As a network becomes larger, it needs the broadcast handling capabilities that are provided through routing. However, it is important to differentiate between routers as a product and routing as a function. Routing can be provided on a number of platforms. In fact, one of the trends in current networking products is to combine routing and LAN switching in a single product. This is how the L3 switchlayer 3 switch emerges in the LAN. I have described LAN switching in depth in my currently available *High-Speed LAN Technology Handbook*. LAN switching is basically very high-speed, hardware-based bridging and has a number of features to offer including QoS. In the same way, L3 switching is basically very high-speed, low-latency hardware-based routing. It is flexible and has all the quality of a layer 2 switchlayer 2 switch as well being capable of providing routing and L3 QoS. Some forms of L3 switching use exactly the same protocols as traditional routing, while others use new protocols to make high-speed processing easier. Some L3 switches have the ability to distinguish between different types of applications, such as file transfers, Web browsing, and real-time applications using the TCP address. With the amount of client/server and real-time trafficreal-time traffic in backbones increasing, customers want differentiation of applications based on service priority levels. The new breed of intelligent LAN switches allows network managers to make more sophisticated decisions relating to such areas as traffic prioritization, bandwidth allocation, access controlaccess control and load balancing by dealing with more information from higher layers. An added benefit is that this increased intelligence enables the switch not only to optimize the use of the network itself but also to better manage network-based resources such as servers.

1.4 IP Addressing

Before we begin, if you plan to connect your enterprise to the Internet please ensure that you have received your legitimate IP address(es) from the Internet Network Information Center (InterNIC). You can do so by visiting http://www.internic.net for the USA. If you are outside the USA please contact your country's InterNIC, local ISP/CLECs or follow http://www.icann.org/registrars/accredited-list.html for a list of accredited registrars appropriate to your country. If you have received a legitimate IP address range which does not meet your demands of addressing, I recommend use of a reserved address from RFC1597. By enabling network address translation (NAT) firewall filtering in the router you can restrict legitimate addresses for use with the Internet only. We will describe one such technique in the following sections. Now, let's get going with the basics of IP, starting with IP addressing.

To understand IP addressing, it is important to be conversant with binary and binary-to-decimal conversion. Binary is represented with either zero (0) or one (1) and each of these values are known as bits. Eight of such bit combinations makes a "byte" which is also known as an octet. The value in one octet can range from 0 to 255 decimal or 00000000 to 11111111 in binary.

A simple way to convert binary octets to decimal is as shown in Table 1.1.

In the table, binary 11111111 is the decimal equivalent of 255. We achieve this value by adding all the decimal values as 128 + 64 + 32 + 16 + 8 + 4 + 2 + 1 = 255. Now, to examine this further, let's consider the binary octet of 11000001. Here the equivalent decimal value can be obtained by following the example of Table 1.2.

Table 1.1. An example of binary-to-decimal or decimal-to-binary conversion for 255

Binary							
1	1	1	1	1	1	1	1
128	64	32	16	8	4	2	1
Decimal number							

Table 1.2. The example of binary-to-decimal conversion for 11000001

Binary							
1	1	0	0	0	0	0	1
128	64						1
Decimal number							

Hence, from the table, the decimal value for binary 11000001 = 128 + 64 + 1 = 193.

Now that we are familiar with binary-to-decimal conversion, let's consider the following example of converting an entire IP address in decimal notation form to binary form, as in Table 1.3.

This example is very important for examining the IP addressing and subnetting scheme. As we progress further, you will find that this simple concept is extremely useful.

An IP address is a 32-bit unique identifier usually represented as four decimal values. Each decimal notation is one octet, which represents the range 0 to 255. Conceptually, each IP address has two parts, "netid" and "hostid", in which "netid" identifies a network and "hostid" identifies the node or host in that network. To support the needs of the Internet community, the IP address is divided into five different classes: Class A, Class B, Class C, Class D and Class E (see Fig. 1.1). Out of these five classes, Classes A, B and C are known as primary address classes. Given an IP address, its class can be determined from the three high-order bits. Each Class A address has an 8-bit network prefix with the highest order bit set to 0, and devotes 7 bits to netid and 24 bits to hostid. In the Class A addressing scheme, a maximum of $(2^7 - 2) = 126$ networks can be defined. The subtraction of 2 is required because the Class A network reserved 0.0.0.0 as the default route and 127.0.0.0 for the "loopback" function. It supports $2^{24} - 2 = 16,777,214$ hosts per network (see Table 1.4). In this case the subtraction of 2 is required for reason of all zeros (this network) and all ones (broadcast). The Class A address begins with 0xxx or 1 to 126 decimal. For example, 10.170.109.1 is a Class A address. Similarly,

IP address of 10.11.120.19			
10	11	120	19
00001010	00001011	01111000	00010011
Binary octets			

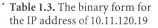

Table 1.3. The binary form for the IP address of 10.11.120.19

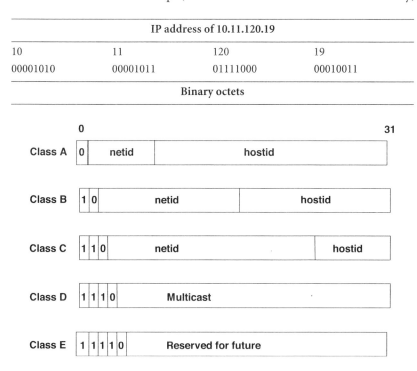

Fig. 1.1. Various IP address classes

Table 1.4. IP address classes and their attributes

IP address class	Purpose	High bit order	Address range	Network/ host bits	Max host
A	Large network size	0	1.0.0.0–126.0.0.0	7/24	16,777,214
B	Intermediate network size	10	128.1.0.0–191.254.0.0	14/16	65,534
C	Small network size	110	192.0.1.0–223.255.254.0	22/8	254
D	Group multicast	1110	224.0.0.0–239.255.255.255	Not for commercial use	N/A
E	Experimental	1111	240.0.0.0–254.255.255.255	N/A	N/A

a Class B network has a 16-bit network prefix with the two highest order bits set to 1 and 0. The hostid field is 16 bits long giving a total of $2^{16} - 2 = 65,534$ hosts per network. The network number for Class B is 16,384 (2^{14}) and it begins with 10xx or 128 to 191 decimal.

A Class C address has a 24-bit netid with the three highest order bits set to 1–1–0 and a 21-bit network number followed by an 8-bit hostid. Therefore, a maximum of $2^{21} = 2,097,152$ networks and $2^8 - 2 = 254$ hosts per network are supported in the Class C network. It begins with 110x or 192 to 223 decimal-decimal. A Class D address has the leading 4 bits set to 1–1–1–0 and is used for multicast. Protocols such as IGMP (Internet Group Membership Protocol) use it for multicast purposes. An example of a Class D address is 224.0.1.29. It starts at 224 and ends at 239. The Class E address is reserved for experimental purposes and the range is 240 to 254.

1.4.1 Subnetting

RFC 950 defines the procedure to support subnetting an IP network. It was introduced to overcome growth issues. As we know, all the hosts in a given network must have the same netid or network number. This attribute of IP addressing causes the following:

- Internet routing tables begin to grow.
- For a newly introduced network, a local administrator has always to request the network number from the network information center.

Both of these issues were addressed by introducing subnetting (Fig. 1.2). It solved the expanding routing table problem by ensuring that the intranet subnet structure is not visible from outside the organization. For example, in a given network the network routing interface of a router connected to the outside world advertises 134.10.0.0 whereas the intranet has a number of different networks within the organization.

Subnetting is a scheme that help network administrators split a network into smaller networks using the same network number assignment. It includes the following advantages:

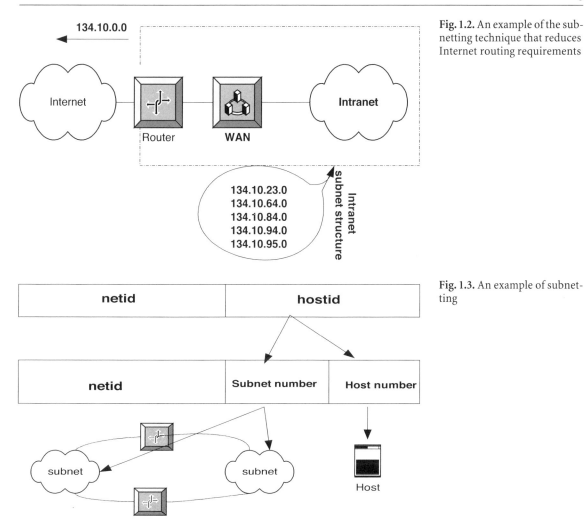

Fig. 1.2. An example of the subnetting technique that reduces Internet routing requirements

Fig. 1.3. An example of subnetting

- Simplified network administration.
- Restructuring and address allocation of the intranet without affecting the external networks.
- Improved security.

Simplified network administration occurs from the partition of a network into two or more routed segments. Each segmented network can be maintained independently and more efficiently. Resource allocation and addressing becomes more effective. For example, a corporation may want to allocate 15 stations for one department and 100 stations to another and yet wants each department to have separate networks for easy administration. Subnetting allows, for example, one Class C IP address to be used effectively in such a scenario. Since intranet subnetting is not visible to external networks, it indirectly improves the security of an organization's network. A subnetwork is obtained by splitting hostid into two: a subnet number and a host number field.

In Fig. 1.3, the router must understand that the hostid field of the IP address is to be treated specially – a part of it is used for the subnet number and another for the host number. Generally, this information is represented to the router as a subnet mask. Routers and hosts use the subnet mask to interpret the hostid field in such a way that they can determine how many bits are being used for subnetting.

1.4.1.1 Subnet Masking

In earlier sections, we learned that a 32-bit IP address is composed of 8-bit integers. Each of these 8-bit integers can be represented by decimal (0 to 255), binary (00000000 to 11111111) and hexadecimal (0 to FF) numbers. Therefore, an IP can be represented in either of the formats in Table 1.5, but the most common form of expression is decimal. The same applies to the case of a subnet mask. A network mask separates the number of network nodes from the host number. Although decimal form is a very common expression of subnet mask, in some networks hexadecimal is also used. Table 1.5 shows the most common decimal and hexadecimal forms of subnet mask related to various IP address classes.

Another form of subnet masking generally used by the software is binary (Fig. 1.4) The subnet mask is a 32-bit number whose value is formed by using the following rules:

- A binary one (1) in the subnet mask corresponds to the netid field and subnet number.
- All zeros (0) in the subnet mask correspond to the position of the host number.

Once you start doing subnet masking for "classful" IP addresses, you will encounter situations in which you need to convert between decimal numbers and their binary values. For example, consider an 8-bit binary number of 10101000 whose decimal value is needed to solve for an IP address. Binary numbers use base 2 or two's complement system whereas a decimal number uses the base 10 system. Table 1.6 shows the two's complements and their corresponding decimal values.

Now to get a binary value for the decimal number 144 (for example), we can add up the bit patterns. Therefore, $144 = 128 + 16 = 10000000 + 00010000 = 10010000$.

As you can see, we have simply done a logical AND operation (please refer to a digital electronics textbook to understand the AND operation). Similar-

Table 1.5. The representation of commonly used subnet mask for various IP address class

IP address class	Subnet mask (hexadecimal form)	Subnet mask (decimal form)
Class A	FF.0.0.0	255.0.0.0
Class B	FF.FF.0.0	255.255.0.0
Class C	FF.FF.FF.0	255.255.255.0

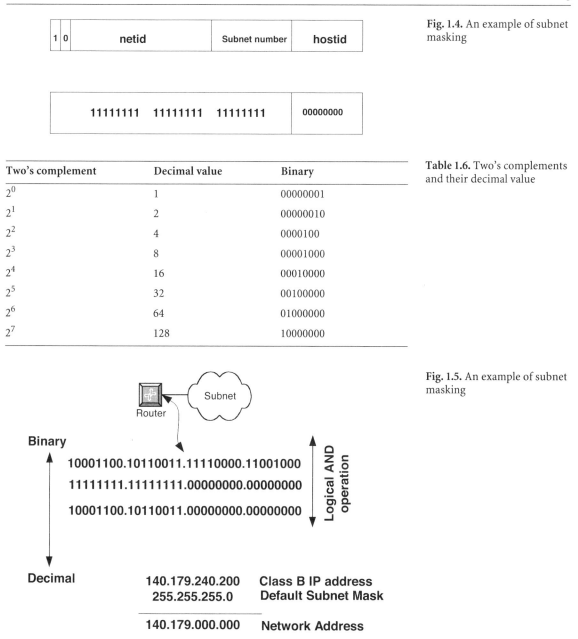

| 1 | 0 | netid | Subnet number | hostid |

Fig. 1.4. An example of subnet masking

| 11111111 11111111 11111111 | 00000000 |

Two's complement	Decimal value	Binary
2^0	1	00000001
2^1	2	00000010
2^2	4	0000100
2^3	8	00001000
2^4	16	00010000
2^5	32	00100000
2^6	64	01000000
2^7	128	10000000

Table 1.6. Two's complements and their decimal value

Fig. 1.5. An example of subnet masking

Subnet

Router

Binary

Logical AND operation

10001100.10110011.11110000.11001000

11111111.11111111.00000000.00000000

10001100.10110011.00000000.00000000

Decimal

140.179.240.200   **Class B IP address**
255.255.255.0   **Default Subnet Mask**

140.179.000.000   **Network Address**

ly, to identify the network and host number a subnet mask is applied to an IP address by performing a bitwise logical AND operation. Let's consider the following example (Fig. 1.5) of doing subnet masking to an IP address by applying a Class B default subnet mask. Here, we have an IP address of 140.179.240.200 and we are going to apply the Class B default subnet mask, which is 255.255.0.0. Hence, the binary value of the IP address and subnet mask is as shown in Tables 1.7–1.9.

	Subnet mask	Subnets	Hosts
Table 1.7. The subnet mask, subnet numbers and hosts for the Class A IP address	255.192.0.0	2	4,194,302
	255.224.0.0	6	2,097,150
	255.240.0.0	14	1,048,574
	255.248.0.0	30	524,286
	255.252.0.0	62	262,142
	255.254.0.0	126	131,070
	255.255.0.0	254	65,536
	255.255.128.0	510	32,766
	255.255.192.0	1022	16,382
	255.255.224.0	2046	8190
	255.255.240.0	4094	4094
	255.255.248.0	8190	2046
	255.255.252.0	16,382	1022
	255.255.254.0	32,766	510
	255.255.255.0	65,536	254
	255.255.255.128	131,070	126
	255.255.255.192	262,142	62
	255.255.255.224	524,286	30
	255.255.255.240	1,048,574	14
	255.255.255.248	2,097,150	6
	255.255.255.252	4,194,302	2

	Subnet mask	Subnets	Hosts
Table 1.8. The subnet mask, subnets and hosts for a Class B IP address	255.255.192.0	2	16,382
	255.255.224.0	6	8190
	255.255.240.0	14	4094
	255.255.248.0	30	2046
	255.255.252.0	62	1022
	255.255.254.0	126	510
	255.255.255.0	254	254
	255.255.255.128	510	126
	255.255.255.192	1022	62
	255.255.255.224	2046	30
	255.255.255.240	4096	14
	255.255.255.248	8190	6
	255.255.255.252	16,382	2

Subnet mask	Subnets	Hosts
255.255.255.192	2	62
255.255.255.224	6	30
255.255.255.240	14	14
255.255.255.248	30	6
255.255.255.252	62	2

Table 1.9. Subnet mask, subnets and hosts for a Class C IP address

1.4.2 Variable Length Subnet Mask (VLSM)

VLSM is a means of allocating IP a ddressing resources to subnets according to their individual need rather than some general network-wide rule. Of the IP routing protocols, OSPF, Dual IS–IS, BGP-4, and EIGRP support "classless" or VLSM routes.

The basic concept of VLSM is to provide more efficient use of available addresses by dividing subnets into variable size multiple subnets. This ensures that an adequate number of hosts are allocated per subnet. All networks requesting additional IP space will be analyzed and designed with VLSM in mind. VLSM allows address blocks to be tailored to your needs. In this way, you can take advantage of subnetting your network to isolate collision domains without losing a significant number of IP addresses. VLSM takes advantage of classless routing algorithms.

Classless algorithms carry information regarding the net mask and do not depend upon the "Class" of an IP address block. This allows the first and last subnet ranges where "classfull" routing forbids their use. An example of VLSM IP subnet design is shown in Tables 1.10 and 1.11 and Fig. 1.6.

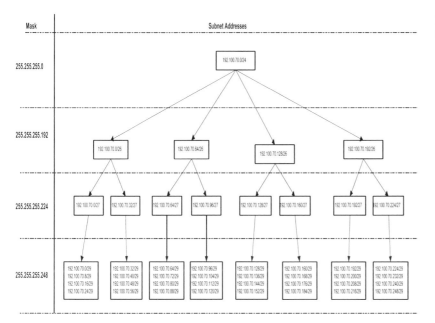

Fig. 1.6. An example of VLSM subnet design

Table 1.10. IP subnet calculation and design

IP class:	C	IP address:	192.100.70.0
Mask1 bits:	2	Subnet Mask1:	255.255.255.192
Mask2 bits:	3	Subnet Mask2:	255.255.255.224
Mask3 bits:	5	Subnet Mask3:	255.255.255.248

Table 1.11. Subnets for VLSM

Subnet address	Hosts from	Hosts to	Broadcast address
192.100.70.0	192.100.70.1	192.100.70.62	192.100.70.63
192.100.70.0	192.100.70.1	192.100.70.30	192.100.70.31
192.100.70.0	192.100.70.1	192.100.70.6	192.100.70.7
192.100.70.8	192.100.70.9	192.100.70.14	192.100.70.15
192.100.70.16	192.100.70.17	192.100.70.22	192.100.70.23
192.100.70.24	192.100.70.25	192.100.70.30	192.100.70.31
192.100.70.32	192.100.70.33	192.100.70.62	192.100.70.63
192.100.70.32	192.100.70.33	192.100.70.38	192.100.70.39
192.100.70.40	192.100.70.41	192.100.70.46	192.100.70.47
192.100.70.48	192.100.70.49	192.100.70.54	192.100.70.55
192.100.70.56	192.100.70.57	192.100.70.62	192.100.70.63
192.100.70.64	192.100.70.65	192.100.70.126	192.100.70.127
192.100.70.64	192.100.70.65	192.100.70.94	192.100.70.95
192.100.70.64	192.100.70.65	192.100.70.70	192.100.70.71
192.100.70.72	192.100.70.73	192.100.70.78	192.100.70.79
192.100.70.80	192.100.70.81	192.100.70.86	192.100.70.87
192.100.70.88	192.100.70.89	192.100.70.94	192.100.70.95
192.100.70.96	192.100.70.97	192.100.70.126	192.100.70.127
192.100.70.96	192.100.70.97	192.100.70.102	192.100.70.103
192.100.70.104	192.100.70.105	192.100.70.110	192.100.70.111
192.100.70.112	192.100.70.113	192.100.70.118	192.100.70.119
192.100.70.120	192.100.70.121	192.100.70.126	192.100.70.127
192.100.70.128	192.100.70.129	192.100.70.190	192.100.70.191
192.100.70.128	192.100.70.129	192.100.70.158	192.100.70.159
192.100.70.128	192.100.70.129	192.100.70.134	192.100.70.135
192.100.70.136	192.100.70.137	192.100.70.142	192.100.70.143
192.100.70.144	192.100.70.145	192.100.70.150	192.100.70.151
192.100.70.152	192.100.70.153	192.100.70.158	192.100.70.159
192.100.70.160	192.100.70.161	192.100.70.190	192.100.70.191
192.100.70.160	192.100.70.161	192.100.70.166	192.100.70.167
192.100.70.168	192.100.70.169	192.100.70.174	192.100.70.175

Subnet address	Hosts from	Hosts to	Broadcast address
192.100.70.176	192.100.70.177	192.100.70.182	192.100.70.183
192.100.70.184	192.100.70.185	192.100.70.190	192.100.70.191
192.100.70.192	192.100.70.193	192.100.70.254	192.100.70.255
192.100.70.192	192.100.70.193	192.100.70.222	192.100.70.223
192.100.70.192	192.100.70.193	192.100.70.198	192.100.70.199
192.100.70.200	192.100.70.201	192.100.70.206	192.100.70.207
192.100.70.208	192.100.70.209	192.100.70.214	192.100.70.215
192.100.70.216	192.100.70.217	192.100.70.222	192.100.70.223
192.100.70.224	192.100.70.225	192.100.70.254	192.100.70.255
192.100.70.224	192.100.70.225	192.100.70.230	192.100.70.231
192.100.70.232	192.100.70.233	192.100.70.238	192.100.70.239
192.100.70.240	192.100.70.241	192.100.70.246	192.100.70.247
192.100.70.248	192.100.70.249	192.100.70.254	192.100.70.255

Table 1.11 (continued). Subnets for VLSM

1.4.3 Classless Interdomain Routing (CIDR)

Now that we understand the principles of IP subnetting, we should explore the concept of CIDR. It was invented to keep the Internet from running out of addresses. It is documented in RFC 1517 to 1520. CIDR is an alternative method for more efficient allocation of IP addresses than the old Class A, B and C address scheme. Instead of IP networks being limited to prefixes of 8, 16 or 24 bits (Class A, Class B and Class C networks respectively) CIDR allows network of prefixes 13 to 27. CIDR addresses look the same as normal IP addresses except they are followed by a slash and then a number denoting the bits assigned to the network. For example, 192.168.1.0/27 denotes an IP network that can address up to 2^5 or 32 hosts (the first 27 bits are for the network with the last 5 bits assigning the host). CIDR functions in much the same way as the phone system does. A high-level backbone network node only looks at the area code information and then routes the packet to the specific backbone node responsible for that area code. The receiving node then looks at the phone number prefix and routes the packet to the subnetwork nodes responsible for that prefix and so on. So each router needs only to know what networks it is serving and the prefixes for those routes. CIDR was introduced as an effective method to stem the tide of IP address as well as routing table overflow. With so many networks connected to the Internet, routers were having trouble keeping up. There are 126 Class A networks that could include up to 16,777,214 hosts each, plus 65,000 Class B networks that could include up to 65,534 hosts each, plus over 2 million Class C networks that could include up to 254 hosts each. The maximum theoretical size of routing tables on today's routers is only 60,000. If the Internet had stayed with the class system of IPv4 the global routing tables would have been exceeded sometime in 1994. With CIDR's ability to route packets to general network address space and not have to address each node, large swaths of address space can be handled easily with a few simple lines in routing tables thus minimizing table size and complexity.

Two main reasons that drove the need for the CIDR method are:

1. Inefficient use of IP address and possibility of running out of IP address space.
2. Inability to manage growing routing table.

In the CIDR concept, the class system is being replaced with a prefix anywhere from 13 to 27 bits as a generalized network prefix. Thus, blocks of addresses can be assigned for networks as small as 32 hosts up to networks with over 500,000 hosts. Hence, a new IP address may look like this: 192.68.10.48/25. It means that the first 25 bits are used to identify the network while the remaining 7 bits are used to identify the host.

Using CIDR helps to solve the two major Internet growth problems:

1. **Class B exhaustion:** CIDR allows more efficient use of multiple Class C addresses to provide Internet users and service providers with more appropriate address space allocation.
2. **Routing table explosion:** CIDR aggregates multiple routes into a single advertisement by limiting the expansion of the ever-expanding route advertisements.

1.4.3.1 The Future

Is CIDR the golden bullet? No. Even if all the ISPs in the world moved over to CIDR we would still run out of address space. IPv6 will increase this address space by expanding bit size from 32 to 128 and use a hierarchical routing scheme. This will allow for more rational assignment of addresses. CIDR blocks could be aggregated on the basis of geographical location or ISP assignment, which enables routers to determine where a network is located by its address. But this will not be until the world decides to adopt IPv6.

1.4.3.2 Subnetting and CIDR Blocks

A CIDR block is simply another term for a subnet. There is no need to worry about the distinction between class-based routing and classless routing; class-based routing is becoming obsolete anyway.

The notation for a CIDR block is an address followed by "/nn", where "nn" is the number of bits of ones in the subnet mask. It is a shorthand way of specifying the start and end of a subnet.

As an example, "128.196.128.131/24" means that subnet which contains address 128.196.128.131 and whose subnet mask begins with 24 ones (the rest are zeros). By convention it is usually the all-zero address which is specified (e.g., "128.196.128.0/24" unlike the example above), but any address in the block along with the subnet mask completely defines the block. CIDR block notation does not allow for non-contiguous subnet masks such as 255.255.128.255. It assumes that once the first zero is reached in a subnet mask, all remaining bits are zero. This is probably not a drawback that anyone will ever care about; although non-contiguous masks are legal, I have never seen one actually in use anywhere.

With a router that supports CIDR, a route advertisement would be made which contains both the starting address (193.21.4.0) and the CIDR mask 255.255.248.0. This tells the network that there are eight contiguous network addresses starting at 193.21.4.0 and ending at 193.21.11.0. This facility can equally be applied to any type of network address, but is most commonly used with Class C addresses (see Table 1.12).

The CIDR (sometimes called the supernet) mask is calculated in much the same way as with a normal subnet mask (Table 1.13). The mask represents the total number of bits which relate to network addresses – the bits on the left-hand side of the address. In the example above, 255.255.248.0 used as a CIDR mask on a Class C address exposes 11 bits of address which would normally be regarded as part of the network address.

One can think of the bits in the CIDR mask as indicating the amount of address which is common to all of the subnetworks within the address range – the common part of the address which does not change. The bits which overlap (those between the CIDR mask and the network mask) indicate the parts of the address which are used to "describe" the subnetworks; these addresses change. In the example in Table 1.14, where the CIDR advertisement is for only eight contiguous network addresses, there are 3 bits of network address which have been exposed: $2^3 = 8$.

CIDR block prefix	Equivalent Class C	Host address (hosts)
/27	1/8 of a Class C	32
/26	1/4 of a Class C	64
/25	1/2 of a Class C	128
/24	1 Class C	256
/23	2 Class C	512
/22	4 Class C	1024
/21	8 Class C	2048
/20	16 Class C	4096
/19	32 Class C	8192
/18	64 Class C	16,384
/17	128 Class C	32,768
/16	256 Class C = 1 Class B	65,536
/15	512 Class C = 2 Class B	131,072
/14	1024 Class C = 4 Class B	262,144
/13	2048 Class C = 8 Class B	524,288

Table 1.12. CIDR block prefix and equivalent Class C address

Class	Address range	Subnet	CIDR (supernet) mask
C	193.21.40 to 193.21.11.0	255.255.255.0 (/24)	255.255.248.0

Table 1.13. An example of CIDR mask

Network mask	CIDR mask
255.255.255.0	255.255.248.0
11111111.11111111.11111111.00000000	11111111.11111111.11111000.00000000

To summarize, the number of networks advertised (A) using CIDR is calculated by taking the number of bits in the CIDR mask (C) minus the number of bits in the original network mask (N) and using that number as the power factor:

$$A = 2^{(N - C)}$$

1.4.3.3 Requirements for CIDR

For routers to be able to support CIDR, they must implement a routing protocol capable of advertising masks as well as addresses. This is one of the driving forces behind producing RIPv2, as the original version of RIP did not support this. OSPF (Open Shortest Path First) can also be used to carry mask information. The other main issue is that the original router software was often written deliberately not to allow users to enter a mask which was less than the network mask. Routing code and lookup tables need to be modified to ensure that they can generate and respond correctly to supernet masks.

There are some other issues which manufacturers need to be aware of, mainly for avoiding loops. But generally, implementation of CIDR has gone a very long way to increase the manageability of Internet address space and the reliability of backbone routers which have to support much fewer routes than before. CIDR has helped the Internet community by getting round the problems of having to advertise routes for multiple IP network addresses. Basically, CIDR allows the router to aggregate multiple contiguous network addresses into a single route advertisement. In the example above, the concentrating router is using CIDR to group the individual addresses together before advertising to the Internet. If the service provider has supplied the three private networks with contiguous blocks of addresses, then the route advertisement would only have to contain a single address because CIDR could be used to aggregate all 24 network addresses.

The only real limitation with CIDR is if you want to change ISP. Because CIDR doles out address space in large chunks to the ISP and not to the end networks directly, if you want to change ISP you have to change all the addresses on all the computers on your network. It is like changing your phone number when you move to a new city. Because phone numbers are tied to local exchanges you cannot have the same number in Chicago as in Denver. There are tricks that network administrators can use to circumvent this limitation but it requires a little more overhead and foresight on the administrator's part.

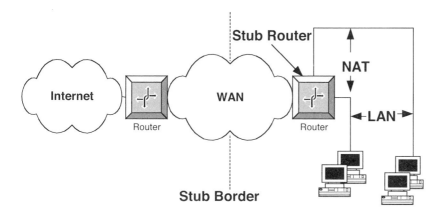

Fig. 1.7. Typical NAT implementation

1.5 NAT (Network Address Translation)

The NAT concept is a part of the corporate firewall, which generally provides address translation between a network with a legitimate IP address and a network with an illegitimate IP address. To overcome the shortage of legitimate IP addresses assigned by the network information center, NAT deployment is extremely significant until IPv6 becomes widely accepted by the industry. RFC 1631 defines NAT for use in the IPv4 network environment. It is generally implemented in a router and only the stub border router can be configured.

To describe it simply, NAT operates in a router connecting two networks together; one with illegitimate addresses and the other with legitimate IP addresses. The translation works in conjunction with routing, so the customer can enable NAT translation when wishing to use address translation for Internet access.

Typical NAT implementation (Fig. 1.7) is capable of providing the following operations:

- static address mapping
- dynamic address translation
- port address translation (PAT).

1.5.1 Static Address Mapping

Static translation is used when a one-to-one mapping is created between inside and outside addresses (Fig. 1.8). Some implementations support both IP address and protocol port numbers. This translation can include pools for both inside and outside addresses as long as there is an equal number on both sides.

The static address mapping remains in the router's address translation table until deleted from the configuration.

Fig. 1.8. A typical example of one-to-one mapping

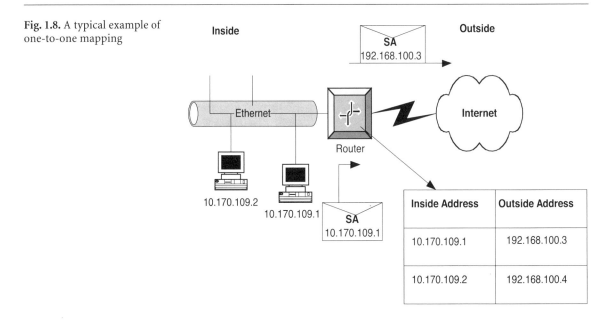

1.5.2 Dynamic Address Translation

Dynamic translation creates a one-to-many, many-to-many or many-to-one mapping between inside and outside addresses. These mappings are created from a pool of IP addresses and remain in the table until cleared or the entry times out.

In one-to-many mapping, one inside address maps to one of a pool of outside addresses or vice versa. The address chosen is the next available address in the pool. Similarly, many-to-many mapping translates one address from a pool of inside addresses to one address from a pool of outside addresses or vice versa. In many-to-one mapping, the router translates many inside addresses into one address. This requires a port range to be supplied in order to provide enough connection.

1.5.3 Port Address Translation (PAT)

The user may choose to conserve addresses in a global (outside) address pool by allowing source ports in TCP or UDP to be translated. Inside addresses will then map to the same outside address with port translation. For example, a station with inside address 10.170.109.1 will map to an outside address 192.168.100.3 at port 512. The rest of the station will follow the same address mapping except the port number would be different. PAT typically works with TCP and UDP suites of protocols only.

1.6 IPv4

The IP we have talked about so far is also known as IPv4. The purpose of the IP is to transport datagrams through an interconnected set of networks. As defined in RFC 791, IP passes the payload from one Internet module to another until it reaches its destination. This payload is routed from one Internet module to another via an individual network known as subnet based on the interpretation of Internet address or IP address. RFC 791 also suggests the possibility of fragmentation which requires that the packet size is bigger than the given maximum transmission unit (MTU) in a link. During transmission of an IP datagram from one local net to another it passes through an important IP module named the gateway (Fig. 1.9). This module implements IP routing and other Internet control information.

During the transmission of the IP datagram, IP uses a header which carries some control information. IP is designed for use in interconnected systems of packet-switched computer communication networks. It provides the means of transmitting blocks of datagrams from source to destination. It was invented by the Department of Defense (DoD) to provide the means for universal communication between different vendor devices and specified in RFC 791. IP implements two basic functions: addressing and fragmentation. An Internet module uses the addresses carried in the packet and forward IP encapsulated datagrams to their destinations. The selection of a path to transmit such packets is called routing. A mechanism in the switch can either listen to the network for MTU or use a preconfigured MTU size to transmit IP encapsulated datagrams. IP does not provide a reliable communications facility and depends on TCP to deliver such a mechanism. IP works as an integral part of TCP/IP or UDP /IP suites. It interfaces on one side to the higher level protocols such as Telnet or FTP and on the other side to the underlying layer 2 protocols such as Token Ring or Ethernet.

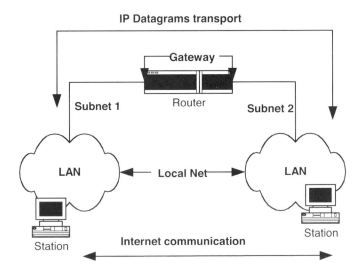

Fig. 1.9. IP datagram transport through the gateway

Since QoS is a vast subject, many have defined it in a different manner; some start the discussion on queuing and others start directly from the core. However, since we will be discussing the IP datagram, its structure and TOS (Type of Service) field elaborately in Chap. 3, let us focus here on some of the common protocols used in IPv4 networks, such as ARP, RARP and BOOTP.

1.6.1 ARP (Address Resolution Protocol)

One of the questions many beginners may ask is: "how do we get from an IP address to a datalink address?". To understand the answer to this question we have to examine the Fig. 1.10.

A system must associate an IP address with its respective MAC (Media Access Control) address. As shown in Fig. 1.10, two ways a node can perform such an association is through ARP or RARP (Reverse Address Resolution Protocol). The ARP as specified in RFC 826 allows a host to find the physical address of a target host on the same network, if the target's IP address is known.

As defined in RFC 826, ARP is used if a host wants to send an IP datagram, but does not know the corresponding Ethernet address of the destination. The source, therefore, will send an ARP request, generally a broadcast to every node in the network (Fig. 1.11). The destination MAC address of the ARP packet would be 0xFFFFFF and the type field value of the packet would be 0x0806.

An ARP packet consists of the fields as depicted in Fig. 1.12.

The first field is a 16-bit field known as the hardware type field. This field can indicate any value depending on the underlying technology in use. Table 1.15 describes the respective hardware type field values.

The next field is the protocol type field, a 16-bit field. For IP the value of this field is 0x800. The following field is the hardware address length, an 8-bit field which indicates the length of hardware address in bytes.

Fig. 1.10. Explanation of exchange of IP to MAC and MAC to IP address information

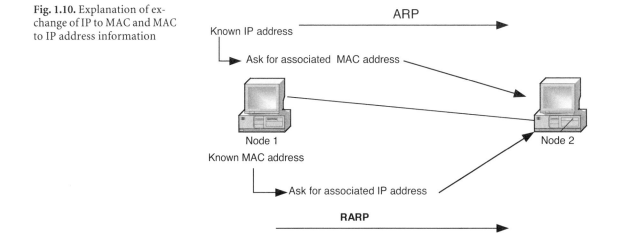

ARP Broadcast

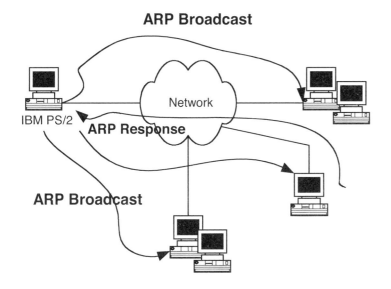

Fig. 1.11. ARP broadcast and response

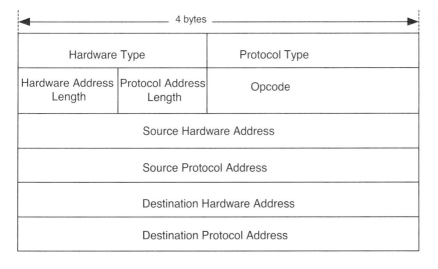

Fig. 1.12. ARP packet format

The protocol address length field is an 8-bit field which indicates the length of the protocol address in bytes.

The next field is a 16-bit "Opcode" field. The value of this field can be within any of the values given in Table 1.16.

The next fields (the source hardware address, source protocol address, destination hardware address and destination protocol address fields) are variable length fields. Generally the destination hardware address field in the ARP request is left blank, which is inserted by the destination node during the ARP reply.

Value	Description
	Table 1.15. The values of the hardware type field

Table 1.15. The values of the hardware type field

Value	Description
1	Ethernet
2	Experimental Ethernet
3	Amateur Radio AX.25
4	Proteon ProNet Token Ring
5	Chaos
6	IEEE 802
7	ARCNET
8	Hyperchannel
9	Lanstar
10	Autonet Short Address
11	Localtalk
12	LocalNet (IBM PCNet or SYTEK LocalNET)
13	Ultra Link
14	SMDS
15	Frame Relay
16	ATM
17	HDLC
18	Fiber Channel
19	ATM
20	Serial Line
21	ATM
22	MIL-STD-188–220
23	Metricom
24	IEEE 1394
25	MAPOS
26	Twinaxial
27	EUI-64
28	HIPARP
29	IP and ARP over ISO 7816–3
30	ARPSec

Value	Description	Reference
1	Request	RFC 826
2	Reply	RFC 826, RFC 1868
3	Request Reverse	RFC 903
4	Reply Reverse	RFC 903
5	DRARP Request	RFC 1931
6	DRARP Reply	RFC 1931
7	DRARP Error	RFC 1931
8	InARP Request	RFC 1293
9	InARP Reply	RFC 1293
10	ARP NAK	RFC 1577
11	MARS Request	
12	MARS Multi	
13	MARS Mserv	
14	MARS Join	
15	MARS Leave	
16	MARS NAK	
17	MARS Unserv	
18	MARS SJoin	
19	MARS SLeave	
20	MARS Gouplist Request	
21	MARS Grouplist Reply	
22	MARS Redirect Map	
23	MAPOS UNARP	

Table 1.16. The values of the "Opcode" field of an ARP packet

1.6.1.1 ARP Helper Address

Section 3.1 of RFC 1433 defines the ARP helper address. A host or router that implements Directed ARP procedures associates an ARP helper address with each routing table entry. If the host or router has been configured to resolve the next-hop IP address IP to its associated link level address (or to resolve the destination IP address, if the next-hop IP address is NULL), the associated ARP helper address is NULL. Otherwise, the ARP helper address is the IP address of the router that provided the routing information indicating that the next-hop address was on the same link level network as the associated physical interface.

1.6.1.2 Directed ARP

Section 2 of RFC 1433 defines Directed ARP, a procedure which enables a router advertising that an IP address is on a shared link level network also to aid in resolving the IP address to its associated link level address. By removing address resolution constraints, Directed ARP enables dynamic routing protocols such as BGP and OSPF to advertise and use routing information that leads to next-hop addresses on "foreign" IP networks. In addition, Directed ARP enables routers to advertise (via Internet Control Message Protocol (ICMP) Redirects) next-hop addresses that are "foreign" to hosts, since the hosts can use Directed ARP to resolve the "foreign" next-hop addresses.

1.6.2 RARP (Reverse Address Resolution Protocol)

As defined in RFC 903, RARP is a datalink layer protocol that allows an IP address to be obtained if the link address is known. Such a protocol is useful if a station does not include a hard drive or other means of suitable storage. RARP requires one or more servers to maintain a database of mapping from a hardware address to a protocol address and respond to the client's request for the stated purpose.

ARP and RARP operation should not be confused. While ARP assumes that every host knows the mapping between its own hardware address and a protocol address, RARP requires a server to maintain mapping databases. RARP and ARP have the same packet format as depicted in Fig. 1.13.

The RARP packet will carry an Ethertype value of 0x8035 in its MAC header, which distinguishes it from ARP. Like an ARP packet the first field of an RARP packet is the hardware type field, a 16-bit field that may have any value as defined in Table 1.17.

The 16-bit protocol type field has the same value as in ARP (i.e., 0x800). All other fields are similar to those specified in ARP except "Opcode" (Table 1.18).

Fig. 1.13. The RARP packet format, which is the same as the ARP packet format

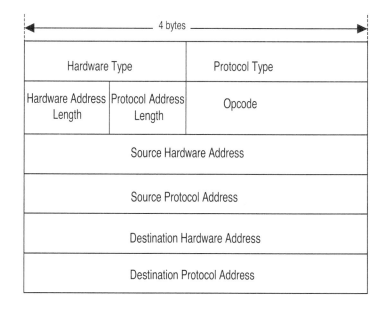

Value	Description
1	Ethernet
2	Experimental Ethernet
3	Amateur Radio AX.25
4	Proteon ProNet Token Ring
5	Chaos
6	IEEE 802
7	ARCNET
8	Hyperchannel
9	Lanstar
10	Autonet Short Address
11	Localtalk
12	LocalNet (IBM PCNet or SYTEK LocalNET)
13	Ultra Link
14	SMDS
15	Frame Relay
16	ATM
17	HDLC
18	Fiber Channel
19	ATM
20	Serial Line
21	ATM
22	MIL-STD-188–220
23	Metricom
24	IEEE 1394
25	MAPOS
26	Twinaxial
27	EUI-64
28	HIPARP

Table 1.17. Hardware type field value and its description of an RARP packet

Value	Description	Reference
3	Request Reverse	RFC 903
4	Reply Reverse	RFC 903

Table 1.18. RARP "Opcode" field value

1.6.3 BOOTP

RFC 951 defines the BOOTSTRP Protocol (BOOTP), which allows a diskless station to discover its own IP address. The BOOTP operation consist of two phases: in the first phase, address determination and the bootfile selection function occur; and in the second phase, file transfer occurs using TFTP (Trivial File Transfer Protocol).

One major advantage of BOOTP can be understood by considering the following network scenario (Fig. 1.14). The site of company ABC has at least four to five multistoried buildings, and every floor of each building has more than 10 to 15 printers. Printers can be moved from one department to another, and these printers are BOOTP-capable Hewlett Packard or similar printers. If each of these printers were configured with a static IP address, it would be a nightmare for the technician as well as network managers. One way to reduce such a headache is to use BOOTP. Assuming that such a company will have powerful minicomputers or servers capable of providing BOOTP support, all that has to be done is to get a self-test result from the printers and configure the BOOTtab file in the server. Once the hardware address of the printer is inserted in this file, it does not matter if that printer is moved from one building to another – the respective server will allocate the IP address accordingly. This reduces the extra overhead for the network managers.

As defined in RFC 951, only a single packet exchange is performed and timeouts are used to retransmit a BOOTP request until a reply is received. The client broadcasts a BOOTPREQUEST packet and the server answers it with a BOOTPREPLY. It is possible that the client may ask for a specific server to boot from if it is configured to do so. Therefore, multiple servers may have the same version of the BOOTtab file.

A BOOTP packet consists of the fields depicted in Fig. 1.15 and described as follows:

Fig. 1.14. A simple example of BOOTP operation

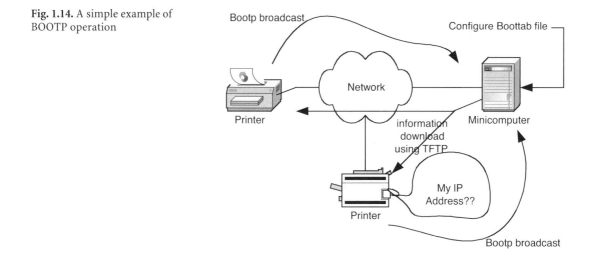

1. "Opcode": This is the first field of a BOOTP packet and consists of two values, one for BOOTREQUEST and the other for BOOTREPLY (Table 1.19).
2. Hardware type: This is an 8-bit field and has the same value as a hardware type field of RARP.
3. Hardware address length: This is an 8-bit field which identifies the hardware address length "6" for 10 Mb/s Ethernet
4. Hope count: This is also an 8-bit field. The client may set this field to zero and it is optionally used by gateways in cross-gateway booting.
5. Transaction ID: This is a 4-byte field, generally a random number used to match the current boot request with the response.
6. Number of seconds: This 16-bit field indicates the elapsed time, in seconds, since the client sent its first BOOTREQUEST message.
7. Flags: This is a 16-bit field as defined in RFC 1542 (Fig. 1.16).

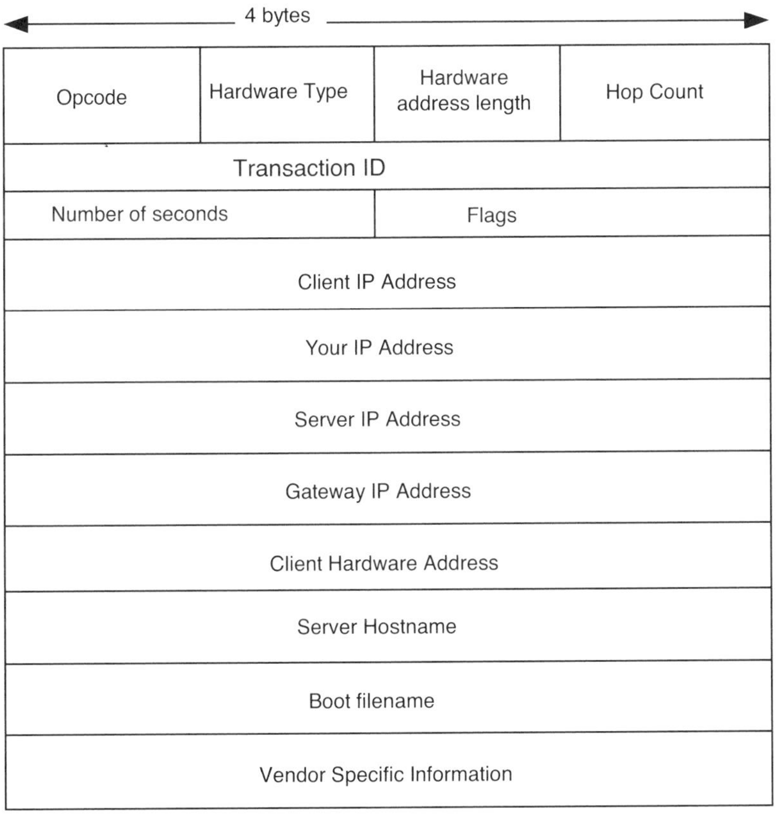

Fig. 1.15. BOOTP packet format

Value	Description
1	BOOTREQUEST, boot request
2	BOOTREPLY, boot reply

Table 1.19. The "Opcode" field value of a BOOTP packet

Fig. 1.16. The flags field of a
BOOTP packet

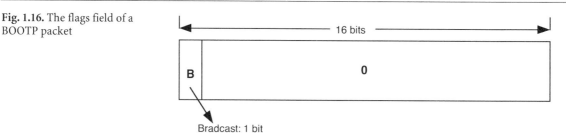

Bradcast: 1 bit

8. Client IP address: This 32-bit field indicates that a client's IP address can
   be specified in the BOOTREQUEST if known.
9. Your IP address: This is also a 32-bit field, generally filled by a server, and
   is the IP address of the client.
10. Server IP address: As its name implies, this is the server's IP address.
11. Gateway IP address: This address is used in optional cross-gateway boot-
    ing.
12. Client hardware address (16 bytes): This is the client's hardware address.
13. Server host name (64 bytes): The optional server host name.
14. Boot filename (128 bytes): The boot filename, a fully qualified directory
    path name in BOOTPREPLY.
15. Vendor specific information (64 bytes): Optional vendor specific informa-
    tion.

1.7 IPv6

The IP and addressing techniques we have talked about so far apply only to
IPv4. As the Internet expands, so does the demand for legitimate IP addresses. With its 32-bit addressing scheme, IPv4 is found to be inadequate to accommodate such demand. In anticipation of the imminent demise of IPv4
addressing, the IETF has developed a comprehensive set of specifications
that define IPng (IP Next Generation) or IPv6. Out of a number of RFCs written for IPng or IPv6, RFC 2460 defines the protocol specification for IPv6.
The changes from IPv4 (RFC 791) to IPv6 can be primarily categorized as follows:

- extended addressing capabilities
- simplified header format
- support for extensions and options
- flow labeling capability
- authentication and privacy capabilities.

In more detail:

- **Extended addressing capabilities:** IPv6 increases IP address size from 32
  bits (as in IPv4) to 128 bits to support a greater number of nodes and more
  levels of addressing hierarchy. The addition of a scope field in multicast

addresses improves the scalability of multicast routing. IPv6 introduces a new type of address known as "anycast address" which is used to send a packet to any one of a group of nodes.

- **Simplified header format:** A number of IPv4 header fields are dropped or made optional in IPv6 header format. This reduces the extra processing cost of packet handling and limits the bandwidth cost of the IPv6 header.
- **Support for extensions and options:** IPv6 provides improved support for extensions and options than those available in IPv4. These changes allow more efficient forwarding, greater flexibility to add new options in future and less stringent limits on the length of options.
- **Flow labeling capability:** This capability is unavailable in IPv4 and added to IPv6. It enables the labeling of packets associated with particular traffic "flows" which requires special services such as non-default QoS as requested by the sender of the packet.
- **Authentication and privacy capabilities:** IPv6 provides extensions to support authentication, data integrity and data confidentiality (optional).

1.7.1 IPv6 Header Format

A good way to understand the header format of IPv6 is to compare it with IPv4. You can use IPv4 as the basis for understanding the IPv6 header. Both IPv4 and IPv6 headers carry version and source/destination address fields. The IPv6 header format (as shown in Fig. 1.17) should be followed and compared with the IPv4 header described earlier in this chapter. IPv6 has a fixed header length of 40 bytes $(4 + 8 + 20 + 16 + 8 + 8 + 128 + 128 = 320$ bits $= 320/8 = 40$ bytes) whilst IPv4 has a variable length. Another comparison between IPv4 and IPv6 concerns the header fields: IPv4 has 14 header fields but IPv6

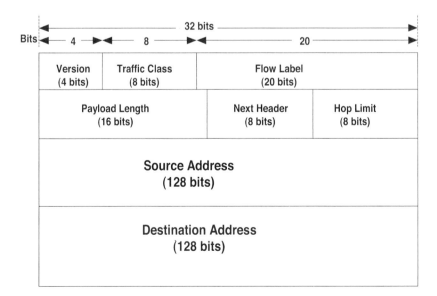

Fig. 1.17. IPv6 header format

has only 8 header fields. This allows router software to optimize the processing of the IPv6 header. Due to fixed header length fields in IPv6, the header length field, which is available in IPv4, is no longer a required criterion. The total length field of IPv4 is retained in the semblance of the IPv6 payload length field. This field can accommodate packets up to 64 KB in length. The time-to-live (TTL) field of the IPv4 header is given a new name in the IPv6 header, the "hop limit". Although the names are different both fields are decremented by routers with a value of 1 for each hop. The function of the TOS field in IPv4 is transferred to the two new fields of the IPv6 header which are the traffic class and flow label fields. In addition, a number of other basic fields in IPv4 such as flags, checksum, identification and fragment offset are eliminated in the IPv6 header. The fragmentation fields (fragment offset, identification and flags) of IPv4 are made optional in IPv6 and we will discuss those extensions later in this section. The IPv6 header assumes that checksum can be done by other levels of the protocol stack and thus checksum was abandoned in IPv6.

The IPv6 header excluding header extensions is 320 bits or 40 bytes. The first field of the header is the version filed, a 4-bit field. The value of this field is 6, which identifies IPv6. The next field after version is the traffic class field, an 8-bit field. With the use of this field originating nodes and/or forwarding routers identifies and distinguishes between different priorities and traffic classes of traversing IPng packets.

This field is yet to be defined in its entirety; however, a number of experiments are under way to provide a service similar to the "IP Differentia ted Service (as in IPv4)" for IPv6 packets. These experiments will continue by considering the following principles as stated in RFC:

(a) The default value of all 8 bits must be zero.
(b) The nodes that support the implementation of IPv6 traffic class should be allowed to change the value of the traffic class bits for service-specific use.
(c) It is not intended that the upper layer protocol will assume the value of traffic class bits of received IPv6 packets as the same as the value asserted by the source.

The next field after traffic class is a 20-bit field known as the flow label. This field can be used by the router to request special handling services. It is still in an experimental state and subject to change on the basis of requirements. Routers and hosts that do not support flow label functions should set this field to zero for originating packets, ignore when received or pass as it is for forwarding packets.

The payload length, a 16-bit field after the flow label field, identifies the length of IPv6 packets in octets. If an extension header is used that is also counted in the payload length field. The next header field is an 8-bit field which identifies the type of header immediately after the IPv6 header. This field has the same value as the protocol field, an 8-bit field of IPv4. RFC 1700 describes $2^8 = 256$ possible values for IPv4 protocol fields. These values are applied also for the next header field in IPv6 and they are as given in Table 1.20.

Decimal value	Keyword	Protocol definition
0		Reserved
1	ICMP	Internet Control Message Protocol
2	IGMP	Internet Group Management Protocol
3	GGP	Gateway-to-Gateway Protocol
4	IP	IP in IP encapsulation
5	ST	Stream
6	TCP	Transmission Control Protocol
7	UCL	UCL
8	EGP	Exterior Gateway Protocol
9	IGP	Any private interior gateway
10	BBN-RCC-MON	BBN RCC monitoring
11	NVP-II	Network Voice Protocol
12	PUP	PUP
13	ARGUS	ARGUS
14	EMCON	EMCON
15	XNET	Cross net debugger
16	CHAOS	Chaos
17	UDP	User Datagram Protocol
18	MUX	Multiplexing
19	DCN-MEAS	DCN measurement subsystems
20	HMP	Host monitoring
21	PRM	Packet Radio Measurement
22	XNS-IDP	XEROX NS IDP
23	TRUNK-1	Trunk-1
24	TRUNK-2	Trunk-2
25	LEAF-1	Leaf-1
26	LEAF-2	Leaf-2
27	RDP	Reliable Data Protocol
28	IRTP	Internet Reliable Transaction
29	ISO-TP4	ISO Transport Protocol Class 4
30	NETBLT	Bulk Data Transfer Protocol
31	MFE-NSP	MFE Network Services Protocol
32	MERIT-INP	MERIT Internodal Protocol
33	SEP	Sequential Exchange Protocol
34	3PC	Third Party Connect Protocol
35	IDPR	Inter-Domain Policy Routing Protocol

Table 1.20. The values of the IPv4 protocol field

	Decimal value	Keyword	Protocol definition
Table 1.20 (continued). The values of the IPv4 protocol field	36	XTP	XTP
	37	DDP	Datagram Delivery Protocol
	38	IDPR-CMTP	IDPR Control Message Transport Protocol
	39	TP++	TP++ Transport Protocol
	40	IL	IL Transport Protocol
	41	SIP	Simple Internet Protocol
	42	SDRP	Source Demand Routing Protocol
	43	SIP-SR	SIP Source Route
	44	SIP-FRAG	SIP Fragment
	45	IDRP	Interdomain Routing Protocol
	46	RSVP	Reservation Protocol
	47	GRE	General Routing Encapsulation
	48	MHRP	Mobile Host Routing Protocol
	49	BNA	BNA
	50	SIPP-ESP	SIPP Encapsulated Security Payload
	51	SIPP-AH	SIPP Authentication Header
	52	I-NLSP	Integrated Net Layer Security Protocol
	53	SWIPE	IP with encryption
	54	NHRP	NBMA Next-Hop Resolution Protocol
	55–60		Unassigned
	61		Any host internal protocol
	62	CFTP	CFTP
	63		Any local network
	64		SATNET and Backroom EXPAK
	65	KRYPTOLAN	Kryptolan
	66	RVD	MIT Remote Virtual Disk Protocol
	67	IPPC	Internet Pluribus Packet Core
	68		Any distributed file system
	69	SAT-MON	SATNET monitoring
	70	VISA	VISA Protocol
	71	IPCV	Internet Packet Core Utility
	72	CPNX	Computer Protocol Network Executive
	73	CPHB	Computer Protocol Heart Beat
	74	WSN	Wang Span Network
	75	PVP	Packet Video Protocol
	76	BR-SAT-MON	Backroom SATNET monitoring

Decimal value	Keyword	Protocol definition
77	SUN-ND	SUN ND PROTOCOL-Temporary
78	WB-MON	WIDEBAND monitoring
79	WB-EXPAK	WIDEBAND EXPAK
80	ISO-IP	ISO Internet Protocol
81	VMTP	VMTP
82	SECURE-VMTP	SECURE-VMTP
83	VINES	VINES
84	TTP	TTP
85	NSFNET-IGP	NSFNET-IGP
86	DGP	Dissimilar Gateway Protocol
87	TCF	TCF
88	IGRP	IGRP
89	OSPFIGP	OSPFIGP
90	Sprite-RPC	Sprite RPC Protocol
91	LARP	Locus Address Resolution Protocol
92	MTP	Multicast Transport Protocol
93	AX.25	AX.25 frames
94	IPIP	IP-within-IP Encapsulation Protocol
95	MICP	Mobile Internetworking Control Protocol
96	SCC-SP	Semaphore Communications Security Protocol
97	ETHERIP	Ethernet-within-IP encapsulation
98	ENCAP	Encapsulation header
99		Any private encryption scheme
100	GMTP	GMTP
101–254		Unassigned
255		Reserved

Table 1.20 (continued). The values of the IPv4 protocol field

Note: For further details about the above-mentioned protocols, please refer to RFC 1700.

The next field after the next header field in an IPv6 header is the hop limit. This is an 8-bit unsigned integer field. For each hop through which a packet traverses, the host decrements its value by one. A packet will be discarded if the value of this field is zero. Both the source address (SA) and the destination address (DA) are 128 bits each. The SA identifies the 128 bit address of the originator of the packet whereas the DA identifies the 128 bit address of the intended recipient of the packet. RFC 2373 defines the addressing architecture of IPv6. We will say more about this in the section on IPv6 addressing.

1.7.1.1 Extension Headers

For the IPv6 packet optional L3 information is encoded in separate headers, which may be placed between the IPv6 header and the layer 4 headers. RFC 2460 describes a small number of such header extensions, each of which is identified by a unique header value (Fig. 1.18).

As identified by RFC 2460, an IPv6 packet may contain zero, one or more extension headers each of which would be identified by the next header field of the preceding header. For example, if the value of the next header field of the IPv6 header identifies TCP as the next level protocol, the IPv6 header will be followed by TCP. Now, a traversing packet can have more headers within it; one such example is as follows:

1. The packet can have an IPv6 header whose next header field identifies routing as the next level header.
2. Therefore, the next header after IPv6 is the routing header whose next header field may indicate TCP as the next header.2.
3. Or, the routing header can indicate the fragment in the next header field and so on.

Figures 1.19 and 1.20 depict these events.

There is one exception when the extension header is not processed: a packet will not be examined by a node along the traveling path of the packet until it reaches its destination. Once it reaches the destination, the node will examine the first extension header if present, otherwise it will process the next layer 4 header. The semantics and contents of each extension header dictate whether or not the next header will be processed. Hence, a receiver should not scan the entire packet to look for a particular extension header and process it. Only one extension header, the hop-by-hop option, is examined by all nodes along the packet delivery path. If this header is present, it immediately follows the IPv6 header. The value 0 of the next header field indicates its presence in a packet. If a node determines that the value of the next header is not recognized it will discard the packet and send an "ICMP parameter problem" to the originating node of the packet. The value for such an ICMP message is ICMP code = 1 (unrecognized next header type encoun-

Fig. 1.18. Example of IPv6 header extension placement

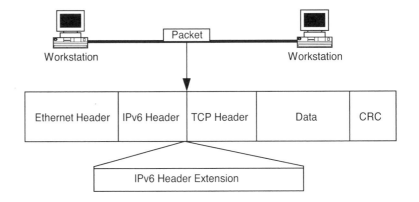

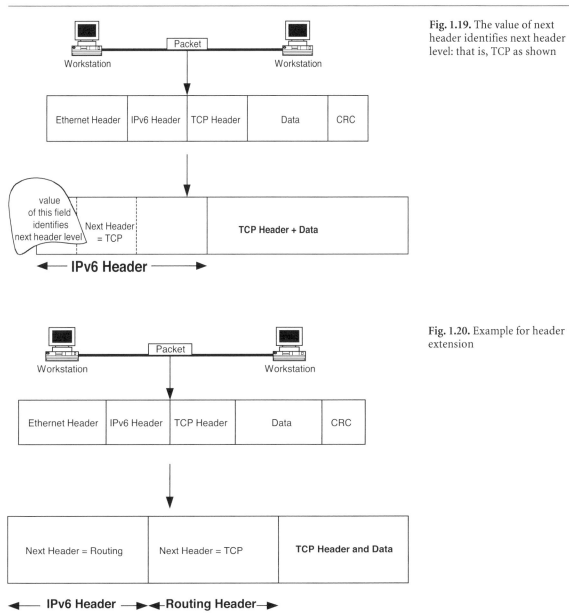

Fig. 1.19. The value of next header identifies next header level: that is, TCP as shown

Fig. 1.20. Example for header extension

tered). The same action may occur if a next header value is set to zero in any header other than the IPv6 header. RFC 2460 described six extension headers as follows:

- hop-by-hop options
- routing (type 0)
- fragment
- destination options

- authentication
- encapsulating security payload (ESP).

The order in which they arranged in a packet is as follows (see Fig. 1.21):

    I.   IPv6 header
   II.   Hop-by-hop option header
  III.   Destination options header – 1
  IV.   Routing header (source routing header)
   V.   Fragment header
  VI.   Authentication header
 VII.   ESP header –2 (IPv6 encr yption header)
VIII.   Destination options header – 2
  IX.   Upper layer headers

The destination options header – 1 is processed by the first destination plus subsequent destinations that are listed in the routing header, and the destination options header – 2 is processed only by the final node.

As suggested in RFC 2460, each extension header is a multiple of an integer 8 octets long. Both the hop-by-hop and destination option extension headers carry a variable number of TLVs (Type-Length-Values) encoded "Options" (Fig. 1.22). The format includes an 8-bit option type field, an 8-bit Opt Data Len and a variable length option data field. The option type field provides an 8-bit identifier for the type of option. Opt Data Len is an 8-bit unsigned integer and identifies the length of option data field in octets. The option data contains specific data in the option type.

The option type identifier is encoded such that its first two highest order bits specify the action which must be taken if the IPv6 processing node does not recognize the option type. The following describe the values of those two highest order ($2^2 = 4$) bit combinations:

Fig. 1.21. Various extension headers with their order of presence in a IPv6 packet

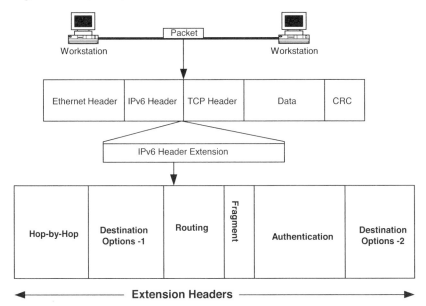

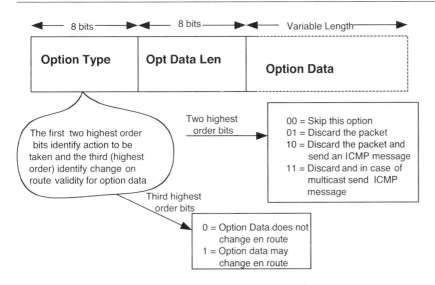

Fig. 1.22. The TLV of the extension header

00 = Skip this option and process the rest of the header.
01 = Simply discard the packet.
10 = Simply discard the packet considering the DA and send an ICMP code 2
    message to the SA pointing to the unrecognized option type.
11 = When discarding the packet consider the DA, only if the DA is not a
    multicast, send an ICMP packet with code 2.

The third highest order bit specifies whether or not option data change "en route":

0 = No en route change for option data.
1 = Option data may change "en route".

Instead of five lower order bits, the entire 8-bit option type field specifies the option type. There are also two padding options that can be inserted into the option area of a header and they are as follows:

1. PAD 1 option = This inserts one octet of padding into the option area of a header.
2. PAD N option = If more octets are required this padding is used.

1.7.1.1.1 Hop-by-hop Options Header

When present in a packet, this header (Fig. 1.23) carries options that are examined by each node along the path as mentioned earlier. It is the first extension header after the initial IPv6 header. The word initial means there may be another IPv6 header after the extension header. Such may happen in the case when the IPv6 header is tunneled over or encapsulated in IPv6. Since every router examine the hop-by-hop header, it is useful for transmitting management information or debugging commands to routers. One such application is the router alert option that informs the router about processing the packet first before forwarding it to the next hop. An example is RSVP's resource reservation message.

Fig. 1.23. Hop-by-hop options header

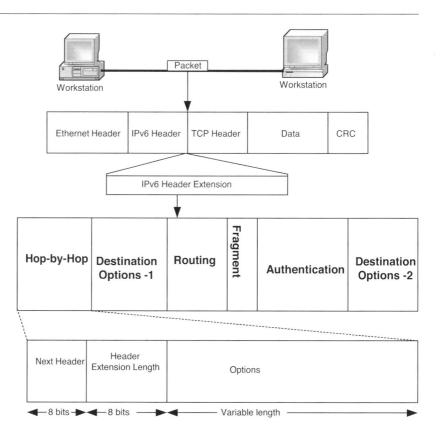

The hop-by-hop header is identified by the next header value of 0. The next header within this extension header is an 8-bit selector field, which identifies the type of header immediately starting after the hop-by-hop option header. It uses the same value as the protocol field of IPv4 (we discussed these values earlier).

The next field is the 8-bit unsigned integer header extension length field. It identifies the length of the hop-by-hop option in eight-octet units. The options field is of variable length and contains one or more TLV-encoded options.

1.7.1.1.2 Destination Options Header

The next extension header in order is the destination options header and used to carry optional information which is required to be examined by the destination node. The next header value of 60 identifies this extension header. This header has an 8-bit next header field similar to the next header field of the hop-by-hop options header. The header extension length and options fields are also the same as in the hop-by-hop options header. There are two possible ways in which optional destination information can be encoded in an IPv6 packet: either through an option in the destination options header or through a separate extension header, that is a fragment header and an authentication header.

When determining which approach to take, the first two highest order bits of the option type field identify the action to be taken. For example, if the value is 11, information such as "discard packet and inform the source through ICMP in case of non-multicast DA" can be encoded either as a separate header or as an option in the destination option header.

Figure 1.24 depicts the format of this field.

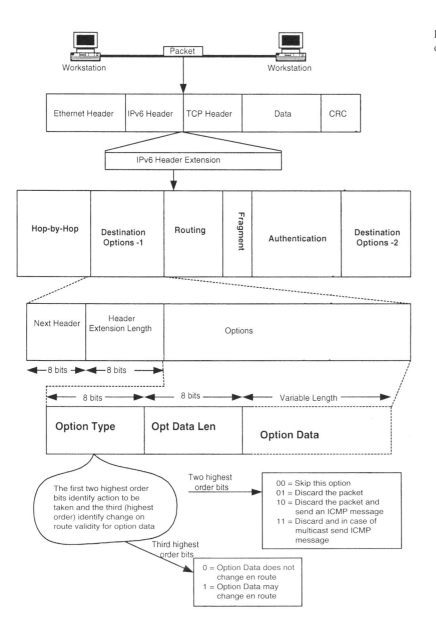

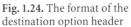

Fig. 1.24. The format of the destination option header

1.7.1.1.3 Routing Header

An IPv6 source node uses this header to identify the list of one or more intermediate hosts to be visited along the delivery path of the packet on its way to the destination. The function of this field is very similar to the loose source and record route option of IPv4. The next header value of 43 identifies the routing header. Figure 1.25 depicts the format of the routing header.

In the routing header, the first field is the next header field, an 8-bit field which identifies the type of header immediately following the routing header. It uses the same value as in the IPv4 protocol field. The header extension length (Hdr Ext Len) is the next 8-bit unsigned integer field. It specifies the length of routing header in eight-octet units excluding the first eight octets. The next field is the routing type field, an 8 bits long field which identifies a particular routing header variant. If the value of this field indicates Route Type = 0, the "Hdr Ext Len" should be equal to two times the number of addresses in the header. The header should also include a 32-bit reserved field

Fig. 1.25. The format of the routing header and type 0 routing header

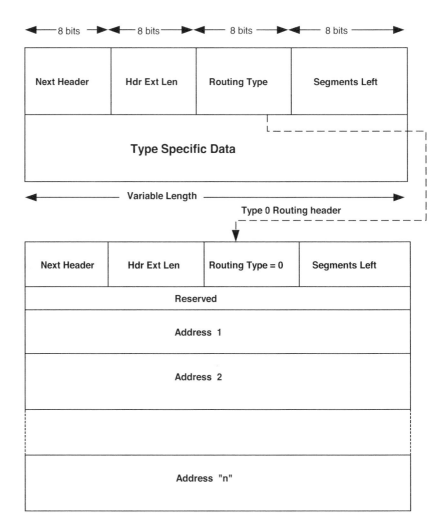

that is initialized to zero during transmission and ignored in reception. Besides an 8-bit segment left field, it will also include an "Address 1 … Address n" field with a vector of 128 addresses numbered 1 to *n*. The routing type 0 header should not contain a multicast address in the address field. If such a header is present in an IPv6 packet the multicast address should not appear in the IPv6 DA field. The next header after the route type is the segment left field which indicates the number of routes remaining. For example, the number of nodes still to be visited before reaching the destination. If it is set to zero, the host must ignore the routing header and process the next header of the packet. If it is set to a non-zero value, the host must discard the packet and send an ICMP message with code 0 (unrecognized route type).

1.7.1.1.4 *Fragment Header*

For IPv6, this header is used by the source to send a packet larger than path MTU (Maximum Transmission Unit). Unlike IPv4, the fragmentation in IPv6 is done at the source, not at the router. As defined in RFC 2460 and RFC 1981, IPv6 requires an MTU of 1280 bytes or more in every link. If a link is unable to convey a 1280-byte packet in one piece, link-specific fragmentation must be done by the underlying protocols, not by IPv6. It is recommended that if there is a possibility to configure MTUs for a link, for that link MTU should be configured as 1500 bytes to accommodate possible encapsulations, namely tunneling if any. RFC 2460 strongly suggests the implementation of path MTU discovery by an IPv6 node as defined in RFC 1981. Nonetheless, the fragment header is identified by the next header value of 44. This header includes an 8-bit selector field known as the next header, an 8-bit reserved field, a 13-bit fragment offset, another 2 bits of "Resor" reserved field, a 1-bit M flag and a 32-bit identifier field.

The next header field of the fragment header identifies the initial header type of the fragmentable part of the original packet. A packet can be considered to include two parts, one the unfragmentable part and the other the fragmentable part. The latter can be divided into multiple parts such as first part, second part and so on. Each fragmented packet is composed of the following:

- The unfragmentable part of the original packet, for which the IPv6 header payload length is changed to indicate the fragment packet only.
- The next header of the fragment header identifying the first header of the fragmented part of the original packet.
- A fragment offset containing the offset of the fragment; for the first fragment this field is set to 0. It also includes the fragment itself.

The IPv6 source node fragments a packet (Fig. 1.26) if the packet is bigger than the MTU supported by the destination node as per the procedure stated above during transmission (Fig. 1.27). Each fragmented packet is identified with a unique identifier.

Once the fragmented packet is received by the destination node, it reassembles the fragments and recovers the original packet. The reserved field value is initialized to zero for transmission and ignored during reception. The reserved field value is also initialized to zero during transmission. If the

Fig. 1.26. Packet fragmentation by IPv6 source node

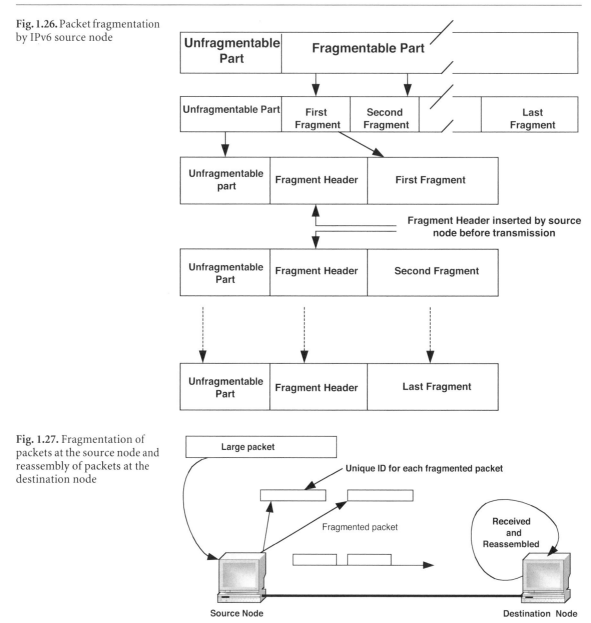

Fig. 1.27. Fragmentation of packets at the source node and reassembly of packets at the destination node

M flag of the fragment header is set to one, it indicates more fragments, otherwise if set to zero it indicates the last fragment. The identifier specifies the unique ID for each fragment as described earlier.

1.7.1.1.5 Authentication Header
The authentication header (AH) is the means to provide strong and connectionless integrity and authentication for IP datagrams. It also provides an op-

tional service which protects against replays. This optional service is used by the receiver once a security association is established. As stated in RFC 2402, the AH provides authentication as much as possible for the IP header as well as for the upper layer protocol data. Although precautions can be taken, some of the IP header field may change in transit, for which the values of these fields may also change. Such behavior is unpredictable by the sender and therefore not protected by the AH. It can function alone or in combination with the IP encapsulating security payload (ESP). RFC 2402 also defines the possibility of its implementation through the use of tunnel mode (see RFC 2401 for further details).

The AH will be identified by the protocol field (IPv4) and next header (IPv6) value of 51 prior protocol headers (IPv4, IPv6 or extension). The AH header includes the following fields as depicted in Fig. 1.28:

- Next header
- Payload length
- Security parameter index (SPI)
- Sequence number
- Authentication data.

In more detail:

Next header: This is an 8-bit field which identifies the type of the next payload following the AH. The value of this field is a set of IP numbers defined in RFC 1700.

Payload length: This is an 8-bit field which identifies the length of the AH in 32-bit word. A value of null in this field identifies that it is used for debugging purposes. For IPv4, the value in this field is 1 and 2 for IPv6.

RESERVED: This is a 16-bit field reserved for future use and is set to zero.

SPI: This is an arbitrary value of 32 which identifies the security association of IP datagrams in combinations of IP DA and security protocol (AH). IANA has reserved the value of this field from 1 through 255 for future use. The value of 0 is reserved for local use and a system must not send it to the wire. For further details and implementation-specific information about this field, please refer to RFC 2401.

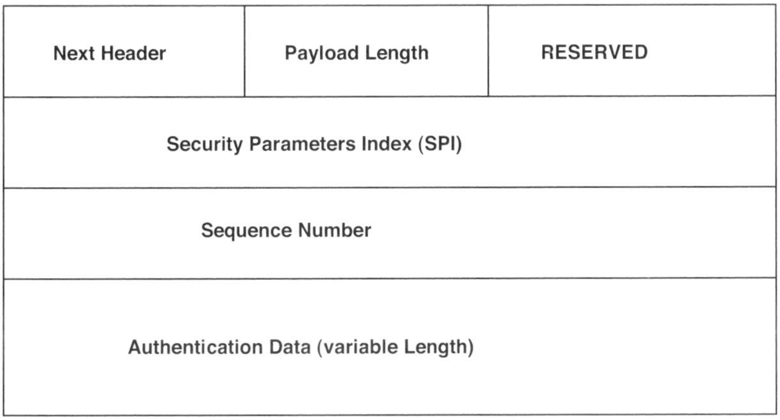

Fig. 1.28. The authentication header (AH)

Sequence number: This is an unsigned 32-bit field which includes a tediously increasing counter value (sequence number). It is always present in the packet and sent by the source although the receiver may or may not act upon it.

Authentication data: This is a variable length field which includes the integrity check value (ICV) for the packet. The AH ICV is calculated over the following:

- IP header fields which are absolute in transit and have predictable value upon arrival,
- the A H and explicit padding bytes, and
- the upper layer protocol data which is also absolute in transit that is not changes value during transport.

On the other hand, if a field can be modified or considered mutable during transit, the value of the field is set to zero for ICV calculation purposes. Nonetheless, the authentication data field may include explicit padding to ensure that the AH is a multiple of 32 bits for IPv4 and 64 bits for IPv6. Generally, all implementation supports such padding.

For IPv4, the AH is inserted immediately after the IPv4 header and upper layer header such as the TCP header. On the other hand, for IPv6, AH is considered as an end-to-end payload and placed after the hop-by-hop, routing and fragmentation headers.

1.7.1.1.6 *ESP Header*

The ESP is designed to provide mixed security services in IPv4 and IPv6. It can be deployed alone, with AH or through the use of IP tunnel mode. In transport mode this header is inserted after the IP header and before the upper layer header such as TCP. On the other hand, in tunnel mode, it is inserted before the encapsulating IP header. The ESP header is used to authenticate data origin, confidentiality, integrity and a form of partial sequence integrity service known as anti-replay. I suggest readers refer to RFC 2401 to understand further these details about security. This will help you to better understand ESP and AH.

The value 50 in the protocol field for IPv4 and the next header field for IPv6 identifies the ESP as subsequent to this header. The ESP header includes the following fields (see Fig. 1.29:

SPI: The SPI has a random 32-bit value, which in combination with the DA and security protocol such as ESP identifies the security association of the datagram. The value set for this field that ranges from 1 to 255 is reserved by IANA. . Unless suggested by RFC for specific implementation, the reserved values are not normally assigned by IANA. This is a mandatory field and used by the destination system upon establishment of security association. The value 0 is reserved for local use and must not be sent on the wire.

Sequence number: This is also a 32-bit field which includes a monotonically increasing counter value or sequence number. Like SPI, it is also a mandatory field. It is always sent by the sender and processing of the field depends on the receiver, which may choose not to act upon it.

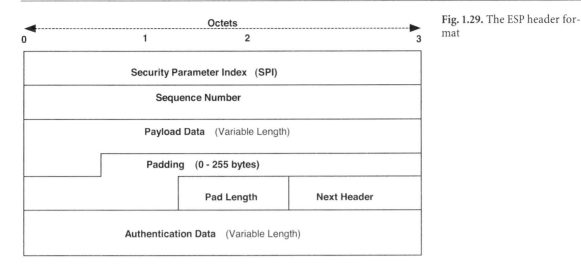

Fig. 1.29. The ESP header format

Payload data: This is a variable length field that contains data described by the next header. It is al)so a mandatory field and may carry an initialization vector (IV) used for payload encryption.

Padding: This is required for encryption and justification of the presence of padding field that depends on the following factors:

- If an encryption algorithm is implemented that needs plaintext to be a multiple number of bytes, padding fills the plaintext up to the size required by the algorithm.
- If even encryption is not used, to ensure that ciphertext terminates on a 4-byte boundary padding is used.
- Padding can be also used to conceal the length of payload to support partial traffic flow confidentiality. The padding is an optional field and can be 0–255 bytes in length.

Pad length: This field indicates the number of bytes in the padding field preceding it. The valid range is 0–255 where value 0 indicates no padding bytes are present.

Next header: This is an 8-bit field which identifies the type of data contained in the payload data field. The payload data can be an extension header or upper layer protocol identifier. The value of this field is taken from IP numbers defined in RFC 1700.

Authentication data: This is a variable length field and includes an ICV computed over the ESP packet minus the authentication data. It is an optional field and used only if the authentication service is selected for security association.

With the ESP header applied, the IPv4 and IPv6 packets will look as depicted in Fig. 1.30.

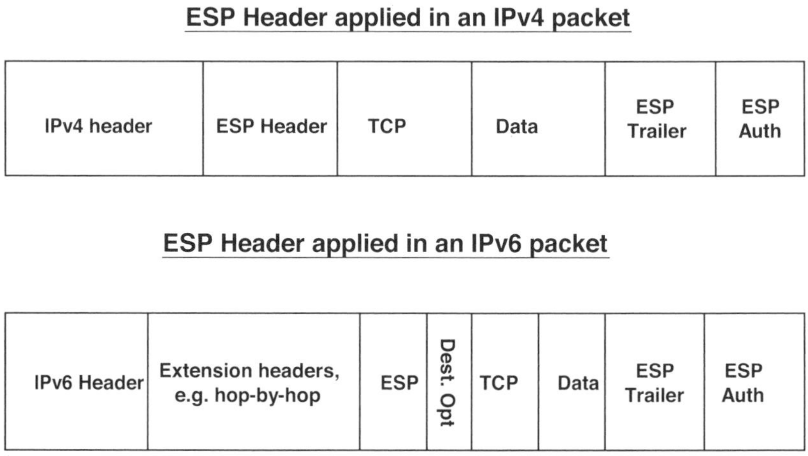

Fig. 1.30. An example of ESP
header in use

ESP Header applied in an IPv4 packet

IPv4 header	ESP Header	TCP	Data	ESP Trailer	ESP Auth

ESP Header applied in an IPv6 packet

IPv6 Header	Extension headers, e.g. hop-by-hop	ESP	Dest. Opt	TCP	Data	ESP Trailer	ESP Auth

1.7.2 IPv6 Addressing Architecture

IPv6 addressing defers very significantly from the addressing structure of
IPv4 due to the 128-bit addressing method that is introduced in IPv6. RFC
2373 defines the addressing architecture of IPv6. As discussed in RFC 2373,
there are three types of addresses that are applied to an IPv6 network and
they are as follows:

1. **Unicast:** This is a one-to-one addressing scheme available in IPv4 also. A
   packet sent with a unicast address is delivered to the endpoint or interface
   identified by the address.
2. **Anycast:** This is new and introduced in IPv6. A packet with an anycast address is delivered to one of the interfaces (the nearest one) identified by
   the address.
3. **Multicast:** This addressing scheme also exists in IPv4. Usually it is an address that can be subscribed to by a group of stations/endpoints /interfac-
   es. A packet with such an address is sent to all subscribed members of the
   group.

It must be remembered that there are no broadcast addresses defined in IPv6.
The broadcast address is superseded by a multicast address. Since IPv6 ad-
dress size is 128 bits, it can accommodate over 6.65×10^{23} network addresses.
This gives an address space of approximately:

$$2^{128} = 340,282,366,920,938,463,463,374,607,431,768,211,456$$

which is certainly enough for future networks. Even if it were considered to
assign addresses by the land mass of the earth, IPv6 address space could provide an average of 2.2×10^{20} addresses per square centimeter. RFC 2373
presents a format for representing addresses in readable text. As such, the
format allows 128 bits to be written as eight 16-bit integers separated by co-

lons. Each of these 16 bit integer pieces is represented by four hexadecimal digits. An example of an IPv6 address is

EFDC:BA98:7654:3210:EFDC:BA98:7654:3210
(ref.: Sect. 2.2 of RFC 2373)

Although hexadecimal notation is relatively compact and straightforward, some see this as a lack of user friendliness since it is difficult to manipulate. One way to make it a little simpler is to allow some abbreviations. As suggested by RFC 2373, we can exclude leading zeros in each hexadecimal component, for example 0 instead of 0000, 8 instead of 0008, etc. With such an abbreviated context an IPv6 address will look like as follows:

1080:0:0:0:8:800:200 C:417 A

The specification suggest yet another simpler way of writing the IPv6 address, that is the use of the :: (double-colon) convention. This indicates multiple groups of 16 bits of null (0) values and also can be used to compress the leading and/or trailing zeros in an IPv6 address. For example, the above address can be written as

1080::8:800:200 C:417 A

We can apply the same rule in the following multicast address:

FF01:0:0:0:0:0:0:101 can be represented as FF01::101

The specification also suggests another compressed textual format of writing addresses when dealing with the mixed environment of IPv4 and IPv6. The mixed address will have x:x:x:x:x:x:d.d.d.d format where the x's represent the hexadecimal values of six high-order 16-bit portions of the address and the d's represent the decimal values of four low-order 8-bit portions of the IPv4 address. An example of this addressing is as follows:

0:0:0:0:0:0:13.1.68.3 or ::13.1.68.3

It must be remembered that 0:0:0:0:0:0:0:0 is known as an unspecified address and must not be used by a node. This indicates the absence of an address. On the other hand, 0:0:0:0:0:0:0:1 is a loopback address and used by a host to send an IPv6 packet to itself. This address also must not be configured to any physical interface.

The representation of prefixes is similar to the way IPv4 address prefixes are written in CIDR notation. For example, IPv6 address/prefix length, where prefix length is a decimal value of the number of leftmost contiguous bits of the address. We can write this as follows:

12AB:0000:0000:CD30:0000:0000:0000:0000/60 or
12AB::CD30:0:0:0:0/60 or 12AB:0:0CD30::/60

The initial address allocation along with the assignment of prefixes are as given in Table 1.21.

Table 1.21. Address allocation and prefix assignment

Address allocation	Prefix in binary format	Address pace (in fractions)
Reserved	00000000	1/256
Unassigned	00000001	1/256
NSAP allocation	0000001	1/128
IPX allocation	0000010	1/128
Unassigned	0000011	1/128
Unassigned	00001	1/32
Unassigned	0001	1/16
Global unicast	001	1/8
Unassigned	010	1/8
Unassigned	011	1/8
Unassigned	100	1/8
Unassigned	101	1/8
Unassigned	110	1/8
Unassigned	1110	1/16
Unassigned	11110	1/32
Unassigned	111110	1/64
Unassigned	1111110	1/128
Unassigned	111111100	1/512
Link local address	1111111010	1/1024
Site local address	1111111011	1/1024
Multicast address	11111111	1/256

The following frame is captured from an IPv6 network. Please verify the IPv6 header section for address format and header format as you understand it by now.

```
- - - - - - - - - - - - - - - - - - - - - Frame 78 - - -
  Frame Status  Source Address    Dest. Address      Size
Rel. Time      Delta Time     Abs. Time
Summary
     78          fe80::200:a2ff:fe ff02::9               86
0:01:00.317   0.050.678      05/18/2000 02:10:37 PM DLC:
Ethertype=86DD, size=86 bytes

IPv6: Priority=7 Flow=0x000000

UDP: D=521 S=521   LEN=32

RIPng: Request Version=1
DLC:  ----- DLC Header -----
      DLC:
      DLC:  Frame 78 arrived at  14:10:37.9498; frame
size is 86 (0056 hex) bytes.
      DLC:  Destination = Multicast 333300000009
      DLC:  Source       = Station AC060600B300
      DLC:  Ethertype    = 86DD
      DLC:
```

```
IPv6: ----- IPv6 Header -----
      IPv6:
      IPv6: Version            = 6
      IPv6: Priority           = 7 (Internet Control
Traffic)
      IPv6: Flow Label         = 0x000000
      IPv6: Payload Length     = 32
      IPv6: Next Header        = 17 (UDP)
      IPv6: Hop Limit          = 255
      IPv6: Source address     =
fe80::200:a2ff:fef7:5249
      IPv6: Destination address = ff02::9
      IPv6:
UDP: ----- UDP Header -----
      UDP:
      UDP: Source port      = 521 (RIPng)
      UDP: Destination port = 521 (RIPng)
      UDP: Length           = 32
      UDP: Checksum         = 06BE
      UDP: [24 byte(s) of data]
      UDP:
RIPng: ----- RIPng -----
      RIPng:
      RIPng: Command          = 1 (Request)
      RIPng: Version          = 1
      RIPng: Reserved         = 0x0000
      RIPng: IPv6 Prefix      = ::
      RIPng: Route tag        = 0
      RIPng: Prefix length    = 0
      RIPng: Metric           = 16 (infinity:
destination unreachable)
ADDR  HEX
ASCII
0000: 33 33 00 00 00 09 ac 06 06 00 b3 00 86 dd 67 00 |
33....¬.......g.
0010: 00 00 00 20 11 ff fe 80 00 00 00 00 00 00 02 00 |
... ..........
0020: a2 ff fe f7 52 49 ff 02 00 00 00 00 00 00 00 00 |
...RI.........
0030: 00 00 00 00 00 09 02 09 02 09 00 20 06 be 01 01 |
........... ....
0040: 00 00 00 00 00 00 00 00 00 00 00 00 00 00 00 00 |
...............
0050: 00 00 00 00 00 10                               |
......
```

1.7.2.1 IPv6 Address Hierarchy

We mentioned earlier that IPv4 addressing was incapable of coping with routing table explosion. To address this problem, IPv6 addresses rely heavily on a hierarchy in which the top level begins with the most significant bits of the address and continues down to the least significant bit (Fig. 1.31). Let's consider the first 64 bits of an IPv6 address, in which the first 3 bits define the top-level hierarchy and are known as format prefix (FP) bits. These FP bits indicate the type of address that follows, namely unicast, multicast, etc.

The next 13 bits define the TLA ID (Top-Level Aggregation Identifier) and are allocated to various TLAs around the world. The size of the TLA ID field that allows for 8192 TLA IDs was chosen to insure that the default-free routing table in top-level routers could be kept within limits. With the current practice of IPv4, the prefix announced 15 times via different paths and cur-

Fig. 1.31. IPv6 address hierarchy (TLA and NLA assignment)

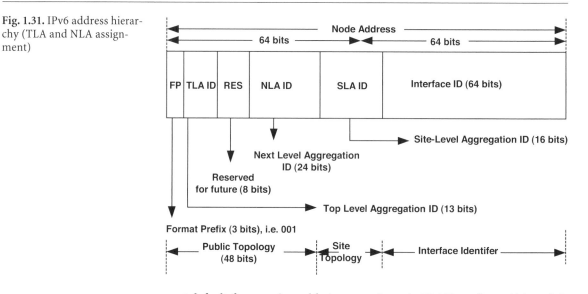

rent default-free routing table is approximately 50,000 prefixes. Although it shows the possibility of supporting more routes than 8192, it can be a matter of debate. Some may think it can cause serious routing issues like stability and providers may not support all prefixes. Therefore, an engineering compromise was the 13-bit size of the TLA field. In future, if the routing technology improves, the TLA field can be expanded to RES or reserved, an 8-bit field. This will provide approximately 2 million TLA IDs. The RES field is chosen since there may be a need to expand the TLA ID or NLA ID (Next-Level Aggregation Identifier) field. The TLAs are the public transit points (exchanges) where telecom/long-haul providers establish peer connections. Therefore, we can consider, at the top of the hierarchy, several international registries assigning blocks of addresses to TLA. The next 24 bits defines NLA ID. The size of the NLA ID field allows up to 16 million NLA IDs. The NLAs are the next level in the hierarchy, which generally represents large providers and global corporate networks. The NLA ID field is followed by the SLA ID (Site-Level Aggregation Identifier), a 16-bit allocation. The size of this field supports up to 65,535 individual subnets per site. The design goal is to provide sufficient subnets; if additional subnets are required they can be obtained from the ISPs. The next field after the SLA ID is the interface ID, a 64-bit field. The size is chosen to support EUI-64-based interface identifiers. This hierarchical approach (Fig. 1.32) is defined in RFC 2450 and the format is describe as part of the global unicast address format.

As mentioned earlier, TLAs are the transit points or providers of transit topology. Therefore, TLA IDs are not assigned to organizations only providing leaf topology and the TLA assignment does not entail ownership but establishes stewardship of valuable Internet resources. The specification (RFC 2450) suggests that the implementation of TLA addresses will be done in two stages. In the first stage, a sub-TLA ID will be allocated. Once the recipient successfully assigns NLA IDs (at least 90% of their sub-TLA ID), the TLA ID will be assigned to the respective transit topology provider. The next field of

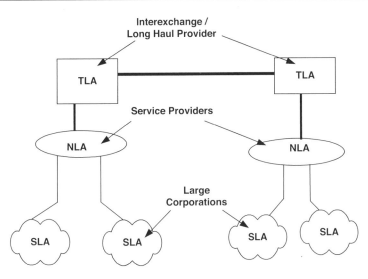

Fig. 1.32. A hierarchical approach to IPv6 address assignment

the global unicast address format is the 64-bit interface ID. The size was chosen to meet the requirements of IPv6 addressing as specified in RFC 2373 to support EUI-64-based interface identifiers. We learned earlier that neither IPv4 nor IPv6 assigns addresses to a host; rather, they are assigned to the interface of that host. The interface address must be unique and 64 bits long to comply with the EUI-64 format defined by the IEEE. The details of EUI-64 are available from http://standards.ieee.org/regauth/oui/tutorials/EUI64.html.

The EUI-64-based interface identifier has a global scope (e.g., IEEE 48-bit MAC address) or local scope (e.g., serial link etc.). The specification suggests the inversion of the "u" bit (universal/local bit in EUI-64) when forming the interface ID from EUI-64. The "u" bit is set to 1 to indicate global scope and to 0 to identify the local scope.

1.7.2.1.1 Unicast Address

IPv6 unicast has several forms of unicast address assignment:

- global unicast address
- NSAP (Network Service Access Point) address
- IPX (Internet Packet Exchange) hierarchical address
- site local address
- link local address, and
- IPv4 address compatibility.

Depending upon their sophistication, IPv6 nodes may have some or little knowledge about the structure of the address (Fig. 1.33).

If the node is a simple host, it may consider its "network" address as the unicast address, whereas a router may be aware of subnet prefixes. In the preceding section we discussed the global unicast format, and therefore we will start exploring unicast addresses with NSAP addresses.

NSAP address: The mapping of an NSAP address into an IPv6 address is defined in RFC 1888. The specification also defines a set of procedures for sup-

Fig. 1.33. An example of unicast address structure that may be realized by a node or a router

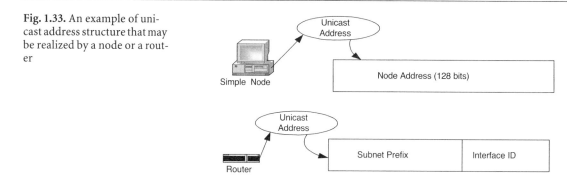

porting OSI NSAP addressing in an IPv6 network. The network of OSI NSAP addressing may use ES–IS [1] and IS–IS [2] routing (ISO 9542 and ISO 10589) protocols. The administrator of such a network must follow the restrictions given here before transitioning to the IPv6 addressing plan:

1. The network that implements the ES–IS/IS–IS model introduces a hierarchical level down to the area level for which all systems may not be in the same subnet or physical link. On the other hand, IPv6 assumes all systems in a subnet are in the same physical link. Therefore, an extra level of hierarchy is needed if chosen so as not to change the physical topology of the network. In other words, the area concept cannot simply be mapped to the IPv6 addressing without change in the physical topology.
2. Another issue which must be considered is that the address prefix used for all the subnets is the same, regardless of whether a particular subnet is using a pure IPv6 addressing schema or CLNP [3] schema.
3. As we have seen earlier, an IPv6 address is assigned to the link, not to the host. In the ES–IS /IS–IS model, a host may have two interfaces with two NSAP addresses but each of them may identify the host as a whole. Therefore, this restriction must be considered for those hosts before mapping into IPv6 addresses.

There are four defined mechanisms that can be used during the IPv6 implementation and/or mapping of the NSAP address (NSAPA) to IPv6 as follows:

1. Mapping a subset of NSAPA< into a 16 byte IPv6 address.
2. Truncated NSAPA for routing, full NSAPA in IPv6 option.
3. Normal IPv6 address, full NSAPA in IPv6 option.
4. IPv6 address carried as OSI address.

These will be now be detailed in the following paragraphs.

---

1. ES (End System) to IS (Intermediate System) is an OSI protocol that allows end systems to announce themselves as intermediate systems. ESs are equivalent to the Internet concept of a host that uses all layers in the communications model. ISs are relay communications nodes or forwarders between ESs and are effectively a subset of ESs.
2. IS (Intermediate System) to IS (Intermediate System) Protocol is an ISO protocol that defines how ISs exchange routing information.
3. Connectionless Network Protocol (CLNP), also known as ISO-IP. This protocol provides a datagram service and is OSI's equivalent to IP.

1. Mapping a subset of NSAPA into a 16 byte IPv6 address: It is more likely that some organizations may choose not to follow the instructions for mapping NSAPA into IPv6 set forth earlier in this section. They may keep their OSI NSAP addressing plan unchanged. Such a decision will adversely affect both internet and intranet for interconnected networks. The routing between the two will not be optimized causing IPv6 routers to have inefficient routing. However, to cover such anomalies, RFC 1888 defines a way to map a subset of NSAPA into IPv6 address space, for which the mapping is algorithmic and reversible within this subset of NSAPA.

Generally, NSAPA uses 20-byte address space. It must be remembered that if the first byte of the IPv6 address is 0×02 (hex) or 00000010 in binary, then the remaining 15 bytes (out of 16 bytes) of the IPv6 address space will include a subset of NSAPA mapping (Fig. 1.34).

2. Truncated NSAPA for routing, full NSAPA in IPv6 option: According to ISO 10589 and ISO 8473 specifications, an NSAP address includes routing information such as routing domain and area/subnet identifiers in the format of the area address. The length and format of this routing information can be represented within first 16 bytes of the IPv6 address space. In this context, readers must consider the following:

- If a truncated NSAPA is used as the SA for IPv6 address space, the address space must be considered as unicast address and be treated accordingly.
- For NSAPA being used as SA or DA or both for IPv6 address space, the packet must establish or include either an NSAPA destination option or a CLNP encapsulation. The action to be taken in this regard is the responsibility of the destination system.
- If an NSAPA destination option is present in the packet and a truncated NSAPA is used to identify a router, then it would be the responsibility of the router to forward the traversing packet.

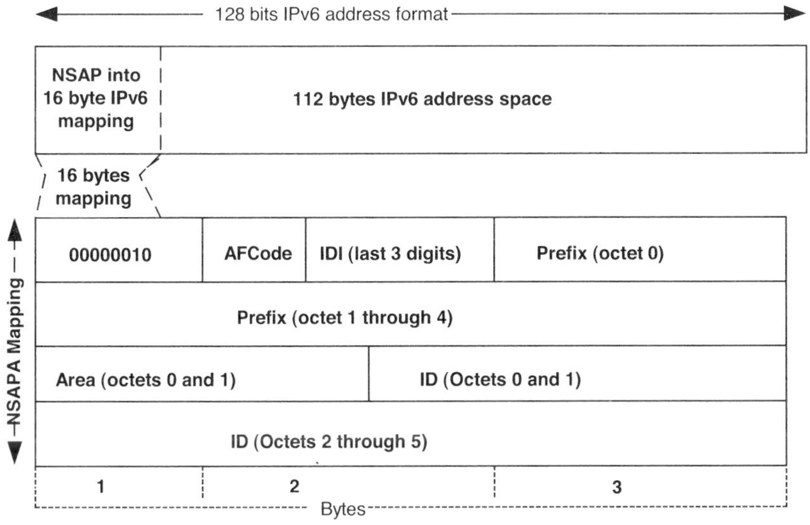

Fig. 1.34. A subset of NSAPA mapping into 16 byte IPV6 address space

Fig. 1.35. The truncated NSA-PA mapping into IPv6 address space

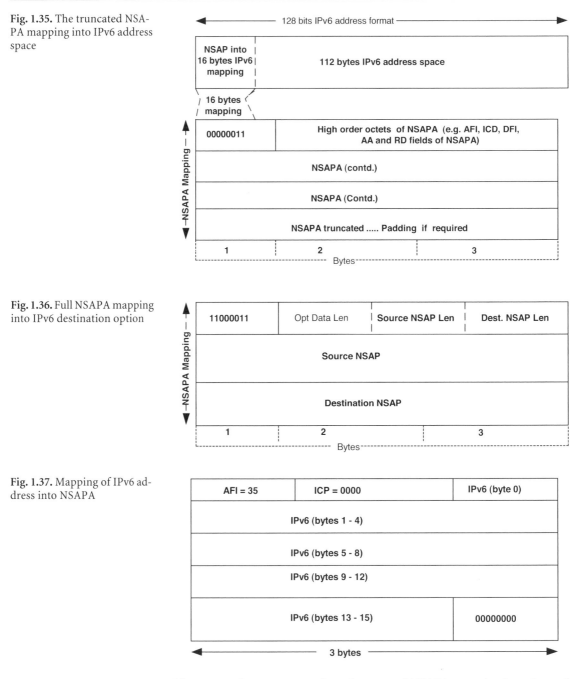

Fig. 1.36. Full NSAPA mapping into IPv6 destination option

Fig. 1.37. Mapping of IPv6 address into NSAPA

The appropriate representation of truncated NSAPA mapping is as shown in Fig. 1.35.

3. Normal IPv6 address, full NSAPA in IPv6 option: The carriage of full NSAPA in the IPv6 destination option has the format shown in Fig. 1.36.

The option type code is 11000011.

4. IPv6 address carried as OSI address: If the IPv6 address is to be embedded within the OSI NSAP address, RFC 1888 defines the methodology the format of which is shown in Fig. 1.37.

For those readers who want to know more about the NSAPA to IPv6 transition, my recommendation would be to study RFC 1888 and other relevant specifications if applicable. Adequate know-how will save you time and effort for such a complex migration.

IPX address: Although there are drafts that are written for IPX address mapping into IPV6, the definition, usage and motivation are still under study. The format that has yet to be defined is considered as having that format shown in Fig. 1.38.

Site local address: The site local address is used for addressing within a site; there is no need for a global prefix for this type of address. A site router must not forward this address outside of the site. The format of the site local unicast address is as depicted in Fig. 1.39.

Link local address: The link local address is used for addressing on a single link for such purposes as auto-address configuration, neighbor discovery or in the absence of a router. This address must not be forwarded by a router to other links. The format is shown in Fig. 1.40.

IPv4 address compatibility: The IPv6 mechanisms include a technique through which routers and hosts can dynamically tunnel IPv6 packets over

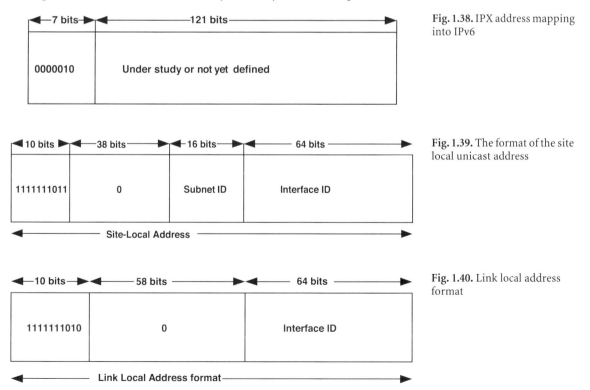

Fig. 1.38. IPX address mapping into IPv6

Fig. 1.39. The format of the site local unicast address

Fig. 1.40. Link local address format

Fig. 1.41. Two types of address mapping for IPv4 compatibility

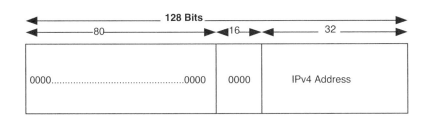

IPv4-mapped IPv6 Address

the IPv4 network infrastructure. Generally, an IPv6 node that uses this technique employs an IPv6 unicast address carrying an IPv4 address. This address format can be understood as shown in Fig. 1.41.

To support nodes that do not understand IPv6, another addressing is also suggested which holds the IPv4 address. This type of format is know as IPv4-mapped IPv6 and shown in Fig. 1.41. We will discuss this subject further in the section on transition criteria of the IPv4 to IPv6 network.

1.7.2.1.2 Anycast Address

The anycast addressing technique is used to send an IPv6 address to more than one interface belonging to multiple nodes. For such an address, a traversing packet can be delivered to the nearest interface having the anycast address. The distance calculation is in the pronouncement of routing protocol being used. These types of addresses are allocated from the unicast address space and would be of any unicast address format discussed earlier. Hence, the anycast address is syntactically discernible from the unicast address. A host treats an anycast address the same way it treats a unicast address, except that in the anycast address, a prefix identifies the topological region where all interface belonging to the anycast address reside. Users may choose to configure routers in their organization to provide Internet services to use anycast address. This way, an IPv6 packet can be delivered via a particular router or routers. Another use can be to identify a set of routers attached to a given subnet or providing entry to a specific routing domain. Even though the use of anycast address is still evolving, it can possibly provide a number of important services. For example, a collection of servers with well-known services can be accessed through this address, or a router using source routing can use the address in source route. RFC 2373 specifies an anycast address format known as "Subnet-Router Anycast". The subnet prefix in this address format identifies the link on which it is connected. The "Subnet-Router Anycast" address format shown here in Fig. 1.42 is defined for all routers within a subnet prefix where the packet sent to this anycast ad-

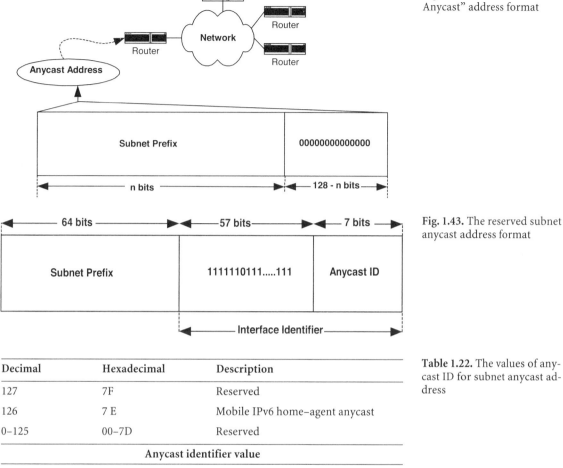

Fig. 1.42. The "Subnet-Router Anycast" address format

Fig. 1.43. The reserved subnet anycast address format

Decimal	Hexadecimal	Description
127	7F	Reserved
126	7 E	Mobile IPv6 home–agent anycast
0–125	00–7D	Reserved
Anycast identifier value		

Table 1.22. The values of anycast ID for subnet anycast address

dress is delivered to one router on the subnet. RFC 2526 suggests the use of additional address space from the unicast address and lists the initial allocation of these reserved anycast addresses.

As stated in RFC 2526, the highest 128 interface identifier values are reserved for subnet anycast addresses. For example, a 64-bit interface identifier can achieve the decimal value of 2^{64} = 18,446,744,073,709,551,616. Therefore, the highest 128 value of subnet anycast will start from 18,446,744,073,709,551,616 − 128 = 18,446,744,073,709,551,488. In other words, 18,446,744,073,709,551,488 to 18,446,744,073,709,551,616 of the interface identifier value is reserved for subnet anycast use. To understand it further we can say that a 7-bit field is reserved (128 = 2^7) or (using two's complement) 7 bits. This 7-bit value identifies the anycast ID (Fig. 1.43).

It must be remembered that, by default, IPv6 address types are required to have a 64-bit interface identifier in EUI-64 format. For all reserved subnet anycast addresses, the universal/local bit should always be set to 0 (local). The anycast ID values for these reserved addresses are shown in Table 1.22.

1.7.2.1.3 Multicast Address

IPv6 does not use broadcast address like the IPv4 network whereas IPv6 multicast addressing can be considered as broadcast in that sense. Similar to IGMP multicast addressing, IPv6 multicast addressing identifies a group of nodes with the flexibility of having a node capable of subscribing to one or more multicast addresses. One of the advantage of IPv6, in this regard, is the flexibility to provide the function of IGMP through the use of the basic ICMP. All routers in an IPv6 network recognize these multicast addresses. The format of a multicast address includes 11111111 as the prefix which if present at the start of an address identifies the address as being multicast.

The multicast address format as shown in Fig. 1.44 includes a 4-bit "flgs" or flags field and a 4-bit "scop" or multicast scope field. The high-order 3 bits of the flag are reserved and initialized to zero. If the "T" bit of the flag is set to 0, it indicates a well-known multicast address, which is typically assigned by the global Internet numbering authority. If this "T" bit is set to 1, it indicates a transient multicast address. The next 4 bit field is "scop" or multicast scope, the values of which are used to limit the scope of the multicast group and shown in Table 1.23.

The next field "Group ID" identifies the multicast group in use, either well known or transient within the given scope. It should be noted that the assignment of scope indicator does not influence the "meaning" of the well-known multicast group. For example, if we assigned a well-known multicast address to a group of NTP (Network Time Protocol) servers with group ID of 101 and various scope indicators, then the meaning would not be changed as depicted in Fig. 1.45.

RFC 2373 has listed a number of well-known multicast addresses as reserved and they are as given in Table 1.24.

The reserved multicast addresses must not be assigned to a node. Users may choose multicast addresses for the assignment of all nodes as follows:

FF01:0:0:0:0:0:0:1
FF02:0:0:0:0:0:0:1

Here scope 1 indicates node local and scope 2 identifies link local attributes of multicast addresses.

Fig. 1.44. The IPv6 multicast address format

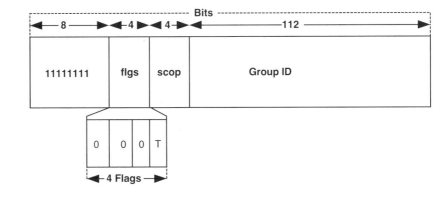

Multicast scope of "scop" values (4 bits = 2^4 = 16)

Table 1.23. Multicast scope of "scop" values (4 bits = 2^4 = 16)

Binary	Hexadecimal	Description
0	0	Reserved
1	1	Node local scope
10	2	Link local scope
11	3	Unassigned
100	4	Unassigned
101	5	Site local scope
110	6	Unassigned
111	7	Unassigned
1000	8	Organizational–local scope
1001	9	Unassigned
1010	A	Unassigned
1011	B	Unassigned
1100	C	Unassigned
1101	D	Unassigned
1110	E	Global scope
1111	F	Reserved

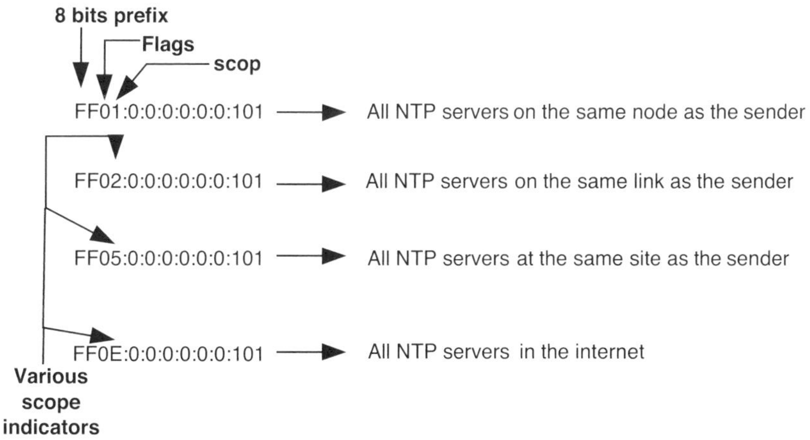

Fig. 1.45. The example of well-known multicast address

Alternatively, for all routers, users should choose multicast addresses as follows:

FF01:0:0:0:0:0:0:2
FF02:0:0:0:0:0:0:2
FF05:0:0:0:0:0:0:2

	Reserved multicast addresses
Table 1.24. The list of reserved multicast addresses	FF00:0:0:0:0:0:0:0
	FF01:0:0:0:0:0:0:0
	FF02:0:0:0:0:0:0:0
	FF03:0:0:0:0:0:0:0
	FF04:0:0:0:0:0:0:0
	FF05:0:0:0:0:0:0:0
	FF06:0:0:0:0:0:0:0
	FF07:0:0:0:0:0:0:0
	FF08:0:0:0:0:0:0:0
	FF09:0:0:0:0:0:0:0
	FF0A:0:0:0:0:0:0:0
	FF0B:0:0:0:0:0:0:0
	FF0C:0:0:0:0:0:0:0
	FF0D:0:0:0:0:0:0:0
	FF0E:0:0:0:0:0:0:0
	FF0F:0:0:0:0:0:0:0

Fig. 1.46. IPv6 transmission over Ethernet

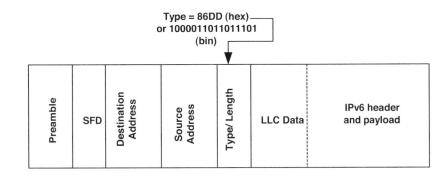

1.7.3 IPv6 Transmission

In the following sections we are going to describe IPv6 packet transmission over broadcast media such as Ethernet and Token Ring. The transmission of IPv6 over Ethernet and Token Ring networks is defined in RFC 2464 and 2470 accordingly. The default MTU size for an IPv6 packet in an Ethernet network is 1500, which can be reduced by the routers or by manual configuration. MTUs over 1500 must be ignored in Ethernet networks for IPv6 packet transmission. During the transmission of an IPv6 packet over Ethernet, the decoded packet format must be as depicted in Fig. 1.46.

The hexadecimal value 86DD in the type field of an Ethernet packet indicates that the data field contains an IPv6 header and payload. Padding may be used if the minimum packet size for Ethernet is not attained. The interface identifier for Ethernet is EUI-64 derived from its 48-bit Ethernet address as described earlier. A link local address for an Ethernet interface (Fig. 1.47) is formed by appending the interface ID to the prefix FE80::/64.

The IPv6 unicast address mapping to the Ethernet link layer is defined in RFC 2461 and 2464. The options packet formats shown in Fig. 1.48 are suggested for the underlying Ethernet link layer.

Since this option is a part of the router's neighbor discovery message, we will describe it in detail again in the neighbor discovery section of Chap. 2. For now, let's consider the IPv6 multicast address mapping to Ethernet's link layer address. RFC 2464 defines a method and a format for such address mapping. For example, the IPv6 packets with a multicast address consisting of 16 bytes are transmitted to an Ethernet multicast address. The Ethernet multicast address for this purpose will have a 16-bit prefix with a hex value of 3333 and the last 32 bits or 4 bytes of the IPv6 address, as clarified in Fig. 1.49.

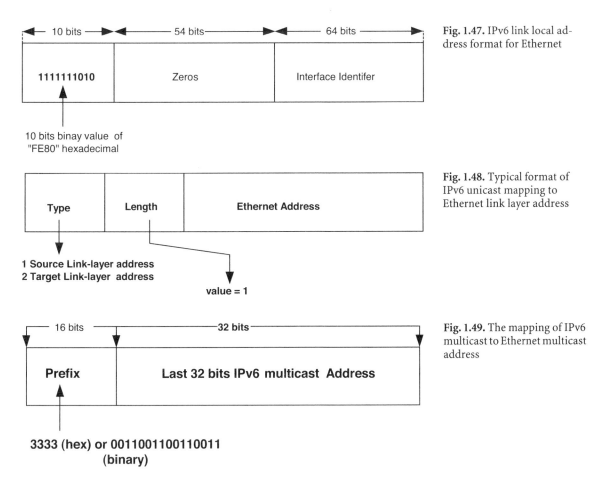

Fig. 1.47. IPv6 link local address format for Ethernet

Fig. 1.48. Typical format of IPv6 unicast mapping to Ethernet link layer address

Fig. 1.49. The mapping of IPv6 multicast to Ethernet multicast address

Now that we understand the transmission of IPv6 packets over Ethernet, let's consider the same thing for the Token Ring network.

1.7.3.1 IPv6 Transmission over Token Ring

The Token Ring is another very important LAN technology for which the transmission compatibility of IPv6 is imperative. RFC 2470 defines the transmission of IPv6 packets over a Token Ring (TR) network. Since the deliberation of this book is limited to unified IP transport, it is not possible to describe the TR in detail here. Therefore, I will suggest readers refer to my *High-Speed LAN Technology Handbook*. However, to study the transmission of IPv6 over TR in further detail, we have to consider the MTU size of the TR network. The TR, which is defined in IEEE 802.5, has a maximum frame size based on "hold token time". Many factors can influence the hold timer including data signaling rate, number of nodes on the ring, etc.

Due to such variation of frame size, suggested MTU can be 2000, 4000 and 8000 as the common default router configuration. If any of these configurations are missing the default MTU will be 1500. In an environment where source route bridging is used, information in the LF (Largest Frame) subfield of the route information field dictates the MTU of that link (Fig. 1.50) .

There are values of LF fields that dictate the MTU size lower than the minimum MTU requirements (1280) for IPv6. In such cases IPv6 transmission is not possible. To support the required MTUs for IPv6 transmission over TR, the values of the LF field are as given in Table 1.25.

It is recommended that users should prioritize the following requirements in order to achieve the desired MTU size for IPv6 transmission over source-route-based TR:

• If no value greater than MTU value is attained from route advertisement, LF MTU values from source route bridges can be used.
• If no value greater than MTU value can be attained from manual and auto configuration, router advertisement MTU size can be used.

Fig. 1.50. The LF field values which dictate the MTU size for source-route-based TR

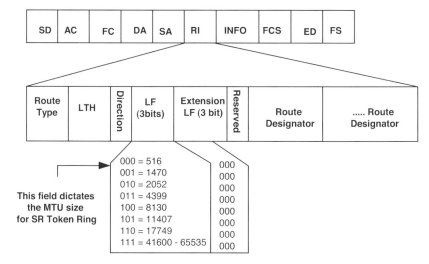

LF	LF extension	TR MTU	IPv6 MTU
001	000	1470	1462
010	000	2052	2044
011	000	4399	4391
100	000	8130	8122
101	000	11,407	11,399
110	000	17,749	17,741
111	000	41,600	41,592

Table 1.25. Supported MTU size for IPv6 transmission in source-routed TR

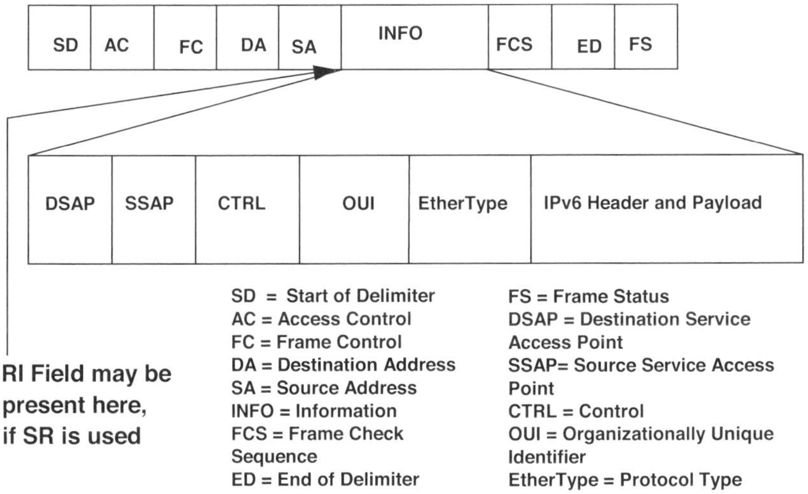
SD
AC
FC
DA
SA
INFO
FCS
ED
FS
DSAP
SSAP
CTRL
OUI
EtherType
IPv6 Header and Payload
RI Field may be present here, if SR is used
SD = Start of Delimiter
AC = Access Control
FC = Frame Control
DA = Destination Address
SA = Source Address
INFO = Information
FCS = Frame Check Sequence
ED = End of Delimiter
FS = Frame Status
DSAP = Destination Service Access Point
SSAP= Source Service Access Point
CTRL = Control
OUI = Organizationally Unique Identifier
EtherType = Protocol Type

Fig. 1.51. TR frame format for IPv6 transmission

- Manual configuration.
- Default MTU 1500.

During the IPv6 transmission over TR, the frame format of the TR will be as depicted in Fig. 1.51.

If the TR is source routed, arouting field (RIF) may appear in the frame immediately after the SA. The RIF will be in the frame if the MSB (Most Significant Bit) of the SA is set to 1. Typically, the RIF is a variable length field that includes a 2-byte RC (Routing Control) header followed by route designator fields (Fig. 1.52).

1.7.4 Transition Criteria

Now that we have some understanding of the technical details of IPv6, let's consider how we should transition the internet or intranet from IPv4 to IPv6. Successful IPv6 deployment depends on the compatibility of the large installed base of the IPv4 network. Although IPv6 is capable of supporting IPv4 infrastructure (i.e., it can send, route and receive IPv4 packets), one problem that still remains is that IPv4 clients are not capable of handling IPv6 packets.

Fig. 1.52. The RI field of the TR

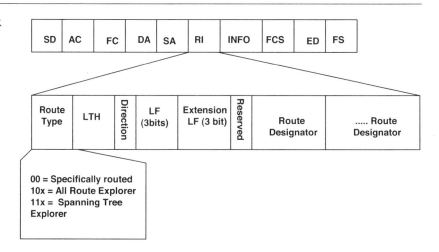

Several options are available to pursue this transition. One might suggest that a "flag day" could be declared when all systems on the earth would be upgraded from IPv4 to IPv6. Even 20 years ago when the NCP to TCP transition occurred, the idea of a "flag day" did not work out. Now, considering the number of systems and the growth of the Internet, it is not conceivable at all. According to RFC 1933 two conceivable methods of transition would be as follows:

1. Dual IP stack
2. IPv6 over IPv4 tunneling.

Both of these approaches can be used alone or together for gradual integration of IPv6 hosts and routers into an IPv4 network. The dual IP stack approach suggests having a client install both IPv4 and IPv6 protocol stacks. This configuration (Fig. 1.53)will allow the system to send and receive IPv4 and IPv6 packets. Such a node or system is known as an IPv6/IPv4 node. Currently a number of operating system vendors are providing IPv6 stacks that can coexist with already installed IPv4 stacks. The IPv6/IPv4 node must be configured with both the IPv6 address and IPv4 address. Furthermore these nodes must also understand whether or not another node is IPv6 capable or IPv4 only.

Since IPv4 implementation comprehends 127.0.0.1 as a "loopback" address, IPv6 /IPv4 implementation may treat IPv4-compatible IPv6 address ::127.0.0.1 as an IPv6 "loopback" address. Therefore, packets with such an address must remain within the node. Another issue to deal with is the DNS (Domain Name Service) resource record. The resource record type named "AAAA" is assigned to IPv6 addresses and "A" is assigned to IPv4 addresses. The IPv6/IPv4 dual stack implementation must provide libraries to deal with both of these DNS record types.

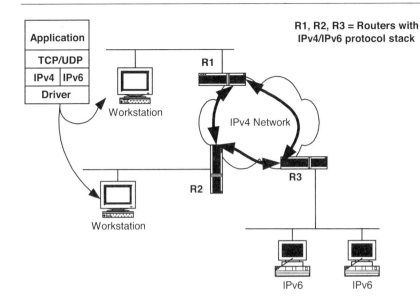

R1, R2, R3 = Routers with IPv4/IPv6 protocol stack

Fig. 1.53. A typical implementation of IPv6 /IPv4 dual stack and IPv6 tunneling

1.7.4.1 IPv6 over IPv4 Tunneling

We mentioned earlier that in most cases the IPv6 routing infrastructure will be built up over time. A more likely deployment would be a still functional IPv4 routin g infrastructure around which the network manager may choose to build an IPv6 infrastructure. In this typical deployment, IPv6 packets must be carried over the IPv4 network. To adopt this, RFC 1933 defines tunneling techniques, which is a way to utilize the existing infrastructure and transport IPv6 traffic through it. The IPv6/IPv4 hosts and routers can tunnel an IPv6 datagram within IPv4 packets to be transported over the IPv4 infrastructure. Such tunneling can be used in several ways:

• Router-to-router: IPv6/IPv4 routers that are connected through the IPv4 infrastructure can tunnel IPv6 packets between themselves.
• Host-to-router: An IPv6/IPv4 host can tunnel to an intermediary IPv6/IPv4 router that is reachable via the IPv4 network.
• Host-to-host: An IPv6/IPv4 host can tunnel to another IPv6/IPv4 host that is reachable through the IPv4 network to transport IPv6 packets.
• Router-to-host: An IPv6/IPv4 router may tunnel IPv6 packets to their final destination.

The common tunneling mechanism is the encapsulation of IPv6 packet in IPv4 as depicted in Fig. 1.54.

A node such as the router, which encapsulates an IPv6 datagram within an IPv4 packet, must handle some more complex issues such as the following:

• Identify when to report an error of ICMP packet too big to the source.
• Determine how to report IPv4 ICMP errors to the source as an IPv6 ICMP error.

RFC 1933 has defined two tunneling techniques which differ primarily on how they identify the tunnel endpoint address, namely configured and automatic.

Fig. 1.54. The encapsulation of IPv6 datagram within IPv4 packet

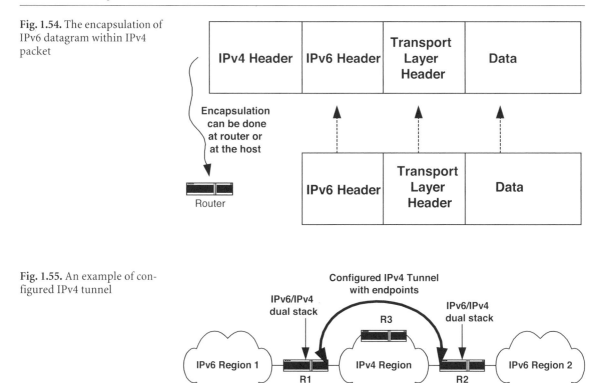

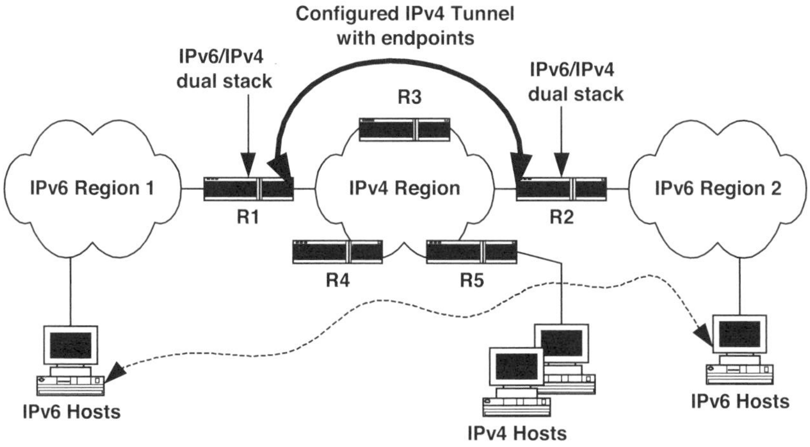

Fig. 1.55. An example of configured IPv4 tunnel

1. Configured or static IPv4 tunnel: This is a mechanism to forward any IPv6 packet through an IPv4 region. Figure 1.55 shows a configured tunnel between an IPv4 interface on router R1 and an IPv4 interface on router R2. Remember that both routers are running IPv6/IPv4 dual protocol stacks.

Now, if the IPv6 host connected to IPv6 region 1 sends a packet addressed to the IPv6 host at IPv6 region 2, the following occur:

- Router R1 receives the IPv6 packet and identifies that it should forward the packet through its tunnel interface.
- Router R1 encapsulates the IPv6 packet in an IPv4 packet. The SA in the IPv4 header will be the IPv4 address of the local tunnel interface on R1. The DA is the IPv4 address of the remote tunnel interface on R2.
- An IPv4 router in the IPv4 region acting as intermediary will forward the packet to router R2 based on IPv4 header information.
- Router R2 will then decapsulate the packet removing the IPv4 header and forwarding it to the destined IPv6 host.

2. Automatic IPv4 tunnel: This mechanism is used to forward a unicast IPv6 packet with an IPv4-compatible address format. It is imperative that we understand the IPv4-compatible address format before studying further. The IPv4-compatible address is a special type of IPv6 address (Fig. 1.56). It is identified by an all-zero 96-bit prefix and an IPv4 address in the low-order 32 bits.

These addresses are assigned to the IPv6/IPv4 node that supports automatic tunneling. Nodes that are configured with IPv4-compatible addresses can use the whole address as their IPv6 address and the embedded IPv4 address as the IPv4 address. It must be remembered that all routers which run automatic tunneling must invoke both IPv4 and IPv6 protocol stacks.

Similar to the configured IPv4 tunnel, the automatic tunnel also works with an intent to forward packets to the destination except that it is dynamic for automatic tunneling. This means that it will only be established by the router for forwarding the IPv6 packets. Once the packet is forwarded, the tunnel no longer exists. In Fig 1.57 an IPv6 host wants to send an IPv6 packet to a host connected to router R6. In this case, R1 will examine the packet and once it determines that a virtual tunnel needs to be established to send the packet to its destination, it will do so followed by encapsulation of the packet. Thus the destination router R6 will decapsulate the packet and will forward it to the destined host.

1.7.5 IPv6 Tunnel

Like the IPv4 tunnel, the IPv6 tunnel also encapsulates IP packets but it is IPv6 within IPv6. This technique is used to establish a virtual link between

Fig. 1.56. The IPv4-compatible address format

Fig. 1.57. An example of automatic IPv4 tunneling

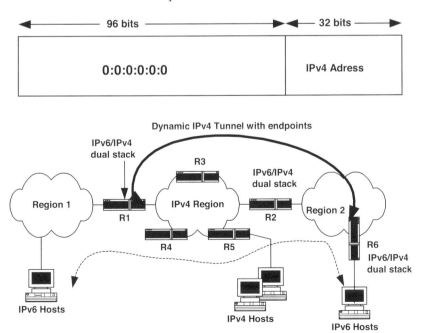

two IPv6 nodes for transmitting data packets as the payload of an IPv6 packet. This technique can be used for various other protocols such as AppleTalk, IPX, etc. (as suggested in RFC 2473). The IPv6 tunnel (Fig. 1.58) is a unidirectional mechanism for which tunnel packet flow occurs in one direction between IPv6 "entry-point" and "exit-point" nodes. The entry point can be considered the encapsulator of the packet (the packets of its own or of others) and the exit point is the decapsulator of the packet (for its own or for others). The entry point can be considered as the encapsulator of the packet (the packets of its own or of others) and the exit point is the decapsulator of the packet (for its own or for others).

Another tunneling technique, namely bidirectional tunneling (Fig. 1.59), is achieved by merging two unidirectional mechanisms. In this approach, two tunnels are configured in opposite directions to each other, having the entry-point node of one tunnel as the exit-point node of the other tunnel.

1.7.6 ICMPv6

The ICMP for IPv6 (ICMPv6) is primarily used by the IPv6 node to report errors in processing packets and some useful Internet layer function such as ICMPv6 "ping". Like currently used ICMP of IPv4, ICMPv6 is an integral part of IPv6. Every ICMPv6 message has an IPv6 header and zero or more extension headers. The IPv6 next header value of 58 identifies ICMPv6 as the subsequent header.

Fig. 1.58. An example of IPv6 tunneling

Fig. 1.59. Bidirectional tunneling

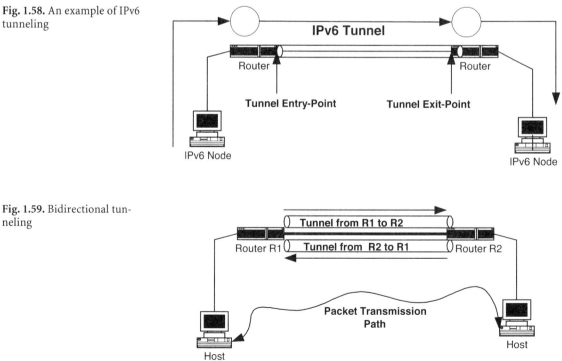

```
- - - - - - - - - - - - - - - - - - Frame 77 - - - -
  Frame Status Source Address   Dest. Address       Size
Rel. Time      Delta Time    Abs. Time
Summary
    77          ::                ff02::1:fff7:5249    78
0:01:00.266   0.239.317     05/18/2000 02:10:37 PM DLC:
Ethertype=86DD, size=78 bytes

IPv6: Priority=15 Flow=0x000000

ICMPv6: Neighbor Solicitation Code=0
DLC:   ----- DLC Header -----
     DLC:
     DLC:  Frame 77 arrived at  14:10:37.8992; frame
size is 78 (004E hex) bytes.
     DLC:  Destination = Multicast 3333FFF75249
     DLC:  Source      = Station AC060600B300
     DLC:  Ethertype   = 86DD
     DLC:
IPv6:  ----- IPv6 Header -----
     IPv6:
     IPv6: Version          = 6
     IPv6: Priority         = 15 (Non-Congestion-
Controlled Traffic)
     IPv6: Flow Label       = 0x000000
     IPv6: Payload Length   = 24
     IPv6: Next Header      = 58 (ICMPv6)
     IPv6: Hop Limit        = 255
     IPv6: Source address   = ::
     IPv6: Destination address = ff02::1:fff7:5249
     IPv6:
ICMPv6: ----- ICMPv6 Header -----
     ICMPv6:
     ICMPv6: Type              = 135 (Neighbor
Solicitation)
     ICMPv6: Code              = 0
     ICMPv6: Checksum          = 0x32A6
     ICMPv6: Reserved          = 0x00000000
     ICMPv6: Target Address    =
fe80::200:a2ff:fef7:5249
     ICMPv6: No Neighbor Discovery options
     ICMPv6:
ADDR   HEX
ASCII
0000: 33 33 ff f7 52 49 ac 06 06 00 b3 00 86 dd 6f 00 |
33..RI¬.......o.
0010: 00 00 00 18 3a ff 00 00 00 00 00 00 00 00 00 00 |
....:...........
0020: 00 00 00 00 00 00 ff 02 00 00 00 00 00 00 00 00 |
................
0030: 00 01 ff f7 52 49 87 00 32 a6 00 00 00 00 fe 80 |
....RI..2......
0040: 00 00 00 00 00 00 02 00 a2 ff fe f7 52 49        |
...........RI
```

Carefully examine Fig. 1.60 and verify the following packet capture to further understand the ICMPv6 message format.

Fig. 1.60. The ICMPv6 message format

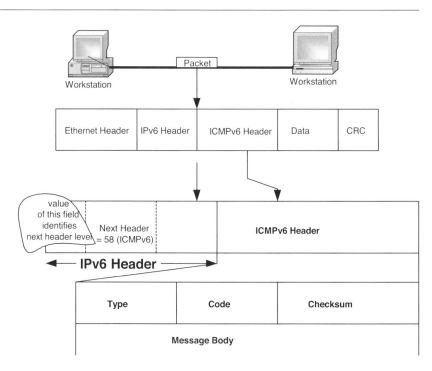

Table 1.26. ICMPv6 messages and their type field values

Type	ICMPv6 error message	ICMPv6 informational message	Type
1	Destination unreachable	Echo request	128
2	Packet too big	Echo reply	129
3	Time exceeded		
4	Parameter problem		

The type field inhe ICMPv6 header indicates the type of message and the value dictates the remaining data. Looking at the packet capture, the type field value of 135 indicates the neighbor solicitation message from a router. The code field indicates the message type and the checksum is used to detect data corruption.

ICMPv6 message.s can be considered as having two groups: one that conveys error message and another that is informational in nature. The error messages are identified with a zero in the high-order bit of the message type field value. As a result, error messages have message types from 0 to 127 whereas informational messages have message types from 128 to 255.

Table 1.26 shows various ICMPv6 messages and their respective type field values. Remember that other messages (not shown here) consist of some that have been defined and some that have yet to be defined. For the sake of discussion these are not necessary here.

1.7.6.1 ICMPv6 Error Messages

The destination unreachable error message occurs if the destination to which the packet is to be transmitted is not reached. It includes the following fields in the ICMPv6 header (Fig. 1.61):

- Type: This one-octet field carries a value of 1 for the destination unreachable message.
- Code: The code is a one-octet field which may carry one of the following values:
  0 = No route to destination
  1 = Communication with destination administratively prohibited
  2 = Not assigned
  3 = Address unreachable
  4 = Port unreachable
- Checksum: This is a two-octet field used for frame error checking.
- Unused: This is a four-octet field which is initialized to zero by the sender and ignored by the receiver.

The destination unreachable is generated by a router or an originating node if a packet is undeliverable to the destination due to reasons other than congestion.

If the failure is due to the lack of matching entry in the forwarding node's routing table then the destination unreachable ICMPv6 error message will indicate a "0" value in the code field. If the packet could not be delivered due to firewall implementation the code field will indicate a "1" as the value of the field. If the value of the code field is set to 3, it indicates either the IPv6 address cannot be resolved or a link-specific problem. If the code field value is set to 4, it indicates that there is no transport protocol listener (e.g., UDP).

The "Packet too big" error message (Fig. 1.62) occurs if the packet to be transported is bigger than the MTU size of the link, and routers generally send this message. The basic frame format for this error message is the same as destination unreachable except the MTU field is inserted instead of the unused field.

The type field value for this error message is 2 and the code field value is set to 0 by the sender which in turn is ignored by the receiver. The MTU field identifies the MTU of the next-hop link.

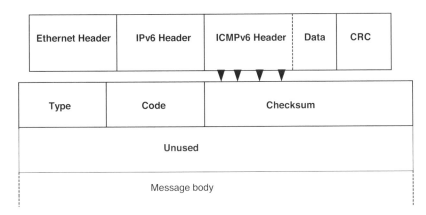

Fig. 1.61. The destination unreachable message (ICMPv6) format

Fig. 1.62. The "Packet too big" ICMPv6 message

Fig. 1.63. The ICMPv6 message format for "Time exceeded" message

Fig. 1.64. The "Parameter problem" message format

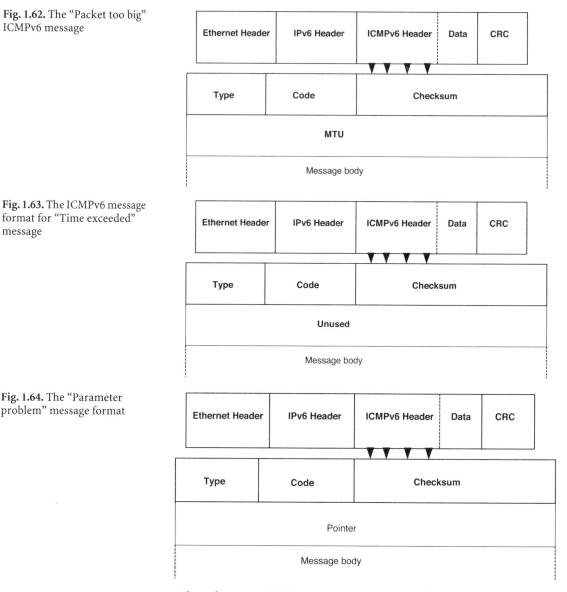

The other two ICMPv6 error messages are "Time exceeded" message (TEM) and "Parameter problem" message. The type field value for the TEM is 3 (Fig. 1.63). In this message the code field can have two values where value "0" indicates hop limit exceeded in transit and value "1" means fragment reassembly time exceeded. The unused field in this message has the same function as in the messages described earlier.

TEM occurs when a router receives a packet with a hop limit of zero or a packet with similar indication; the router discards such packets and sends out a TEM ICMPv6 error message.

PPM (Fig. 1.64) occurs when the processing of an IPv6 header was unsuccessful due to a problem in the header. If such a problem exists the IPv6 node that is processing the packet may discard it and send out PPM indicating the type and location of the problem.

Table 1.27 shows various fields of the PPM and their values.

1.7.6.2 ICMPv6 Inform ational Message

As described earlier, "Echo request" and "Echo reply" are the two information- al ICMPv6 messages. Every node in the IPv6 network must implement an echo responder function that receives echo request and replies back and can also send echo reque st and receiveecho reply for diagnostics purposes (Fig. 1.65). The type field value for echo request is 128 and the code field value is 0. The identifier field in this message is used to aid in matching echo replies to the echo request being sent. The data field value is set to zero or may include more data in this message.

The echo reply is sent in response to echo request. The echo reply message (Fig. 1.66) includes a type field with value 129 and a code value of 0.

Field name	Values and descriptions
Type	4
Code	0 – erroneous header field encountered 1 – unrecognized next header type 2 – unrecognized IPv6 option
Pointer	Identifies the location with the packet where error has occurred

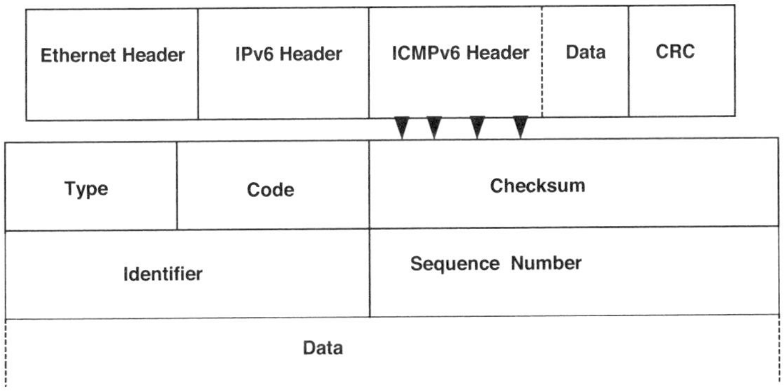

Table 1.27. ICMPv6 PPM fields and their descriptions

Fig. 1.65. The ICMPv6 echo re- quest message format

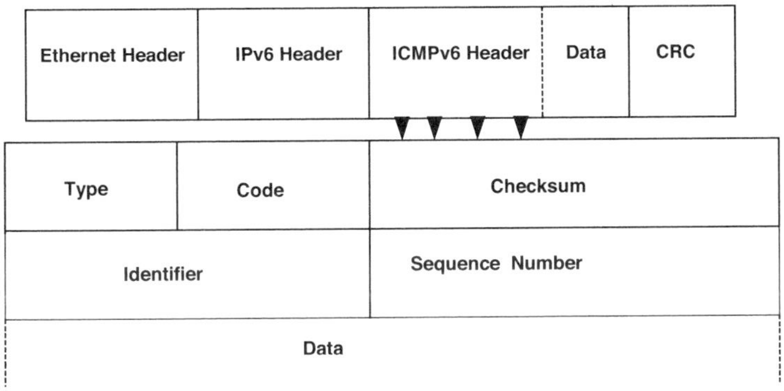

Fig. 1.66. The echo reply mes- sage

1.7.7 Address Autoconfiguration

IPv6 provides a means for hosts to autoconfigure its interface. The autoconfiguration includes creating a link local address and verifying the uniqueness of this address in a link. IPv6 suggests two mechanisms through which a host can obtain an address for its interface: stateless autoconfiguration and stateful autoconfiguration.

Typically, to start the process of autoconfiguration, a node will perform the following:

- Configures a link local address to use temporarily. The host can obtain this address by adding a generic local address prefix to a unique token (e.g., the host's IEEE LAN interface address).
- The host sends out an ND (NeighborDiscovery) message to the created address to ensure that it is unique. This is ensured by monitoring that the previously transmitted ND message was not received back, and therefore it is unique. If a message comes back indicating that the link local address is already in use, the host will use a different token (e.g., an administrative token or a randomly generated token).
- The host will use the IPv6 multicast service to send out an ND router s olicitation request, which will be done by using the new link local address as a source address. It should be remembered that the ND multicast solicitations are not necessarily processed by all nodes on the link. IPv6 defines several permanent multicast groups for finding resources on a local node or link, including an all-routers group, an all-hosts group, and a Dynamic Host Configuration Protocol (DHCP) server group.

Routers respond to the solicitation messages from hosts with a unique router advertisement that includes prefix information indicating a valid range of addresses for the subnet. Routers can also send these advertisements periodically to local multicast groups, whether or not they receive solicitations.

Using the router advertisement message that it sends in response to a solicitation from a host, an IPv6 router can control whether the host uses stateful or stateless autoconfiguration.

In stateful autoconfiguration, the host contacts a DHCP or similar address server, which assigns an address from a manually administered list.

In stateless autoconfiguration, a host can automatically configure its own IPv6 address without the help of a stateful address server. The host uses the globally valid address prefix information in the router advertisement message to create its own IPv6 address. The host concatenates the valid prefix with its link layer address (or a similar unique token) to create an IPv6 address.

Table 1.28 shows the difference between stateless and stateful autoconfiguration in IPv6.

Stateless autoconfiguration is defined in RFC 2462 while stateful autoconfiguration is still under research and a recommendation is specified in Internet draft: draft-ietf-dhc-dhcpv6-15.txt. If the stateful autoconfiguration Internet draft becomes an RFC the protocol will be known as DHCPv6.

Stateless autoconfiguration	Stateful autoconfiguration
A system uses link local address as source and multicasts to "All routers on this link"	Routers ask the new system to go DHCP server (by setting managed configuration bit)
Router replies and provides all the needed prefix information	System multicasts to "All DHCP servers"
Disadvantages: anyone can connect	DHCP server assigns an address

Table 1.28. Stateless and stateful IPv6 address autoconfiguration

2 Routing Technologies

2.1 Introduction

This chapter is specifically written for those who are interested in not only the routing technologies but also the trend of routing techniques. Although a number of books have been written about routing technologies, most of them have specifically addressed a protocol or two. Very few books have so far addressed the routing technologies in a complete manner. I have tried to accommodate as much "routing technology" information as possible in this one chapter. The wealth of information is enough for anyone to become conversant in the subject. The chapter is so designed that anybody with a first-hand approach will be able to understand the details about routing technology and its current trend. The chapter covers the beginning of the routing idea to its state-of-the-art protocols, which should be enough to make you conversant with the subject.

The chapter includes the basics of routing, routing techniques, routing protocols such as RIP, OSPF and BGP (Border Gateway Protocol), and the recently introduced MPLS routing technique. It is a fact that you will find the use of routing protocols almost everywhere. Routing provides much of the transport advantages if the implementation is correct. It does not matter which vendor has manufactured a product, so long as knowledge of the underlying technology is crystal clear. At least that is my experience. The key idea is understanding the technology. You will find that most routing books primarily address the routing technology with vendor-specific implementation; only a few of them describe the technology as a whole. This chapter only addresses the technologies and it is often possible to apply such an approach to almost any vendor's product.

Once you are through with this chapter, reading relevant RFCs will enhance your know-how. The RFCs also will provide you with the latest modifications of a protocol and any further information therein. One of the main advantages you will get out from reading this chapter is that it will act as a teacher to slowly improve your knowledge and let you digest easily an enormous wealth of information. After finishing this chapter you should be capable of not only deploying the routing protocols but also verifying that a product or products are deploying the underlying protocol correctly. So why wait? Let's get started ...

2.2 Routing

We have used the term "routing" during our discussions about switching and also in various other sections of this book. Therefore, it is imperative to learn more about this technique. IETF documentation (generally RFCs) also refers to the router as an Internet Gateway, which in another sense is the IP-level router. RFC 1009 has defined the requirements for an Internet Gateway or a router. To describe it we should first observe the behavior of a bridge. The bridges monitor all frames at the media access control (MAC) layer, that is it operates as a promiscuous device. But the router is specifically addressed at the network layer and it does not examine all frames or its mode of operation is non-promiscuous. A router only examines frames selectively for those frames explicitly destined for it. Another important difference between the bridge and router is the address structure on which they operate. For example, a bridge typically examines the MAC address whereas the router examines the IP address or network layered address. Like bridges, routers make forwarding decisions using tables. However, a bridge generally implements a simple table lookup procedure whereas the router implements a sophisticated table lookup procedure. For example, a router is capable of selecting an optimal path to the destination from several existing paths by using a routing algorithm. This provides several advantages over use of a bridge, namely flow control mechanism, frame fragmentation, optimal path for traffic, QoS, and interconnection of dissimilar networks. Routing in a network involves a complex collection of algorithms that work more or less independently and yet support each other by exchanging services or information. One example of such a configuration is implementation of RIP and OSPF in an intranet.

The complexity in a router is inherited from several sources. First, routing requires coordination between all nodes of a subnet rather than just a pair of modules such as datalink and network protocols. Second, the routing system must cope with link and node failures, requiring redirection of traffic and updating the database maintained by the system. Third, to achieve high performance, a router may need to modify its routes when some areas within the network become congested. Use of a routing algorithm substantially affects two main performance measures: throughput and average packet delay. Routers use a flow control mechanism to determine these measures. For example, when traffic load is relatively low, it will be fully equal to the throughput:

Throughput = Offered traffic load

When the offered traffic load is excessive and/or the network is congested, a portion of the incoming traffic will be rejected:

Throughput = Offered traffic – Rejected load

Therefore, in a congested network, traffic accepted into the network will experience an average delay per packet that will depend on the routes chosen by the router. The effect of good routing is to increase throughput for the same value of average delay per packet under high traffic conditions and to decrease average delay per packet under low traffic conditions.

According to RFC 1009, an IP-level gateway or router must perform the following functions:

1. Conform to the protocols specified in RFC 1009 including IP and ICMP.
2. Have interfaces to two or more packet networks. For each network, it should also implement the functions required by the said network and generally these are as follows:
    (a) Capability to encapsulate and decapsulate IP datagrams with the underlying framing concept (e.g., Ethernet header and checksum).
    (b) Capability to receive and send IP datagrams up to the maximum size supported by the underlying layer 2 networking concept. This packet size is considered as the MTU for that network.
    (c) Capability to translate an IP DA into the underlying network-level address (e.g., Ethernet MAC address).
    (d) Capability to respond to the network flow control or error indication if any.

In an internet with a hop-by-hop routing model, a router that handles a packet by examining the DA in the IP header computes the next hop that will bring the packet one step closer to its destination, and delivers the packet to the next hop, where the process is repeated. To make this work, two things are needed. First, routing tables match DAs with next hops. Second, routing protocols determine the contents of these tables.

2.2.1 Routing Tables

An internetworking device (i.e., router or L3 switch) uses routing tables to compute the next hop for a packet. Routing tables help a router to determine how it should route packets. For a given network, where two or more minimum hops exist, routes are chosen arbitrarily to minimize the number of hops to reach the destination. The routing tables indicate, for each destination, the next router to which a packet should be sent. Let's consider the network in Fig. 2.1 for example.

In our given network, information from R1 to R5 is sent from R1 to R4 first, then directly to R5. Therefore, the routing table at R1 should be as stated in Table 2.1 and that at R4 as in Table 2.2.

For a router, inconsistent tables may cause unsuccessful routing and lead to ping-ponging, looping and similar phenomena. More often it is difficult to completely eliminate such glitches in a complex network. Routing tables can take many forms. To describe what we stated in Tables 2.1 and 2.2, here is a simple real-world example that can explain most Internet routing. Each entry in a routing table has at least two fields – the IP address prefix and the next hop. The next hop is the IP address of another host or router that is directly

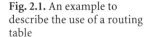

Fig. 2.1. An example to describe the use of a routing table

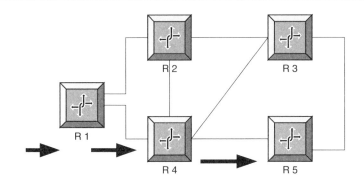

Packet is sent to R4 first in order to send to R5

Table 2.1. Routing table at R1

Destination router	2	3	4	5
Next router	2	2	4	4

Table 2.2. Routing table at R4

Destination router	1	2	3	5
Next router	1	2	3	5

reachable via an Ethernet, serial link, or some other physical connection. The IP address prefix specifies a set of destinations for which the routing entry is valid. In order to be in this set, the beginning of the destination IP address must match the IP address prefix, which can have from 0 to 32 significant bits. For example, an IP address prefix of 128.8.0.0/16 would match any destination IP address of the form 128.8.X.X.

Bridged networks are regarded as single connections. If no routing table entries match a packet's DA, the packet is discarded as undeliverable (possibly with an ICMP notification to the sender). If multiple routing table entries match, the longest match is preferred. The longest match is the entry with the most 1 bits in its routing mask.

To avoid routing entries for every possible Internet destination, most hosts and routers use a default route (some routing tables contain nothing but a single default route). A default route has a routing address/mask pair of 0.0.0.0/0.0.0.0. In other words, it matches every IP address, but since there is no 1 bit in its routing mask, any other match would be selected by the longest match rule. The default route will only be used if there are no other matches in the routing table – hence its name. Default routes are quite common, and are put to best use on networks with only a single link connecting to the global Internet. On such a network, routing tables will have entries for local nets and subnets, as well as a single default route leading to the outbound link. However, remember that all next hops must be directly reachable, so the default routes will not necessarily point to the same IP address. Also, some networks (large ISPs, mostly) use defaultless routing tables that must be able to match every IP address in the global net.

2.2.2 Routing Protocols

"Real network engineers construct routing tables by hand", but the rest of us use routing protocols. Routing protocols form the core of the hacker's internet, because it is here that all the decisions are made. Network engineers assign costs to network paths, and routing protocols select the least-cost path to the destination.

I find that routing protocols bear an uncanny resemblance to capitalist market economics. In both systems, there is a large group of "nodes", the decisions of each being driven by a cost-minimization algorithm. The end result is a reasonably efficient distribution of "resources". Furthermore, cost determination is done in similar ways. A router, like an import/export firm, will compute its cost, add on profit for its part in the transaction, and pass this cost along to customers. Both systems use this method to achieve reasonable efficiency. However, in today's complex internetworking world a number of routing protocols are used and they are part of the following protocol class specifications: distance-vector routing protocols, link state routing, interior routing and exterior routing.

2.2.2.1 Distance-Vector (D-V) Routing Protocols

This type of routing protocol requires that each router simply inform its neighbors of its routing table. In the D-V algorithm, each router maintains a table known as "Vector" for example. A vector supplies the information about the best-known distance to every destination and the path to get there. These vectors or tables are updated periodically by exchanging information among the neighboring routers. The D-V routing algorithm is sometimes known as the distributed *Bellman–Ford* routing algorithm or the *Ford–Fullkerson* algorithm. These algorithms are named after the scientists who developed them (Bellman in 1957, Ford and Fullkerson in 1962). Actually, Ford and Fullkerson are the authors of this algorithm, though Bellman's name comes from the fact that the formulation is based on Bellman's equation. This protocol is the original ARPANET routing algorithm and used in the Internet as RIP. For each network path, the receiving routers pick the neighbor advertising the lowest cost, then add this entry into the routing table for re-advertisement. In addition, it includes a "metric" measuring the total distance to the router or connected entity. The "metric" used here can be number of hops, time delay in milliseconds, total number of packets queued along the path, or something very similar. The router assumes the distance by looking at the "metric". If the metric is in hops, the distance is just one hop. If the metric is in delay, the router measures it directly with special echo packets that the receiving router just timestamps and sends back immediately. To summarize the D-V algorithm, we can say routers work together and do the following:

1. Each router maintains a table (vector) giving the best-known distance to destination and the line to use for sending to there. Tables are updated by exchanging information with neighbors.

2. Each router knows the distance (cost) of reaching its neighbors (e.g., send echo requests).
3. Routers periodically exchange routing tables with each of their neighbors.
4. Upon receipt of an update, for each destination in its table, a router compares the metric in its local table with the metric in the neighbor's table plus the cost of reaching that neighbor. If the path via the neighbor has a lower cost, the router updates its local table to forward packets to the neighbor.

This algorithm was used in the original ARPANET. Unfortunately, it suffers from the problem that good news travels quickly, bad news travels slowly (count-to-infinity problem). The fundamental problem with the old ARPANET algorithm is that it continues to use "old" information that is invalid, even after newer information becomes available.

Hello and RIP are common D-V routing protocols. Common enhancements to D-V algorithms include split horizon, poison reverse, triggered updates, and holddown. RFC 1058 discusses D-V or Bellman–Ford algorithms in RIP's specification. Besides RIP, Novell's IPX, early versions of DECnet and AppleTalk can be considered as D-V routing protocols. While using D-V protocols in general, many vendors may introduce their own proprietary protocols among the same vendor products. As stated in RFC 1058, in a D-V routing scenario these proprietary protocols must be used as the "Interior Routing Protocol".

The RIP is a straightforward implementation of the D-V algorithm. It allows hosts and gateways to exchange information for computing routes through an IP-based network. Since RIP is a D-V protocol, it acquired significant attributes of the D-V algorithm. In general, it conveys information about routes to "destinations", which may be individual hosts, networks, or a special destination used to convey a default route. RIP can be implemented as active or passive. Usually routers or IP gateways use RIP in active mode whereas a host runs it in passive mode. In active mode, routers send out broadcasts every 30 seconds. A host that implements RIP in passive mode does not broadcast but listens and updates its routes based on advertisements. Normally, a participant in RIP is assumed to have a routing table. The routing table keeps an entry for every destination that is reachable. It is imperative that each entry contains at least the following information (as stated in RFC 1085):

1. The IP address of the destination.
2. A "hop count" metric to measure the total cost of getting a datagram from the host to the destination. Here, the metric is the sum of the costs associated with the networks that would be traversed in getting to the destination.
3. The IP address of the next gateway along the path to the destination.
4. A flag to indicate that information about the route has changed recently. This will be referred to as the "route change flag."
5. Various timers associated with the route.

Let's understand the RIP function by examining the network given in Fig. 2.2. Here, router R1 will broadcast a message to network B, which contains infor-

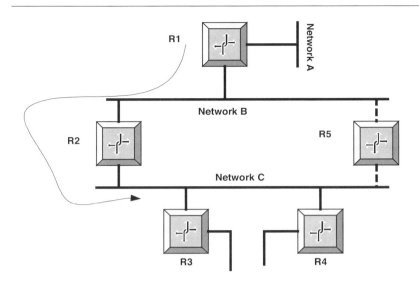

Fig. 2.2. An example of RIP function

mation that it can reach network A at cost 1. Now, gateways R2 and R5 will receive the broadcast and add a route to network A through R1 (at cost 2, for example). Later, R2 and R5 will include this information in their broadcast RIP message to network C. Eventually, all routers will update their route table and add the route entry. It is important to know that RIP implements some rules to prevent routes from oscillating between two or more equal-cost paths. For example, if R2 and R5 both broadcast or advertise network A at cost 2, routers R3 and R4 will update the route based on the first advertised message. Also RIP specifies that routers should retain existing routes until a new route is discovered with a lower cost.

2.2.2.2 Link State Routing Protocols

This type of routing protocol requires each router to maintain at least a partial map of the network. When a network link changes state (up to down, or vice versa), a notification, called a link state advertisement (LSA) is flooded throughout the network. All the routers note the change, and recompute their routes accordingly. This method is more reliable, easier to debug and less bandwidth intensive than D-V. It is also more complex and more computing and memory intensive. OSPF and OSI's IS–IS are link state routing protocols.

The old ARPANET routing algorithm was replaced in 1979. Problems with the old algorithm included:

1. High-priority routing update packets were large, adversely affecting traffic.
2. The network was too slow in adapting to congestion, too fast to react to minor changes.
3. Average queue length was used to estimate delay. This works only if all lines have the same capacity and propagation delay, and does not take into account that packets have varying sizes.

In the new algorithm:

1. Each router maintains a database describing the topology and link delays between each router. That is, each router keeps track of the full graph of links and nodes.
2. Each router periodically discovers its neighbors (sends a "Hello" message on booting) and measures the delays across its links (echo requests – should load be taken into account?), then forwards that information to all other routers (link state packets).
3. Updates are propagated at high priority using flooding. They contain sequence numbers, and a router forwards "new" copies of the packet. Why use flooding? Because that way routing updates propagate even when routing tables are not quite correct. Acknowledgements (ACKs) are sent to neighbors.
4. Each router uses an SPF (Shortest Path First) algorithm to calculate shortest paths based on the current values in its database.
5. Because each router makes its calculation using the same information, better routing decisions are made.

Limitations of the new algorithm are as follows:

1. It does not take link capacity into consideration. A 1200 baud link with a 100 ms delay is favored over Ethernet having a 200 ms delay.
2. It does not scale well, as each router receives updates from all other routers. Today, we need to think of scaling to a system with a million nodes and many more links! After all, 5 billion people will (eventually) be on the network! Widely used today, it replaced D-V in the ARPANET. Link state improves the convergence of DV by having everybody share the idea of the state of the net with everybody else (more information is available to nodes, so better routing tables can be constructed).

The basic outline is:

1. Discover your neighbors.
2. Measure the delay to your neighbors.
3. Bundle all the information about your neighbors together.
4. Send this information to all other routers in the subnet.
5. Compute the shortest path to every router with the information you receive.

It is described in the following subsections.

2.2.2.2.1 Neighbor Discovery
Send a Hello packet out. Receiving routers respond with their addresses, which must be globally unique.

2.2.2.2.2 Measure Delay
Time the round-trip for an echo packet, divide by 2. Question arises: do you include time spent waiting in the router (i.e., load factor of the router) when measuring round-trip echo packet time or not?

2.2.2.2.3 Bundle Your Info

Put information for all your neighbors together, along with your own ID, a sequence number and an age.

2.2.2.2.4 Distribute Your Info

Ideally, every router would get every other router's data simultaneously. This cannot happen, so in effect you have different parts of the subnet with different ideas of the topology of the net at the same time. Changes ripple through the system, but routers that are widely spread can be using very different routing tables at the same time. This could result in loops, unreachable hosts, other types of problems.

A flooding algorithm is used to get the data out as soon as possible. The sequence number is used to control the flooding. Each router keeps track of the routing data packets it has seen by router/sequence number pair. If the pair is new, then it is forwarded on all lines but the one it arrived on; if it has been seen before it is not forwarded.

The age of a data packet is used to prevent corruption of the sequence number from causing valid data to be ignored. The age field is decremented once per second by the routers which forward the packet. When it hits zero it is discarded.

2.2.2.2.5 Compute Shortest Path Tree

Using an algorithm like Dijkstra's, and with a complete set of information packets from other routers, every router can locally compute a shortest path to every other router. The memory to store the data is proportional to nk, for n routers each with k neighbors. Time to compute can also be large. Bad data (e.g., from routers in error) will corrupt the computation.

2.2.2.3 Interior Routing

Interior routing occurs within an autonomous system. Most common routing protocols, such as RIP and OSPF, are interior routing protocols. The basic routable element is the IP network or subnetwork, or CIDR prefix for newer protocols.

2.2.2.4 Exterior Routing

Exterior routing occurs between autonomous systems, and is of concern to service providers and other large or complex networks. The basic routable element is the autonomous system, a collection of CIDR prefixes identified by an autonomous system number. While there may be many different interior routing schemes, a single exterior routing system manages the global Internet, based primarily on the BGP-4 exterior routing protocol.

2.3 RIP (Routing Information Protocol)

Of Internet interior routing protocols, RIP is probably the most widely used (see Table 2.3). It is a D-V protocol based on a 1970s' Xerox design. Ported to

Parameter	RIP default value
Infinity	16 (fixed)
Update time	30 s
Invalid time	180 s
Flush time	120 s
Holddown	Not used

Table 2.3. RIPv1 parameters and their values

TCP/IP when LANs first appeared in the early 1980s, RIP has changed little in the past decade and suffers from several limitations, some of which have been overcome with RIP-2; RFC 1058 documents RIP.

Its disadvantages are as follows:

- **With restriction:** RIP uses a 4 bit metric to count router hops to a destination. An RIP network can be no wider than 15 hops (16 is infinity). If hop counts are elevated on slower or less reliable links, this can quickly become a problem.
- **No direct subnet support:** RIP was deployed prior to subnetting and has no direct support for it. It can be used in subnetted environments, subject to restrictions. VLSM cannot be used in RIP networks.
- **Bandwidth consumptive:** Every 30 seconds or so, an RIP router will broadcast lists of networks and subnets it can reach. Depending on the lengths of these lists, which depend on the size of the network, bandwidth usage can become prohibitive on slow links.
- **Difficult to diagnose:** Like any D-V routing protocol, RIP can be difficult to debug, since the routing algorithm is distributed over many different routers. Most reported RIP problems could probably be traced to poor understanding, incorrect configuration and inadequate diagnosis.
- **Weak security:** RIP itself has no security features, but some developers have produced RIP implementations that will only accept updates from configured hosts, for example. Various security attacks can be imagined.

However, RIP has several benefits. It is in widespread use and the only interior gateway protocol that can be counted on to really run everywhere. Configuring an RIP system requires little effort, beyond setting path costs. Finally, RIP uses an algorithm that does not impose serious computation or storage requirements on hosts or routers.

2.3.1 Message Format

RIP is a UDP-based protocol. Routers or the host send and receive RIP PDU (Protocol Data Unit) in UDP port 520. In general, all routing updates and messages are sent to UDP port 520. The maximum size of an RIPv1 datagram is 512 bytes besides IP or UDP header. The first octet of an RIP message is the command field, which is followed a one-octet version field.

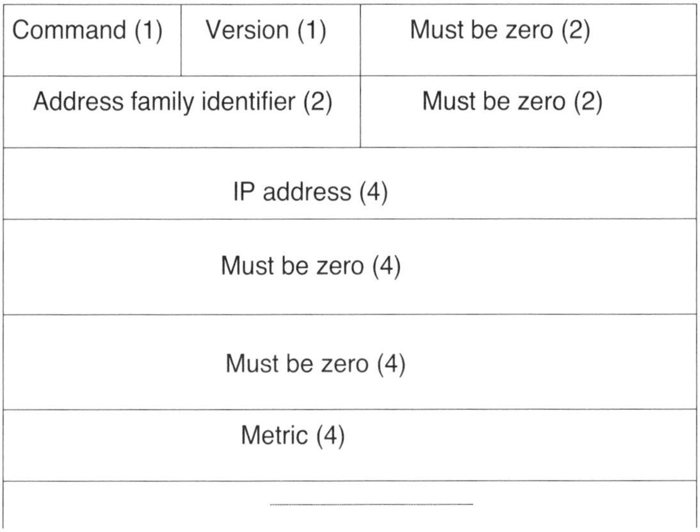

Command (1)	Version (1)	Must be zero (2)
Address family identifier (2)		Must be zero (2)
IP address (4)		
Must be zero (4)		
Must be zero (4)		
Metric (4)		

Fig. 2.3. The RIPv1 message format

Every RIP message contains a command field and it is used to specify the purpose of the packet. The following commands are implemented in RIPv1 (see Fig. 2.3) :

1. Request: A request for information from the responding system.
2. Response: This is a message containing routing table information of the sender, which may be sent as response to a request/poll.
3. Traceon: This is obsolete now. A router generally ignores a message with this command.
4. Traceoff: This is also obsolete and is ignored.
5. Reserved: This is used by Sun Microsystems for its proprietary purposes.

The version field in an RIPv1 message indicates version protocol. The address family identifier for IP is 2. The IP address is usually the Internet address and comprises four octets. The metric identifies the current metric and can be between 1 and 15.

The first four octets of the new RIPv2 message format (Fig. 2.4) contain the RIP header and the remaining portion of the message contains 1–25 route entries with 20 octets each. The command, address family identifier (AFI), IP address and metric have the same meaning as in RIPv1 that is defined in RFC 1058. For RIPv2 messages, the version field specifies version 2 and uses authentication. The authentication is a two-octet field but it may use the space of an RIP entry. If the value of AFI is 0xFFFF, then the rest of the entry contains the authentication message (Fig. 2.5). The authentication type is a simple password and currently the value is 2. The rest of the authentication is a 16-octet field with a simple text password. The route tag field is used to identify the internal route from the external route. It is recommended that routers with other protocol support should be configured to allow the route tag to be configured for routes imported from different sources. The subnet mask field is used to identify the subnet mask for the IP address. The next

Fig. 2.4. The RIPv2 message
format

Command (1)	Version (1)	Unused
Address family identifier (2)		Route Tag (2)
IP address (4)		
Subnet Mask (4)		
Next Hop (4)		
Metric (4)		

Fig. 2.5. The authentication
message

Command	Version	Unused
0xFFFF		Authentication Type
Authentication		

field is NEXT HOP, which identifies the destination route where this packet should be forwarded. If configured to 0.0.0.0, it means that the routing should be via the originator of the RIP message.

2.4 OSPF Protocol

OSPF is an SPF or link state protocol. It was developed by an IETF OSPF working group to introduce a high functionality non-proprietary Internal Gateway Protocol[1] (IGP) for the TCP/IP family. The first RFC (RFC 1131) for OSPF was written by Jon Moy in October 1989. RFC 1131 clearly defines the specification for OSPF. It has been designed to provide explicit support for

---

1 **IGP:** Interior Gateway Protocol (IGP) is an Internet Protocol which distributes routing information to the routers within an autonomous system. The term "gateway" is historical; "router" is currently the preferred term.

IP subnetting, TOS-based routing and tagging of externally derived routing information. This information (e.g., routes learned from EGP or BGP) is passed transparently through the autonomous system[2] (AS) and is kept separate from OSPF's internally derived data. Each external route can also be tagged by the advertising router, enabling the passing of additional information between routers on the borders of the AS.

OSPF is capable of providing authentication for routing updates and uses IP multicast to receive and send them. It is an IGP that distributes routing information between routers in a single AS. It can be viewed as a departure from the Bellman–Ford algorithm traditionally used by other Internet routing protocols such as RIP. OSPF has introduced new concepts such as authentication of routing updates, variable length subnet masks (VLSMs), route summarization, etc. Since its inception OSPF has been modified and written in several RFCs such as RFC 2178 (defines OSPF version 2). The current URL for the OSPF working group is http://www.ietf.org/html.charters/ospf-charter.html. OSPF uses an SPF algorithm to calculate loop-free path among the routers in a hierarchical network. OSPF as indicated by its acronym is an open standard and does not require licensing fees for vendors to implement it in their routers. The SPF algorithm which OSPF routers implement uses Dijkstra's algorithm to compute loop-free optimal path for traffic transport.

In the following sections, we will discuss the OSPF terminology, algorithm and the pros and cons of the protocol in designing the large and complicated networks of today.

2.4.1 Dijkstra SPF Algorithm

The Dijkstra SPF algorithm is the basis for OSPF operation. Besides the Bellman–Ford-Moore algorithm, the Dijkstra is another popular shortest path algorithm. Edsger W. Dijkstra, who invented this algorithm, was born in 1930 in Rotterdam, the Netherlands. He obtained his Ph.D. in computer science in 1959 from the University of Amsterdam. Currently he is the Schlumberger Centennial Chair in Computer Sciences and Professor of Mathematics at the University of Texas. His URL is http://net.cs.utexas.edu/users/UTCS/report/1994/profiles/dijkstra.html.

The Dijkstra algorithm is used in OSPF to compute the loop-free shortest path from one endpoint to another. The algorithm emphasizes the length of a path and finds the shortest path based on weight or cost (Fig. 2.6). It first finds the shortest path from some node (i.e., router) to the destination and establishes this path. It then finds the next shortest path and establishes it, and so forth. The algorithm assumes that all arc lengths are positive. The very shortest path from node 1 (i.e., router 1) must be a single-arc path to the clos-

---

2 **Autonomous System** (AS): A collection of routers under a single administrative authority using a common Interior Gateway Protocol for routing packets.

Fig. 2.6. A set of nodes (P_c) in a given network where each link has weight

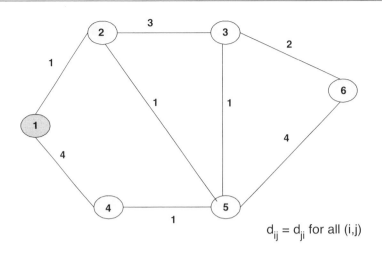

$d_{ij} = d_{ji}$ for all (i,j)

est neighbor router 1. Since it is based on a positive length assumption, multiple-arc paths must be longer than the first arc.

To formulate it in an algorithm, let P_c represent a set of routers that are presently connected with the destination where D_j is the distance of router j from the destination.

Now, initially $P_c = \{1\}$, $D_1 = 0$, $D_j = d_{ij}$ for $j \neq 1$.

Step 1. (Updating labels.) For all $j \notin P_c$ set

$$D_j = \min[D_j, D_i + d_{ij}]$$

Step 2. (Find the next closet router or node.) Find $i \notin P_c$ for which

$$D_i = \min Dj \text{ where } i \notin P_c$$

Set $P_c = P_c \cup \{I\}$. If $P_c = P$ stop; algorithm is completed. Otherwise return to Step 1.

To understand this further, let's imagine a network as shown Fig. 2.7. The shortest path from point 1 to j is calculated based on the weight of each link. In this example, the shortest path from router or node 1 to 2 has a weight of 1.

Therefore, mathematically,

$$D_2 \text{ (distance of router or node 2)} = d_{1 \rightarrow 2} = 1 \text{where } P_c = \{1,2\}$$

Now, applying step 2,

$$D_i = \min Dj \text{ (where } j \notin P_c) = 1 \text{ (where } i = 2)$$

Using step 1,

$$D_2 = 1$$

therefore the link with weight 1 is the shortest path from 1 to 2.

A similar method applies to all other nodes where $P_c = \{1,2,3,4,5\}$ (see Figs. 2.7 and 2.8).

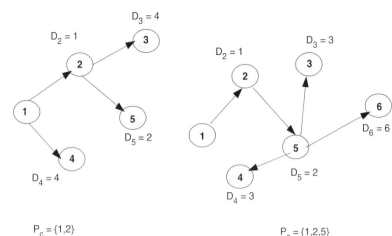

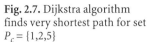

Fig. 2.7. Dijkstra algorithm finds very shortest path for set $P_c = \{1,2,5\}$

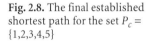

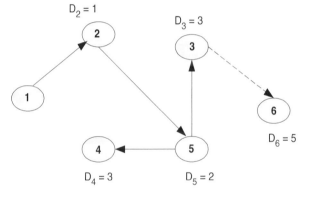

Fig. 2.8. The final established shortest path for the set $P_c = \{1,2,3,4,5\}$

2.4.2 OSPF Concept

OSPF chooses the least-cost path as the best path. It routes IP packets based on the IP DA and IP TOS byte representations found in the IP header. The IP packets are sent "as is" without further encapsulating. OSPF is a dynamic protocol: that is, it can detect topological changes very quickly and provide loop-free routes. The loop-free route convergence time is very short. Suitable for complex networks with a large number of routers, OSPF provides equal-cost multipath routing where packets to a single destination can be sent via more than one interface simultaneously.

OSPF supports three different types of networks: point-to-point, broadcast and non-broadcast multiple access (NBMA) networks.

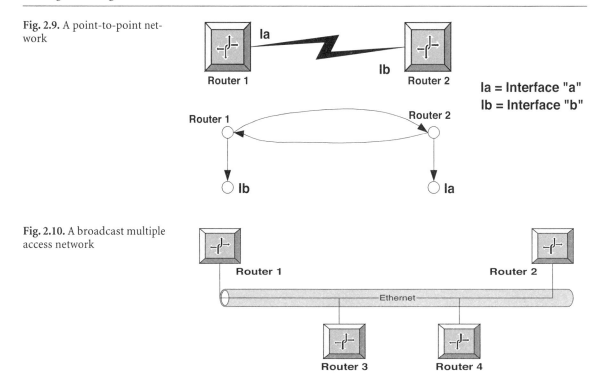

Fig. 2.9. A point-to-point network

Ia = Interface "a"
Ib = Interface "b"

Fig. 2.10. A broadcast multiple access network

1. **Point-to-point networks:** This type has a direct link between two routers. A 56 Kb/s serial line is an example of a point-to-point network (Fig. 2.9) . In a directed graph, two routers joined by a point-to-point network are represented as being directly connected by a pair of edges.

It is not required to assign an IP address to the physical interface of a router for a point-to-point network. Such a network is called unnumbered. When an IP address is assigned to the links, they are known as stub links, in which each router advertises a stub connection to the IP subnet.

2. **Broadcast multiple access networks:** This type of network (Fig. 2.10) supports many attached routers with the capability to address a single physical message to all attached routers. A protocol called Hello is used to dynamically discover all routers in the network.

Ethernet is an example of a broadcast network. OSPF is capable of using multicast if it exists.

3. **NBMA networks:** OSPF can be run in an NBMA network (Fig. 2.11) such as frame relay using one of two methods: NBMA or point-to-multipoint mode.

In NBMA mode, a designated router is chosen for the network, which originates the LSA. The NBMA is the most efficient way to run OSPF over a nonbroadcast network. However, one significant restriction is that all routers at-

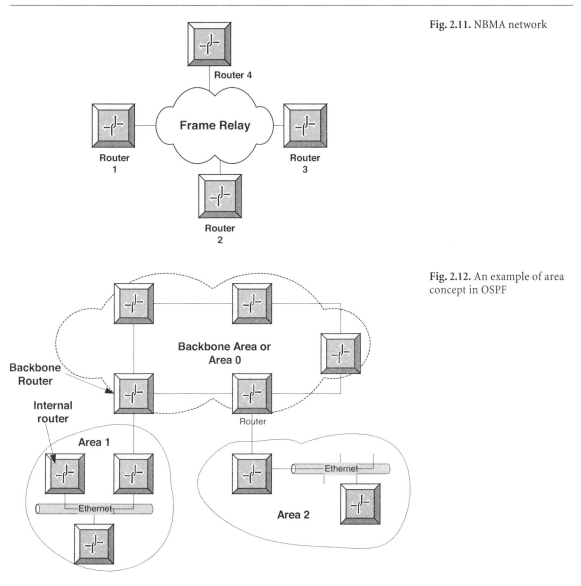

Fig. 2.11. NBMA network

Fig. 2.12. An example of area concept in OSPF

tached to NBMA should communicate directly. In point-to-multipoint mode, the OSPF mechanism treats all router-to-router interconnecting links in an NBMA network as point-to-point links. No designated router (DR) is needed for this configuration and there are no LSAs generated for the network.

2.4.2.1 Area Concept

Since OSPF allows routers to flood on the network to exchange information through the LSA message format, an area concept (Fig. 2.12) can help to ease CPU use, memory use and the number of LSAs being transmitted. In other words, area is introduced to put a boundary on LSAs in the network. These areas are defined on the routers and ultimately interfaces are assigned to the areas. In fact, areas are similar to the concept of a subnet and they are the contiguous logical segments of the network. The default area is area 0 and denoted as 0.0.0.0. As more areas are added 0.0.0.0 becomes the backbone area. All areas must be connected to the backbone area. Each area maintains its own link state database (LSDB). Routers within an area are only responsible for the modification of the SPF specific to that area. Another benefit of area is that networks within an area can be advertised as a summary, which reduces the size of the routing table and the processing of such information by the external routers to that area.

2.4.2.1.1 *Backbone Area*

A backbone area is the key ingredients of the AS and is attached to multiple areas. It is responsible for the distribution of routing information between non-backbone areas. To configure the backbone area, one should follow the following guidelines:

1. Since backbone is the critical area, redundancy is a must in this configuration.
2. Ensure all routers are connected to the backbone area or area 0.
3. The OSPF backbone should be configured as contiguous.
4. The backbone area should be simple, that is fewer interconnected routers.
5. A backbone area should be stable and free from shared resources.

2.4.2.1.2 *Stub Area*

A stub area is an area which is on a limb with no routers or areas beyond it (Fig. 2.13). It carries default routes and inter-area routes but does not allow external routes. It can be configured by setting "Import AS external" parameter to "No". Therefore, as the parameter suggests, stub area does not allow AS external LSA to be flooded into the stub area. Since the default routing

Fig. 2.13. An example of stub area

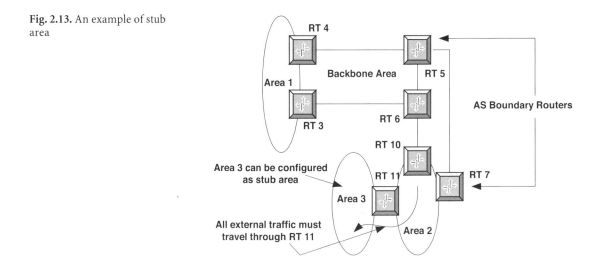

technique is used in this area, the LSDB is reduced and so is the load in the CPU and memory of a router. Also, it should be remembered that summary LSA should not be sent to this area. So, any parameter such as "Import Summaries" should be configured as "False". A stub area can be configured as normal stub, totally stubby area (TSA) and not-so-stubby area (NSSA).

2.4.2.2 Classification of Routers

In OSPF with area configuration, a number of routing functions are defined for various routers within an AS (Fig. 2.14) . RFC 2178 has defined four types of routers in OSPF according to their functions: internal routers, area border routers, backbone routers and AS boundary routers.

1. **Internal routers (IRs):** These are routers with all directly connected networks within the same area. They will have a single LSA database and run a single basic routing algorithm.
2. **Area border routers (ABRs):** These types of routers are attached to multiple OSPF areas. Therefore, there can be multiple ABRs in a given OSPF network. ABRs run multiple copies of the basic algorithm and will have multiple copies of LSAs. ABRs will run one database for each area that will be summarized and presented to the backbone area for distribution to other areas. In turn, the backbone will distribute the information to other areas.
3. **Backbone routers (BRs):** These routers typically will have an interface to the backbone area. This includes ABRs and any other routers that interface to more than one area.
4. **AS border routers (ASBRs):** These routers connect more than one AS and exchange route information with routers in another AS. ASBRs advertise the exchanged external route information throughout their AS. ASBRs may be IRs or ABRs and may or may not participate in the backbone area. Every router in the AS knows how to get to each ASBR. Besides OSPF, an ASBR may run other routing protocols such as RIP or BGP.

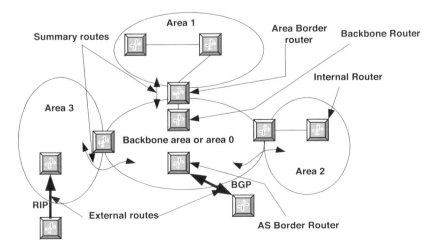

Fig. 2.14. A network running OSPF shows various routing functions

2.4.2.2.1 Designated Router and Backup Designated Router

In general, the designated router (DR) and backup designated router (BDR) on a LAN have the most OSPF work to do. The DR is responsible for two main functions for the routing protocol:

1. It originates the network LSA on behalf of the network which lists the set of routers attached to the network including the DR itself. The IP address of the DR is given as link state ID in the LSA. Then the IP network number can be obtained by using the network's subnet mask.
2. The DR becomes adjacent to all routers in the network. The DR plays an important role for synchronization of the LSDB.

The election of the DR and BDR is done via the Hello Protocol. In a network, Hello messages are exchanged through IP multicast on each segment. A Hello packet contains the "router priority" for a router, which is configurable per interface basis. It is recommended to select routers that are not already heavily loaded to be the DR and BDR. In general, when a router is first attached to an OSPF network, it checks to see whether there is a DR present in the network. If there is, it accepts it regardless of its router priority. Otherwise the router itself becomes the DR if it has the highest router priority on the network. On the other hand, a BDR is used to make the transition to a new DR smoother. Therefore, a BDR is recommended for each broadcast or NBMA network. Similar to a DR, a BDR is adjacent to all other routers in the network and becomes the DR when a DR fails.

2.4.2.2.2 Adjacencies

To form an adjacency, an OSPF router must first have discovered its neighbors; it is the next step after the neighboring process. Adjacency is formed for the purpose of exchanging routing information. Multiple adjacency is possible between two routers if they have multiple networks in common. Not all the routers will form an adjacency. The collection of adjacencies on a network can be viewed as forming an undirected graph for which vertices consist of routers with an edge joining two routers if they are adjacent. Such a graph describes the flow of routing protocols as well as LSA updates in an AS. In a point-to-point network or point-to-multipoint network neighboring routers become adjacent whenever they can communicate directly. On the other hand, in a broadcast or NBMA network only the DR and BDR become adjacent to all other routers. Therefore, considering this, only two graphs are possible as depicted in Fig. 2.15.

Since the BDR performs less function than the DR during flooding, the dotted line in the figure from RT3 indicates lesser function of a BDR. Not all the routers in a network will form adjacency. There are certain conditions under which an adjacency can be formed and they are as follows:

1. In a point-to-point network, all routers are adjacent.
2. The network connectivity is achieved through virtual link.
3. If the router is a DR or BDR.

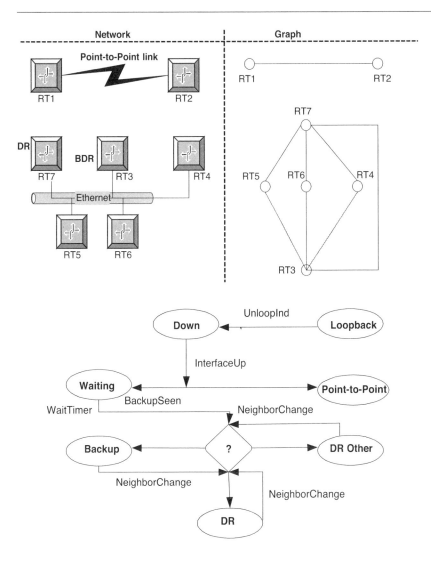

Fig. 2.15. The graph of adjacency

Fig. 2.16. The interface state changes as defined in RFC 2178

Routers that become adjacent will have the exact LSDB. The following is a brief summary of the various interface states of a router (Fig. 2.16), which dictate its adjacency to another router:

- **Down:** This is the initial interface state of a router. No protocol traffic at all will be sent or received in this state and the parameters should be set to their initial values. In this state, all interface timers should be disabled and there are no adjacencies associated with the interface.
- **Loopback:** This is a condition of the router interface and it can be done through hardware or software. In this state, the interface is unavailable for regular traffic, but one can still gain information through ICMP ping to the interface or through some sorts of bit error test.
- **Waiting:** In this state, the router tries to gain the identity information of the DR or BDR of the network. To do that it monitors the received Hello

packets. At this state, the router is not allowed to elect the DR or BDR unless it is out of waiting state.

- **Point-to-point:** In this state, the interface becomes operational and connects to either a virtual link or a point-to-point network. Once a routing interface enters this state, it tries to form an adjacency with a neighboring router. Hello packets are sent at every HelloInterval seconds to the neighboring router.
- **DR other:** In this state, the router forms adjacency to both the DR and BDR if they exist.
- **Backup:** This state denotes that the router itself is the BDR on the attached network. It may change to DR if a DR fails. In a backup state, the router establishes adjacency to all other routers and performs lesser functions than a DR during the flooding procedure.
- **DR:** In this state, the router itself is the DR and forms the adjacency with all other routers attached to that network. It also originates network LSA and identifies its IP address as the link state ID.

2.4.2.2.3 OSPF Implementation Requirements

The router which will implement OSPF should be capable of supporting the following elements:

- **Timers:** There are two kinds of timers, "single-shot timer" and "interval timer". The first kind of timer, if fired once, helps the protocol event to be processed. The second kind is fired at a regular interval. Such a timer is used to send Hello packets.
- **IP multicast:** Certain OSPF packets can be considered as IP multicast datagrams. A router that implements OSPF must support sending and receiving of such IP multicast datagrams.
- **Variable length subnet:** A router must also support the ability to divide a single IP Class A, B or C network number into many subnets of various sizes.
- **IP supernetting:** This is the proposed technique to improve the scaling of IP routing in the Internet. A router that implements OSPF should support IP supernetting.
- **Lower level protocol:** This support can be interpreted as the support for network access protocols such as Ethernet. A router must provide the means of communication from such a protocol to the OSPF as an interface goes up and down.
- **Non-broadcast lower level protocol:** This is used on non-broadcast networks such as X.25 to indicate to the Hello Protocol when an attempt is made to send a packet to a dead or non-existent router.
- **List manipulation primitives:** A router that implements OSPF should be able to manipulate lists of LSAs as required by adding or deleting them.
- **Tasking:** An OSPF router must support the instruction to schedule a task; that is, to identify when a procedure should be invoked.

2.4.2.2.4 Virtual Links

In case a newly introduced area does not have direct connectivity to the backbone area or any area that is connected to the backbone through other areas,

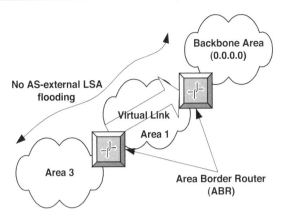

Fig. 2.17. An example of a virtual link

a virtual link (Fig. 2.17) will have to be configured for such a situation. A virtual link provides the path between two ABRs that are not directly connected. Such a link is treated as an unnumbered point-to-point link to the backbone. Therefore, an attempt is made to establish adjacency over the virtual link. It is to be noted that AS external LSAs are never flooded over virtual adjacencies. The cost for a virtual link should not be configured since it is defined to be the cost of the inter-area path between two ABRs. Also, a virtual link should not be configured on an unnumbered link or through a stub area.

2.4.3 Basic Operation

In a link state protocol, each router maintains a database describing the entire AS topology, which it builds out of the collected LSAs of all routers. Each participating router distributes its local state (i.e., the router's useable interfaces and reachable neighbors) throughout the AS by flooding. Each multiple access network that has at least two attached routers has a DR and a BDR. The DR floods an LSA link or the multiple access network and has other special responsibilities.

The DR concept reduces the number of adjacencies required on a multiple access network.

OSPF allows networks to be grouped into areas. Routing information passed between areas is abstracted, potentially allowing a significant reduction in routing traffic. OSPF uses four different types of routes, which are, in order of preference: intra-area, inter-area, type 1 external and type 2 external. Intra-area paths have destinations within the same area, inter-area paths have destinations in other OSPF areas and AS external (ASE) routes are routes to destinations external to the AS. Routes imported into OSPF as type 1 routes are supposed to be from IGPs whose external metrics are directly comparable to OSPF metrics. When a routing decision is being made, OSPF will add the internal cost to the ASBR to the external metric. Type 2 ASEs are used for EGPs whose metrics are not comparable to OSPF metrics. In this case, only the internal OSPF cost to the ASBR is used in the routing decision.

From the topology database, each router constructs a tree of the shortest paths with itself as the root. This shortest path tree gives the route to each destination in the AS. Externally derived routing information appears on the tree as leaves. The LSA format distinguishes between information acquired from external sources and information acquired from internal routers, so there is no ambiguity about the source or reliability of routes.

OSPF optionally includes TOS routing and allows administrators to install multiple routes to a given destination for each type of service (e.g., low delay or high throughput.) A router running OSPF uses the DA and TOS to choose the best route to the destination. OSPF intra- and inter-area routes are always imported into the gated routing database with a preference of 10. It would be a violation of the protocol if an OSPF router did not participate fully in the area's OSPF, so it is not possible to override this. Although it is possible to give other routes lower preference values explicitly, it is ill advised to do so. Hardware multicast capabilities are also used where possible to deliver link status messages.

OSPF areas are connected by the backbone area, the area with identifier 0.0.0.0. All areas must be logically contiguous and the backbone is no exception. To permit maximum flexibility, OSPF allows the configuration of virtual links to enable the backbone area to appear contiguous despite the physical reality.

All routers in an area must agree on that area's parameters. A separate copy of the link state algorithm is run for each area. Because of this, most configuration parameters are defined on a per area basis. All routers belonging to an area must agree on that area's configuration. Misconfiguration will lead to adjacencies not forming between neighbors, and routing information might not flow, or even loop.

2.4.3.1 Authentication

All OSPF exchanges are authenticated. The OSPF packet header includes an authentication type field. Authentication guarantees that routing information is only imported from trusted routers, to protect the Internet and its users. OSPF currently specifies that the authentication type be configured per area with the ability to configure separate passwords per interface. A variety of authentication schemes can be used but a single scheme must be configured for each area. This enables some areas to use much stricter authentication than others. There are three defined authentication types: 0, 1 and 2. The "All others" authentication type is reserved for future use (Table 2.4).

Table 2.4. OSPF authentication types and their description

Authentication type (AuType)	Description
0	Null
1	Simple password
2	Cryptographic authentication
All others	Reserved by the IANA for experimental purposes (iana@ISI.edu)

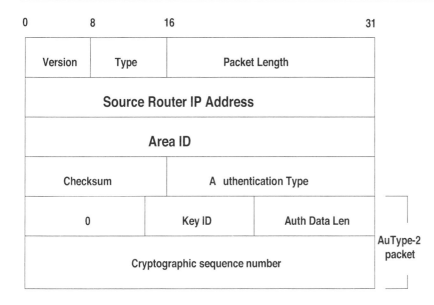

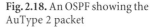

Fig. 2.18. An OSPF showing the AuType 2 packet

The first type (0 or null) of authentication is used if routing exchanges are not authenticated. The 64-bit AuType field can contain anything and when employed the entire OSPF packet's checksum is calculated to detect data corruption. The second type (1) is a simple authentication key of up to eight characters and guards against routers inadvertently joining the routing domain. The next authentication type (2) uses a share secret key. For each OSPF packet, the key is used to generate or verify a "message digest" that is appended to the end of the OSPF packet. When using cryptographic authentication the OSPF AuType is set to 2 (Fig. 2.18) and the checksum is not calculated and set to 0.

The key ID is set to the chosen KEY ID and "Auth Data Len" field is set to bytes in the message digest appended to the OSPF packet. For example, if the MD5 authentication algorithm is used, it will be set to 16.

2.4.4 OSPF Message Format

Encapsulated with the IP header, every OSPF packet (Figs. 2.19 and 2.20) starts with a standard 24-byte header. This header contains information required to determine processing criteria, that is whether the packet should be accepted for further processing. When a protocol packet is received by the router, it is marked with the port or interface it was received on.

An OSPF packet should pass through a number of tests in IP level before it is forwarded to the OSPF engine in the router or L3 switch for processing. Here is a list of those tests:

1. IP checksum must be correct.
2. The IP destination address must be one of the IP multicast group addresses designated for OSPF.

Fig. 2.19. An overview of an OSPF packet

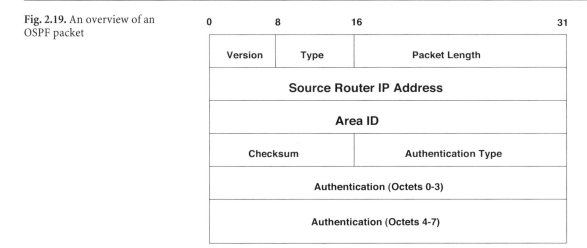

Fig. 2.20. The practical look of an OSPF packet

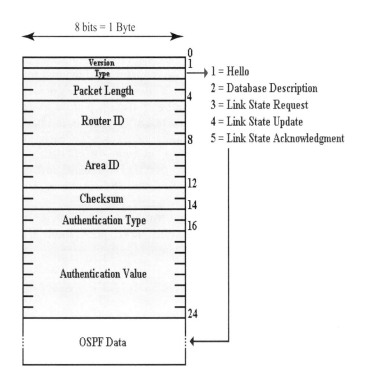

3. The specified IP must be OSPF.
4. The source IP address of the packet must be verified to ensure that it is not a multicast packet which the router itself generated.

Once the OSPF header of the incoming packet is verified, the process will ensure whether or not the fields specified in the header match those configured in an interface. If there is no match, the packet should be discarded. The following tests ensure the criteria for packet discard:

1. The version field must specify protocol version 2.
2. The area ID must be verified (Fig. 2.20). If the following cases fail, the packet should be discarded:
   (a) As described in RFC 2178, the OSPF process will match the area ID of an OSPF packet with those configured in the interface. For packets traversing a single hop, the IP source address is required to be in the same network as the receiving interface. This is verified by masking both the IP source address of the packet and IP address of the interface with the interface mask. For a point-to-point network this comparison should not be performed. In a point-to-point network, the interface addresses of each end of the link are assigned independently.
   (b) The area ID specified in the OSPF header should indicate the backbone. In this scenario, the packet is sent over a virtual link and the receiving router must be the border router. The router ID specified in the packet must be in the other end of the virtual link. Also, the receiving end must be attached to the virtual link's configured transit area.
3. The packets whose IP destination is "AllDRouters" should only be accepted if the receiving interface is in the DR or BDR state.
4. The authentication type field value should match the AuType specified for the associated area.
5. The packet must be authenticated.

```
- - - - - - - - - - - - - - - - Frame 1 - - - - - - -
- - - - - - - - SUMMARY  Delta T     Destination
Source         Summary
  M   152    0.18133  [224.0.0.5]     [10.170.111.1]
OSPF   Hello ID=[22.89.90.0]

   OSPF:  ----- OSPF Header -----
   OSPF:
   OSPF:  Version = 2,   Type = 1 (Hello),   Length = 44
   OSPF:  Router ID       = [22.89.90.0]
   OSPF:  Area ID         = [10.128.0.0]
   OSPF:  Header checksum = 081A (correct)
   OSPF:  Authentication: Type = 0 (No Authentication),
Value = 00 00 00 00 00 00 00 00
   OSPF:
   OSPF:  Network mask         = [255.255.255.0]
   OSPF:  Hello interval       = 10 (seconds)
   OSPF:  Optional capabilities = X2
   OSPF:                .... 0... = router is not NSSA
capable
   OSPF:                .... .0.. = no multicast
capability
   OSPF:                .... ..1. = external routing
capability
   OSPF:                .... ...0 = no Type of Service
routing capability
   OSPF:  Router priority      = 1
   OSPF:  Router dead interval = 40 (seconds)
   OSPF:  Designated router    = [10.170.111.1]
   OSPF:  Backup designated router = [0.0.0.0]
   OSPF:
```

Table 2.5. OSPF packet types and their description

Type	Description
1	Hello
2	Database description
3	Link state request
4	Link state updates
5	Link state acknowledgement

Returning to the packet format of OSPF, the first field is "Version". A router that complies with RFC 1131 may use the value of 1 for this field. Since RFC 2178 replaced RFC 1131 and is now widely used, the currently suggested value for this field is 2. The length of the field is 8 bits or one octet. The next field after "Version #" is "Type". This is also a one-octet field, which defines the OSPF packet types. Table 2.5 describes the various OSPF packet types.

2.4.4.1 Hello Packet

The OSPF packet type 1 is the "Hello" packet. These packets are periodically sent to all interfaces to establish and maintain neighbor relationships. Although it depends on how a vendor implements it, the router usually sends out Hello packets every 10 seconds. The Hello packet is a multicast packet designed for neighborhood discovery. All routers or L3 switches in a network agree to certain parameters such as network mask, Hello and dead intervals. A Hello packet includes those parameters so that the differences can inhibit the formation of neighborhood relationships. It contains the following fields: network mask, option, HelloInterval, Rtr Pri, RouterDeadInterval, DR, BDR and neighbor.

Readers should note that all Hello packets start with the OSPF header as described in Fig. 2.21. Please observe the sniffer trace as shown in Fig. 2.21 to verify it. All OSPF packets including the Hello packet are encapsulated with the IP header.

2.4.4.1.1 Network Mask

The first field of the Hello packet after the OSPF header is the network mask, a 32-bit field. It is associated with the interface of a router or L3 switch. For example, if the interface is to a Class A network, the network mask is 0xff000000.

2.4.4.1.2 HelloInterval

This field value indicates the interval between two Hello packets, that is 10 seconds.

2.4.4.1.3 Option

This field indicates the optional capabilities supported by a router. It is present in OSPF Hello packets, database description packets and all LSAs. Routers or L3 switches use this field to communicate their capability level with the peers. This mechanism allows mixing of different capability routers

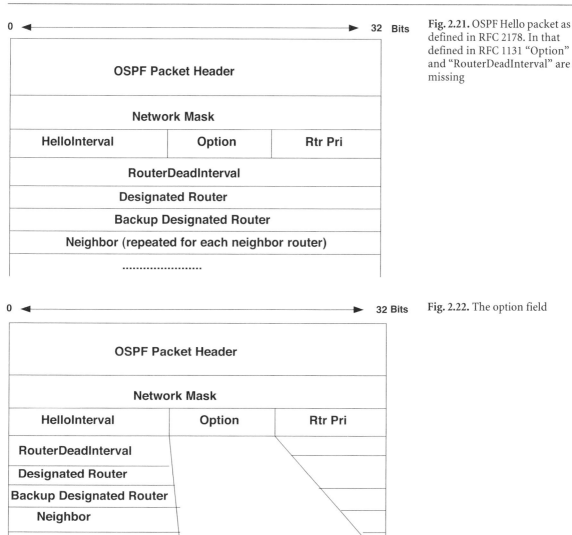

Fig. 2.21. OSPF Hello packet as defined in RFC 2178. In that defined in RFC 1131 "Option" and "RouterDeadInterval" are missing

Fig. 2.22. The option field

or switches in a network. If this field is used in the Hello packet, it will help a router to reject a neighbor because of capability mismatch. Alternatively, for a database description packet, this field helps the router to forward or not to forward certain LSAs to a neighbor because of its reduced functionality. So far, 5 bits of the option field have been identified out of which only the E bit is defined by RFC 2178. A router encountering an unrecognized option bit in Hello, database description packets or LSAs should ignore the capability and process the packet normally. The 5-bit fields in the option field (Fig. 2.22) are E bit, MC bit, N/P bit, EA bit and DC bit.

- **E bit:** This bit field describes how ASE LSAs are flooded. In some ASs, the majority of the LSDB may consist of AS LSAs. Normally ASE LSA is flooded throughout the entire AS but OSPF has certain areas configured as stub areas where ASE LSA is not flooded.
- **MC bit:** This bit describes whether IP multicasts are forwarded according to the specification as defined in RFC 2178, ref. 18.
- **N/P bit:** This describes the handling of Type-7 LSAs (defined in RFC 2178, ref. 19).
- **EA bit:** This field described a router's willingness to receive and forward external attribute LSAs (defined in RFC 2178, ref. 20).
- **DC bit:** This denotes the router's handling of demand circuit (defined in RFC 2178, ref. 21).

2.4.4.1.4 Rtr Pri

This describes the router's priority. It is normally used in BDR election. If it is set to 0, the router is ineligible to be a BDR.

2.4.4.1.5 RouterDeadInterval

This describes the number of seconds before declaring a silent router down.

2.4.4.1.6 DR

This field describes the identity of the DR for the network. If there is no DR in the network, it is set to 0.0.0.0.

2.4.4.1.7 BDR

This field describes the identity of the BDR . If set to 0.0.0.0, there is no BDR in the network.

2.4.4.1.8 Neighbor

This field indicates the router ID from which a valid Hello packet has been seen recently (in the last RouterDeadInterval seconds) in the network.

2.4.4.2 Database Description Packet

OSPF type 2 packets are exchanged when adjacency is being initialized. This describes the contents of the LSDB and multiple packets may be used to describe the database. Due to this condition, a poll-response procedure is used in which one router is designated to be the master and the other is the slave. In this scenario, the master sends out a database description packet (pools) which is then in turn acknowledged the slave. In the acknowledgement phase, the slave sends out a database description packet as response. The DD sequence number of the database description packet is used to identify "poll-response".

A database description packet (Fig. 2.23) , besides the OSPF header, contains the following fields: interface MTU, options, I bit, M bit, MS bit, DD sequence number and an LSA header.

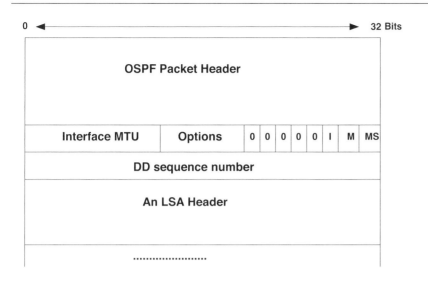

Fig. 2.23. The database description packet

2.4.4.2.1 Interface MTU
This describes the size of an IP datagram that can be sent out without fragmentation and should be set to 0 in database description packets sent over virtual links. Table 2.6 shows MTUs of common Internet link types as defined in RFC 1191, Table 7–1.

2.4.4.2.2 Options
This field describes the capability of a router. Please refer to the Hello packet option field above for further details.

2.4.4.2.3 I Bit
This is an initialization bit; when set to 1 it indicates that the conveyer packet is the first in sequence of the database description packet.

2.4.4.2.4 M Bit
This is a more bit; when set to 1 it indicates that more database description packets are to follow.

2.4.4.2.5 MS Bit
This is the master/slave bit; when set to 1 it indicates that the router is master, otherwise the router is slave.

2.4.4.2.6 DD Sequence Number
This bit is used in the database description packet to indicate the sequence of collection. The initial value should be unique as indicated by the I bit being set. The DD sequence then increments until completion.

2.4.4.2.7 LSA Header
The rest of the database description packet consists of an LSA header (Fig. 2.24). It is a 20-byte header usually used in an LSA packet. All LSAs begin

Table 2.6. MTUs of common Internet link types

MTU	Description	Reference
65,535	Official maximum MTU	RFC 791
65,535	Hyperchannel	RFC 1044
17,914	16 Mb/s IBM Token Ring	RFC 1191, ref. 6
8166	IEEE 802.4	RFC 1042
4464	IEEE 802.5 (4 Mb/s max)	RFC 1042
4352	FDDI (revised)	RFC 1188
2048	Wideband network	RFC 907
2002	IEEE 802.5 (4 Mb/s recommended)	RFC 1042
1536	Exp. Ethernet	RFC 895
1500	Ethernet	RFC 894
1500	Point-to-point (default)	RFC 1134
1492	IEEE 802.3	RFC 1042
1006	SLIP	RFC 1055
1006	ARPANET	BBN 1822
576	X.25 networks	RFC 877
544	DEC IP portal	RFC 1191, ref. 10
512	NETBIOS	RFC 1088
508	IEEE 802/Source route bridge	RFC 1042
508	ARCNET	RFC 1051
296	Point-to-point (low delay)	RFC 1144

Fig. 2.24. An LSA header

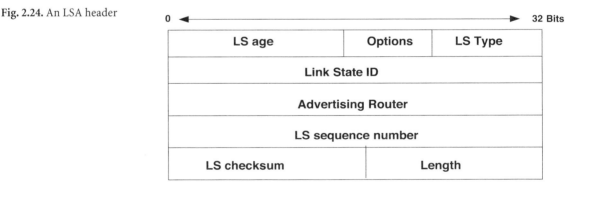

with this header. It contains enough information to identify each LSA uniquely (LSA type, link state ID, and advertising router). If multiple instances of the LSA exist in a routing domain at the same time, LS age is used with LS sequence number and LS checksum to determine the most recent one.

- **LS age:** This describes the time in seconds since the LSA was generated.
- **Options:** As described earlier, this identifies the capability of a router.
- **LS type:** This identifies LSA types and each LSA has its own advertisement format. Table 2.7 shows LS type values and their descriptions.

LS type	Description
1	Router LSAs
2	Network LSAs
3	Summary LSAs (IP network)
4	Summary LSAs (ASBR)
5	ASE LSAs

Table 2.7. LS types and descriptions

2.5 Border Gateway Protocol (BGP)

The routing technique involves two basic functions: determination of optimal paths and transmission of information groups (i.e., packets). The transport of packets through an internetwork is fairly straightforward. Path determination, on the other hand, is very complex. The BGP addresses the task of path determination apparently well. It is an Exterior Routing Protocol (EGP) meaning that it performs routing between multiple ASs[3] or domains.

The commonly used term EGP (a routing protocol, used in ARPANET days) is a particular instance of EGP; care should be taken not to confuse the two. The legacy "EGP" is replaced by BGP as being the only routing protocol recommended for exchanging information between ASs. The EGP was developed from 1982 to 1984 and replaced by BGP in 1989 as it emerged in June 1989 as RFC 1105. Two pioneers in routing technology, namely K. Lougheed of Cisco Systems and Y. Rekhter of IBM, proposed this protocol through RFC 1105.

The primary function of a BGP router is to exchange network "destination path" information with other routers that support BGP. The initial RFC for BGP version 1 or BGP-1 was written from the experience gained through the implementation of EGP (RFC 904). Therefore, it is obvious that BGP addresses most of the issues raised by the EGP users. There are some major differences between EGP and BGP, but perhaps the most important innovation within BGP is the "path vector" concept. The "path vector" algorithm enables loop prevention in complex topologies. If we recall our discussions in previous sections about distance-vector routing protocols, all the information about routes to a destination is concentrated in the "metric" value. This is inadequate for fast loop prevention. A number of proposals were proposed to install additional protection by providing more information. In BGP, the approach is more radical: each routing update carries the full list of transit networks, or rather ASs, traversed between the source and destination. Therefore, a loop may only occur if one of the ASs is listed twice, in which

---

3 The autonomous system (AS) is a set of routers under a single technical administration. An Interior Gateway Protocol (IGP) is used to route information between various routers within a single AS, whereas an Exterior Gateway Protocol (EGP) is used to exchange information between routers of one AS to the routers of another AS.

case it is an error. Hence, the loop protection algorithm is very simple. An exterior router checks route advertisements to ensure that the AS listed in the message is not its own. In such cases, it will refuse to use the "local path identification"; otherwise, it will insert local identification before advertising.

2.5.1 BGP Analysis

BGP is an inter-autonomous system routing protocol that uses TCP as the transport protocol. It is designed to operate as a routing protocol between multiple ASs. The routing within an AS is not the function of BGP; it is done by interior routing protocols such as OSPF. BGP exchanges sufficient information to construct a graph of AS connectivity and decision at the AS level may be enforced (Fig. 2.25).

This information is used to eliminate routing loops. The algorithm used in BGP cannot be classified either as pure distance-vector or pure link state. It carries a complete AS path in the AS-PATH attribute that allows BGP to reconstruct the overall topology.

Initially BGP speakers[4] establish connection using TCP followed by messages containing open and confirm connection parameters. The initial dataflow is the entire BGP routing table. As the routing table changes, incremental updates are sent by the BGP speakers. It should be remembered that BGP does not require periodic updates of the entire routing table. Hence, a BGP speaker retains the current version of the entire BGP routing table that learned from its peers for the duration of the connection. To ensure that the connection is live, BGP speakers also send out "KeepAlive" messages. If an error or a special condition occurs, the BGP speaker sends out "Notification" messages. For a connection in which an error has been detected, BGP routers will close the connection after sending out the "Notification" message. A connection between BGP speakers of different ASs is known as "External" link. On the other hand, connection between BGP speakers within the same AS is known as "Internal" link. The initial version of BGP was version 1 which after one year was rendered obsolete by BGP version 2. Therefore, we will ex-

Fig. 2.25. The BGP and its operation

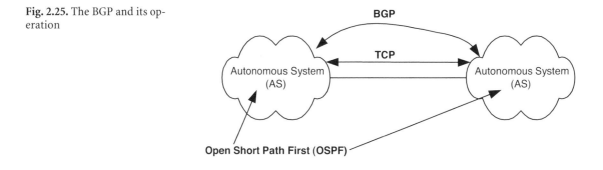

---

4   A system or router that supports the BGP routing protocol is considered as the BGP speaker.

plore BGP-2 (or version 2) first and end with BGP-4 (version 4), the currently
used version of BGP.

2.5.2 BGP-2 Message

The maximum message size for BGP-2 is 4096 bytes and such a message is
only processed after it is received entirely. The minimum message type with
the BGP-2 header (Fig. 2.26) only can be 19 bytes. Each BGP-2 header has a
fixed header length and may or may not include a data portion depending
upon the message type.

"Marker" is a 16-byte field and the value of this field can be predicted by
the receiver. For example, if the "Type" of the message is OPEN or if the authentication code used in the OPEN message is zero, then the marker must
be set to all ones. Otherwise, the value of this field can be computed as part
of the authentication mechanism that is being used. The marker field can be
used to detect loss of synchronization between BGP peers, and for authentication of incoming BGP messages.

The length field is a 2-byte unsigned integer that specifies the total length
of the message. The value of this field must be always 19 octets at the least and
4096 bytes maximum.

The type field is one octet long and specifies the type code of the message.
There are four type field values identified for BGP-2 messages as follows:

1. OPEN
2. UPDATE
3. NOTIFICATION
4. KEEPALIVE

2.5.2.1 OPEN Message Format

Once the TCP connection is established between BGP peers, the first message
exchanged from each side is an OPEN message. If this message is acceptable
a KEEPALIVE message is sent in turn. This confirms successful processing of
the OPEN message. Once the OPEN message is confirmed, UPDATE, KEEP-
ALIVE and NOTIFICATION messages can be exchanged between the BGP
peers.

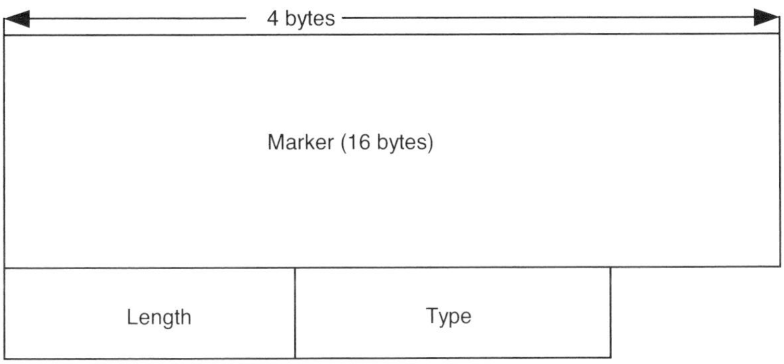

Fig. 2.26. The BGP-2 message
header

Fig. 2.27. The OPEN message format of BGP-2

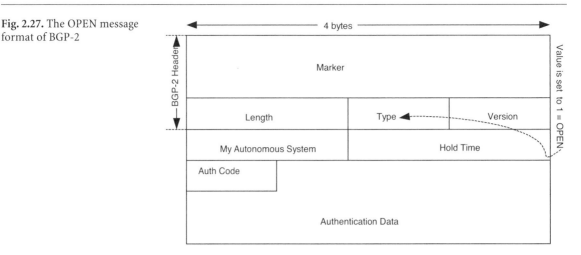

The OPEN message includes the BGP-2 header as an addition to its contents. The first field in the OPEN message is "Version", a one-octet field. The value of this field is 2 (for BGP-2) (Fig. 2.27).

The next field is "My Autonomous System". It is a two-octet unsigned integer that specifies the AS number of the sender. The "Hold Time" is a two-octet unsigned integer that specifies the maximum number of seconds elapsed between the receipt of successive KEEPALIVE and/or UPDATE and/or NOTIFICATION messages.

The "Auth Code" or authentication code is a one-octet unsigned integer that specifies the underlying authentication mechanism. Any time an authentication mechanism is used within BGP, three things must be included in the specification:

1. the value of the authentication code that identifies the mechanism,
2. an algorithm for computing the values in the marker field, and
3. the form and meaning of authentication data.

The authentication data field is a variable field and its length depends on the authentication code. For example, if the value of the authentication code field is zero, this field must be zero in length.

The minimum length of the OPEN message is 25 bytes including the message header.

2.5.2.2 UPDATE Message Format

These messages are used to exchange routing information between BGP peers. The information within the UPDATE message is used to construct a graph identifying the relationships of the various ASs. In addition to the BGP-2 header, the UPDATE message includes the following fields (Fig. 2.28):

- Total path attribute length
- Path attributes
- Network 1–*n*.

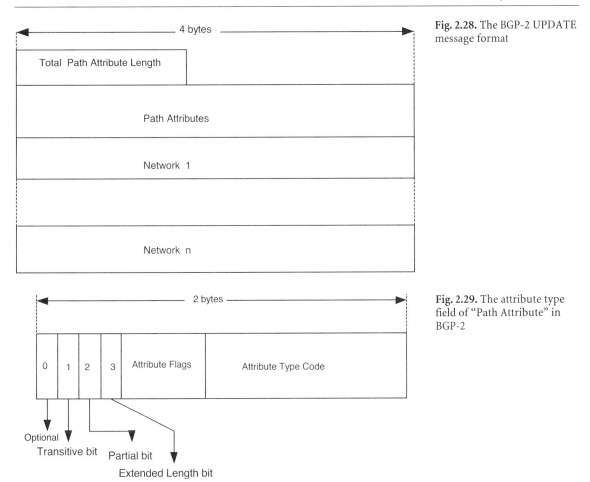

Fig. 2.28. The BGP-2 UPDATE message format

Fig. 2.29. The attribute type field of "Path Attribute" in BGP-2

"Total Path Attribute Length" is a 2-byte unsigned integer which specifies the total length of the path attribute field in bytes. Its value must specify the number of network fields to be determined.

"Path Attribute" is a variable length field containing a sequence of path attributes that is present in every UPDATE message. Each path attribute includes attribute type, attribute length and attribute value within its variable length field.

"Attribute Type" is a 2 byte field which consists of attribute flags and attribute type code (Fig. 2.29).

The high-order (bit 0) bit of the attribute flags byte is considered as optional. If set to 1 it indicates the attribute is optional; if set to 0 it indicates "well known".

The second high-order bit (bit 1) is the transitive bit . If set to 1 it indicates the attribute is transitive; if set to 0 it indicates non-transitive.

The third high-order bit (bit 2) is the partial bit. If set to 1 it indicates that the information contained in the optional transitive attribute is partial; if set to 0 it indicates it is complete.

Table 2.8. Attribute type code values

Attribute name	Type code	Length (bytes)	Attribute category
ORIGIN	1	1	Well known, mandatory
AS_PATH	2	Variable	Well known, mandatory
NEXT_HOP	3	4	Well known, mandatory
UNREACHABLE	4	0	Well known, discretionary

The fourth high-order bit (bit 3) is the extended length bit. If set to 0 it indicates that the attribute length is one octet, otherwise two octets (if set to 1).

The lower 4 bits of "Attribute Flags" are unused and must be set to 0.

Table 2.8 shows the attribute type code values supported.

The network is a 4-byte internetwork number field that indicates one network whose inter-AS routing is described in the path attributes.

2.5.2.3 KEEPALIVE Message Format

BGP-2 does not use any transport-protocol-based keep-alive mechanism to determine whether or not its peer is reachable. The KEEPALIVE message only includes the BGP-2 header and a length of 19 bytes.

2.5.2.4 NOTIFICATION Message Format

As we have discussed earlier, the NOTIFICATION message is only sent when an error condition has occurred. The BGP-2 connection is closed immediately after sending it.

In addition to the BGP-2 header, this message includes the following (Fig. 2.30):

- Error code
- Error subcode
- Data.

Fig. 2.30. The BGP-2 NOTIFICATION message format

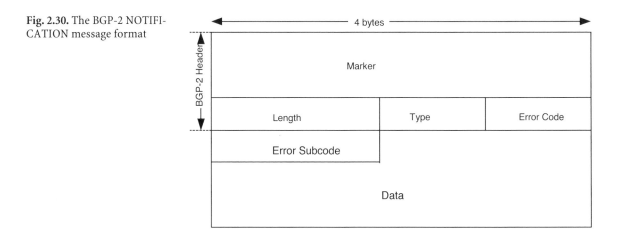

Error code	Symbolic name
1	Message header error
2	OPEN message error
3	UPDATE message error
4	Hold timer expired
5	Finite state machine error
6	Cease

Table 2.9. The BGP-2 NOTIFI-CATION message error code

Error subcode name	value
Message header error	1 – Connection not synchronized 2 – Bad message length 3 – Bad message type
OPEN message error	1 – Unsupported version number 2 – Bad peer AS 3 – Unsupported authentication code 4 – Authentication failure
UDPATE message error	1 – Malformed attribute list 2 – Unrecognized well-known attribute 3 – Missing well-known attribute 4 – Attribute flags error 5 – Attribute length error 6 – Invalid ORIGIN attribute 7 – AS routing loop 8 – Invalid NEXT_HOP attribute 9 – Optional attribute error 10 – Invalid network field

Table 2.10. Error subcodes

The error code is a 1-byte unsigned integer that specifies the type of NOTIFI-CATION. A list of error code values are given in Table 2.9.

The error subcode is a 1-byte field that provides specific information about the nature of the error being reported. Each of the error codes will have one or more error subcodes; if no error subcode is defined for a specific error code, the error subcode value would be 0.

Table 2.10 lists error codes and their associated error subcode values.

The data field of the NOTIFICATION message is a variable length field that is used to diagnose the reason for the NOTIFICATION. The contents of this field depend upon the error code and error subcode field values.

2.5.2.5 BGP-2 FSM

Table 2.11 lists the transitions between states in the BGP FSM (Finite State Machine) in response to BGP events.

Table 2.12 shows BGP-2 FSM state transitions and the associated actions (as specified in RFC 1163).

Table 2.11. The BGP-2 FSM transition and actions

BGP-2 states	BGP-2 events
1 – Idle	1 – BGP<index>BGP</index> start
2 – Connect	2 – BGP stop
3 – Active	3 – BGP transport connection open
4 – OpenSent	4 – BGP transport connection closed
5 – OpenConfirm	5 – BGP transport connection open failed
6 – Establish	6 – BGP transport fatal error
	7 – ConnectRetry timer expired
	8 – HoldTime timer expired
	9 – KeepAlive timer expired
	10 – Receive OPEN message
	11 – Receive KEEPALIVE message
	12 – Receive UPDATE message
	13 – Receive NOTIFICATION message

Table 2.12. BGP FSM state transition and associated events

Event	Actions	Message sent	Next state
Idle (1)			
1	Resource initialization	None	2
	Start ConnectRetry timer		
	Initiation of transport connection	None	
Others	None		1
Connect (2)			
1	None	None	2
3	Complete initialization	OPEN	4
	Clear ConnectRetry timer		
5	ConnectRetry timer restart	None	3
7	ConnectRetry timer restart	None	2
	Transport connection initiation		
	Release resources		
Others		None	1
Active (3)			
1	None	None	3
3	Complete initialization	OPEN	4
	Clear ConnectRetry timer		
5	Close connection		3
	Restart ConnectRetry timer		
7	Restart ConnectRetry timer	None	2
	Initiate a transport connection		
	Resources release		
Others		None	1
OpenSent (4)			
1	None	None	4
4	Transport connection close		3
	Restart ConnectRetry timer		
	Release resources		
6	Process OPEN is OK	None	1
10	Process OPEN is failed	KEEPALIVE	5
	Close transport connection	NOTIFICATION	1
Others	Release resources	NOTIFICATION	1

Event	Actions	Message sent	Next state
OpenConfirm (5)			
1	none	None	5
4	Release Resources	None	1
6	Release Resources	None	1
9	Restart KeepAlive Timer	KEEPALIVE	5
11	Complete Initialization Restart HoldTime Timer	None	6
13	Close Transport connection Release Resources		1
Others	Close Transport connection Release Resources	NOTIFICATION	1
Established (6)			
1	none	None	6
4	Release Resources	None	1
6	Release Resources	None	1
9	Restart KeepAlive Timer	KEEPALIVE	6
11	Restart HoldTime Timer	KEEPALIVE	6
12	Process UPDATE is ok	UPDATE	6
	Process UPDATE is failed	NOTIFICATION	1
13	Close Transport connection Release Resources		1
Others	Close Transport connection	NOTIFICATION	1

Table 2.12. (continued) BGP FSM state transition and associated events

2.5.3 BGP-3

BGP-2 and BGP-3 are almost same in terms of message format and FSM. During the proposal of RFC 1267 that defines BGP-3 the following topics were a matter of discussion, which shows the need of having BGP-3 and its differences with BGP-2.

1. In view of the overhead of processing the message and update headers and the attribute lists of each BGP-2 update message, the inclusion of many routes per update message is an extremely important efficiency concern.
2. In BGP-3 this is seriously considered by letting the next-hop attribute of an update message default to the IP address of the speaker. This would not only simplify the implementation, but allow an identical update message to be sent to several peers in even more cases than at present. There is a problem with the FSM in the case when two peers try to connect to one another at the same time. This causes a "BGP transport connection open" event in the OpenSent state, which causes both ends to disconnect and return to the idle state, all with no particular reason to think it will not happen again. An improved FSM would fix this.
3. Also, there is a need for a default inter-AS metric attribute. Without one, it is not clear how to compare an advertisement from one peer with an explicit metric to an advertisement from another peer with no metric.

According to RFC 1207, the following are considered as the major differences between BGP-2 and BGP-3:

Fig. 2.31. The BGP-3 OPEN message that includes the BGP identifier

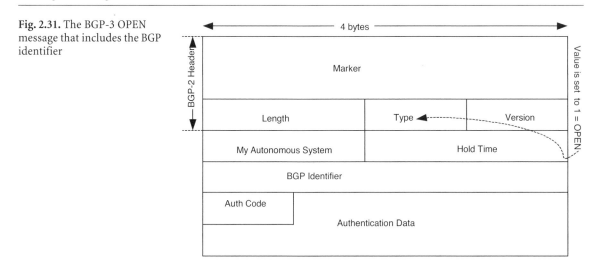

- During BGP connection a collision may occur; a new field (BGP identifier) is required in the OPEN message to detect and recover from the BGP connection collision. The BGP identifier included in the BGP-3 OPEN message is a four-octet field that specifies the BGP identifier of the sender (Fig. 2.31). A BGP speaker will set the value of this field as the IP address of its interface (the interface through which it can reach the other BGP speaker).

If a local system supports TCP PUSH function, a BGP message should be transmitted with the push flag set. As such, it will force the BGP message to be transmitted immediately to the receiver. Also, if a local system supports the setting of IP precedence bits for certain TCP connections, then BGP should set IP precedence as internetwork control (110) for that connection.

2.5.3.1 BGP Timer
BGP-3 employs three timers: ConnectRetry, HoldTime and KeepAlive. The suggested value for them is as follows:

> ConnectRetry = 120 seconds
> HoldTime = 90 seconds
> KeepAlive = 30 seconds.

It is recommended that BGP implementation must allow these timers to be configurable.

2.5.3.2 Processing Message on TCP
As we discussed earlier, BGP uses TCP as the transport protocol and TCP port 179 for establishing connection. Due to the stream nature of TCP, all data for a message is not necessarily received at the same time. In some situations it is difficult to process the data as messages; for example, in BSD UNIX it is not possible to determine how much data has been received and not yet been processed. One method which can be used to address this issue is to first try reading just the header of a message. Except for the KEEPALIVE

message, for other message types the header should be verified first, in particular the total length.

If all checks are done, the size of the data left to read is the specified length in the total length field minus the message header.

Setting up a message buffer (4096) per peer and filling it with data as available may reduce the "hang" situation of the routing information process for a particular implementation.

2.5.4 BGP-4

RFC 1771 defines BGP-4. It was developed on the basis of experience gained from earlier version of BGP. For BGP-4 messages are sent over TCP and TCP port 179 is used for establishing connection. BGP-4 provides a new set of mechanisms for supporting CIDR. This includes support for IP prefix advertisement and abolishes the concept of network class within BGP. BGP-4 also allows route aggregation including aggregation of AS paths. With these changes BGP-4 supports the proposed supernetting scheme described in RFC 1518 and 1519.

BGP-4 does not modify the BGP header, which was described earlier, but there is a slight modification in various message formats.

2.5.4.1 OPEN Message
The OPEN message includes BGP identifier, Opt Parm Len and optional parameters fields other than those specified earlier in BGP-2 (Fig. 2.32) .

The version field in the BGP-4 OPEN message indicates the current protocol version, that is 4 for BGP-4. The value for "My Autonomous System" and "Hold Time" is unchanged from those specified in BGP-2 OPEN message.

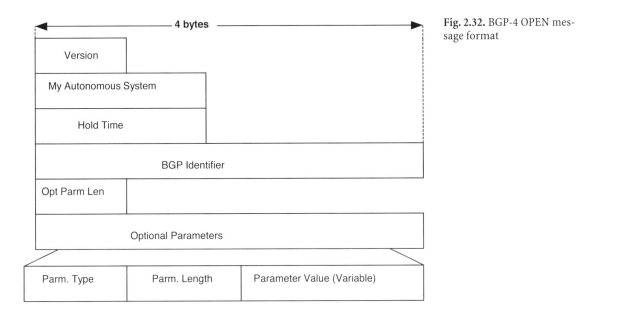

Fig. 2.32. BGP-4 OPEN message format

The BGP identifier is a 4-byte unsigned integer that indicates the BGP identifier of the sender. For a given BGP speaker, the value of this field is the IP address of its interface.

"Optional Parameters Length" is a one-octet field that indicates the total length of the optional parameters field in bytes. If the value of this field is set to zero, no optional parameters are present. The optional parameters field may contain a list of optional parameters for which each parameter is encoded as a triplet (parameter type, parameter length and parameter value).

The parameter type is a 1-byte field which identifies individual parameters. The parameter length is also a 1-byte field which contains the length of the parameter value field in octets. The parameter value is a variable length field that is deduced as per the value of the parameter type field.

2.5.4.2 UPDATE Message

As mentioned earlier, UPDATE messages are the conveyers of routing information between BGP peers. The information in UPDATE messages is used to construct a graph describing relationships among ASs. This message is also used to advertise a single feasible route to a peer or to withdraw multiple unfeasible routes from service, and these can happen simultaneously. For BGP-4 an UPDATE message includes a fixed BGP header and may optionally include the following fields (Fig. 2.33):

• Unfeasible route length
• Withdrawn routes
• Total path attribute length
• Path attribute
• Network layer reachability information.

The UPDATE message is used either to advertise a single feasible route to a peer, or to withdraw multiples of such routes from service. It may also simultaneously do both. The unfeasible route length field is a 2-byte field which indicates the total length of the withdrawn routes field in bytes. A value of 0 in

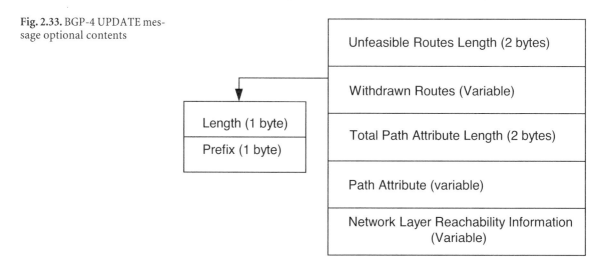

Fig. 2.33. BGP-4 UPDATE message optional contents

this field indicates that no routes are being withdrawn and also suggests that there is no withdrawn routes field present in this message. The withdrawn routes field is a variable length field which includes a list of IP address prefixes for withdrawn routes. Each of these IP prefixes is encoded in 2-tuple form (length, prefix).

The length field of the withdrawn routes field is a 1-byte field which indicates the length in bits of the IP address prefix. A length value of 0 indicates a prefix that matches all IP addresses. The prefix on the other hand is a variable length field and contains IP address prefixes followed by enough trailing bits to make the end of the field fall on a byte boundary.

The next field is the total path attribute length field. It is a 2-byte field which indicates the total length of the path attribute field in bytes. The value of this field identifies the network layer reachability. A value of 0 indicates that there is no network layer reachability information field present in the given UPDATE message.

ORIGIN (type code 1):
ORIGIN is a mandatory attribute that specifies the origin of path information. This data octet may have the values given in Table 2.13.

AS_Path (type code 2):
This is also a mandatory attribute that is composed of a sequence of AS path segments. Each of these segments is represented by a 3-tuple (path segment type, path segment length and path segment value). This 1-byte field may have the values given in Table 2.14.

NEXT_HOP (type code 3):
This mandatory attribute defines the IP address of the border router that should be used as the next hop to the destinations listed in the network layer reachability field of the UPDATE message. A BGP speaker must not advertise an address of a peer to that peer as a NEXT_HOP, for a route that the speaker is originating. Also, a BGP speaker must not install a route with itself as the next hop. The BGP speaker should not modify the NEXT_HOP attribute when advertising a route to a peer located in its own AS.

Value	Meaning
0	IGP – The network layer reachability information is interior to originating AS.
1	EGP – The network layer reachability information learned via EGP
2	Incomplete – The said information is learned via other means

Table 2.13. The type code 1 value of the attribute type code

Value	Segment type
1	AS_SET: A route in the UPDATE message has traversed for an unordered set of ASs
2	AS_Sequence: A route in the UPDATE message has traversed for an ordered set of ASs

Table 2.14. The values of AS_Path (type 2 code)

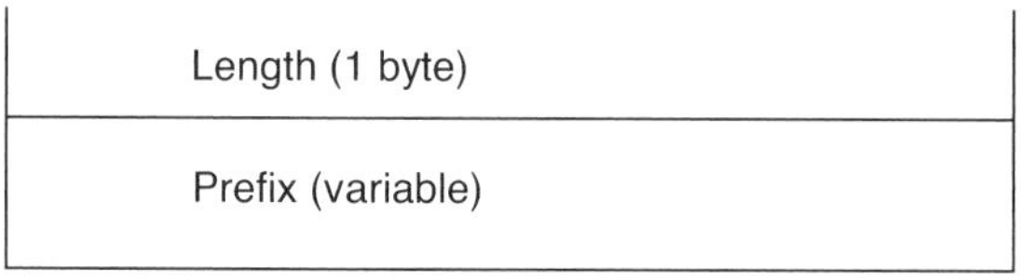

Fig. 2.34. The 2-tuple form of network layer reachability information

Length (1 byte)
Prefix (variable)

MULTI_EXIT_DISC (type code 4):
This is an optional non-transitive attribute that is a 4-byte non-negative integer. A BGP speaker to discriminate among multiple exit points to a neighboring AS may use the value of this field.

LOCAL_PERF (type code 5):
This is a well-known discretionary attribute that is a 4-byte long non-negative integer. A BGP speaker uses this field in an UPDATE message within its own AS and must not include it when sending an UPDATE message to neighboring ASs.

ATOMIC_AGGREGATE (type code 6):
This is also a well-known discretionary attribute of length 0. A BGP speaker uses it to inform other BGP speakers that the local system selected a less specific route rather than a specific route.

AGGREGATOR (type code 7):
This is an optional non-transitive attribute of length 6. This attribute includes the last AS number that formed the aggregate route followed by the IP address of the BGP speaker that formed the aggregate route.

Now, the next field after the path attribute in an UPDATE message is the network layer reachability information. It is a variable length field which includes a list of IP address prefixes. The information within this field is encoded in one or more 2-tuples, length and prefix (Fig. 2.34).

The length field indicates the length in bits of the IP address prefix, for which a length of zero indicates a prefix that matches all IP addresses.

The prefix field includes the IP prefix followed by enough trailing bits to make the end of the field fall on a byte boundary.

2.5.4.3 KEEPALIVE Message

BGP-4 or BGP in general does not use any transport-protocol-based keepalive mechanism to determine the reachability of its peer. Instead, KEEPALIVE messages are exchanged often so as not to cause the hold timer to expire.

The reasonable maximum time between two KEEPALIVE messages is one-third of the hold time interval. There is no difference in KEEPALIVE messages to what we described earlier in BGP-2 and BGP-3.

2.5.4.4 NOTIFICATION Message

We described the NOTIFICATION message in BGP-2; there is no difference between BGP-4 and BGP-2 NOTIFICATION messages.

2.5.5 BGP-4 Routes Advertisement and Storage

A route is defined as a unit of information which pairs a destination with the attribute of a path to that destination.

In BGP-4 routes are advertised between BGP peers in UPDATE messages, the destination of which is the systems whose IP addresses are reported in the network layer reachability information (NLRI), and the path is the information reported in the path attribute fields of the same UPDATE message.

Routes are stored in the routing information bases (RIBs) such as Adj-RIBS-In, the Loc-RIB, and Adj-RIBs-Out. The routes that will be advertised to other BGP speakers should be present in the Adj-RIB-Out. The routes that are used by the local BGP speaker must be present in the Loc-RIB and routes that are received from other BGP speakers must be present in Adj-RIB-In. The Adj-RIBs-In store routing information that is being learned from inbound UPDATE messages. The Loc-RIB includes the local routing information that the BGP speaker has selected by applying the information learned from Adj-RIBS-In . The Adj-RIBS-Out store the information that the local BGP speaker has selected for advertisement to its peer.

2.6 Multi-Protocol Label Switching (MPLS)

In summer 1999, a small design team led by Eric C. Rosen of Cisco Systems, Arun Viswanathan of Lucent Technologies and Ross Callon of IronBridge Networks produced a joint document which specifies the architecture of MPLS. The primary objective of MPLS is to standardize a base technology that integrates the layer 2 (L2) forwarding paradigm with network layer (L3) routing. The MPLS is an emerging protocol that should soon be standardized by the IETF. According to the Internet draft "A Framework for MPLS", the initial effort of MPLS will focus on IPv4; later it will include support for IPv6, IPX, CLNP etc.

It is expected that this base technology will be used with any media types such as asynchronous transfer mode (ATM) , Ethernet or frame relay. The MPLS has been developed almost to a full-blown technology from the proprietary approaches developed by Cisco (Tag Switching), IBM (ARIS), Toshiba (CSR) and, to some extent, Ipsilon (IP Switching). It provides connection-oriented (label-based) switching with IP routing and control protocols. MPLS can be compared to a thin layer that is used to provide connection services to IP and utilizes link layer services from L2 (Point-to-Point Protocol, ATM, Ethernet, etc.) (Fig. 2.35).

The term "Multi-Protocol" is used to specify the support of various network layer protocols although initial work is based on IPv4. The term "label"[5]

---

5 Label: As defined in the internet draft "A Framework for MPLS", a label is a short, fixed length, physically contiguous, locally significant identifier that is used to identify a stream.

Fig. 2.35. An imaginary layered concept for MPLS

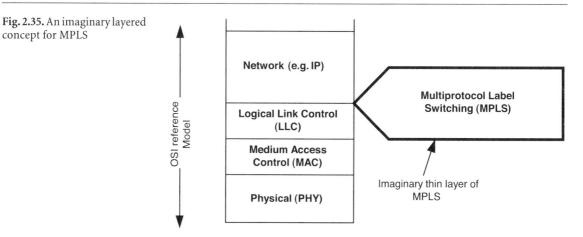

means tag or identification that is associated each packet and applied at the ingress of the data path. It is removed at the egress of the data path. MPLS provides a simple core set of mechanisms that can be grouped in three different methods of operation:

1. Label assignment: Each stream is identified with a label.
2. Forwarding: Labels are used to forward the packets. Forwarding includes simple functions such as looking up a label in a table, swapping labels, and where possible decrementing and checking TTL. In certain scenarios, MPLS may directly use L2 switching as seen in ATM or Ethernet.
3. Label distribution: It allows the nodes to determine which labels to use for specific streams. It can be obtained through some sorts of control exchange and/or piggybacked on a routing protocol.

To consider the advantage of MPLS over existing switching technologies, MPLS Internet drafts described consideration of two commonly used campus networking methodologies. The first uses a router as the core of the network and the second uses ATM as the core with IP routers operating over ATM (Table 2.15). Although the campus network is now based on L3 switching rather than slow processing routers, we will consider the described methodologies for the sake of discussion and to understand the advantages of deploying MPLS in such a network.

Table 2.15. A comparison between legacy routing and MPLS

	Datagram Rrouters	**Multi-Protocol Label Switching (MPLS)**
Simplified forwarding	Datagram forwarding is based on longer match algorithm applied to longer address	Datagram forwarding is based on exact match for a short label
	Protocol headers are used. Often protocol header has more complex information than needs to be processed such as IP header	Simple label header is used and overall simple forwarding technique

	Datagram Rrouters	Multi-Protocol Label Switching (MPLS)
Efficient explicit routing	Carries complete explicit or source route with each packet during the application of source routing	MPLS allows explicit or source route that can be carried only at the time "label switched path" is not set up.
Traffic engineering	Traffic engineering provides balanced traffic load on the various links. It is difficult to accomplish with datagram routing, although currently some degree of load balancing can be obtained	Using MPLS traffic engineering is much easier since streams from ingress to egress node pair can be individually identified
QoS routing	For some reason information available for QoS routing in a datagram router may be outdated due to particular node or nodes not having available resources	MPLS can provide QoS by allowing ingress node to inform the network elements about which path is capable of carrying streams and through the use of explicit routing
Mapping from IP packets to FEC	Datagram routers allow mapping from IP packet to FECs (Forward Equivalent Classes) but packets that are mapped will be indistinguishable	MPLS allows mapping from IP packets to FECs only once and at the ingress of MPLS domain. This type of mapping is important for ISPs to identify who is transmitting and in turn apply appropriate packet classification for specific traffic treatment
Single forwarding paradigm with service level differentiation	This TOS is partially missing in datagram routers	MPLS allows multiple TOS through the use of single forwarding model. Due to the forwarding technique, it is possible to carry different services through the use of same network elements. The support of multiple services simultaneously requires partitioning of the label space, which can be supported by the LDM (Label Distribution Management) protocols

Table 2.15. (continued) A comparison between legacy routing and MPLS

2.6.1 MPLS Overview

As a packet encapsulated by the connectionless network layer protocol traverses through the routers, each router analyzes the packet header, runs a routing algorithm, chooses a next hop for the packet based on header analysis and learning from the routing algorithm, all done independently. To choose the next hop, distinctively two functions are required. The first is to partition the packets into a set of forwarding equivalence classes (FECs). The second is to map each FEC to a next hop.

Considering Fig. 2.36, networks where different packets get mapped into the same FEC are indistinguishable. For datagram routers, as a packet traverses through each hop, the router maps packets into an FEC; since each hop reexamines the packet header and provides FEC assignment, the initial assignment at ingress might not match the FEC assignment at egress.

In MPLS, FEC assignment is done once at the ingress of the MPLS domain. The packet assigned to an FEC will be identified by a short prefix known as "label". Each packet carries a label when the packet is forwarded to the next hop; those packets are known as labeled packets. For the subsequent hops there is no further analysis of network layer headers in the packet. These packets are also known as labeled packets. Each hop considers the label of the packet as an index and maps this into the table replacing the old entry (Fig. 2.37).

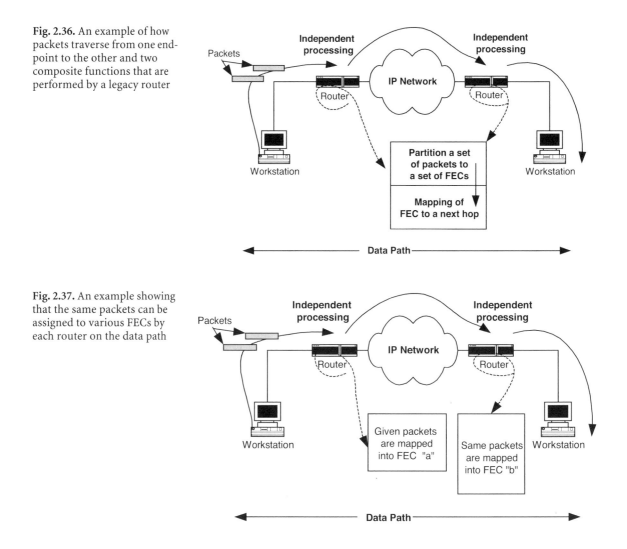

Fig. 2.36. An example of how packets traverse from one endpoint to the other and two composite functions that are performed by a legacy router

Fig. 2.37. An example showing that the same packets can be assigned to various FECs by each router on the data path

In MPLS, since there is no further analysis of the network layer header, all forwarding is driven by the label; the result introduces a number of advantages over conventional L3 forwarding.

The advantages of MPLS forwarding are as follows:

1. The forwarding as suggested in the MPLS paradigm can be done by switches that are not capable of doing network layer header analysis.
2. In MPLS, since FEC assignment is done only once at ingress and the information that is obtained may not be gleaned from the network layer header, packets arriving in different ports, for example, can be assigned to different FECs. This particular behavior is difficult to impose in conventional L3 forwarding.
3. Packetsentering one router can be labeled differently to the same packet entering the network through a different router, and as a result forwarding decisions can be easily made. In conventional routing, this is reasonably difficult to do.
4. In some cases, it is necessary for a packet to take a certain data path; through use of traffic engineering this is possible for MPLS devices. In conventional forwarding this requires special encoding.

Note that a router that supports MPLS is known as an LSR (Label Switching Router).

Now let's consider a simple network (that is using conventional L3 forwarding) as given Fig. 2.38 to understand the MPLS forwarding paradigm further. In our example, we have four routers R1–R4 and three subnets A–C. For the sake of discussion, those routers are running an OSPF routing algorithm to determine the best path to each destination. The tables as shown in Fig. 2.38 depict the forwarding information bases (FIBs) that are constructed by the routing protocol in use at each router. Now, if R2 receives a packet destined for network "Net 3" from R1, R2 knows through the use of the routing algorithm that it should forward it to R3. To ensure R2 is making the correct

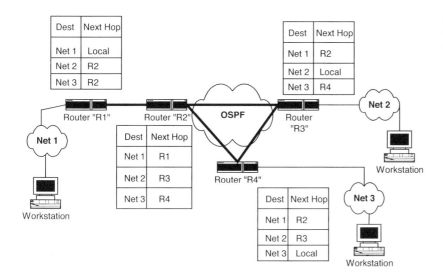

Fig. 2.38. An example of conventional forwarding paradigm

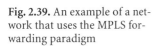

Fig. 2.39. An example of a network that uses the MPLS forwarding paradigm

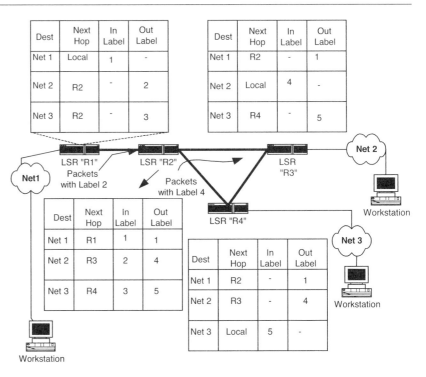

decision, it will search its FIB to find the longest destination prefix that matches the destination IP address of the traversing packet.

Let's consider the same network using the MPLS forwarding paradigm where the conventional routers are replaced with LSRs. The LSRs are using LDP (Label Distribution Protocol) to exchange labels for each route, otherwise known as LSP (Label Switched Path), in their FIBs. The labels are exchanged between neighboring LSRs and are unique on a link. For simplicity, the LSRs in Fig. 2.39 are using the same incoming label in all links. Now, considering the same forwarding of a packet as we described earlier, R2 receives a packet from R1 destined for "Net 2". Since we are using LSR instead of legacy routers, R1 puts label 2 on the traversing packet. In this case, R2 can search for incoming label 2 and determines label 4 for output towards R3. This procedure is much simpler since LSRs are only performing an exact match for the label instead of the longest prefix. Moreover, if the receiving LSR chooses the incoming labels to be used (known as "downstream label allocation"), the LSRs can use an index on their FIB as a label. This method of label assignment allows the LSR to do a direct lookup in the FIB for forwarding information that takes a single-access instead of a multiple access search.

2.6.2 MPLS Basics

The major protocol introduced by MPLS is an LDP that is used to set up and tear down LSP. An alternative to LDP is RSVP. We mentioned earlier that a

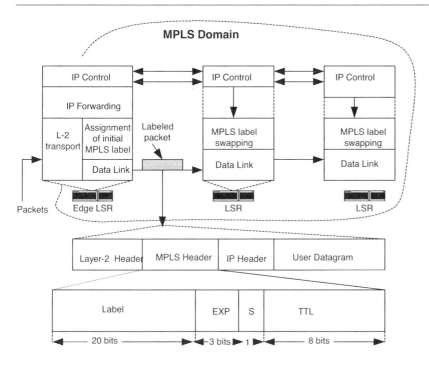

Fig. 2.40. An example of MPLS encapsulation with label and other information

packet traversing through an MPLS router or LSR carries a label, which is a short, fixed length, locally significant identifier. The label that is placed in a packet represents the FEC to which the packet is assigned.

At the time of writing MPLS is not yet an RFC. Therefore, the text here is based on the manufacturer's implementation of MPLS and available Internet drafts.

According to the Internet draft "A Framework for MPLS", the label-based forwarding makes use of information including label or stack label and possibly additional information such as TTL field. In some cases, this information would be encapsulated using the MPLS header, otherwise it may be encoded with the L2 header. It should be noted that there may be multiple types of MPLS header. For example, a header used in one medium may be different than other media types. Therefore, encapsulation will vary with the underlying L2 technology. The initial suggestion about the content of MPLS encapsulation was that it would include the following fields as contents (Fig. 2.40):

- Label
- TTL
- Class of service
- Stack indicator
- Next header type indicator
- Checksum.

According to a later released Internet draft "MPLS Label Stack Encoding", the suggested MPLS header is four octets or 32 bits long. This header appears after the datalink or L2 header. In a typical network that employs LSRs, pack-

Fig. 2.41. An example of label stack

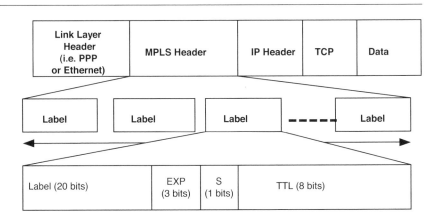

ets enter at edge LSR where they are labeled; that is, an MPLS header is inserted after the L2 header and before the L3 header. There can be multiples of labels inserted in the MPLS header. These multiples are known as label stacks (Fig. 2.41) and useful for situations where both IGP and BGP are used as routing protocols. Thus, both IGP and BGP labels allow routers in the interior of an AS to be free of BGP information. In this case, the IGP label is used to steer through the AS and the BGP label is used to switch between ASs.

The label stack encapsulation format shown in Fig. 2.41 can be represented as a sequence of label stack entries. Each label stack entry is four octets.

"S", a 1-bit field, identifies the last entry in the label stack or bottom of the stack when set to 1, and set to 0 for other entries.

The TTL is an 8-bit field. It includes a time-to-live value. If the value is set to 0 for the outgoing TTL of a labeled packet, that packet should not be forwarded. When an IP packet is first labeled, the TTL value of the label stack must be set to the value of the IP TTL field.

"EXP" is a 3-bit field and reserved for experimental use.

"Label" in the label stack entry is a 20-bit field. A value of 0 represents "IPv4 Explicit Null Label". This label value indicates that the label stack needs to be popped and its packet forwarding should be based on the IPv4 header. A value of 1 identifies "Router Alert Label" and it can be anywhere in the label stack except at the bottom. The use of this label is similar to the use of "Route Alert Option" in the IP packet. A value of 2 identifies the "IPv6 Explicit Null Label" and indicates that the packet should be popped and its forwarding based on the IPv6 header. A value of 3 identifies "Implicit Null Label" assigned by the LSR for use with LDP. The values 4–15 are reserved.

2.6.2.1 Label Processing

Once the last label is removed and processed from a packet label stack, further processing of the packet is done based on the network layer header, that is the IP header (Fig. 2.42). The LSR, which removes and processes the last label from the label stack also identifies the network layer protocol header of the packet. The label stack entry does not carry any field that explicitly identifies the network layer header that is followed. But the LSR must be able to identify the network layer header and it does so from the value of the label.

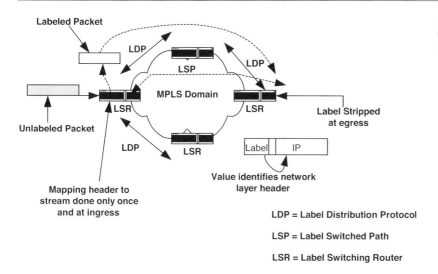

Fig. 2.42. Label processing and other packet forwarding information

For example, we have said that a label value of 0 indicates that the packet must be forwarded based on the IPv4 header. Therefore, if the label value is set to 0, the LSR assumes the network layer header is IPv4. If for any reason the label value does not meet the criteria, the LSR will not be able to identify the network layer header.

If a packet exceeds the MTU size of a datalink layer (i.e., Ethernet), and the label value does not meet the criteria or there are no protocol-dependent rules for handling error conditions, then such a packet must be silently discarded.

There may be a situation when the network administrator is using MPLS to tunnel through a transit routing domain and the external routes are not liked into the interior routers. For example, imagine a network where several ASs are connected using BGP and OSPF is running within the AS. In this scenario, BGP is not distributed into OSPF and the LSRs that are not ASBRs do not run BGP. In this example, only the ASBRs know how to route packets between the ASs. If an interior router wants to send an ICMP message to the packet origin, it will not know how to route the message. One solution is to inject "default" into the OSPF packet by one or more ASBRs. This will not cause any loops and will work given the fact that the ASBRs have complete routing information and the packets have globally unique addresses.

2.6.2.1.1 Fragmentation and Path MTU Discovery (PMTUD)

It is sometimes possible that the labeled packet is too large to be transmitted on the output link. It is also possible that a packet which was originally within the MTU size of the underlying technology has grown to exceed that due to multiple labels being pushed on. As specified in the Internet draft "MPLS Label Stack Encoding", the nodes that adhere to the rules provided in this do not need to apply fragmentation. If a labeled IPv4 packet is considered "too big" and the DF (Don't Fragment) bit in the IPv4 header is not set, then the LSR will silently discard the packet.

In the case when an LSR decides not to discard a "too big" IPv4 datagram, this is perhaps due to the DF bit being set in the IPv4 header; the LSR will execute an algorithm similar to the one depicted in Fig. 2.43.

The above discussion was based on the IPv4 header, but now, considering the packet to be encapsulated with the IPv6 header, in the case of a "too big" packet the algorithm depicted in Fig. 2.44 will be executed by an LSR. (Bear in mind that this is just an imaginary flowchart to aid understanding.)

2.6.2.1.2 Label Packet over PPP

The PPP (Point-to-Point Protocol) defined in RFC 1661 is a standard protocol for transporting various PDUs over a point-to-point link. It has mainly three components:

1. Encapsulation method for multiprotocol datagram
2. Link Control Protocol (LCP) for configuring, testing and establishing the link.
3. A family of network control protocols (NCPs) for configuring and establishing L3 potocols.

During the establishment of a point-to-point link, each side of the link sends LCP packets to configure and test the link. Once the link is established and the other optional criteria as needed by LCP are negotiated, PPP send an MPLSCP (MPLS Control Protocol) packet in order to transmit label packets. The label packets are rsent only after MPLSCP has reached the opened state (Fig. 2.45).

Fig. 2.43. An example of the algorithm invoked by the LSR to determine how to handle a "too big" packet

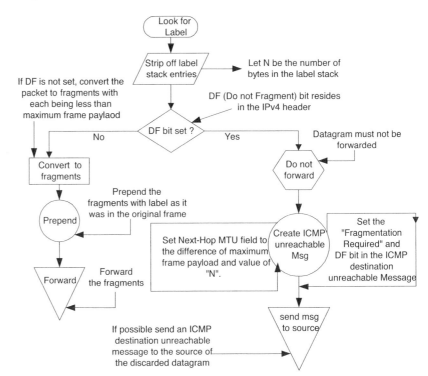

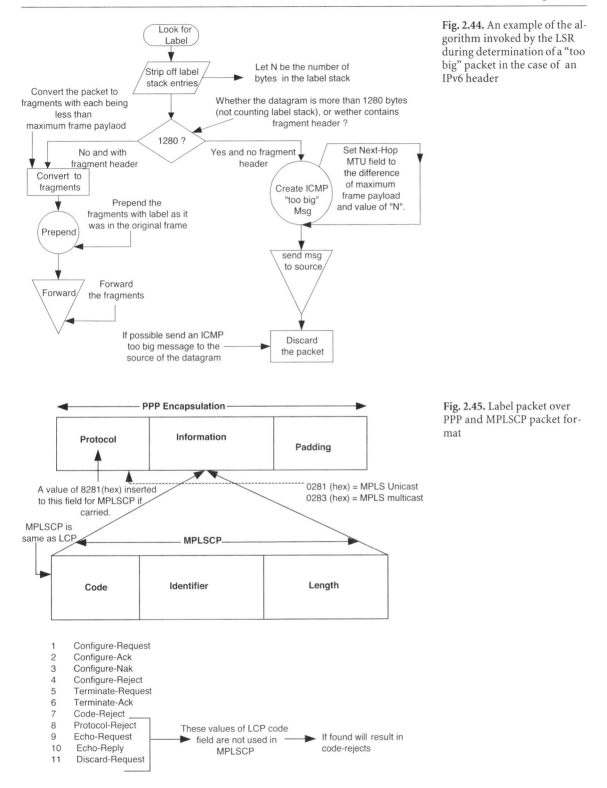

Fig. 2.44. An example of the algorithm invoked by the LSR during determination of a "too big" packet in the case of an IPv6 header

Fig. 2.45. Label packet over PPP and MPLSCP packet format

Fig. 2.46. An example of how label stack entry is encapsulated within an Ethernet packet

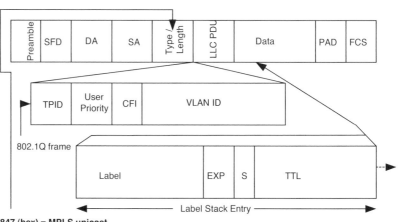

8847 (hex) = MPLS unicast
8848 (hex) = MPLS multicast

The link will remain open until LCP or MPLSCP closes the connection. MPLSCP is almost the same as LCP except for the following:

- The packet, which is being sent during the link establishment phase, may be modified.
- Exactly one MPLSCP will be encapsulated with the information field of PPP, where the protocol field indicates type 8281(hex).
- The code field of LCP will carry only 1 through 7 other values will and result in code-rejects.
- The MPLSCP may not be exchanged until PPP has completed its negotiation phase.

2.6.2.1.3 Label Packet over LAN Media

The label stack entries must be after any datalink layer headers including the 802.1q header if it exists (Fig. 2.46). The "ethertype" field value 8847(hex) is used to identify MPLS unicast packets or else if this field value is 8848 (hex), it indicates MPLS multicast packets.

2.6.3 Label Distribution Protocol

The Label Distribution Protocol (LDP) is a set of procedures through which an LSR informs the other LSRs about the meaning of labels used to forward traffic between and through them. This set of procedures and messages provides the means for LSRs to establish LSPs through a network by mapping network layer routing information directly to datalink layer switched paths. These LSPs may connect an immediate neighbor or an egress node thus allowing switching via all intermediary nodes. The LDP provides an FEC association with each LSP that it creates. This association specifies which packets are mapped to which LSP. Two LSRs that exchange label/FEC mapping information through LDP are known as "LDP peers". Note that LDP is bidirectional; in other words, a single session allows each LSR in "LDP peers" to learn the others' label mappings.

There are four categories of LDP messages:

1. Discovery message: This message is used by the LDP of an LSR to announce and maintain LSR presence in the network. It is a mechanism through which LSRs indicate their presence in the network by sending periodic Hello messages. Such a message will be carried by a UDP packet destined for an LDP port at the group multicast address "all routers on this subnet".
2. Session message: Once a Hello is received and an LSR wishes to establish a session with the peer, it initializes LDP through the use of a session advertisement over TCP. The session message is used to establish, maintain and terminate sessions between LSR peers.
3. Advertisement message: An LSR uses this LDP message to create, change and delete label mapping for FECs. Assuming that the LSR successfully completes the session through the use of session message, the two LSRs that are considered "LDP peers" may now initiate advertisement messages.
4. Notification message: This is used for advisory and signal error information. The notification message can be of two kinds, one that is used for signaling fatal errors known as "Error Notification", and the other "Advisory Notification". If an LSR receives the error notification, it will close the TCP connection and discard all label mappings learned via session. The advisory notification passes information about the LDP session or the status of previous message received to LSR in "LDP peers".

2.6.3.1 LDP PDU

The LDP uses TCP as the transport and exchanges message through the use of LDP PDUs. Each LDP PDU can be considered as an LDP header followed by one or more LDP messages. The LDP header includes a two-octet version field followed by a 2-byte PDU length field and a six-octet LDP identifier field. The version field includes a two-octet unsigned integer containing the version number of the LDP. Currently the value specifies version 1 of this protocol.

The next field, the PDU length, specifies the total length of the PDU in bytes excluding the version and PDU length. The maximum length allowed for LDP PDU is 4096 bytes and negotiable during LDP sessions (Fig. 2.47).

The LDP identifier field identifies the label space of the LSR that is sending the PDU. The first 4 bytes of this 6-byte field use a globally unique value to identify the LSR. It should be a 32-bit router ID that is assigned to the LSR. The last 2 bytes identify a label space within the LSR.

The LDP uses a special encoding scheme for carrying information in LDP messages, which is known as TLV (Fig. 2.48).

The LDP uses 14 bits of the first two octets to specify the type of an LSR. The 2 bits before the type field specify the behavior of an LSR when that LSR does not recognize the type field. The TLV field also includes a 2-byte length field and a variable length value field. The first 2 bits of TLV are known as the U and F bits. If the U or "Unknown" bit of TLV in a message is set to 0, the message is ignored and a notification is sent to the message originator. If the

Fig. 2.47. The frame format of LDP PDU

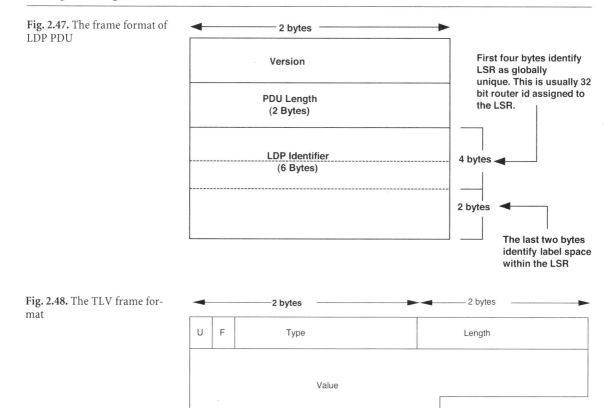

U bit is set to 1, the unknown TLV is ignored and the message is processed. The F bit is the "Forward" unknown TLV bit. If this bit is set to 0, the message is not forwarded, else if set to 1, the message with unknown TLV is forwarded.

The type field indicates how the value field is to be read. The length field identifies the length of the value field. Since an LDP message uses several parameters with TLV encoding, it is important that we discuss them before examining the details on LDP messages. Some of these parameters are:

- FEC TLV
- Label TLV
- Address list TLV
- Hop count TLV
- Path vector TLV
- Status TLV.

2.6.3.1.1 *FEC TLV*

The labels are mapped to FECs. Each FEC has a list of one or more FEC elements. Therefore, FEC TLV encoding includes FEC element 1 to element *n* (Fig. 2.49). These elements' encoding depends on the type of FECs.

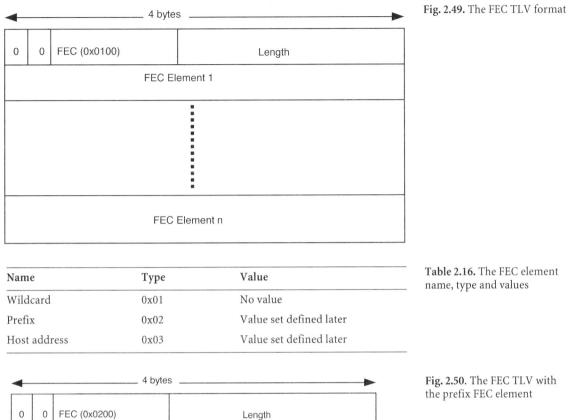

Fig. 2.49. The FEC TLV format

Name	Type	Value
Wildcard	0x01	No value
Prefix	0x02	Value set defined later
Host address	0x03	Value set defined later

Table 2.16. The FEC element name, type and values

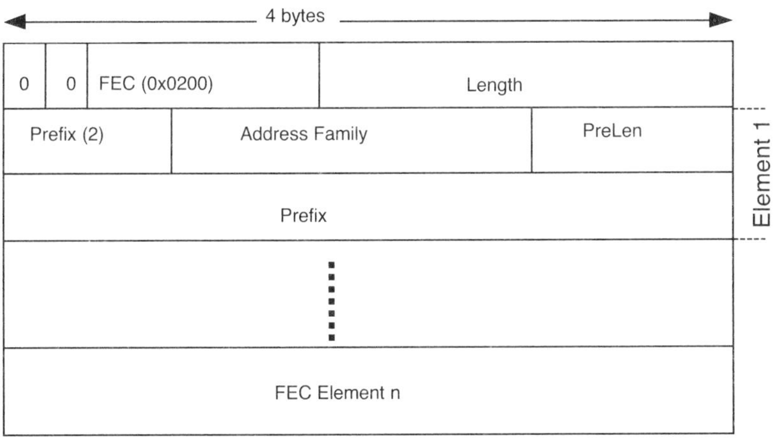

Fig. 2.50. The FEC TLV with the prefix FEC element

The FEC element value is encoded within several octet fields for which the one-octet field specifies type, and a variable length field includes type-dependent element value.

Table 2.16 gives the type and value of the FEC elements.

The wildcard FEC element is only used in the label withdraw and label release messages. It indicates the withdraw and release of all FECs that are associated with label within "Label TLV".

The prefix FEC element value encoding includes the prefix, address family and PreLen fields (Fig. 2.50).

Fig. 2.51. The host address FEC element encoding

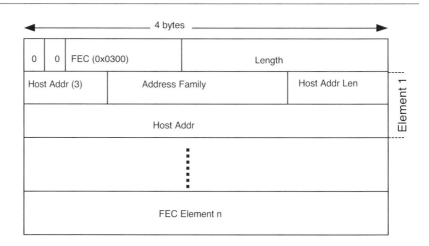

The address family field is a 2-byte field that contains the value from the address family number as defined in RFC 1700.

The prefix field contains an address prefix as per the value of the address family field. The length of this field is specified in the PreLen field.

The next element type is the host address FEC element. This element includes a Host Addr field, an address family and a Host Addr Len field (Fig. 2.51). The address family field includes the address family number from RFC 1700. The Host Addr Len field specifies the length of the host address in bytes. Host Addr contains an address as per the value of the address family field.

2.6.3.1.2 *Label TLV*

The label TLVs encode the label and are carried by the message used to advertise, request, release and withdraw label mappings.

There are several kinds of label TLVs:

- Generic label TLV
- ATM label TLV
- Frame relay label TLV.

Since ATM label TLV and frame relay label TLV require readers to be familiar with the subject, I will therefore omit them here. Interested readers may wish to refer to my third book *High Speed Enterprise Networking Handbook* for further details.

As for the generic label TLV, this is used by the LSR to encode labels associated with links. Examples of such links are PPP and Ethernet.

The generic label TLV (Fig. 2.52) includes a generic label field, a length field and a 4-byte label field that specify a 20-bit label value.

2.6.3.1.3 Address List TLV

This particular TLV (Fig. 2.53) appears in the address and address withdraw messages.

This encoding includes a 2-byte address family field that conains the value specified in address family number in RFC 1700. The address list TLV also in-

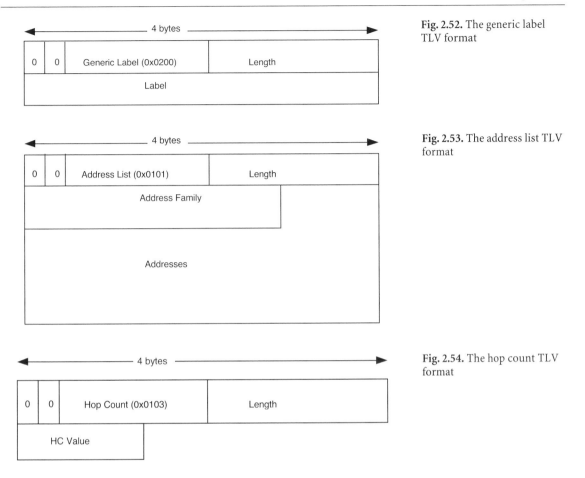

Fig. 2.52. The generic label TLV format

Fig. 2.53. The address list TLV format

Fig. 2.54. The hop count TLV format

cludes a length field and an addresses field. A list of addresses from the specified address family are included in this latter field.

2.6.3.1.4 Hop Count TLV

This TLV appears as an optional field in messages that set up LSPs and also calculates the hop numbers along an LSP during the setup of an LSP.

The HC value is a 1-byte field that indicates hop count value (Fig. 2.54).

2.6.3.1.5 Path Vector TLV

This TLV is used with the hop count TLV in label request and label mapping messages to implement the LDP loop (optional) detection mechanism. The TLV encodes a list of router IDs indicating the path of LSRs through which the message has traversed (Fig. 2.55).

2.6.3.1.6 Status TLV

A notification LDP message carry status TLV to specify the event that is being signaled. The encoding includes a U bit, an F bit, a status code field, and message type and message ID fields. The U bit is set to 0 when status TLV is sent

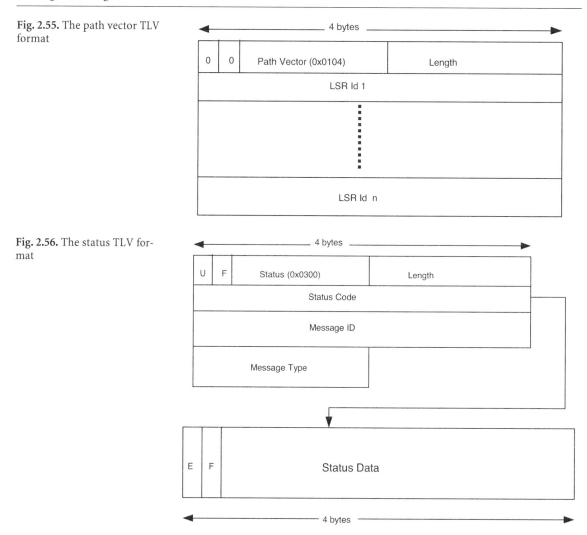

Fig. 2.55. The path vector TLV format

Fig. 2.56. The status TLV format

in a notification message. Otherwise, if set to 1, it indicates that status TLV is sent in other message.

The F bit is the same as setting the F bit in the status code field. This field is a 32-bit unsigned integer that encodes the event being signaled. Figure 2.56 shows the structure of the status code field. This field starts with E and F bits. The E bit is fatal error bit which, when set to 1, indicates a fatal error notification. Otherwise, if set to 0, it indicates an advisory notification.

The F bit is the forward bit and, if set to 1, the notification should be forwarded for the next hop or previous hop for an LSP. If set to 0, it indicates that the notification should not be forwarded. The status data in the status code field specifies status information. It is a 30-bit unsigned integer field.

The next field is the message ID field which, if non-zero, indicates the peer message. Otherwise, if it is zero, it indicates no peer message. The message type identifies the type of peer message if set to non-zero, otherwise, if set to zero, it indicates that no peer message type exists.

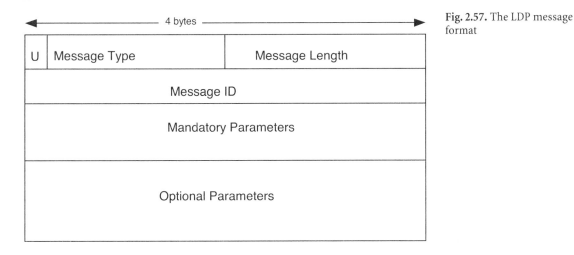

Fig. 2.57. The LDP message format

2.6.3.2 LDP Message Structure

We earlier talked about various LDP message types and now in the succeeding sections we will explore them. It is important to understand the basic structure first. All LDP messages have the same format as depicted in Fig. 2.57.

The first bit is the U bit or unknown message bit. If a message received with this bit set to 0, a notification is sent to the message originator. Otherwise, if it is set to 1, the unknown message is discarded silently.

Next there is a message type field which identifies the type of message. The message length specifies the length in octets for the message ID, mandatory parameters and optional parameters.

The next field is a 32-bit message ID field which identifies the message. It is used by the sending LSR to identify notification messages that may apply to this message.

The mandatory parameter is a variable length field which some messages will use and some not.

"Optional Parameters" is a variable length field that includes some optional parameters for a message, but often many messages do not use it.

2.6.3.2.1 Notification Message

The notification message is used by an LSR to inform its LDP peers about a significant event. It may signal a fatal error or provide advisory information regarding the LDP session or the outcome of processing an LDP message.

The message includes a 32-bit message ID field, a status TLV field and an optional parameters field among other fields.

As we mentioned earlier, the message ID field identifies the message in which it is included.

The status TLV field indicates an event that is being signaled. We discussed status TLV in an earlier section.

The optional parameters field is a variable length field which contains zero or more parameters. Each of these parameters is encoded with TLV. The op-

Table 2.17. Various optional parameters for notification message

Optional parameters	Type	Length
Extended status	0x0301	Four octets
Returned PDU	0x0302	Variable
Returned message	0x0303	Variable

Fig. 2.58. The notification message structure

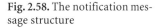

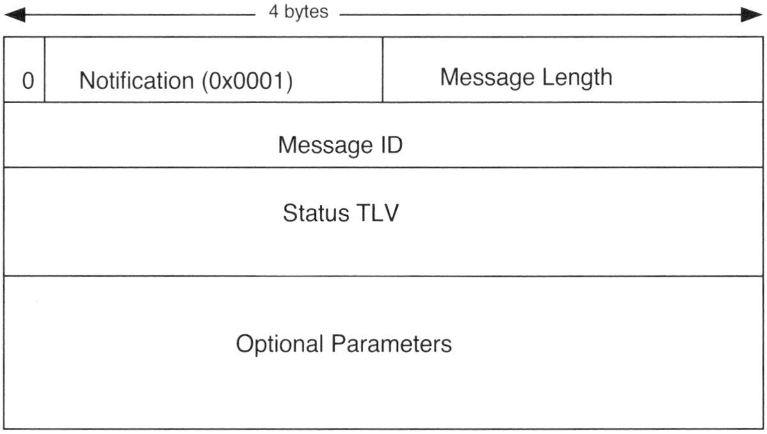

tional parameters that are depicted in Table 2.17 may be included in a notification message.

The extended status is a four-octet value. It is an extended status code, which encodes information supplementary to the notification message status code (Fig. 2.58) .

"Returned PDU" is used by an LSR to return a part of the LDP to the originator. "Return Message" is also used by an LSR to return part of an LDP to the originator.

In the notification message procedure, if an LSR detects a condition which requires it to notify its peer with some advisory or error information, it sends a notification message to the peer. If the condition is a fatal error the status TLV within the message will indicate that.

2.6.3.2.2 Hello Message

During the LDP discovery mechanism a Hello message is exchanged. The message includes the message length, message ID, common Hello parameter TLV, and optional parameters fields as depicted in Fig. 2.59.

The message ID is a 32-bit field which identifies the message. The common Hello parameter TLV field specifies the common parameters for all Hello messages. It includes a hold time field and T and R (Target and Request) fields. The hold time specifies Hello hold time in seconds. The LSR exchanges the Hello message to maintain the Hello adjacency. It also maintains the Hello hold timer and updates it once it receives another Hello. If for any reason the timer expires the LSR discards the Hello adjacency. A pair of LSRs negotiate hold times through the use of Hellos. Each proposes a hold time. A value of 0

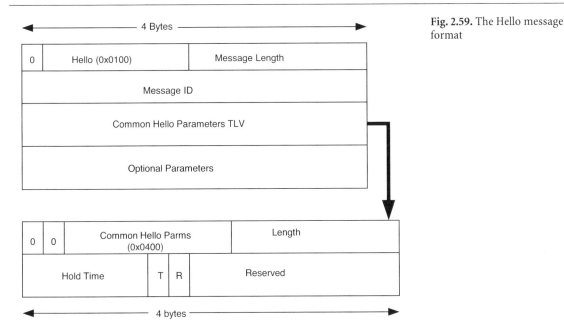

Fig. 2.59. The Hello message format

indicates use of the default. This means 15 seconds for link Hellos and 45 seconds for targeted Hellos. The value of 0xffff for the hold time means infinite.

The T and R fields are used for "Target Hello" and "Request Send Targeted Hellos" accordingly. If the T is set to 1, the Hello message is "Targeted Hello". Otherwise, if set to 0, it indicates a "Link Hello". The value of R, if set to 1, indicates a request to the receiver to send periodic targeted Hellos to the source of this Hello. A value of 0 indicates no request.

The reserved field is always set to zero during transmission and ignored upon receipt.

2.6.3.2.3 Initialization Message

During an LDP session the initialization message is exchanged between LSRs. This message includes the encoding depicted in Fig. 2.60.

The common session parameter TLV includes the parameters (identified by the sending LSR) that need to be negotiated during the LDP session. The common session parameter includes (among other fields) a protocol version field the value of which is currently set to 1. It also includes a keep-alive time, an A bit, a D bit, a PVLim, MAX PDU length and receiver LDP identifier fields.

The keep-alive time is a two-octet field with non-zero integer values that indicate the number of seconds in the keep-alive time proposed by the sending LSR. The receiver must calculate this value by using the least value of its own proposed keep-alive time and that of the received PDU. The A bit is the label advertisement discipline and indicates the type of label advertisement. When set to 0, it means the downstream "unsolicited advertisement". Otherwise, if set to 1, it indicates downstream on demand. The D bit is known as loop detection; when set to 0 it means it is disabled, and when set to 1 it means the loop detection is enabled.

Fig. 2.60. The initialization
message format

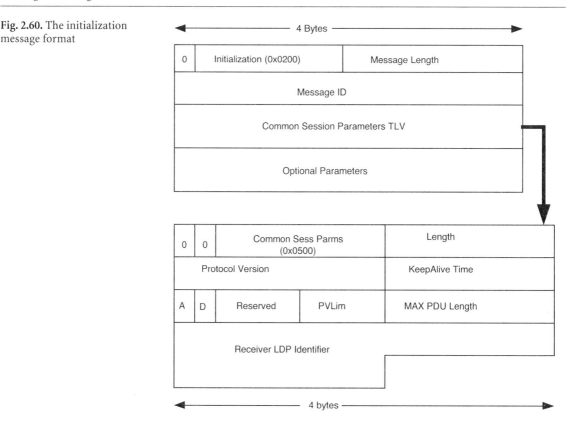

The next field is reserved and has the same value as described for earlier messages. PVLim is the "Path Vector Limit" field and set to 0 when loop detection is disabled. If the value exceeds the limit of this field, the LSR behaves as if a loop is being detected. "Max PDU length" specifies the maximum PDU length during an LDP session. A value of 255 or less indicates the default maximum length of 4096 bytes.

2.6.3.2.4 *Keep-alive Message*
An LSR sends the keep-alive message as part of the mechanism that monitors the integrity of the LDP session. The encoding is as shown in Fig. 2.61.

The message ID is a 32-bit field which identifies the message. Yet no optional parameter is defined for the keep-alive message.

2.6.3.2.5 *Address Message*
An LSR sends this message to an LDP peer in order to advertise its interface address. The address message includes a message ID field, an address list TLV field and an optional parameters field among others (Fig. 2.62).

2.6.3.2.6 *Address Withdraw Message*
This message is sent by an LSR to its peer in order to withdraw a previously advertised interface address. The encoding for this message is as shown in Fig. 2.63.

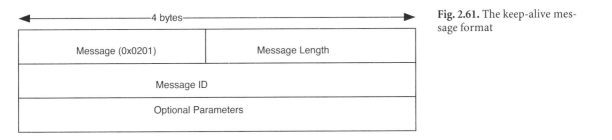

Fig. 2.61. The keep-alive message format

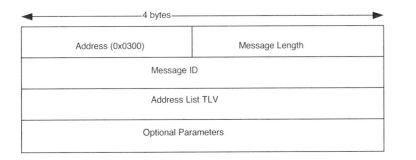

Fig. 2.62. The address message format

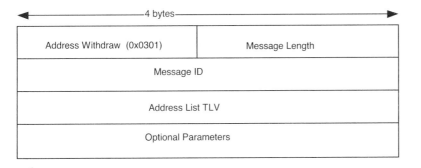

Fig. 2.63. The address withdraw message format

2.6.3.2.7 Label Mapping Message

When an LSR chooses to advertise FEC–label bindings, it does so by sending a label mapping message to the peer. The encoding includes FEC TLV, label TLV and optional parameter fields among others (Fig. 2.64).

The FEC TLV field specifies the FEC component of the FEC–label mapping that is advertised. On the other hand, the label TLV field specifies the label component of the FEC–label mapping.

The optional parameter field includes parameters as shown in Table 2.18.

2.6.3.2.8 Label Request Message

In order to request a mapping for an FEC, the LSR sends out this message to its peer. The encoding includes an FEC TLV and an optional parameters field among other fields (Fig. 2.65).

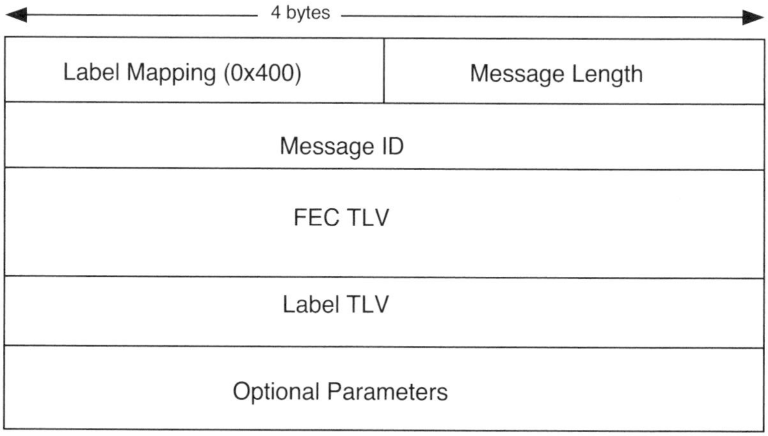

Fig. 2.64. The label mapping message format

Table 2.18. Optional parameters for label mapping message

Optional parameters	Length
Hop count TLV	One octet
Path vector TLV	Variable

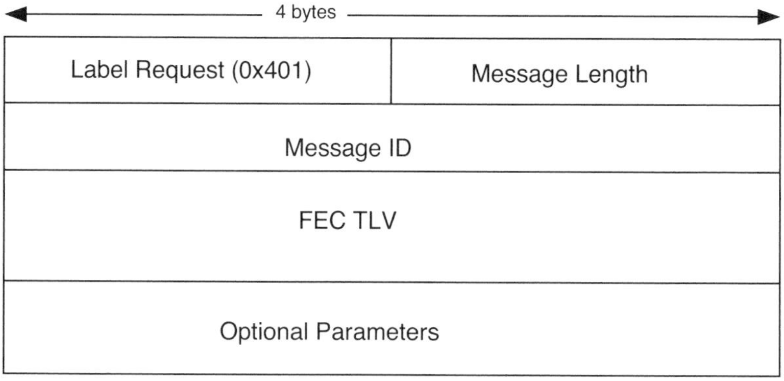

Fig. 2.65. The label request message format

Table 2.19. Optional parameters for the label request message

Optional parameters	Length
Label request message ID TLV	Four octets
Hop count TLV	One octet
Path vector TLV	Variable

The FEC TLV encodes the FEC for which a label is being requested. The optional parameters field includes the encoding in Table 2.19.

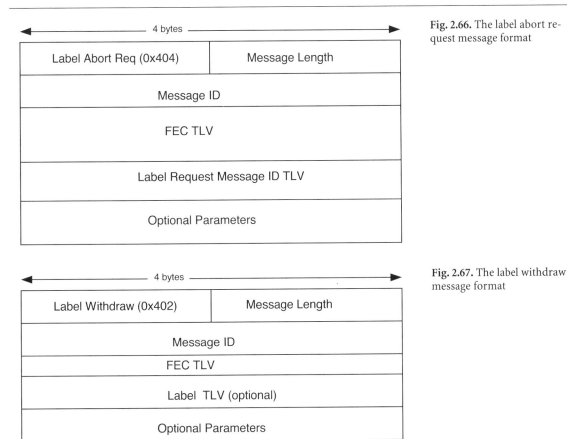

Fig. 2.66. The label abort request message format

Fig. 2.67. The label withdraw message format

2.6.3.2.9 Label Abort Request Message
This may be used to abort an outstanding label request message (Fig. 2.66).

The label request message ID TLV is the newest field in this message. This field specifies the message ID of the label request message to be aborted. There is no optional parameter carries in this message.

2.6.3.2.10 Label Withdraw Message
If for any reason an LSR decides that the peer is not able to continue specific FEC–label mapping, it sends out this message (Fig. 2.67) to alert other LSRs in the peer.

This breaks the mapping between the FECs and the labels.

2.6.3.2.11 Label Release Message
If an LSR decides that it no longer needs FEC–label mappings which it previously requested, it sends out a label release message (Fig. 2.68) to its peer.

This concludes the discussion on MPLS. Although MPLS cannot be considered a regular routing protocol, it combines both L2 and L3 switching functionality (i.e., routing capability) also. Therefore, it is obvious that we need to discuss it in the context of a routing technology.

Fig. 2.68. The label release
message format

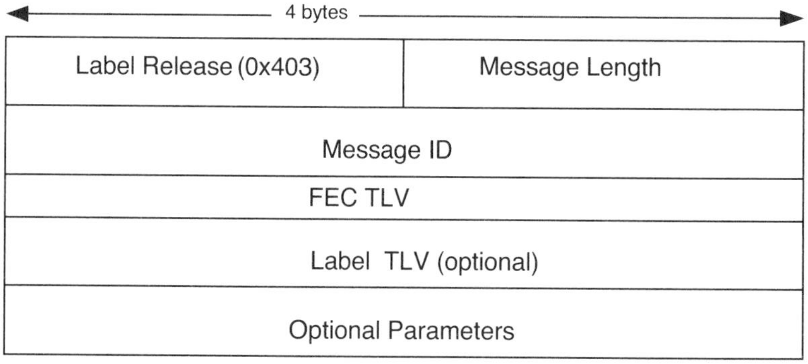

Now that you are conversant with routing technology, it should be easy to pursue more in-depth discussions of unified internetworking as you will see in the following chapters.

3 IP and Policy Services

3.1 Introduction

Networks are changing and growing more multifaceted than those of the 1990s. The merger mania of data and the telecom industries in 1999 created a new type of networking concept for information transport. It is now known as a converged network and IP is considered the best transport means of such a network system. With end-to-end QoS and policy-based management mechanisms, today's network is more intelligent and sophisticated. Now, more than ever before, the idea of data and means of telecom transport are unified into a single, more efficient network infrastructure. Such a unified network has so far been extensively adaptable with the IP internetworking technique. Building such a state-of-the-art internetwork requires in-depth understanding of IP as well as of the behavior and constraint of various traffic. Another and most important aspect of such a complex network is how to manage it. In this regard, PEN provides significant enhancements, automata and intelligence than that of a network based on SNMP (Simple Network Management Protocol). Now traffic can be controlled and managed as per the requirements of the users.

The technique to manage a unified IP network is the proper use of policy, and also the need to understand the policy or rules and means to convey them. Even if we understand policy, we still need to define what is important for a network rather than impose some rules. Also, having a rule defined for a particular transport may not be enough – it also requires an enhanced deployment schema. QoS, security and other key parameters should be seamlessly deployed throughout the intranet.

Sounds confusing? This chapter will make it easy for you to grasp the complexity of unified IP networks. Moreover, the theory and practice of IP and policy services will be explicitly examined.

After completing this chapter, you should be able to deploy a QoS mechanism perfectly tuned for your intranet traffic. This deployment will embrace the sophistication of PEN and thus provide a self-managed network.

It is often difficult to furnish the bits and bytes of a technology due to presenting that technology in a timely manner. Although every step is taken to

present very timely and adequate information, sometimes it is important
that readers study the relevant RFCs and standards for the latest information.

3.2 IP QoS

A QoS can be viewed as providing some special service to a specific traffic
class over various underlying technologies (i.e., 802.3 network, SONET,
ATM, etc.). To define it more clearly, we can say that a QoS is the network
service that specifies the performance of traffic through one or more networks. For example, mission-critical and time-sensitive traffic such as voice
traffic should receive higher QoS guarantees than less time-sensitive traffic
such as FTP or email. Including more bandwidth may not resolve some issues of congestion in a network. Therefore, optimal utilization and differentiated use of the existing bandwidth becomes a critical issue (Fig. 3.1).

In my *High-Speed LAN Technology Handbook*, I have discussed how a
switch can provide QoS by allocating a specific amount of bandwidth for a
specific class of traffic. The internetworking community has tried to invent
some sorts of QoS method for each service class such as ATM and IP. One of
the important ideas included in a QoS is to provide a means of congestion
management. Congestion management allows you to control congestion by
determining the order in which packets are transmitted from an interface
based on priorities assigned to those packets. Why do we need congestion
management? The answer is simple: for the efficient handling of different
traffic in a given data path. In today's heterogeneous network, different protocols and different types of traffic sharing a data path may interact with one
another in ways that affect their application performance. For example, if a
network is designed to support different types of traffic such as voice, video
and data that share a single data path between routers, the network administrator should consider using congestion management techniques to ensure
fairness of treatment across different types of traffic. Therefore, a QoS for the
IP network includes technologies such as queuing, Integrated Service
(IntServ) and Differentiated Service (DiffServ). The technology focus is on
router actions or behavior for flows, but the customer focus is on the services

Fig. 3.1. An example of IN network with QoS

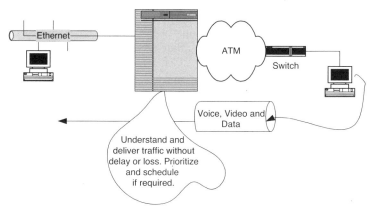
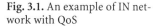

provided. A number of reasons that drove the need for QoS, especially IP QoS in today's networks, are as follows:

- Increasing number of network users and applications.
- New applications and traffic dynamics – for example, multimedia and Web traffic.
- Service providers wanting to offer varying levels of service as value added.
- Work differentiation in intranets – assigning business priorities to traffic.

To understand all these driving factors of QoS, let's imagine what it would be like if a network had to support multimedia traffic as well as the demands of bandwidth from hundreds of users. Throwing bandwidth at the problem would not resolve such issues and would require special handling of traffic. On the other hand, ISPs are driven by their business needs. They would like to differentiate between customers based on the amounts paid for traffic transport. Therefore, in simple English, if a customer pays X amount of money, certain bandwidth will be reserved or otherwise delivered without any guarantee. In the case of an enterprise network, QoS will provide the ability to control bandwidth allocation to specific users through policies. An application can request bandwidth and be allocated it on an as-needed basis, end to end. Also, customers will be able to manage their sensitive traffic (jitter or delay sensitive) and cost will be ultimately minimized through efficient traffic management. A QoS such as IP QoS resolves some of these issues by introducing the following in a network:

- Varying levels or tiers of service relative to business priorities.
- More control over delay- and jitter- sensitive traffic such as multimedia and interactive audio/video.
- Additional services to customers that can be offered by an ISP.

As we can see in Fig. 3.2, a special service is provided to a client based on priority, access level and application. An IP QoS takes almost the same approach for end-to-end traffic transport.

We mentioned earlier that the components of QoS include queuing, IntServ and DiffServ technologies. To understand QoS further, we will explore each of these areas in the following sections. The queuing technologies mainly reside in a router or L3 switch. There are a number of queuing tech-

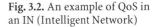

Fig. 3.2. An example of QoS in an IN (Intelligent Network)

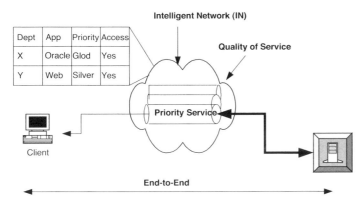

niques introduced by various routing vendors, of which I would like to discuss the four more commonly used techniques. They are FIFO (First-In, First-Out), weighted fair queuing (WFQ), custom queuing (CQ) and priority queuing (PQ).

3.2.1 First-in, First-out (FIFO)

This type of queuing requires no concept of priority or traffic class. In FIFO, packet transmission occurs in the order in which it was received. It is also known as first-come, first-served (Fig. 3.3). If the network is congested, FIFO stores the packets and delivers them in order of arrival when it no longer congested.

   FIFO has only one queue and all traffic flows are fed into the same queue. Higher priority packets are not transmitted faster than lower priority traffic. Issues may arise when an ill-behaved source starts transmitting continuously; as such the source may consume all the bandwidth. A bursty source can cause delays in time-sensitive traffic and even important traffic may get dropped. FIFO is the fastest queuing method and is effective for large links that have little delay and minimum congestion. A slight variation to FIFO is the FIFO++ queuing algorithm (Fig. 3.4). It uses class differentiation techniques and provides per flow queues with priority. Favored traffic gets better service in FIFO++ but all the other disadvantages of FIFO still exist.

3.2.2 Weighted Fair Queuing (WFQ)

WFQ was developed from the fair queuing (FQ) algorithm. FQ was proposed by John Nagle in 1987 to solve the fair bandwidth allocation problem. He ob-

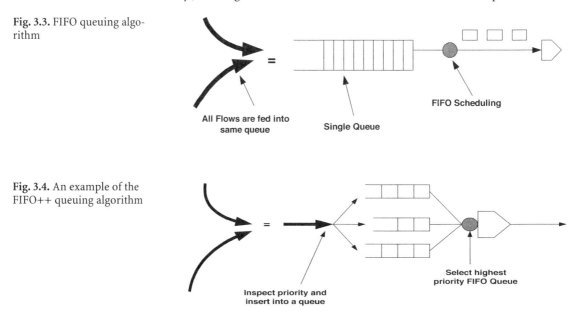

Fig. 3.3. FIFO queuing algorithm

Fig. 3.4. An example of the FIFO++ queuing algorithm

served that if a router is swamped with packets from four sources, for example, it sends out choke packets to all sources. As in reality, one source is supposed to cut back (as a normal behavior) while others blast away. As a result, the honest source will not get an even smaller share of bandwidth than it had before. FQ was proposed on the essence that a router would have multiple queues for each output line, one for each source. Once a line becomes idle, the router scans the queues in a round-robin fashion. This way, competing hosts get a chance at least to send one out of every n packets. To define it, FQ is a scheduling method in which each queue is treated fairly in a round-robin fashion. In FQ, each queue gets a FAIR share of the bandwidth, each flow has its own queue and cannot affect other flows. The FAIRNESS criteria are based on a fair packet rate and bitwise round-robin algorithm (Fig. 3.5).

Although FQ provides some fairness, it still gives more bandwidth to hosts that use large packets than to those that use small packets. In 1990, Alan Demers *et al.* suggested an improvement in which the round robin is done byte by byte instead of packet by packet. Later this model was modified and named weighted fair queuing (WFQ) (Fig. 3.6) WFQ also provides fair bandwidth allocation but it applies priority or weight to identified traffic to classify it into conversations and determine how much bandwidth each conversation is allowed in regard to other conversations. It is a flow- based algorithm which reduces response time and fairly shares the remaining bandwidth among high-bandwidth flows. For example, WFQ can provide low-volume traffic such as Telnet sessions higher priority over high-volume traffic such as FTP sessions.

3.2.3 Custom Queuing (CQ)

CQ is a method of guaranteeing bandwidth for various protocols or incoming interfaces (Fig. 3.7). This is done by assigning protocols or interfaces to any of 16 possible queues. These queues are then handled in a round-robin fash-

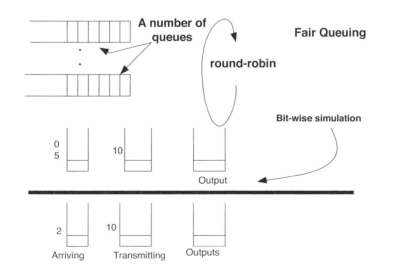

Fig. 3.5. Bitwise FQ simulation with packets

Fig. 3.6. WFQ

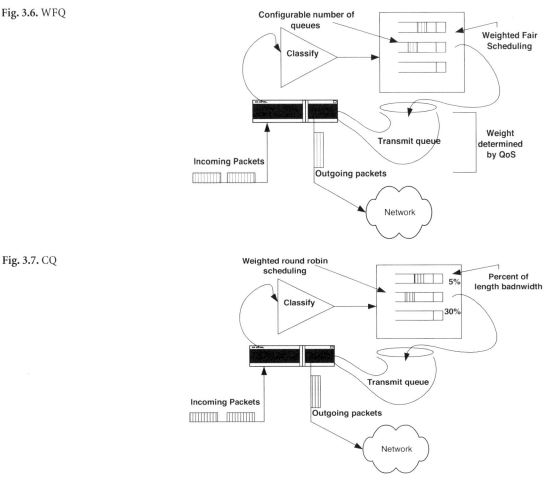

Fig. 3.7. CQ

ion. One can define how much is transmitted from each queue at a time so that some queues can transfer more than other queues, which means that they will be able to have a greater share of the bandwidth than other queues. There is one queue that cannot be changed called queue 0. This is the system queue and will be emptied before all others; it handles system packets such as KeepAlives.

The advantages of CQ are as follows:

• 16 queues which are services in round-robin fashion.
• Full control over which traffic gets what proportion of bandwidth.
• Allocates full bandwidth.
• Suitable for high-bandwidth links.

3.2.4 Priority Queuing (PQ)

Packets to be transmitted on an interface with a priority queue applied are done in such a way that all packets from the high queue are transmitted be-

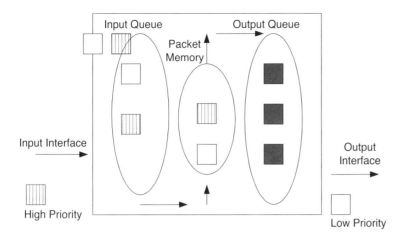

Fig. 3.8. Operation of PQ

fore any packets from the medium queue; when the high queue is empty then packets from the medium queue will be transmitted until that is empty, next will be the normal queue and lastly the low queue. Because of the way PQ works packets from the lower queues might not get transmitted in a timely manner, or possibly never get transmitted at all.

To create any kind of queuing priorities must be assigned to different types of traffic: for example, if IPX is required to have a higher priority than IP packets. The other way of assigning priorities is to assign them based on which interface they enter the router. The priorities that are available with PQ are high, medium, normal and low (Fig. 3.8). One of these must be assigned to the default queue. The default queue is where packets not matching the priority list will end up.

The following are some of the reasons why PQ is used:

- Best on low-bandwidth links.
- Assigns one of four priorities to traffic – high, medium, normal, low.
- High traffic given priority over all others so they might never get access.

3.3 IP Datagram

Today's most commonly used network layer protocol is IP. It is designed for use in interconnected systems of packet-switched computer communication networks. It provides the means of transmitting blocks of datagrams from source to destination, and was invented by the DoD to provide universal communication means for different vendor devices as specified in RFC 791. IP implements two basic functions: addressing and fragmentation. An Internet module uses the addresses carried in the packet and forwards IP encapsulated datagrams to their destinations. The selection of a path to transmit such packets is called routing. A mechanism in the switch can either listen to the network for MTU or use a preconfigured MTU size to transmit IP encapsulated datagrams. IP does not provide a reliable communication facility and depends on TCP to deliver such a mechanism. IP works as an integral part of

TCP/IP or UDP/IP suites. It interfaces on one side to the higher level protocols such as Telnet or FTP and on the other side to the underlying L2 protocols such as Token Ring or Ethernet.

Since QoS is a vast subject, many have defined it in different ways, some starting their discussion on queuing first and others starting directly from the core. However, I feel that an appropriate place to start our study of IP QoS is the format of the IP datagram itself, assuming that readers have learned some queuing techniques.

An IP packet consists of a header and a text part (Fig. 3.9). The header is a 20-byte fixed part and a variable length optional part.

The first field of an IP packet is the version field, which is a 4-bit field and describes the version of IP (i.e., v4). RFC 790 defines a list of values for this field as in Table 3.1.

The next field is the IHL (Internet Header Length), a 4-bit field. It indicates the length of the IP header in 32-bit words and thus indicates the beginning of data. The minimum value of a correct IP header is 5. The next field is the TOS (Type of Service) field, an 8-bit field which provides an indication of the abstract parameters of the desired QoS. Although some bits of the TOS were used for some specific treatment capability, it was not widely used until deployment of IntServ and DiffServ. However, these parameters were intended

Fig. 3.9. An IP packet

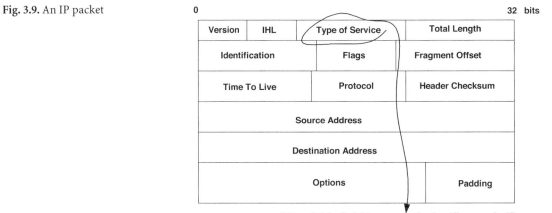

Bits of this field have much significance in IP QoS mechanism

Table 3.1. The value of version field as defined in RFC 790

Decimal	Octal	Version
0	0	Reserved
1–3	1–3	Unassigned
4	4	Internet Protocol
5	5	ST Datagram Mode
6–14	6–16	Unassigned
15	17	Reserved

to be used to guide the selection of the actual service parameters during transmission of a datagram. Some networks offer service precedence, which aims to treat high-precedence traffic more importantly than other traffic. In fact the TOS field is further subdivided into precedence and TOS fields. IP precedence is a 3-bit field and TOS is also a 3-bit field (Fig. 3.10). The remaining 2 bits of the 8-bit TOS field are reserved.

We will say more about TOS bytes in the IP precedence and TOS byte section. For now, please treat it as a reference. Concerning the IP header, the next field after the TOS byte is a 16-bit total length field. It indicates the total length of the datagram measured in octets including the IP header and data. This field allows the length of the datagram to be up to 65,535 bytes. Such a value is impractical but RFC 791 suggest that all hosts should support 576 bytes of IP datagram whether they arrive whole or fragmented. The next field is the identification field, a 16-bit field. It uses an identifying value assigned by the sender to aid in assembling the fragment of an IP packet. Flags, a 3-bit field, is next to the identification field and uses various control flags (Fig. 3.11).

Bit 0 in the flags field is reserved and must be set to zero. Bit 1 is the DF bit, which, when set to 0, provides "May Fragment" indication, otherwise for "Don't Fragment" indication it is set to 1. The MF is 0 = Last Fragment if set, otherwise 1 = More Fragments.

The next field is the fragment offset field which indicates where in the datagram this fragment belongs. It is measured in units of 8 bytes. The first fragment has offset zero. The TTL field is an 8-bit field which indicates the maximum time the datagram is allowed to remain in the Internet system. If

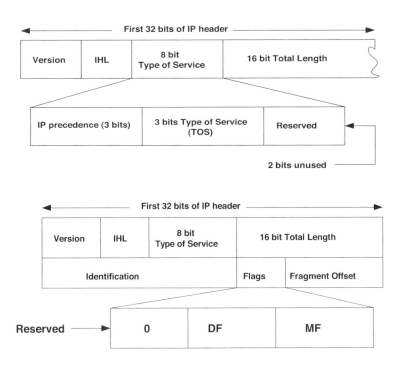

Fig. 3.10. The TOS byte and IP precedence

Fig. 3.11. The flags field of the IP header

the field has the value 0 then the packet must be destroyed. The units of TTL are seconds. As a packet travels through the IP network, every Internet module it passes through changes its TTL value by one even if it processes the datagram in less than a second. The TTL value signifies the upper bound on the time a datagram may exist. The next field is an 8-bit protocol field which indicates the next level protocol used in the datagram, for example UDP. The value of this field for various protocols is defined in RFC 790 (assigned numbers) and they are given in Table 3.2.

Table 3.2. The value of various protocols in the protocol field of the IP header as defined in RFC 790

Decimal	Octal	Protocol numbers
0	0	Reserved
1	1	ICMP
2	2	Unassigned
3	3	Gateway-to-gateway
4	4	CMCC gateway monitoring message
5	5	ST
6	6	TCP
7	7	UCL
8	10	Unassigned
9	11	Secure
10	12	BBN RCC monitoring
11	13	NVP
12	14	PUP
13	15	Pluribus
14	16	Telnet
15	17	XNET
16	20	Choas
17	21	User datagram
18	22	Multiplexing
19	23	DCN
20	24	TAC monitoring
21–62	25–76	Unassigned
63	77	Any local network
64	100	SATNET and Backroom EXPAK
65	101	MIT subnet support
66–68	102–104	Unassigned
69	105	SATNET monitoring
70	106	Unassigned

Decimal	Octal	Protocol numbers
71	107	Internet packet core utility
72–75	110–113	Unassigned
76	114	Backroom SATNET monitoring
77	115	Unassigned
78	116	WIDEBAND monitoring
79	117	WIDEBAND EXPAK
80–254	120–376	Unassigned
255	377	Reserved

Table 3.2 (continued). The value of various protocols in the protocol field of the IP header as defined in RFC 790

The header checksum (HC) is a 16-bit field after the protocol field. It is used on the IP header only because some header field (e.g., TTL) changes. HC is recomputed to be verified at each point where the Internet header is processed. This is a simple checksum; it is provisional and may be replaced by a CRC procedure depending upon further experience.

The next two fields are the SA and DA, both of which are 32 bits in length. They provide source and destination IP addresses for a host. The IP addresses used in this field can be from any of the IP address classes (e.g., A, B and C) as discussed before.

3.3.1 IP Options

The next field after the DA is the options field (Fig. 3.12), which may or may not appear in a datagram. The IP options field is a variable length field used primarily for testing, debugging and there may be zero or more options. This capability must always be implemented with IP. Options appear contiguously in the field (not separated) and consist of a single-octet option code for one-octet options, or vary in length for longer options.

The first 1-bit field of the options field is COPY that determines how gateways treat options during fragmentation:
1 => copy option to ALL fragments.
0 => copy options to first fragment only.

The second 2-bit field is OPTION CLASS which specifies the general class of the option (Table 3.3), and the third is OPTION NUMBER (5 bits) which determines the specific option within that class (Table 3.4).

Several options can be added to the IP header; included here are record route, source route, timestamp and security.

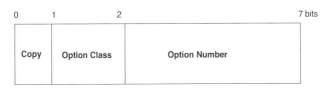

Fig. 3.12. The options field

3.3.1.1 Record Route Option

This allows the source to create an empty list of IP addresses and arranges for each gateway that handles the datagram to add its IP address to the list. In the record route field (Fig. 3.13):

CODE (8 bits): The code field should equal 7 for record route.
LENGTH (8 bits): Total length of the option field, including the header.
POINTER (8 bits): Incremented in four-octet intervals, it points to the next available address slot in the option field.
IP ADDRESS (variable length): Allocated space in blocks of 32 bits to hold each IP address encountered..

Since the header is of limited size, the number of IP addresses recorded is also limited. All gateways that handle the datagram add their IP addresses (outgoing link only) and, if space is full, simply forward the datagram without making any changes.

3.3.1.2 Source Route Option

This provides a way for the sender to dictate a path through the Internet. Source route can force a datagram to traverse a path, even if it would not nor-

Table 3.3. IP options class and its meanings

Option class	Meaning
0	Datagram or network control
1	Reserved for future use
2	Debugging and measurement
3	Also reserved for future use

Table 3.4. IP options class, number and length

Option class	Option number	Length	Description
0	0	N/A	End of option list
0	1	N/A	No operation. Used to align octets in an option list
0	2	11	Security. Used for security in IPv4
0	3	Variable	Loose source routing
0	7	Variable	Record route (used to trace a route)
0	8	4	Stream identifier (obsolete)
0	9	Variable	Strict source routing
2	4	Variable	Internet timestamp

Fig. 3.13. The record route field

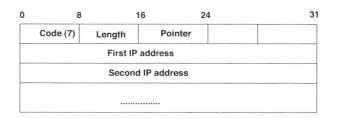

mally be chosen by a gateway. It is good for testing a physical path and debugging problems with it. In the source route option field (Fig. 3.14):

CODE (8 bits): The code field should equal 37 for record route.
LENGTH (8 bits): The total length of the option field, including the header.
POINTER (8 bits): Incremented in four-octet intervals, it points to the next available address slot in the option field.
IP ADDRESS OF NEXT HOP (variable length): Allocated space in blocks of 32 bits to hold each IP address that a datagram must traverse. Since the header is of limited size, the number of hops is limited. Usually five or less gateways are included in the next hop addresses, due to the limited size of the header fields.

There are two forms of source routing:

1. Strict source routing, which specifies the path via included IP addresses in the option field. It must strictly follow the path, and errors occur if any path is NOT specified. All addresses must be included.
2. Loose source routing, which also specifies the path, but allows for multiple hops between each specified address (more flexible).

3.3.1.3 Timestamp Option
This records each gateway's IP address (32 bits) along the path and a 32-bit timestamp generated by that gateway. It is similar to the record route option, but can only record half as many addresses. In the timestamp option field (Fig. 3.15):

CODE (8 bits): The code field should equal 68 for record route.
LENGTH (8 bits): The total length of the option field, including the header.
POINTER (8 bits): Incremented in four-octet intervals, it points to the next available address slot in the option field.
OFLOW (4 bits): Integer count of gateways which could not supply the timestamp due to lack of header space.

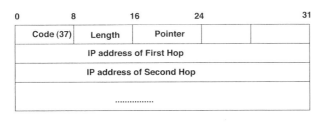

Fig. 3.14. The source route option field

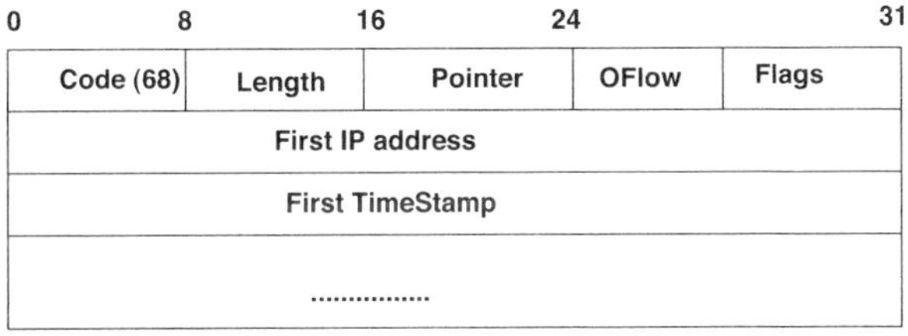

Fig. 3.15. The timestamp option field

Flag value	Meaning
Table 3.5. Timestamp option flags	

Flag value	Meaning
0	Record timestamps, not IP address<index>IP address</index>
1	Record IP, then timestamp<index>timestamp</index>.
3	Record timestamp if IP is found in the list of addresses specified

FLAGS (4 bits): Specifies the exact format of the timestamp and option fields (Table 3.5).

FIRST IP ADDRESS (32 bits): Allocated space to hold the IP address of a gateway that is required to produce a timestamp value.

FIRST TIMESTAMP (32 bits): A 32-bit timestamp is produced and recorded at each participating gateway hop.

Timestamps give the time (in milliseconds) and date (Universal Time – at the prime meridian). Recording IP addresses with timestamps eliminates ambiguity as to who set the timestamp.

3.3.1.4 Security Option

This allows a datagram to have different levels of secure status. The option values are assigned by the US Defense Intelligence Agency, and range from unclassified to top secret. Routers detect the security status and, based on the value, determine whether packets should route beyond certain gateway boundaries.

3.3.2 Padding

This is the last field in an IP header. It is usually of variable length and used to ensure the IP header ends on a 32-bit boundary. The padding is zero.

3.3.3 IP Precedence and TOS Byte

Earlier we talked about the TOS byte and IP precedence in an IP datagram. In this section, we are going to explore IP precedence and the 3-bit TOS field of a TOS byte with respect to IP QoS. The IPv4 TOS field is divided into two sections: a 3-bit IP precedence field and a 3 bit TOS field (Fig. 3.16).

3.3.3.1 TOS

As we described earlier, the TOS byte in the IP header is divided into three sections. The first high-order 3 bits are the precedence field, the next 4-bit field that is customarily called the TOS field, and a reserved bit (the low-order bit). A router should consider the TOS field in a packet's IP header when deciding how to forward it. The router must also maintain a TOS value for each route in its routing table. Routes learned through a routing protocol that does not support TOS must be assigned a TOS of zero (the default TOS).

To choose a route to a destination, a router MUST use an algorithm equivalent to the following:

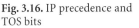

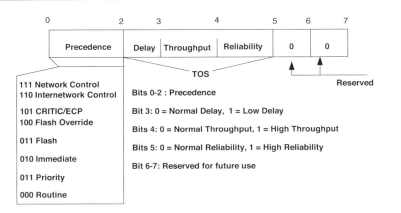

Fig. 3.16. IP precedence and TOS bits

1. The router locates in its routing table all available routes to the destination.
2. If there are none, the router drops the packet because the destination is unreachable.
3. If one or more of those routes have a TOS that exactly matches the TOS specified in the packet, the router chooses the route with the best metric.
4. Otherwise, the router repeats the above step, except looking at routes whose the TOS is zero.
5. If no route was chosen above, the router drops the packet because the destination is unreachable. The router returns an ICMP Destination Unreachable error specifying the appropriate code: either Network Unreachable with Type of Service (code 11) or Host Unreachable with Type of Service (code 12).

Although TOS has been little used in the past, its use by hosts is now mandated by the Requirements for Internet Hosts RFCs. Support for TOS in routers may become essential in the future but up till now it has been an advisory feature.

Various people have proposed that TOS should affect other aspects of the forwarding function. For example:

1. A router could place packets that have the low-delay bit set ahead of other packets in its output queues.
2. If a router is forced to discard packets, it could try to avoid discarding those which have the high-reliability bit set.

3.3.3.2 Precedence

IP precedence is used for allocating resources in the network based on the relative importance of different traffic flows. As defined by RFC 791 there are some specific values to be used in this field for various types of traffic. The basic mechanisms for precedence processing in a router are preferential resource allocation, including both precedence-ordered queue service and precedence-based congestion control, and selection of link layer priority features. The router also selects the IP precedence for the routing, management and control traffic it originates.

Precedence-ordered queue service includes but is not limited to the queue for the forwarding process and queues for outgoing links. It is intended that a router supporting precedence should also use the precedence indication at whatever points in its processing are concerned with the allocation of finite resources, such as packet buffers or link layer connections. The set of such points is implementation dependent.

Although the precedence field was originally provided for use in DoD systems where large traffic surges or major damage to the network are viewed as inherent threats, it has useful applications for many non-military IP networks. Although the traffic handling capacity of networks has grown greatly in recent years, the traffic generating ability of the users has also grown, and network overload conditions still occur at times. Since IP-based routing and management protocols have become more critical to the successful operation of the Internet, overloads present two additional risks to the network:

1. High delays may result in routing protocol packets being lost. This may cause the routing protocol to falsely deduce a topology change and propagate this false information to other routers. Not only can this cause routes to oscillate, but an extra processing burden may be placed on other routers.
2. High delays may interfere with the use of network management tools to analyze and perhaps correct or relieve the problem in the network that caused the overload condition to occur.

Implementation and appropriate use of the precedence mechanism alleviates both of these problems.

3.3.3.2.1 Precedence-ordered Queue Service

Routers should implement precedence-ordered queue service. This service means that when a packet is selected for output on a (logical) link, the packet of highest precedence that has been queued for that link is sent. Routers that implement precedence-ordered queue service must also have a configuration option to suppress the service in the Internet layer.

Any router may implement other policy-based throughput management procedures that result in other than strict precedence ordering, but it must be configurable to suppress them (i.e., use strict ordering).

Routers that implement precedence-ordered queue service discard low-precedence packets before discarding high-precedence packets for congestion control purposes. Preemption (interruption of processing or transmission of a packet) is not envisioned as a function of the Internet layer. Some protocols at other layers may provide preemption features.

3.3.3.2.2 Lower Layer Precedence Mappings

Routers that implement precedence-ordered queuing must implement lower layer precedence mapping (LLPM). Other routers may implement LLPM with respect to the requirements.

A router that implements LLPM:

1. would be able to map IP precedence to link layer priority mechanisms for link layers that have such a feature defined;

2. would have a configuration option to select the link layer's default priority treatment for all IP traffic and should be able to configure specific non-standard mappings of IP precedence values to link layer priority values for each interface.

Some research questions the workability of the priority features of some link layer protocols, and some networks may have faulty implementations of the link layer priority mechanism. It seems prudent to provide an escape mechanism in case such problems show up in a network.

On the other hand, there are proposals to use novel queuing strategies to implement special services such as multimedia bandwidth reservation or low-delay service. Special services and queuing strategies to support them are current research subjects and in the process of standardization.

Implementers may wish to consider that correct link layer mapping of IP precedence is required by DoD policy for TCP/IP systems used on DoD networks. Since these requirements are intended to encourage (but not force) the use of precedence features in the hope of providing better Internet service to all users, routers supporting precedence-ordered queue service should default to maintain strict precedence ordering regardless of the type of service requested.

3.3.3.2.3 Precedence Handling for All Routers
A router (whether or not it employs precedence-ordered queue service) does the following:

1. Accepts and processes incoming traffic of all precedence levels normally, unless it has been administratively configured to do otherwise;
2. Implements a validation filter to administratively restrict the use of precedence levels by particular traffic sources. If provided, this filter must not filter out or cut off the following sorts of ICMP error messages: Destination Unreachable, Redirect, Time Exceeded, and Parameter Problem. If this filter is provided, the procedures required for packet filtering by addresses are required for this filter also. Precedence filtering should be applicable to specific source/destination IP address pairs, specific protocols, specific ports, and so on.
   An ICMP Destination Unreachable message with code 14 is sent when a packet is dropped by the validation filter, unless this has been suppressed by choice of configuration.
3. Implements a cutoff function that allows the router to be set to refuse or drop traffic with precedence below a specified level. This function may be activated by management actions or by some implementation-dependent heuristics, but there must be a configuration option to disable any heuristic mechanism that operates without human intervention. An ICMP Destination Unreachable message with code 15 is sent when a packet is dropped by the cutoff function, unless this has been suppressed by choice of configuration. A router does not refuse to forward datagrams with an IP precedence of 6 (Internetwork Control) or 7 (Network Control) solely due to precedence cutoff. However, other

criteria may be used in conjunction with precedence cutoff to filter high-precedence traffic. Unrestricted precedence cutoff could result in an unintentional cutoff of routing and control traffic. In the general case, host traffic should be restricted to a value of 5 (CRITIC/ECP) or below; this is not a requirement and may not be correct in certain systems.

4. Does not change precedence settings on packets it did not originate.

5. Is able to configure distinct precedence values to be used for each routing or management protocol supported (except for those protocols, such as OSPF, which specify which precedence values must be used).

6. Is able to configure routing or management traffic precedence values independently for each peer address.

7. Responds appropriately to link layer precedence-related error indications where provided. An ICMP Destination Unreachable message with code 15 is sent when a packet is dropped because a link cannot accept it due to a precedence-related condition, unless this has been suppressed by choice of configuration.

The precedence cutoff mechanism described in point 3 is somewhat controversial. Depending on the topological location of the area affected by the cutoff, transit traffic may be directed by routing protocols into the area of the cutoff, where it will be dropped. This is only a problem if another path that is unaffected by the cutoff exists between the communicating points. Proposed ways of avoiding this problem include providing some minimum bandwidth to all precedence levels even under overload conditions, or propagating cutoff information in routing protocols. In the absence of a widely accepted (and implemented) solution to this problem, great caution is recommended in activating cutoff mechanisms in transit networks.

A transport layer relay could legitimately provide the function prohibited by point 4 above. Changing precedence levels may cause subtle interactions with TCP and perhaps other protocols; a correct design is a non-trivial task.

The intent of points 5 and 6 (and the discussion of IP precedence in ICMP messages) is that the IP precedence bits should be appropriately set, whether or not this router acts upon those bits in any other way. We expect that in the future specifications for routing protocols and network management protocols will specify how the IP precedence should be set for messages sent by those protocols.

The appropriate response for point 7 depends on the link layer protocol in use. Typically, the router should stop trying to send offensive traffic to that destination for some period of time, and should return an ICMP Destination Unreachable message with code 15 (Service not Available for Precedence Requested) to the traffic source. It also should not try to reestablish a preempted link layer connection for some time.

3.4 QoS Architecture

As we discussed earlier, QoS is the ability to define or predict the performance of a network and provide a better service to a specific traffic class. The original goal was to use IP TOS bits to indicate the QoS desired for a network. The QoS can be configured within a single network element which includes queuing, scheduling and traffic shaping. Signaling techniques such as RSVP are used for coordinating QoS end to-end between network elements. In QoS, policing and management functions are also required to control and administer end-to-end traffic across a network. The two important network elements for QoS are edge router and backbone router. The edge router provides packet classification, admission control and configuration management for data flows whereas the backbone router provides congestion management and congestion avoidance for a network. To provide end-to-end QoS for an IP network three service elements are defined and they are Best-effort Service, Integrated Service (IntServ) and Differentiated Service (Diff-Serv). The Best-effort Service is a single-service model in which an application sends data whenever it must, in any quantity, and without requesting permission or first informing the network. A router that implements Best-effort Service has FIFO queuing. Best-effort Service is suitable for a wide range of networked applications such as general file transfers or email. The traditional Internet provides a best-effort service to all of its applications. The Best-effort Service does not make any promises about the QoS that an application will receive. Furthermore, the traditional Internet does not allow delay-sensitive multimedia applications to request any special treatment. At the routers, all packets are treated equal, including delay-sensitive audio and video packets. However, several recently developed distributed applications such as teleconferencing, video-on-demand and virtual reality are very sensitive to the QoS treatment received from the network. In particular, delivery of traffic with traditional Best-effort Service, which provides correct and fair delivery by trading off delay, is not acceptable. Therefore, the IP network design has to be modified to support real-time QoS and controlled end-to-end delays. One of the ways to overcome this issue is to use IntServ at the edge and DiffServ in the core of the network (Fig. 3.17).

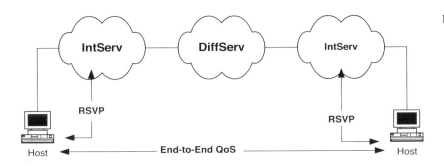

Fig. 3.17. End-to-end QoS

3.4.1 IntServ

Recently, the architecture of the Internet is extended to support multiservice provision, that is classical data and video/audio traffic. One of this internetwork system components is known as IntServ. It specifies a nature of packet delivery service which is described by parameters such as packet delay, packet loss and achieved bandwidth. A router that supports IntServ must perform admission control and resource allocation based on the information contained in a Tspec (Traffic Specification). As defined in RFC 2215 and 2216, Tspecs convey information about the data rate using a token bucket and range of packet sizes of the flow in question. The Tspec can be described as a traffic pattern for which service is being requested. On the other hand, a flow is a stream of packets with common source address, destination address and port number. An IntServ router is required to maintain state information on each flow and determines what flows get what resources based on available capacity. A setup protocol is used to carry QoS-related information from the end nodes requesting QoS control, which is known as RSVP (Resource ReSerVation Protocol). Such a setup protocol can also be used to collect QoS-related information from the network along the dataflow path of application to ensure ultimate delivery to end systems. RSVP is defined in RFC 2205 and the use of RSVP with IntServ is defined in RFC 2210. We will say more about the use of RSVP and the protocol itself in the succeeding sections.

The components of the IntServ architecture are as follows:

1. Traffic classes
   - Best effort
   - Controlled load
   - Guaranteed load.
2. Traffic control
   - Admission control
   - Packet classification
   - Packet scheduler.

The best-effort component is the general traffic class, which specifies no commitment and admission control.

The controlled load (CL) service is specified in RFC 2211. A client will request this service for the following reasons if the network is functioning correctly:

- Successful packet delivery at a very high percentage.
- Minimize packet transit delay.

The CL will ensure that these requirements are met for the network. Interested clients may request CL service by the use of Tspec. In turn, CL ensures that network resources are available to process the traffic as described in the Tspec. Although CL is intended to support a broad class of applications, it is prone to overloaded network conditions.

We have so far learned that a client requesting CL services specifies a flow requirement using Tspec and the token bucket. This flow requirement can be further analyzed by means of service elements which compute various parameters as well as the maximum delay a data packet will experience in a given dataflow path. A delay has two parts: fixed delay and queuing delay. The fixed delay is associated with the dataflow path, which is determined by the setup mechanism. On the other hand, the queuing delay is a functional parameter of the token bucket and data rate, which is determined by the guaranteed load (GL). The GL service provides strict guarantees on throughput and delay. It ensures that the datagram is within the guaranteed delivery time and not delayed due to queue overflow. This service is most suitable for the application that requires data exchange within strictly specified time limits. For example, audio and video "playback" applications.

In admission control, in order to obtain QoS, a client must request admission: that is, provide Tspecs. Once admission is granted packet classification and packet scheduling mechanism are initiated.

In packet classification, incoming packets are put in the right service class matching the IP address, ports, etc.

The packet scheduler is used to enforce the commitment service.

3.4.1.1 RSVP

To provide and improve the quality of audio and video in a multiservice network, it is desirable to introduce the services into the Internet which provides QoS guarantees to applications. But QoS guarantees require a mechanism to allow applications running in hosts to reserve resources in the Internet. RSVP, a new Internet standard, is one such mechanism that allows applications to reserve resources. When people talk about resources in the Internet context, they usually mean link bandwidth and router buffers. To keep the discussion concrete and focused, however, we shall assume that the word resource is synonymous with bandwidth. For our pedagogic purposes, RSVP stands for Bandwidth Reservation Protocol. RSVP provides a host with the ability to request specific QoS from the network for an application of dataflow. Routers also use RSVP to provide QoS requested by a host (Fig. 3.18). An RSVP request generally results in resources being reserved by all nodes along the given data path. It is a simplex flow, which means that the request flows in one direction. RSVP can be used with IPv4 or IPv6 protocols and will act as a transport layer protocol for an IP network. However, it does not provide application data transport but rather operates as an Internet control protocol such as ICMP or IGMP. Like routing protocols, RSVP is executed in the background, not in the data path.

RSVP is not a routing protocol and is designed for use with the IntServ network. It is designed so that current and future unicast and multicast routing protocols will be well suited to RSVP. It is merely a protocol that allows the applications to reserve the necessary link bandwidth. Once the reservations are in place, it is up to the routers in the IP network to actually provide the reserved bandwidth to the dataflows. This provisioning will likely be done by having each router interface service the packets of the various flows passing through the interface with a generalized round-robin scheduling policy such as WFQ. In RSVP, the sender specifies the characteristics of outgo-

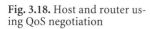

Fig. 3.18. Host and router using QoS negotiation

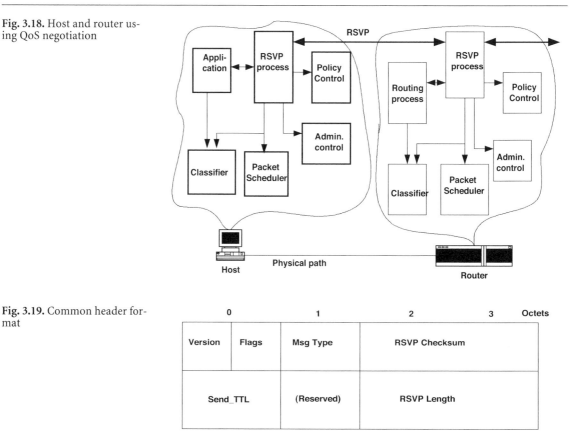

Fig. 3.19. Common header format

ing traffic in terms of delay, jitter and bandwidth limits. The protocol sends out path messages from the sender to either a unicast or multicast DA. The path message contains Tspec information. A router that implements RSVP along the downstream is known as an edge router.

3.4.1.1.1 *Message Format*

RSVP messages consist of a common header followed by a message body containing a typed "object" (Fig. 3.19). There are two fundamental message types: path and reservation. There are a set of rules for choice of object type permitted for each message type. These rules are specified in RFC 2205 (defines RSVP version 1) using BNF (Backus–Naur Form) extended with square brackets surrounding optional subsequences. BNF means an order for the objects in a message.

The version field is a 4-bit field which indicates the RSVP protocol version number (version 1). The version is followed by the flags field which is also a 4-bit field and values 0x01–0x08 are reserved. No flag is defined yet. Msg Type (the message type field) is an 8-bit field. Table 3.6 shows various values for Msg Type.

The next field is the RSVP checksum, a 16-bit field initially set to all zeros. The all zeros mean no checksum was transmitted. Send_TTL is an 8-bit field

Value	Meaning
1	Path
2	Resv
3	PathErr
4	ResvErr
5	PathTear
6	ResvTear
7	ResvConf

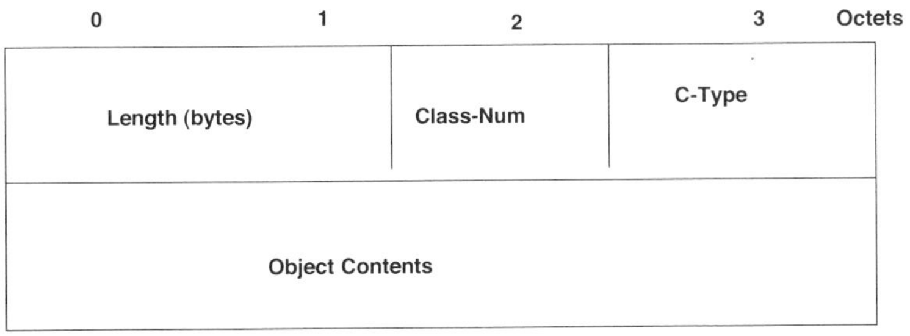

Table 3.6. Msg Type values

Fig. 3.20. The object format for RSVP message

after the RSVP checksum that indicates the IP TTL value for the message. The last field of the common header is the RSVP length, a 16-bit field which identifies the length of this RSVP message in bytes (including common header and object format) (Fig. 3.20).

An object header has fields Length, Class-Num and C-Type, as follows:

Length: A 16-bit field that indicates the total object length in bytes and is always a multiple of 4 or at least 4.

Class-Num: This identifies the object class and each object class has a name which an RSVP implementation must recognize.

The following are those object classes:

NULL: The NULL object has a Class-Num value of zero and the C-Type of the object class is ignored. The length for this object class is at least 4, but can be multiple of 4. Usually, the receiver ignores the contents of a NULL object.

SESSION: This defines a specific session for the other object that follows and contains the IP DA, IP ID and destination port for that purpose. It must appear in every RSVP message. In this object class C-Types are defined for IPv4 and IPv6. For other address classes, additional C-types can be defined as required. For IPv4/UDP SESSION (Fig. 3.21), Class = 1 and C-Type = 1 whereas for IPv6/UDP SESSION (Fig. 3.22), Class = 1 and C-Type = 2.

All unused fields are set to zero and ignored upon receipt. DestAddress is the unicast or multicast IP address and the field must be non-zero. The protocol ID must also be a non-zero field. The flags field has a value 0x01 = E_Police flag. The E_Police flag is used in path messages to control traffic policing and determine the edge of the network. DestPort is the next field and

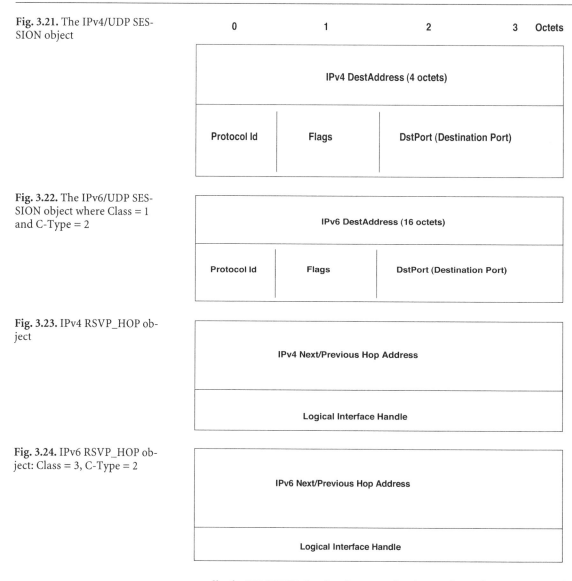

Fig. 3.21. The IPv4/UDP SES-SION object

Fig. 3.22. The IPv6/UDP SES-SION object where Class = 1 and C-Type = 2

Fig. 3.23. IPv4 RSVP_HOP object

Fig. 3.24. IPv6 RSVP_HOP object: Class = 3, C-Type = 2

normally the UDP/TCP destination port for the session. If no UDP/TCP destination port is used a zero can be used to identify this condition.

RSVP_HOP: RSVP_HOP: This object class consists of Class = 3 and C-Type = 1. It carries the IP address of the RSVP capable node which has sent this message (Figs. 3.23 and 3.24). The LIH (Logical Interface Handle) is used to distinguish outgoing interfaces. If there is no logical interface, the value is set to zero. A node that receives the LIH from a path message save its value and returns it in the Resv message back to the originating node.

TIME_VALUES: This contains the refresh period time parameter. There are two time parameters associated with each elements of RSVP path or reservation state in a host or node. The refresh period "R" is the period between successive refreshes for the state (Fig. 3.25). Each path or Resv message car-

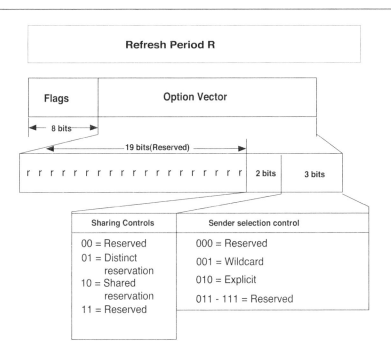

Fig. 3.25. The TIME_VALUES object class

Fig. 3.26. The STYLE object class

ries a TIME_VALUES object containing the refresh time "R" used to generate refreshes. The current suggested default for "R" is 30 seconds. It consists of Class = 5 and C-Type = 1.

STYLE: This defines the reservation style and provides style-specific information that is not in FLOWSPEC or FILTER_SPEC. Every Resv message should have this object class. It consists of Class = 8 and C-Type = 1 values and has a 8-bit flags field followed by a 24-bit option vector field. The value for the flags field is not assigned yet. The option vector field provides the value for reservation options. Of the bits assigned in this field 19 bits are reserved. The bit assignments are shown in Fig. 3.26.

FLOWSPEC: This defines a desired QoS in a Resv message. The values for this object include Class = 9 and C-Type = 1. It is further clarified in RFC 2210 beyond the discussions of RFC 2205. FLOWSPEC is a reservation request that includes a service class and two different numeric parameters. They are "Rspec" and Tspec. Rspec (R for reserve) defines the desired QoS and Tspec (T for traffic) describes the dataflow.

FILTER_SPEC: This defines a specific flow of data packets that should receive the desired QoS in a Resv message. This object class includes the value of Class = 10 and C-Type = 1. Class = 10 also for IPv4 and IPv6 FILTER_SPEC objects but C-Type = 2 for IPv6 (Figs. 3.27 and 3.28).

SENDER_TEMPLATE: This contains a sender IP address and some additional demultiplexing information.

SENDER_TSPEC: This defines traffic characteristics and is required in a path message.

ADSPEC: This carries OPWA (One Pass With Advertising) data in a path message.

Fig. 3.27. IPv4 FILTER_SPEC object class

Fig. 3.28. IPv6 FILTER_SPEC object: Class = 10 and C-Type = 2

Fig. 3.29. IPv4 SCOPE list object: Class = 7 and C-Type = 1

Fig. 3.30. IPv4 RESV_CONFIRM object class

Fig. 3.31. IPv6 RESV_CONFIRM object class

ERROR_SPEC: This object class specifies the error in PathErr, ResvErr or ResvConf messages.

POLICY_DATA: This object class carries the policy regarding the permission of reservation and may appear in Path, Resv, PathErr or ResvErr messages. It not fully defined yet.

INTEGRITY: This provides the means for authentication and carries cryptographic data.

SCOPE: This carries the list of sender hosts towards which the information is to be forwarded and may be seen in Resv, ResvErr or ResvTear messages (Fig. 3.29).

RESV_CONFIRM: This object class carries the IP address of a receiver which requested a confirmation. Class = 15 and C-Type = 1 for IPv4 (Fig. 3.30) and C-Type = 2 for IPv6 (Fig. 3.31) .

3.4.1.2 RSVP with IntServ

The requirements and operations of RSVP with IntServ are defined in RFC 2210. RSVP works as a setup protocol mechanism for IntServ to correctly invoke QoS control services. It carries authentication, accounting, and policy information needed to manage the use of IntServ. RSVP carries the traffic description (Tspec) generated by the sender through the router to a receiver using RSVP SENDER_TSPEC objects. This information is not modified by the intermediate network elements such as a router. A network element may only modify the following information:

- Services available
- Network delay
- Bandwidth estimates
- Operation parameters.

The information is used by QoS control services, collected from the network elements and carried towards receivers in RSVP ADSPEC objects. There are three RSVP objects important for IntServ operation and they are:

1. RSVP SENDER_TSPEC: This object carries sender Tspec generated by a data source within an RSVP session and transported unchanged through the network to the receiving applications.
2. RSVP ADSPEC: This carries information that can be updated by the network which includes both parameters describing the data path properties and parameters required for QoS control services.
3. RSVP FLOWSPEC: This object carries RSVP request both Receiver_Tspec and Rspec that are generated by a receiver. The information in FLOW-SPEC flows upstream toward the data source which can be used or updated by the intermediate network elements.

3.4.1.2.1 Operation of RSVP

To initiate the RSVP operation a data source application must first send a Tspec to an RSVP mechanism describing the traffic the application wishes to generate. RSVP uses the information to construct an RSVP SENDER_TSPEC object for use with RSVP PATH messages that are generated for the application (Fig. 3.32).

The source application also constructs an initial RSVP ADSPEC object which carries information regarding QoS control parameters, requirements of the sending application and path properties. This object is added to the RSVP PATH message by the RSVP mechanism and transmitted out into the network. The intermediate network elements are capable of modifying the ADSPEC object along the path to the receiving end. The receiving application accepts the PATH message through its local RSVP application program interface (API) to the application. The parameters within the ADSPEC object are used by IntServ mechanisms such as the GL service (RFC 2212) to calculate a mathematical bound on the delivered packet delay, for example. The receiving application on the other hand imparts to its local RSVP mechanism its reservation parameters (i.e., QoS control parameter such as CL or GL), Tspec and Rspec. These parameters are composed within RSVP FLOWSPEC

Fig. 3.32. An example of RSVP operation

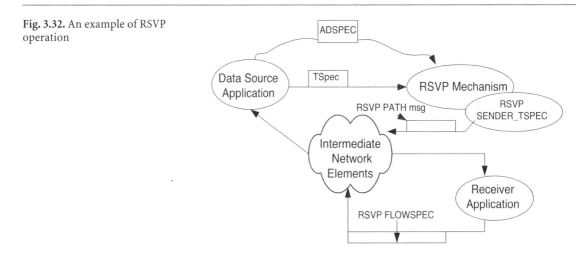

which is in turn transmitted upstream. At a given RSVP point in the network the SENDER_TSPEC arriving in the PATH message and FLOWSPEC arriving in the RESV message are used to determine the required resource reservation.

3.4.2 DiffServ

The traditional approach of internet/intranet traffic transport for both enterprise and ISPs were Best-effort Service which provides all customers with the same level of performance. The traffic differentiation was in the pricing structure of individual vs. business rate and the connectivity type such as dial-up access vs. leased lines. Therefore, the DiffServ model was developed to give better service to some traffic at the expense of giving worse service to other. DiffServ provides the framework of a service architecture within which both enterprise and ISPs can offer differentiated services to their customers on the basis of performance in addition to the pricing tiers used in the past. It is done by allowing the customers to request specific services by marking the DS (DiffServ) field of the IP packet with a specific value. The DS field is just the reanimation of the TOS byte field in the IP packet (Fig. 3.33). The DS field replaces the IPv4 TOS octet (and the corresponding IPv6 traffic class octet).

RFC 2474 defines the DS byte for IPv4 and IPv6. Although the DS byte is defined and approved by IETF as an RFC, it is to be noted that much of Diff-Serv's works are still in draft stage. Recently IETF has approved DiffServ architecture as RFC 2475, where 6 bits in the DS field are known as the DSCP (Differentiated Service CodePoint) . It is used as a codepoint to select PHB (Per Hop Behavior) packet experiences at each node. A PHB is realized by an implementation mechanism internal to the node, whereas DSCPs are mapped into PHBs available in a given node (Fig. 3.34). To further define them, PHBs are the packet forwarding treatment that delivers the DiffServ to packets at the network node output and includes policing, shaping, possible remarking of DSCP, queuing treatment and scheduling.

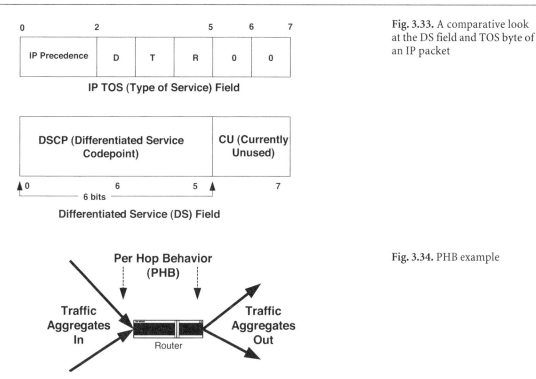

Fig. 3.33. A comparative look at the DS field and TOS byte of an IP packet

Fig. 3.34. PHB example

Currently IETF has defined the following PHBs: expedited forwarding (EF), assured forwarding (AF) and default (DE). The EF forwarding treatment requires that at each node the egress rate should exceed the ingress rate for a conforming aggregate. The EF can be used to build a low-loss, low-latency, low-jitter and assured bandwidth end-to-end service throughout the DS domain.

On the other hand, AF provides delivery of packets in four AF classes. Each class is in each DS (DiffServ) node and allocated a certain buffer and bandwidth space. Customer- or provider-assigned IP packets require services from AF PHB groups. Within each AF class, IP packets are marked with one of the three "drop precedence" values. We will say much about these when we start exploring the DS field. Refer to the PHB section for further details on various PHB classes.

Concerning the DS byte, a 2-bit field is still undefined and known as CU (Currently Unused). The DiffServ- compliant nodes ignore CU bits when determining the PHB to be applied to a packet received. The DSCP field is capable of conveying 64 distinct codepoints. RFC 2474 defines DSCP value notation as "xxxxxx" where "x" may equal 0 or 1 and where the leftmost bit identifies bit 0 and the rightmost bit signifies bit 5 of the DSCP. For the purpose of management and code assignment (Table 3.7), the codepoint space is divided into three pools as follows:

- Pool 1: A pool of 32 recommended codepoints to be assigned by Standard Action as defined by RFC 2434.

Table 3.7. The DS codepoint assignment

Pool	Codepoint space	Assignment policy
1	xxxxx0	Standard Action
2	xxxx11	EXP/LU
3	xxxx01	EXP/LU(*)

- Pool 2: A pool of 16 codepoints to be reserved for Experimental or Local Use (EXP/LU) as defined in RFC 2434.
- Pool 3: A pool of 16 codepoints that are initially available for EXP/LU but can be used if Pool 1 is exhausted.

3.4.2.1 DiffServ Architecture

DiffServ provides two distinct services: Better Best Effort and Virtual Leased lines. The Better Best-Effort Service provides finer control of relative bandwidth allocation particularly under heavy load. On the other hand, Virtual Leased lines provide end-to-end absolute bandwidth allocation, independent of other traffic. They are independent of applications and protocols; that is, DiffServ will work with various protocols such as IP, UDP, TCP, OSPF and BGP. One of the major advantages of DiffServ is that it helps the scale of the Internet (e.g., millions of networks) at the physical speed (i.e. Gbs/link). There are three elements that work together to deliver a DiffServ service. They are the PHB, traffic conditioner (TC) and bandwidth broker (i.e., the policy manager). The PHB deliver special treatment to packets at forwarding time. The TC alters the packet aggregate to enforce rules for services. Finally, the bandwidth broker applies and communicates policy. The policy can be defined as a network service that specifies the performance of traffic flows through one or more networks. The architecture of DiffServ is based on a simple model where traffic entering a network is first classified and conditioned at the boundaries of the network and assigned to different aggregates. A single codepoint identifies each behavior aggregate. In the core of the network, packets are forwarded based on PHBs, which in turn are identified by DS codepoint. A number of DS nodes implement PHB groups and service provisioning policy for the DS domain through which traffic should traverse. A DS domain includes adjacent set of DS nodes and has a well-defined boundary known as the DS boundary (Fig. 3.35) . A node in the DS boundary classifies and conditions incoming traffic to ensure that the traversing packets are marked to select the PHB from PHB groups that are supported in the domain.

A node within the DS domain is responsible for selecting the forwarding behavior of the traversing packets based on their DSCPs (Fig. 3.36) .

It then maps the value to one of the supported PHBs by either using DSCP to PHB mapping or locally customized mapping. If a non-DS-compliant node is included with a DS domain, it may result in unpredictable performance and may hinder the SLA (Service Level Agreement).

A DS domain may include several networks under one administration, for example an intranet.

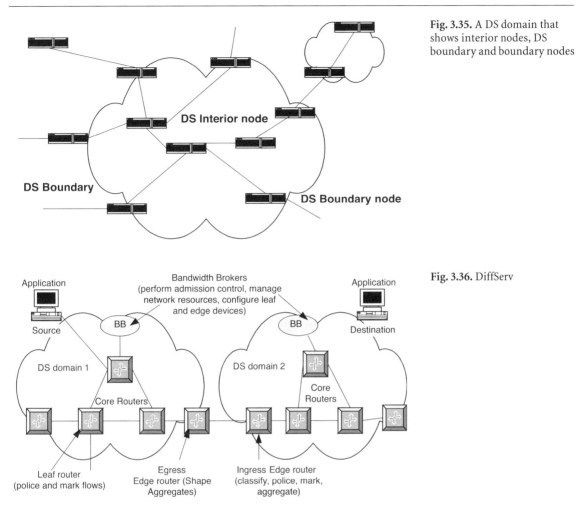

Fig. 3.35. A DS domain that shows interior nodes, DS boundary and boundary nodes

Fig. 3.36. DiffServ

3.4.2.1.1 DS Boundary Nodes and Interior Nodes

A DS domain consists of nodes that are a combination of DS boundary nodes and DS interior nodes. The DS boundary nodes interconnect a DS domain to other DS or non-DS domains. On the other hand, DS interior nodes connect DS interior or boundary nodes within the same DS-capable domain (Fig. 3.37).

The rule is that both DS interior and DS boundary nodes must implement the desired PHB to packets based on the DSCPs. In addition, a DS boundary node may need to perform traffic conditioning functions as defined by the TCA (Traffic Conditioning Agreement). The TCA is an agreement which specifies the rules governing metering, marking, discarding and shaping. These rules are applied to traffic streams selected by the classifier. Although the DiffServ architecture assumes that the traffic classification and conditioning would be done at egress and/or ingress DS boundary nodes, interior

Fig. 3.37. The block diagram of a DS boundary router

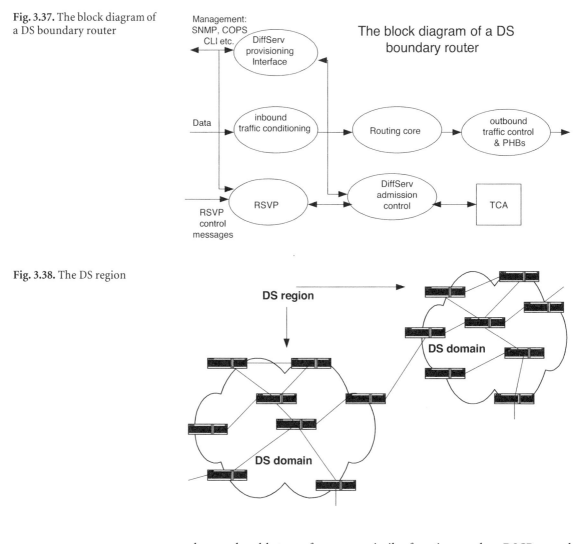

Fig. 3.38. The DS region

nodes are also able to perform some similar functions such as DSCP remarking. A DS boundary node acts as an ingress or egress node for traffic with a different direction. In the ingress function, a DS boundary node ensures that the incoming traffic conforms to a specific TCA between it and other domains to which it may connected. On the other hand, in the egress function, a DS boundary node may perform traffic conditioning depending on the TCA between its domain and the other domain.

3.4.2.1.2 DS Region
A DS region is a set of DS domains capable of supporting DiffServ among the DS domains along the paths (Fig. 3.38). The DS domains within a DS region are capable of supporting different PHB groups and DSCP to PHB mappings. However, in order to support services across the domains, the adjacent domains must establish a peering SLA.

3.4.2.2 Traffic Conditioning (TC)

The SLA is used to extend DiffServ across the DS domain boundary between an upstream network and a downstream DS domain. It may specify traffic profile, classification and remarking rules. The temporal properties of traffic flow selected by a classifier are known as traffic profile. As RFC 2475 defines it, a traffic profile provides the rule to determine whether a packet is in profile or out of profile. For example, a profile based on a token bucket may look like

Codepoint = X, use token – bucket r, b

The profile indicated here can be described as packets market with codepoint X should be measured with a token bucket meter whose rate is r and burst size is b.

In this example, out of profile means the packets in the traffic stream that arrive when the token bucket has insufficient tokens available. Different conditioning or accounting may be applied to the in-profile and out-of-profile packets. The DSCP of in-profile packets may be changed or they may be allowed to enter the DS domain without further conditioning.

A traffic conditioner may or may not apply its four elements (classifier, meter, marker and dropper/shaper) to a packet. For example, a packet with no traffic profile may only pass through the classifier and a marker (Fig. 3.39).

The function of the meter is to measure the temporal properties of the traffic flow selected by a classifier, which in turn learned the traffic profile of the flow from the TCA. A meter imparts the information regarding temporal properties of the stream to other functions to trigger the appropriate action for each in- or out-of-profile packet. A marker on the other hand sets the DSCP in the DS field to indicate certain DiffServ behavior aggregate. The marker can be configured to mark all packets with one single DSCP or one of a set of codepoints to a packet. The set of codepoints can be used to select a specific PHB from a PHB group. The change done by a marker in the codepoint is known as "remarked". The shaper mechanism may impose a delay to all or some packets in order to bring it into compliance with a traffic pro-

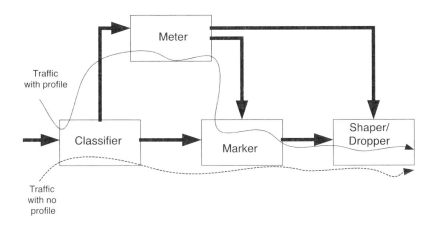

Fig. 3.39. The traffic conditioner and classifier

file. It usually has a calculable size buffer, and therefore a packet may be discarded if the buffer is not available. Similarly, a dropper may discard some or all packets in a traffic flow in order to ensure that the stream complies with a given traffic profile. This is known as "policing" the traffic flow. In special cases, a dropper is implemented by reducing the buffer size of the shaper to zero. The TC and classifiers (i.e., multifield (MF)) are implemented in an egress or ingress DS boundary node but may also be implemented within the DS interior node.

3.4.2.3 PHB

We talked a little about PHB earlier; in this section we will explore further details about PHB and its various classes. As described in RFC 2475, the PHB is an externally observable "Forwarding Behavior" that is applied in a DS node (Fig. 3.40). This directly results in a DS behavior aggregate. For example, a stream of IP packets is marked with a certain priority at the DS edge, the observable forwarding behavior (i.e., loss, delay, jitter) often depending on the relative loading of the link. This means that the buffer and bandwidth allocation by the DS node for that particular flow may affect the forwarding behavior. Some behavioral distinctions will occur when multiple DS behavior aggregates compete for the DS node's resources.

A DS node allocates resources based on packet classification, which means packets are marked with a certain DSCP. The marked packets are then passed through a scheduling discipline and queuing mechanism within the DS node that results in forwarding behavior for the particular flow. The procedure within a DS node can be imagined as PHB and this mechanism will be continued throughout the domain on hop-by-hop basis. This provides a useful differentiated service. A set of PHBs can be identified as a PHB group only if a common constraint such as queue servicing or queue management can be applied to them. The relationship between PHBs in a PHB group is in terms of absolute or relative priority. A single PHB defined in isolation is a special case of a PHB group.

The implementation of PHBs in DS nodes can be considered as the implying means of some buffer management and packet scheduling mechanisms.

Fig. 3.40. The explanation of PHB and forwarding behavior

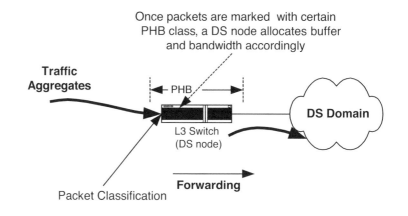

Note especially that these PHBs are defined in terms of behavior characteristics pertaining to service provisioning policies, and not in terms of particular implementation mechanisms. It should also be noted that in some circumstances more than one PHB group may be implemented on a DS node and utilized within a domain.

So far, IETF has defined three PHB classes: default, AF and EF. Although not clearly defined in DS RFCs, it is possible to define the relationship between two classes of PHBs to make a PHB group.

3.4.2.3.1 Default PHB

This particular already exists in routers and is known as the best-effort forwarding behavior that is defined in RFC 1812. If no specific packet treatment is defined, it is assumed that packets belong to the best-effort aggregate. These types of packets are sent to the network without allocating resources; instead the forwarding is based on available resources. The implementation of these PHBs enforces compatibility with the non-DiffServ network. The recommended DSCP for this PHB is the bit pattern of 000000. It should to be noted that the packets that are marked with default PHB DSCP can be remarked with another DSCP as it passes a boundary into a DS domain (Fig. 3.41).

3.4.2.3.2 AF PHB

For an enterprise network with geographically distributed sites, the network engineer would prefer IP packets within the intranet to be forwarded with assurance and high probability as long as the traffic does not exceed a certain threshold. It is also desirable that if the aggregate requirement is exceeded, out-of-profile traffic should be transported with not so high a probability as for in-profile traffic. In other words, in-profile traffic will have a higher priority than out-of-profile traffic. The former can be considered as the traffic that follows the requirements for AF PHB (Fig. 3.42) whereas the latter can be default PHB (DE).

Note that a DS-compliant node is not required to implement AF PHB in order to comply with DiffServ requirements. The implementation of AF PHB in a DS node if deployed must conform to RFC 2597.

For a DS node the assurance of IP packet forwarding actually depends on the available forwarding resources out of which a certain amount is allocated to certain AF classes.

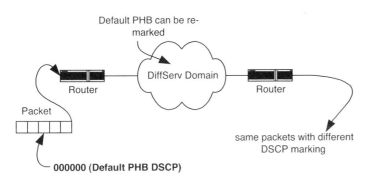

Fig. 3.41. Default PHB can be remarked in the DS domain

Fig. 3.42. The AF PHB example

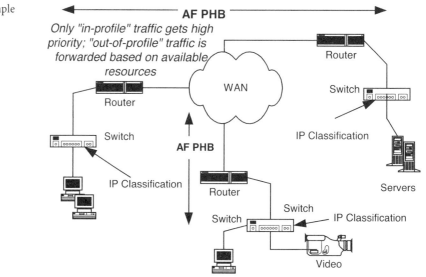

Table 3.8. Recommended DSCP for AF PHB classes

Drop prece-dence	AF PHB recommended DSCP							
	Class 1		Class 2		Class 3		Class 4	
Low	001010	AF 11	010010	AF 21	011010	AF 31	100010	AF 41
Medium	001100	AF 12	010100	AF 22	011100	AF 32	100100	AF 42
High	001110	AF 13	010110	AF 23	011110	AF 33	100110	AF 43

There are four PHB classes defined and given in Table 3.8.

If two classes of AF PHB try to access the same resources in a DS node, the AF class with lower drop precedence will get priority over the other. In other words, the lower the drop precedence the higher the probability of receiving the allocated resources, and the higher the drop precedence the bigger the probability of packets getting dropped, if the DS node is congested.

The AF PHB group has a number of PHB classes that can be denoted with A_n, each with a number of drop precedence level D_p. Currently RFC 2597 defines $A_n = 4$ and $D_p = 3$.

3.4.2.3.3 EF PHB

According to RFC 2598, EF PHB is not a mandatory requirement for a DS-complaint device. EF PHB provides a special service known as Virtual Leased line from end to end. In other words, to the end-user it is like a point-to-point link. This PHB can be used to implement low-latency, low-jitter, assured bandwidth, point-to-point service within a DS domain.

Traffic experiences queues during its transiting of the network if the incoming aggregate is higher than the serviceable aggregate. For EF PHB, there is no queue and thus such traffic experiences low latency, low jitter and low

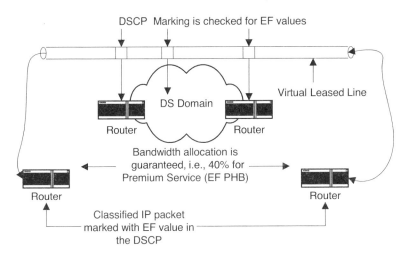

Fig. 3.43. An example of EF PHB forwarding

loss (Fig. 3.43). As mentioned earlier, the question of queuing arises when the arrival rate of the traffic is higher than departure rate at some nodes. Therefore, for traffic that experiences no queue the bounding rate is such that, at every transit node, the traffic maximum arrival rate is less than the minimum departure rate.

Several types of queue scheduling mechanisms may be employed to deliver the forwarding behavior described in the previous section.

A simple priority queue will give the appropriate behavior as long as there is no higher priority queue that could preempt the EF queue for more than a packet time at the configured rate. This could be accomplished by having a rate policer such as a token bucket associated with each priority queue to bound how much the queue can starve other traffic.

It is also possible to use a single queue in a group of queues serviced by a weighted round-robin scheduler where the share of the output bandwidth assigned to the EF queue is equal to the configured rate.

Another possible implementation is a CBQ (Class-Based Queuing) scheduler that gives the EF queue priority up to the configured rate.

Another procedure would be a simple queue that is serviced by a weighted round-robin scheduler in which the bandwidth share assigned for the packets with EF is equal to the configured rate.

RFC 2598 suggests that the DSCP value for EF PHB is 101100 (0x2E in hex), but remember that the actual marking should be only 6 bits instead of 8 bits. Some implementations consider the entire TOS field to define the DSCP value for EF PHB as B8 (hex). This is wrong and must not be followed. If packets are marked for EF PHB then their DSCP can be marked again at a DS domain boundary only if the new DSCP satisfies the EF PHB. Also the packets that are marked with for EF PHBs should not be changed to any other type of PHB by a DS domain.

In order to protect itself against denial of service attacks, the edge of a DS domain must police all EF marked packets to the negotiated rate with the upstream domain. This value should be less than the configured rate. Packets in excess of the negotiated value should be discarded.

Since the end-to-end premium service constructed from the EF PHB requires that the upstream domain police and shape EF marked traffic to meet the rate negotiated with the downstream domain, the downstream domain's policer should never have to drop packets. Any drops should be noted (e.g., via SNMP traps) as possible security violations or serious misconfiguration. Similarly, since the aggregate EF traffic rate is constrained at every interior node, the EF queue should never overflow. If it does, the drops should be noted as possible attacks or serious misconfiguration.

3.4.2.3.4 *Class Selector Codepoints*

The DS field values of xxx000 and CU field unspecified are reserved as a set of class selector (CS) codepoints (Table 3.9). For CS code points "x" can be either 0 or 1. CS codepoints CS1–CS7 may be mapped to different DSCPs as long as the CS and DiffServ PHB requirements are met.

The PHBs that are mapped by these codepoints must satisfy the CS PHB requirements in addition to preserving the default PHB requirements on codepoint 000000. The CS PHB and associated codepoints are used to support legacy (non-DS-compliant) routers and switches in a DS-compliant network. Support for the CS PHB is mandatory for the DS-compliant node.

A DS-compliant node implements eight CS codepoints. According to RFC 2474, the CS codepoints must yield at least two independently forwarded classes of traffic. To deploy this in a DiffServ network, the CS PHB maps to the currently defined DiffServ PHBs, that is EF, AF and DE. Also, in CS codepoint mapping, the eight CS codepoints MUST map into the currently defined 14 DSCPs, namely 1 EF, 12 AF and 1 DE DSCP. The CS PHB MUST inherit the PHB associated with the DiffServ PHB to which the CS codepoint is mapped. For example, if the CS7 codepoint is mapped to the EF codepoint then packets marked with CS7 must receive EF PHB treatmentPackets marked with higher value CS codepoints must be forwarded with a higher

Table 3.9. CS codepoints

Name	Value
CS7	11100000
CS6	11000000
CS5	10100000
CS4	10000000
CS3	01100000
CS2	01000000
CS1	00100000
CS0 [**]	00000000

[**] *The CS0 codepoint and PHB are equivalent to the DE DSCP and PHB.*

probability than packets marked with a lower value CS codepoint. For example, a packet marked with a CS5 codepoint must be forwarded before a packet marked with a CS3 codepoint. This is consistent and compatible with the 3-bit TOS IP precedence field specified in RFC 791.

3.4.2.4 L2 Traffic Class to DiffServ Mapping

Although we have not defined the L2 traffic class (TC) in this book, it is clearly defined in my *High-Speed LAN Technology Handbook*. I will suggest that readers use this handbook as the basis for improving their knowledge of the layer 2/layer 3 technology concept and LAN know-how. Besides, L2 TC is defined in the IEEE 802.1p standard: it is a 30-bit field that is carried in an IEEE 802.1Q frame or otherwise known as a tagged frame. Both IEEE 802.1Q and IEEE 802.1p are now combined in the IEEE 802.1D standard. The IEEE 802.1Q frame is a 4-byte VLAN tagged frame which is inserted right after the SA (Source Address) in an Ethernet frame format. The intention of the .1Q frame is to carry VLAN information from one part of the LAN to the other. The VLAN tagged frame (Fig. 3.44) is identified with a value for Tag Identifier as 8100. The TCI (Tag Control Information) field contains the 3-bit priority subfield, the 1-bit CFI (Canonical Form Indicator) subfield, and the 12-bit VID (VLAN ID) field.

For Ethernet this bit is set to 0. If a network includes Ethernet and Token Ring that are connected together using a translation bridge, then this bit will be set to 1, otherwise it is always set to 0.

Under the 802.1p priority mechanism, a packet destined for an output port is assigned one of eight priority levels. Within a priority level, traffic is served in FIFO order. Higher numbered traffic classes have higher priority than lower numbered traffic classes.

Note that the 802.1q tag is optional and therefore an Ethernet frame may arrive "untagged" with no 802.1p user priority setting.

A priority scheduler is used for 802.1p tagged traffic by L2 switches. A DS node should also use a priority scheduler for packets egressing over an Ethernet link.

L2 switches do not recognize L3 DSCPs and hence need to map incoming 802.1p tagged traffic to a default queue structure. This is required to be con-

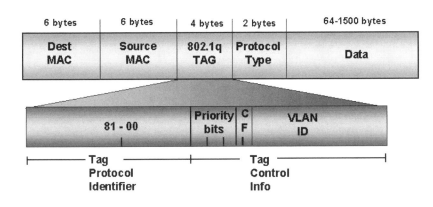

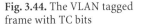

Fig. 3.44. The VLAN tagged frame with TC bits

sistent with DS nodes ("L3-aware" nodes) mapping between 802.1p, DSCP and queues.

A packet may arrive from a downstream L2 switch with its set to 0 default PHB (DE) but have an 802.1p user priority set. However, the DSCP will not be remarked by L2 switches that are not "L3 aware".

Table 3.10 provides the required default mapping between 802.1p user priorities to products with differing numbers of queues. Note that there may be a different number of queues on different ports within the same product.

Mapping 802.1p user priorities to DSCPs is required because some L2 devices such as Ethernet switches or NICs can only mark 802.1p and are not L3 aware. Hence they cannot mark the DSCP nor apply the appropriate behavioral treatment for the DSCP. Therefore, the traffic is reliant on an L3 device to provide the appropriate DSCP marking and behavioral treatment. Furthermore, 802.1p information is temporary but DSCP information remains with the packet to its destination regardless of the link layer transport.

A packet may arrive from a downstream L2 switch with its DSCP set to the default DSCP but have an 802.1p user priority set. If the packet ingresses an L3-aware DS node, the packet can be classified and remarked with a DSCP based upon network policy. However, if no policy manager is present, a default mapping between 802.1p and the DSCP is required since an upstream L3 device may not support 802.1p but can prioritize traffic based on the DSCP.

A packet may ingress an L3-aware DS node from a "trusted" source and does not require remarking. In this case, the default mapping of DSCP to queue specified in must be used.

Table 3.10. The L2 TC and queue mapping

Incoming 802.1p User Priority	Number of queues				
	Eight	Six	Four	Three	Two
7	1 (highest priority)	1	1	1	1
6	2	2	2	2	2
5	3	3			
4	4	4	3		
3	5	5			
0	6				
		6	4	3	
2	7				
1	8 (lowest priority)				

When a packet ingresses to a DS node, it may not have the 802.1q tag and hence no 802.1p user priority setting. In this case, IP classification can be performed on the DSCP if from a trusted source or MF (Multi-Field) or BA (Behavior Aggregate) classification for the general case. The DSCP will then determine the queue in which the packet is placed.

Table 3.11 provides the required default mapping of 802.1p to DSCP to queue. These are to be used as the standard defaults as the device is powered up.

Table 3.11. The L2 TC to IP DiffServ mapping

IP service class	Incoming 802.1p user priority	Default DSCP	Number of queues
			Eight
Critical		CS7	1 (highest priority)
	7 (or untagged)		
Network		CS6	
Premium	6 (or untagged)	EF	2
Platinum	5 (or untagged)	AF41	3
Gold	4 (or untagged)	AF31	4
Silver	3 (or untagged)	AF21	5
Bronze	2 (or untagged)	AF11	6
Standard	0 (or untagged)	DE*	7
Custom	1 (or untagged)	(user defined within allowable DSCP values of xxxxx0, where x = 0 or 1)**	8 (lowest priority)

Notes:
* If no custom DSCP is defined, then the incoming traffic tagged with 802.1p user priority 1 must be mapped to the DE DSCP.

** Any DSCP other than the user-defined custom DSCP, EF, AF1x–AF4x, DE and CS0–CS7 must be mapped to 802.1p user priority 0.

3.4.3 IntServ and DiffServ Comparison

The service achieved after deploying either IntServ or DiffServ varies in several key areas as follows:

- Scalability
- Flow state and PHB
- Resource allocation
- Signaling
- Deployment
- Backward compatibility
- Transport technology
- Utilization.

Scalability: This issue is based on the characteristics of the flow state of both the architectures. While IntServ maintains a per flow basis on the packets, DiffServ concentrates on aggregated flows. Due to this reason, DiffServ can create connections between DS-compliant and DS-non-compliant domains in addition to connections between DS-compliant domains. This increases scalability.

Flow state and PHB: IntServ uses a "soft-state" flow in its per flow signaling, in which there is periodic expiration of resource reservations, whereas in the case of DiffServ there is no soft state. It concentrates on aggregated flows and PHB. The PHB is implemented in the routers inside the DS-compliant domain, which provides the routers to monitor all the packets traversing their path so that they adhere to the SLAs.

Resource allocation: IntServ uses the RSVP in order to allocate the required bandwidth for the path. DiffServ implements the marking, metering, shaping and policing of packets, and based on these criteria working in conjunction with the DSCPs the required bandwidth is allocated to each packet.

Signaling: With regards to signaling, IntServ uses point-to-point signaling since it has to maintain a per flow soft state. At the same time DiffServ cannot support an end-to-end QoS architecture all by itself.

Deployment: Classification, marking, policing and shaping are to be implemented only on the ingress and the egress routers only. Hence DiffServ can be deployed in a less harder way as compared to IntServ which deals with the fact that there is a per flow soft state to be maintained and the timer also has to be taken into consideration, so it is a bit cumbersome.

Backward compatibility: The DiffServ architecture supports backward compatibility by reserving the first 3 bits of the IPv4 ToS octet. With this setup, a DS-compliant domain can be connected to a non-DS-compliant domain. IntServ does not have any such setup.

Transport technology: IntServ implements RSVP which supports multicasting, whereas the DiffServ architecture does not support multicasting because a multicast packet after arrival may exit from the DS domain from multiple DS egress nodes which enter multiple downstreams. So keeping the SLA legal and not violating it for the downstream nodes is difficult.

Utilization: The last point is more one of incorporating both architectures under one roof. A DS domain can support an IntServ architecture inside its domain. This is particularly useful because, since IntServ supports multicasting, it is helpful for the DS architecture also. This sort of combination helps both the architectures in maintaining QoS.

3.5 COPS (Common Open Policy Service)

The new developments in IP QoS such as IP DiffServ and the need for PEN have identified the importance of COPS deployment in an optimized IP network. Although COPS is not yet standard, a number of vendors have already deployed it in their product combinations to strengthen the PEN for users – for example, Nortel Network's Optivity COPS server and ARN series of routers. COPS is a server/client model which supports policy control over QoS signaling protocols and allows QoS resource management. RFC 2748 defines COPS for supporting policy control over QoS signaling protocols. The protocol specifies a means to exchange policy information between a policy server (policy decision point or PDP) and its clients (policy enforcement point or PEP). It is a simple query and response protocol, which uses TCP as its transport protocol. Thus there is no additional mechanism required for reliable communication. The COPS draft specifies in an example that a router that must exercise policy-based admission control can be considered as the policy client. The PEP simply updates, deletes and sends requests to the remote PDP and the PDP returns decisions back to the PEP. COPS is designed to leverage off self-identifying objects and can support diverse client-specific information without modifying the COPS protocol itself. It also provides message-level security for authentication, replay protection and message integrity. COPS may also use IPSEC (IP Security Protocol) or TLS (Transport Layer Security) to authenticate and secure the channel path between the PEP and PDP (Fig. 3.45).

The PEP and LDP (Local Decision Point) are implemented in a network node or router, for example. On the other hand, remote PDP is implemented in a server such as a network management server; Nortel Network's Optivity COPS software bundle is a good example of PDP deployment. The policy client uses LDP if somehow a remote PDP is not available. Fault tolerance is achieved by allowing both the PEP and PDP to constantly verify their connection to each other via keep-alive messages. If a failure occurs, the PEP tries to establish a connection with a remote or backup PDP. The PEP also imparts to the PDP any deleted state or new events during next association after the connection is lost. Since the implementation of the COPS protocol is strictly

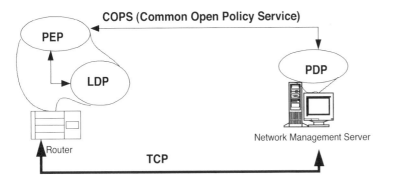

Fig. 3.45. An illustration of COPS

associated with a network that provides IP QoS, a number of methods are defined in various RFCs and drafts. At the beginning, COPS-DS or COPS for DiffServ network was written in an IETF draft. The COPS-DS draft suggested some specific COPS objects and a method of updating but unfortunately it has not yet become an RFC, although a number of vendors have already implemented COPS-DS in their products. In 1999, an effort was made to define a similar IETF draft known as COPS-PR or COPS provisioning. The latest available COPS-PR draft is valid until January 2001. More likely this draft will be accepted. COPS-PR is currently used with the IP DiffServ network. Similarly, RFC 2749 and RFC 2750 define COPS-OutSource, otherwise known as COPS-RSVP.

Therefore, for simplicity of discussion we can consider two kinds of COPS object implementations, namely COPS-PR and COPS-RSVP.

3.5.1 COPS Message Format

The message carries information between the PEP and remote PDP. Each COPS message consists of a COPS header known as a common header (Fig. 3.46).

The first field in the common header message format is a 4 bits long version field, which indicates the COPS version. Currently the value is 1. The next field is also 4 bits long and known as the flags field. This flag is set when the message is solicited by another COPS message, otherwise it is set to 0. The "Op Code" is an 8 bits long field which has the values given in Table 3.12.

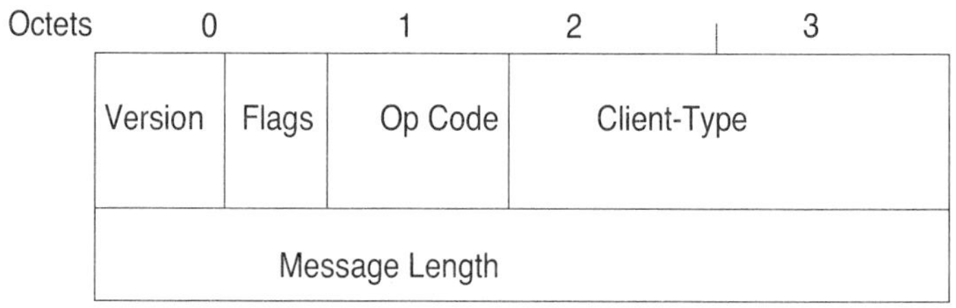

Fig. 3.46. Common header message format

Table 3.12. "Op Code" field values and their description

Value	Description
1	Request (REQ)
2	Decision (DEC)
3	Report state (RPT)
4	Delete request state (DRQ)
5	Synchronize state request (SSQ)
6	Client-Open (OPN)
7	Client-Accept (CAT)
8	Client-Close (CC)
9	Keep-Alive (KA)
10	synchronize complete (SSC)

The next field is a 16 bits long client-type field, which identifies the policy client. If the MSB is set in this field those values are enterprise specific and are 0x8000–0xFFFF. For the keep-alive message, the client-type is set to 0. The message length field is a 32-bit field, which includes the standard COPS header and all encapsulated objects. It must be aligned on a four-octet interval.

3.5.1.1 COPS Object Format
All COPS objects follow the same format (Fig. 3.47) and each of them consists of one or more 32-bit words with a four-octet header.

The length field in an object format has two-octet value, which describes the number of octets in the header and in the object. Generally, "C-Num" (a one-octet field) identifies the class of information contained in the object. The bit values and their description for the C-Num field are given in Table 3.13.

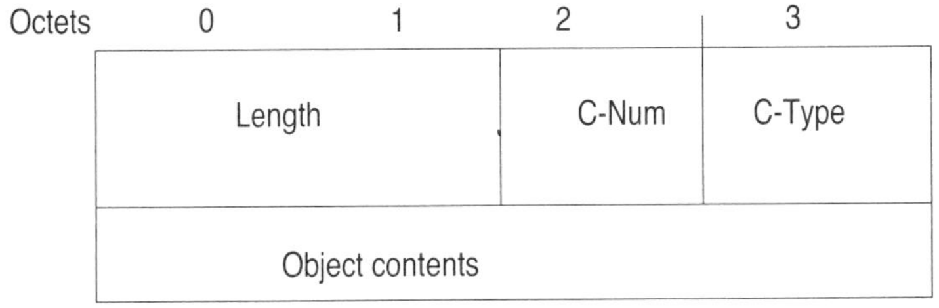

Fig. 3.47. The COPS object format

Bit value	Description
1	Handle
2	Context
3	In interface
4	Out interface
5	Reason code
6	Decision
7	LDP decision
8	Error
9	Client-specific information
10	Keep-alive timer
11	PEP identification
12	Report type
13	PDP redirect address
14	Last PDP address
15	Accounting timer
16	Message integrity

Table 3.13. The C-Num bit values and their description

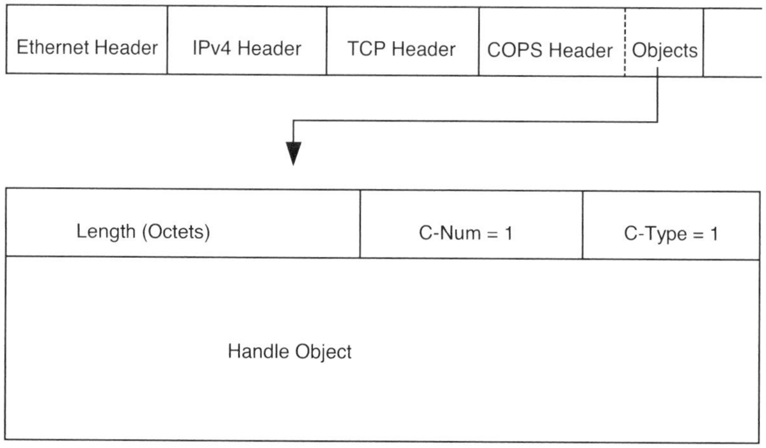

Fig. 3.48. An example of the handle object, showing the object within a IP packet

"C-Type" is a one-octet field that identifies the subtype or version of the information contained in the object. As we mentioned earlier, a C-Num value identifies the content of the object: if C-Num = 1, it identifies that the content in the object field is "Handle Object". For this, C-Type = 1. The object carries a unique value that identifies an installed state.

This identification is used by most COPS messages. The handle that corresponds to a state should be deleted when it is no longer applicable. The PEP uses the handle object to identify a unique request state for a client type. The handle object is a variable length field (Fig. 3.48).

To further clarify the frame format and understanding of how an object is being exchanged, consider the following packet decode. Please note that the value of the client type in the COPS common header is 2, which means it is a COPS-PR message. We will describe COPS-PR later in the section.

```
Frame 245 (350 on wire, 350 captured)
    Arrival Time: Oct 11, 2000 21:21:03.8991
    Time delta from previous packet: 0.001576 seconds
    Frame Number: 245
    Packet Length: 350 bytes
    Capture Length: 350 bytes
Ethernet II
    Destination: 00:e0:16:7f:58:83 (00:e0:16:7f:58:83)
    Source: 00:c0:4f:28:c1:d3 (00:c0:4f:28:c1:d3)
    Type: IP (0x0800)
Internet Protocol
    Version: 4
    Header length: 20 bytes
    Differentiated Services Field: 0x00 (DSCP 0x00:
Default)
        0000 00.. = Differentiated Services Codepoint:
Default (0x00)
        .... ..00 = Currently Unused: 0
    Total Length: 336
    Identification: 0x504f
    Flags: 0x04
```

```
           .1.. = Don't fragment: Set
           ..0. = More fragments: Not set
       Fragment offset: 0
       Time to live: 128
       Protocol: TCP (0x06)
       Header checksum: 0xf870 (correct)
       Source: 10.170.129.29 (10.170.129.29)
       Destination: 192.168.100.120 (192.168.100.120)
   Transmission Control Protocol, Src Port: 3288 (3288),
   Dst Port: 1068 (1068), Seq: 41799503, Ack: 2210126298
       Source port: 3288 (3288)
       Destination port: 1068 (1068)
       Sequence number: 41799503
       Acknowledgement number: 2210126298
       Header length: 32 bytes
       Flags: 0x0018 (PSH, ACK)
           ..0. .... = Urgent: Not set
           ...1 .... = Acknowledgment: Set
           .... 1... = Push: Set
           .... .0.. = Reset: Not set
           .... ..0. = Syn: Not set
           .... ...0 = Fin: Not set
       Window size: 15952
       Checksum: 0x5110
       Options: (12 bytes)
           NOP
           NOP
           Time stamp: tsval 350434, tsecr 1014
   Common Open Policy Service
       Version: 1, Flags: None
           0001 .... = Version: 1
           .... 0000 = Flags: None (0x00)
       Op Code: Decision (DEC) (2)
       Client Type: 2
       Message Length: 284
       Object Type:  Handle Object (Handle)
           Object Length: 8
           C-Num:  Handle Object (Handle) (1)
           C-Type: 1
           Object contents: 4 bytes
       Object Type:  Context Object (Context)
           Object Length: 8
           C-Num:  Context Object (Context) (2)
           C-Type: 1
           Object contents: 4 bytes
       Object Type:  Decision Object (Decision)
           Object Length: 8
```

3.5.1.1.1 *Context Object*

When C-Num = 2 and C-Type = 1, the contents in the object field will include "Context object". It specifies the type of event or events triggered by this query and is generally used with request messages. Multiple flags can be set for the same request; currently two types of flags are defined for context object, namely "R-Type" and "M-Type" (Fig. 3.49).

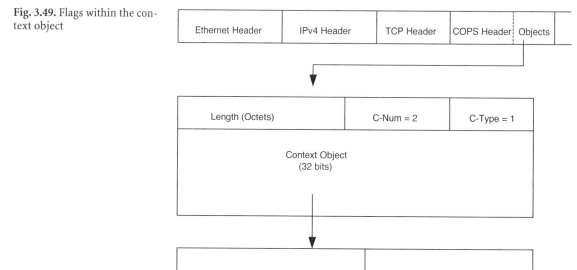

Fig. 3.49. Flags within the context object

The R-Type (Request- Type) flag includes the following:

0x01 = Incoming-Message/Admission control request
0x02 = Resource-Allocation request
0x04 = Outgoing-Message request
0x08 = Configuration request

The M-Type (Message-Type) includes 16-bit values of protocol message types.

3.5.1.1.2 In Interface (IN-Int) Object

The IN-Int is used to identify the interface on which the incoming request applies and the IP address of the message originator.

If C-Num = 3 and C-Type = 1 in the COPS object format, it identifies that the object followed is "In Interface Object". Generally, for flows or messages originated from the PEP's local host, the loopback address and ifindex are used (Fig. 3.50).

For the IPv4 network, the IPv4 address identifies the originating interface of the message whereas ifindex is typically relative to the flow of the underlying protocol messages. The ifindex is the interface where the message is received.

For the IPv6 network, C-Type would be 2 and the object would carry the IPv6 address format and ifindex fields (Fig. 3.51).

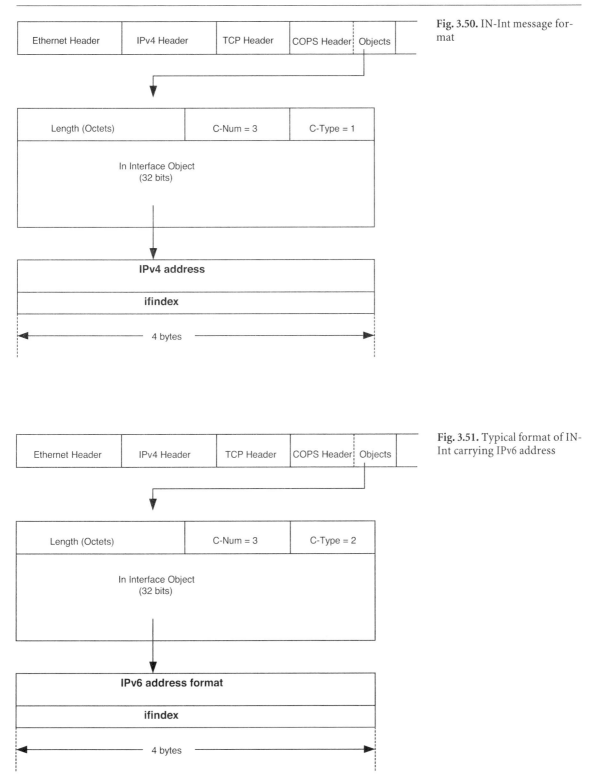

Fig. 3.50. IN-Int message format

Fig. 3.51. Typical format of IN-Int carrying IPv6 address

Fig. 3.52. A example of OUT-Int object for IPv4 address

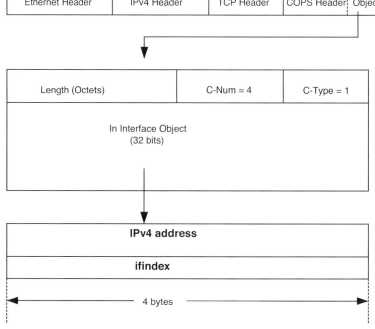

Fig. 3.52. A example of OUT-Int object for IPv4 address

3.5.1.1.3 Out Interface (OUT-Int) Object

The OUT-Int is used to identify the outgoing interface for which a specific request applies. It also includes the forwarding address and has the same format as IN-Int object. C-Num = 4 and C-Type = 1 identify the OUT-Int for IPv4 (Fig. 3.52) whereas C-Type = 2 identifies IPv6.

3.5.1.1.4 Reason Object

The reason object is used to specify the basis for which a request state has been deleted. This object appears in the delete request (DRQ) message. C-Num = 5 and C-Type = 1 identify the object will be "Reason Object".

The object field should include a 2-byte "Reason Code" and a 2-byte "Reason Subcode" (Fig. 3.53). The values of the reason code are as follows:

1 = Unspecified
2 = Management
3 = Preempted
4 = Tear
5 = Timeout
6 = Route change
7 = Insufficient resources
8 = PDP's directive
9 = Unsupported decision
10 = Synchronize handle unknown
11 = Transient handle

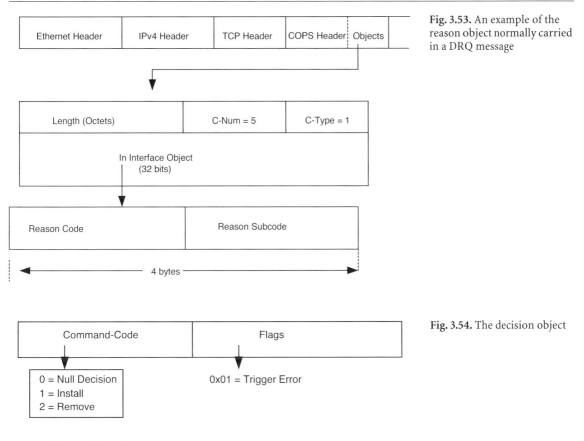

Fig. 3.53. An example of the reason object normally carried in a DRQ message

Fig. 3.54. The decision object

12 = Malformed decision

13 = Unknown COPS object from PDP: the subcode contains unknown object's C-Num and C-Type.

The reason subcode is reserved client-specific information.

3.5.1.1.5 Decision Object

The decision is made by the PDP for the PEP and generally appears in replies. C-Num = 6 and C-Type = 1 identify the object followed is the decision object (Fig. 3.54). The object includes a mandatory "Decision Flags" field.

For the decision object when C-Type = 2, the object carries additional stateless data that can be applied by the PEP locally. With C-Type = 3, the decision object carries replacement data which is used to replace existing data in a signaled message. For C-Type = 4, the decision object carries a client-specific decision data object. This is a variable length object and is an optional object decision message. For C-Type = 5, the object carries "Named Decision Data" in response to configuration requests.

3.5.1.1.6 LDP Object

The LDP or LPDP object is the consequence of the decision made by the PEP's local policy decision point (LPDP or sometimes known as LDP). C-

Fig. 3.55. The error object

Num =7 and C-Type = same value as in the decision object identify the object followed will be the LPDP or LDP object.

3.5.1.1.7 Error Object
This object identifies a particular error for the COPS protocol. The object is divided into two fields: error code and error subcode. C-Num = 8 and C-Type = 1 indicate the object contents are the error object (Fig. 3.55).

The error code field includes the following values:

1 = Bad handle
2 = Invalid handle reference
3 = Malformed message
4 = Unable to process
5 = Mandatory client-specific information missing
6 = Unsupported client type
7 = Mandatory COPS object missing
8 = Client failure
9 = Communication failure
10 = Unspecified
11 = Shutting down
12 = Redirect to preferred server
13 = Unknown COPS object
14 = Authentication failure
15 = Authentication required

3.5.1.1.8 Client-specific Information (ClientSI) Object
C-Num = 9 indicates that the object followed is CientSI. Various ClientSI is used for requests, reports and opens. The object includes client-type specific information. When C-Type = 1, the object is considered signaled ClientSI. This is a variable length field and all attributes in the object pertain to signaling protocol or internal state information. This information may be contained within one or more signaled ClientSI.

C-Type = 2 indicates the variable length field for the object content, named ClientSI. The object includes named configuration information useful for relaying certain information about the PEP, a request or configured state to the PDP.

3.5.1.1.9 Keep-Alive Timer Object
C-Num = 10 and C-Type = 1 indicate the object followed is the keep-alive timer. The times are encoded within 2-byte integer values and the units of measurement are seconds.

Fig. 3.56. The keep-alive timer object

This timer object (Fig. 3.56) carries information in terms of maximum allowed interval over which a COPS message must be sent or received. The range is 1 to 65,535 seconds.

3.5.1.1.10 PEP Identification Object (PEPID)
The PEPID is used to identify the PEP client to the PDP. It is conveyed in "Client-Open" messages. C-Num = 11 and C-Type = 1 indicate that the object followed is the PEPID. It can be either the IP address or the DNS name.

3.5.1.1.11 Report-Type Object
C-Num = 12 and C-Type = 1 indicate the object is "Report-Type", which is used to indicate the type of request on the request state associated with a handle.

Report-Type = 1 means that the decision was successful at the PEP, whereas a value of 2 means a failure or could not complete the decision. Report-Type = 3 means accounting update for a installed state (Fig. 3.57).

3.5.1.1.12 PDP Redirect Address (PDPRedirAddr) Object
C-Num = 13 and C-Type = 1 indicate the object is PDPRedirAddr (Fig. 3.58). Once a PDP closes the PEP session with a particular client type, it may optionally redirect the PEP to a specified server address (IPv4) and TCP port number. C-Type would be 2 if the object carries the IPv6 address.

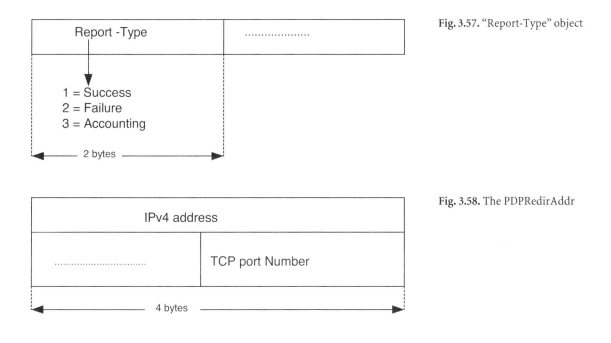

Fig. 3.57. "Report-Type" object

Fig. 3.58. The PDPRedirAddr

3.5.1.1.13 Last PDP Address (LastPDPAddr)

C-Num = 14 indicates the object is LastPDPAddr. When C-Type = 1, the object carries the IPv4 address, otherwise when C-Type = 2 it carries the IPv6 address. This object is used in Client-Open messages.

When the PEP sends the Client-Open message to the PDP for a particular client type, it indicates the last PDP address it successfully opened a session. If no PDP was used during the last reboot, the LastPDPAddr is not included in the Client-Open message.

3.5.1.1.14 Accounting Timer (AcctTimer) Object

C-Num = 15 and C-Type = 1 indicate the object followed is AcctTimer and the value of the accounting timer is encoded within 2 bytes.

The use of this object is optional and it is used by the PDP to describe to the PEP an acceptable interval for accounting updates (Fig. 3.59). The object is carried via the Report message.

3.5.1.1.15 Message Integrity Object (Integrity)

C-Num = 16 and C-Type = 1 indicate that the object followed will be "Integrity".

The object includes a sequence number and a message digest useful for authentication and integrity validation of the COPS message (Fig. 3.60).

Fig. 3.59. The AcctTimer object

Fig. 3.60. The message integrity object

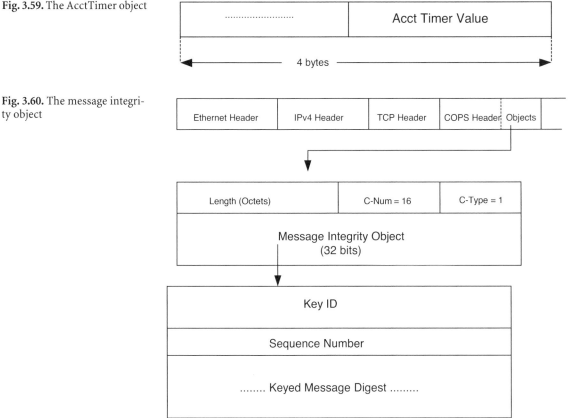

The object includes a 32-bit key ID that identifies a specific key shared between a particular PEP and its PDP and the cryptographic algorithm to be used.

3.5.2 COPS Operation

The COPS protocol is used over the TCP connection between a PEP and a PDP (Fig. 3.61). The COPS implementation at the PDP server must listen on a well-known TCP port number (Port = 3288).

The PEP is implemented in a LAN switch or router and is responsible for inititiating TCP connection with the PDP. Usually the PDP is implemented in the network management server station (e.g., Nortel's Optivity server). In the PEP's COPS configuration web GUI or console, the IP address of the PDP is specified and thus the PEP knows the PDP to initiate a TCP connection. A PEP can support multiple client types, for example a switch or router that supports RSVP and IP DiffServ implementation. Let's imagine a network that includes a stub network on one end, a transit network and a stub network on the other end. The stub network is usually used RSVP as being IntServ at the edge. The transit network on the other hand is a DiffServ network. Therefore, a device known as a border router can sit between IntServ and DiffServ, and should be able to support RSVP and IP DiffServ at the same time. A device such as this should be considered to include multiple client types, that is Client-Type = 1 (RSVP) and Client-Type = 2 (DiffServ) (Fig. 3.62).

The PDP has the capability to accept or reject multiple client types. It is also possible that the PEP has an open connection with multiple PDPs for multiple client types.

If a PDP fails and/or is rebooted, the PEP should initiate a connection with the backup PDP and in that case inform the backup PDP about the previous state in which it was unable to contact the primary PDP.

Once a TCP connection is lost, the PDP can clean up the outstanding request state with the PEP. Once the PEP detects a connection timeout, it sends a Client-Close message for each client type with an object containing communication failure "Error-Code".

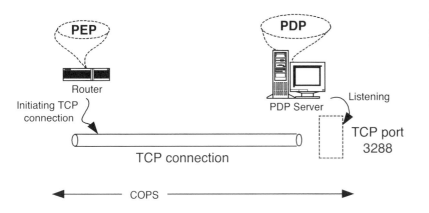

Fig. 3.61. The COPS protocol operation and communication between a PEP and a PDP

Fig. 3.62. Multiple client types can be used in a device at the IntServ/DiffServ border

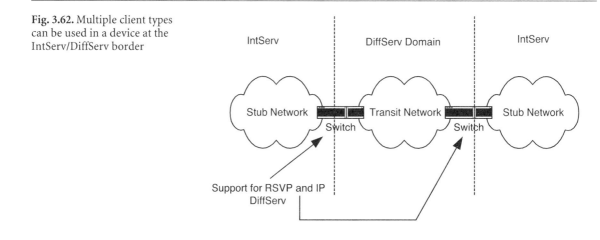

3.5.3 COPS Message Exchange

We identified earlier in the common header discussion that up to 10 "Op Codes" can be carried by COPS messages, and a number of COPS messages can be subdivided based on the Op Code. The REQ or request message is identified by the Op Code value of 1. This message is sent from the PEP to PDP to request a state client handle. The REQ is also used to request a new state whenever a local state is changed in the PEP. The REQ message includes the following fields:

- Common header
- Client handle
- Context
- IN-Int
- Out-Int
- ClientSI
- LPDP decision
- Integrity.

The DEC or decision message is the response of REQ and is sent from the PDP to the PEP. The Op Code value 2 in the common header identifies that the message is a DEC. The DEC message includes the following fields:

- Common header
- Client handle
- Decision | Error
- Integrity
- Decision.

In the following DEC message decode, please note that Client-Type = 2 indicates a COPS-PR message.

```
Frame 225 (370 on wire, 370 captured)
    Arrival Time: Oct 11, 2000 21:21:03.8704
    Time delta from previous packet: 8.197346 seconds
    Frame Number: 225
    Packet Length: 370 bytes
    Capture Length: 370 bytes
Ethernet II
    Destination: 00:e0:16:7f:58:83 (00:e0:16:7f:58:83)
    Source: 00:c0:4f:28:c1:d3 (00:c0:4f:28:c1:d3)
    Type: IP (0x0800)
Internet Protocol
    Version: 4
    Header length: 20 bytes
    Differentiated Services Field: 0x00 (DSCP 0x00:
Default)
        0000 00.. = Differentiated Services Codepoint:
Default (0x00)
        .... ..00 = Currently Unused: 0
    Total Length: 356
    Identification: 0x5023
    Flags: 0x04
        .1.. = Don't fragment: Set
        ..0. = More fragments: Not set
    Fragment offset: 0
    Time to live: 128
    Protocol: TCP (0x06)
    Header checksum: 0xf888 (correct)
    Source: 10.170.129.29 (10.170.129.29)
    Destination: 192.168.100.120 (192.168.100.120)
Transmission Control Protocol, Src Port: 3288 (3288),
Dst Port: 1068 (1068), Seq: 41798223, Ack: 2210126298
    Source port: 3288 (3288)
    Destination port: 1068 (1068)
    Sequence number: 41798223
    Acknowledgement number: 2210126298
    Header length: 32 bytes
    Flags: 0x0018 (PSH, ACK)
        ..0. .... = Urgent: Not set
        ...1 .... = Acknowledgment: Set
        .... 1... = Push: Set
        .... .0.. = Reset: Not set
        .... ..0. = Syn: Not set
        .... ...0 = Fin: Not set
    Window size: 15952
    Checksum: 0xfc63
    Options: (12 bytes)
        NOP
        NOP
        Time stamp: tsval 350433, tsecr 1014
Common Open Policy Service
    Version: 1, Flags: None
        0001 .... = Version: 1
        .... 0000 = Flags: None (0x00)
    Op Code: Decision (DEC) (2)
    Client Type: 2
    Message Length: 304
    Object Type:  Handle Object (Handle)
```

```
            Object Length: 8
            C-Num:  Handle Object (Handle) (1)
            C-Type: 1
            Object contents: 4 bytes
        Object Type:  Context Object (Context)
            Object Length: 8
            C-Num:  Context Object (Context) (2)
            C-Type: 1
            Object contents: 4 bytes
        Object Type:  Decision Object (Decision)
            Object Length: 272
            C-Num:  Decision Object (Decision) (6)
            C-Type: 5
            Object contents: 268 bytes
```

The report state (RPT) is used by the PEP to communicate its success or failure to the PDP. In the message it may carry PDP's decision, or accounting updates. Report-Type specifies the kind of report and ClientSI carry additional information per client type. The message includes the following fields:

- Common header
- Client handle
- Report-Type
- ClientSI
- Integrity.

Consider the following decode to understand the RPT message further.

```
Frame 268 (82 on wire, 82 captured)
    Arrival Time: Oct 11, 2000 21:21:10.8002
    Time delta from previous packet: 2.207939 seconds
    Frame Number: 268
    Packet Length: 82 bytes
    Capture Length: 82 bytes
Ethernet II
    Destination: 00:c0:4f:28:c1:d3 (00:c0:4f:28:c1:d3)
    Source: 00:e0:16:7f:58:83 (00:e0:16:7f:58:83)
    Type: 802.1Q Virtual LAN (0x8100)
802.1q Virtual LAN
    000. .... .... .... = Priority: 0
    ...0 .... .... .... = CFI: 0
    .... 0000 0000 0011 = ID: 3
    Type: IP (0x0800)
Internet Protocol
    Version: 4
    Header length: 20 bytes
    Differentiated Services Field: 0x00 (DSCP 0x00:
Default)
        0000 00.. = Differentiated Services Codepoint:
Default (0x00)
        .... ..00 = Currently Unused: 0
    Total Length: 64
    Identification: 0x403e
    Flags: 0x00
        .0.. = Don't fragment: Not set
        ..0. = More fragments: Not set
```

```
      Fragment offset: 0
      Time to live: 63
      Protocol: TCP (0x06)
      Header checksum: 0x8a92 (correct)
      Source: 192.168.100.120 (192.168.100.120)
      Destination: 10.170.129.29 (10.170.129.29)
Transmission Control Protocol, Src Port: 1068 (1068),
Dst Port: 3288 (3288), Seq: 2210126346, Ack: 41799787
      Source port: 1068 (1068)
      Destination port: 3288 (3288)
      Sequence number: 2210126346
      Acknowledgement number: 41799787
      Header length: 20 bytes
      Flags: 0x0018 (PSH, ACK)
            ..0. .... = Urgent: Not set
            ...1 .... = Acknowledgment: Set
            .... 1... = Push: Set
            .... .0.. = Reset: Not set
            .... ..0. = Syn: Not set
            .... ...0 = Fin: Not set
      Window size: 8192
      Checksum: 0x2ee7
Common Open Policy Service
      Version: 1, Flags: Solicited Message Flag Bit
            0001 .... = Version: 1
            .... 0001 = Flags: Solicited Message Flag Bit
(0x01)
      Op Code: Report State (RPT) (3)
      Client Type: 2
      Message Length: 24
      Object Type:  Handle Object (Handle)
            Object Length: 8
            C-Num:  Handle Object (Handle) (1)
            C-Type: 1
            Object contents: 4 bytes
      Object Type:  Report-Type Object (Report-Type)
            Object Length: 8
            C-Num:  Report-Type Object (Report-Type) (12)
            C-Type: 1
            Object contents: 4 bytes
```

The DRQ or delete request state is sent from the PEP to PDP imparting that the state identified in the earlier client handle is no longer available or valid. The PDP will use this message to do appropriate housekeeping actions. The reason object identifies the reason of the removal. The message includes the following fields:

• Common header
• Client handle
• Reason
• Integrity.

The following decode may be used to understand the DRQ message, but remember that the frame is malformed. It is not a general behavior of the DRQ message but a consequence of a bug in the product.

```
Frame 244 (270 on wire, 270 captured)
    Arrival Time: Oct 11, 2000 21:21:03.8975
    Time delta from previous packet: 0.000486 seconds
    Frame Number: 244
    Packet Length: 270 bytes
    Capture Length: 270 bytes
Ethernet II
    Destination: 00:e0:16:7f:58:83 (00:e0:16:7f:58:83)
    Source: 00:c0:4f:28:c1:d3 (00:c0:4f:28:c1:d3)
    Type: IP (0x0800)
Internet Protocol
    Version: 4
    Header length: 20 bytes
    Differentiated Services Field: 0x00 (DSCP 0x00:
Default)
        0000 00.. = Differentiated Services Codepoint:
Default (0x00)
        .... ..00 = Currently Unused: 0
    Total Length: 256
    Identification: 0x5049
    Flags: 0x04
        .1.. = Don't fragment: Set
        ..0. = More fragments: Not set
    Fragment offset: 0
    Time to live: 128
    Protocol: TCP (0x06)
    Header checksum: 0xf904 (correct)
    Source: 10.170.129.29 (10.170.129.29)
    Destination: 192.168.100.58 (192.168.100.58)
Transmission Control Protocol, Src Port: 3288 (3288),
Dst Port: 1081 (1081), Seq: 41981094, Ack: 507736182
    Source port: 3288 (3288)
    Destination port: 1081 (1081)
    Sequence number: 41981094
    Acknowledgement number: 507736182
    Header length: 32 bytes
    Flags: 0x0018 (PSH, ACK)
        ..0. .... = Urgent: Not set
        ...1 .... = Acknowledgment: Set
        .... 1... = Push: Set
        .... .0.. = Reset: Not set
        .... ..0. = Syn: Not set
        .... ...0 = Fin: Not set
    Window size: 16376
    Checksum: 0x6ac6
    Options: (12 bytes)
        NOP
        NOP
        Time stamp: tsval 350434, tsecr 21004
Common Open Policy Service
    Version: 0, Flags: Solicited Message Flag Bit
        0000 .... = Version: 0
        .... 0001 = Flags: Solicited Message Flag Bit
(0x01)
    Op Code: Delete Request State (DRQ) (4)
    Client Type: 301
```

```
    Message Length: 67240194
    Object Type: Unknown
        Object Length: 257
        C-Num: Unknown (22)
        C-Type: 0
        Object contents: 253 bytes
[Malformed Frame: COPS]
```

The SRQ or synchronization state request is a query message to indicate that the PDP wishes the client to resend its state. The message includes the following fields:

- Common header
- Client handle
- Integrity.

Client-Open or OPN is sent from the PEP to PDP to specify the client types that the PEP can support. The message includes the following fields:

- Common header
- PEPID
- ClientSI
- LastPDPAddr
- Integrity.

The CAT or Client-Accept message is sent from the PDP to PEP in order to positively respond to an OPN message. The CAT includes the following fields:

- Common header
- Keep-Alive timer
- Accounting timer
- Integrity.

Consider the following decode to understand the CAT message further.

```
Frame 287 (118 on wire, 118 captured)
    Arrival Time: Oct 11, 2000 21:21:24.5123
    Time delta from previous packet: 0.001971 seconds
    Frame Number: 287
    Packet Length: 118 bytes
    Capture Length: 118 bytes
Ethernet II
    Destination: 00:c0:4f:28:c1:d3 (00:c0:4f:28:c1:d3)
    Source: 00:80:2d:ca:23:e1 (00:80:2d:ca:23:e1)
    Type: 802.1Q Virtual LAN (0x8100)
802.1q Virtual LAN
    000. .... .... .... = Priority: 0
    ...0 .... .... .... = CFI: 0
    .... 0000 0000 0011 = ID: 3
    Type: IP (0x0800)
Internet Protocol
    Version: 4
    Header length: 20 bytes
```

```
                   Differentiated Services Field: 0x00 (DSCP 0x00:
            Default)
                       0000 00.. = Differentiated Services Codepoint:
            Default (0x00)
                       .... ..00 = Currently Unused: 0
                   Total Length: 100
                   Identification: 0xeb40
                   Flags: 0x00
                       .0.. = Don't fragment: Not set
                       ..0. = More fragments: Not set
                   Fragment offset: 0
                   Time to live: 30
                   Protocol: TCP (0x06)
                   Header checksum: 0x99c6 (correct)
                   Source: 10.170.129.28 (10.170.129.28)
                   Destination: 10.170.129.29 (10.170.129.29)
            Transmission Control Protocol, Src Port: 21777 (21777),
            Dst Port: 3288 (3288), Seq: 3433124952, Ack: 2255038688
                   Source port: 21777 (21777)
                   Destination port: 3288 (3288)
                   Sequence number: 3433124952
                   Acknowledgement number: 2255038688
                   Header length: 32 bytes
                   Flags: 0x0018 (PSH, ACK)
                       ..0. .... = Urgent: Not set
                       ...1 .... = Acknowledgment: Set
                       .... 1... = Push: Set
                       .... .0.. = Reset: Not set
                       .... ..0. = Syn: Not set
                       .... ...0 = Fin: Not set
                   Window size: 4096
                   Checksum: 0x69c7
                   Options: (12 bytes)
                       NOP
                       NOP
                       Time stamp: tsval 3433124959, tsecr 0
            Common Open Policy Service
                   Version: 1, Flags: None
                       0001 .... = Version: 1
                       .... 0000 = Flags: None (0x00)
                   Op Code: Client-Accept (CAT) (7)
                   Client Type: 2
                   Message Length: 48
                   Object Type:  Report-Type Object (Report-Type)
                       Object Length: 17
                       C-Num:  Report-Type Object (Report-Type) (12)
                       C-Type: 1
                       Object contents: 13 bytes
                   Object Type:  PEP Identification Object (PEPID)
                       Object Length: 8
                       C-Num:  PEP Identification Object (PEPID)(11)
                       C-Type: 1
                       Object contents: 4 bytes
                   Object Type: Keep-Alive Timer Object (KATimer)
                       Object Length: 12
                       C-Num: Keep-Alive Timer Object (KATimer) (10)
                       C-Type: 3
                       Object contents: 8 bytes
```

The CC or Client-Close message can be issued either by the PEP or PDP to notify the other about the inability to support a particular client type which may been supported earlier. The message includes the following fields:

- Common header
- Error
- PDPRedirAddr
- Integrity.

The error object describes the reason for close.

The KA or Keep-Alive message must be sent by the PEP within the period identified by the minimum of all KA timer values. This is conveyed in the received CAT messages for the connection. The KA includes the following fields:

- Common header
- Integrity.

Consider the following message decode for further details.

```
Frame 278 (66 on wire, 66 captured)
    Arrival Time: Oct 11, 2000 21:21:15.1033
    Time delta from previous packet: 0.001322 seconds
    Frame Number: 278
    Packet Length: 66 bytes
    Capture Length: 66 bytes
Ethernet II
    Destination: 00:c0:4f:28:c1:d3 (00:c0:4f:28:c1:d3)
    Source: 00:e0:16:7f:58:83 (00:e0:16:7f:58:83)
    Type: 802.1Q Virtual LAN (0x8100)
802.1q Virtual LAN
    000. .... .... .... = Priority: 0
    ...0 .... .... .... = CFI: 0
    .... 0000 0000 0011 = ID: 3
    Type: IP (0x0800)
Internet Protocol
    Version: 4
    Header length: 20 bytes
    Differentiated Services Field: 0x00 (DSCP 0x00:
Default)
        0000 00.. = Differentiated Services Codepoint:
Default (0x00)
        .... ..00 = Currently Unused: 0
    Total Length: 48
    Identification: 0x4048
    Flags: 0x00
        .0.. = Don't fragment: Not set
        ..0. = More fragments: Not set
    Fragment offset: 0
    Time to live: 63
    Protocol: TCP (0x06)
    Header checksum: 0x8a98 (correct)
    Source: 192.168.100.120 (192.168.100.120)
    Destination: 10.170.129.29 (10.170.129.29)
Transmission Control Protocol, Src Port: 1068 (1068),
Dst Port: 3288 (3288), Seq: 2210126466, Ack: 41799787
```

```
Source port: 1068 (1068)
Destination port: 3288 (3288)
Sequence number: 2210126466
Acknowledgement number: 41799787
Header length: 20 bytes
Flags: 0x0018 (PSH, ACK)
    ..0. .... = Urgent: Not set
    ...1 .... = Acknowledgment: Set
    .... 1... = Push: Set
    .... .0.. = Reset: Not set
    .... ..0. = Syn: Not set
    .... ...0 = Fin: Not set
Window size: 8192
Checksum: 0x8ca0
Common Open Policy Service
    Version: 1, Flags: None
        0001 .... = Version: 1
        .... 0000 = Flags: None (0x00)
    Op Code: Keep-Alive (KA) (9)
    Client Type: 0
    Message Length: 8
```

The SSC or Synchronization State Complete is transmitted by the PEP to the PDP after the PDP sends an SSQ and the PEP has finished the synchronization. The message includes the following fields:

- Common header
- Client handle
- Integrity.

3.5.4 COPS-PR

The work on COPS-PR (COPS usage for Policy Provisioning) is still an IETF draft. While COPS-RSVP is a one-to-one correlation between PEP events and the PDP decision, the COPS-PR model does not makes any assumption as such. In other words, COPS-PR uses $N{:}M$ correlation where provisioning is performed in bulk (i.e., the entire router QoS configuration) or in portions. Unlike COPS-OutSource, the COPS-PR provisioning (Fig. 3.63) is done by the PDP in a somewhat flexible timing and not in real time.

At first, if the COPS-PR model is in use, the PEP describes itself through its REQ message and the configurable parameters rather than an operational event to the PDP. If a change occurs, an update REQ is sent. Therefore, requests are issued infrequently. Generally, the PDP's decision is not an exact mapping of the PEP's REQ; the DEC may be issued also when the PDP responds to external events or policy/SLA updates.

Let's understand the interaction between the PEP and PDP (Fig. 3.64) with a real-world example. For this discussion, consider you have Nortel's BPS 2000 switch as the packet classifier and sitting at the edge of your DiffServ domain.

Being on the edge BPS 2000 allows customers to specifically configure packet classification information through a Web GUI to Nortel's BPS. On the

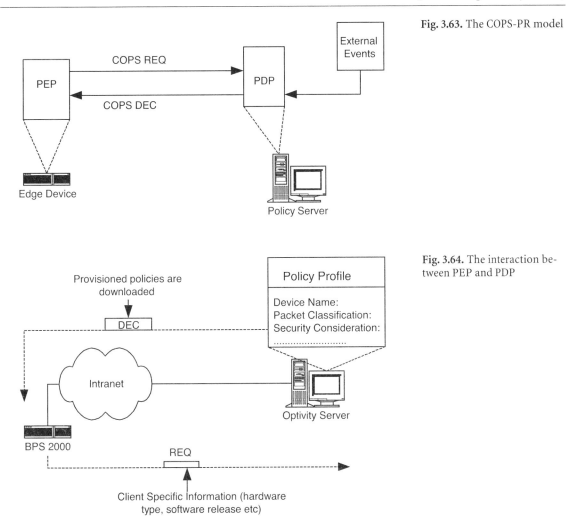

Fig. 3.63. The COPS-PR model

Fig. 3.64. The interaction between PEP and PDP

intranet an optivity server is installed with support for the PDP. Now customers may choose the optivity server to provide packet classification information to the BPS instead of doing it through BPS's own Web user interface. One of the advantages of downloading such information is that if the BPS somehow fails or resets to default, the entry QoS, the security configuration can be downloaded at any time after the reboot. Another advantage is that if an MDA (Media Adaptor) fails and a new MDA is inserted, the BPS will inform the optivity server of such a change and download appropriate policies for that interface. Like those described here, numerous other advantages are available through the implementation of COPS. A network that is based on COPS and defined policies is normally known as PEN.

The data carried by COPS-PR can be considered as a set of policy rules and, therefore, a named data structure is required. COPS uses PIB (Policy Information Based) as the named data structure to identify the type and pur-

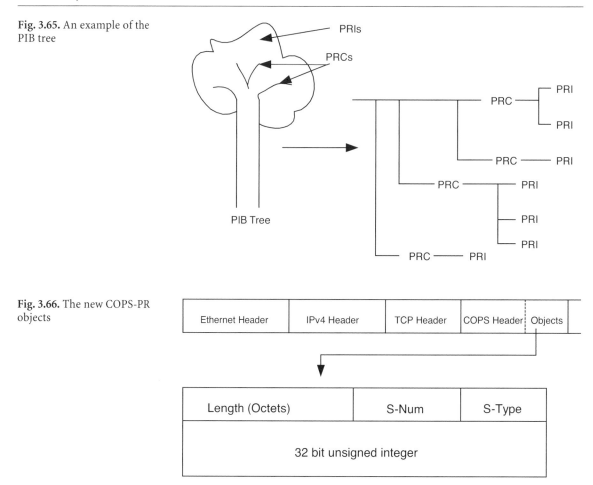

Fig. 3.65. An example of the PIB tree

Fig. 3.66. The new COPS-PR objects

poses of unsolicited policy information that is downloaded from the PDP to the PEP for provisioning policy.

One can describe as the conceptual tree namespace where the branches represent rules or policy rule classes (PRCs) and the leaves are various instantiations of policy rule instances (PRIs) (Fig. 3.65).

The instances of PRIs are each identified by a PRID (Policy Rule Identifier). The PRID is a name carried in a named ClientSI or named decision data object and identifies a particular instance of a rule.

The COPS-PR clients encapsulate a number of new objects within the existing named ClientSI object and named decision data object. A binding is a combination of PRI and PRID encoded within the context of the provisioning PIB. COPS-PR uses these bindings to classify data.

The newly defined object format for COPS-PR is as depicted in Fig. 3.66.

S-Num and S-Type are similar to C-Num and C-Type used in the regular COPS objects. The difference is that S-Num and S-Type are only used for COPS-PR. When S-Num = 1 and S-Type = 1 and length = variable, the object is used to carry the PRID (Fig. 3.67) of a PRI.

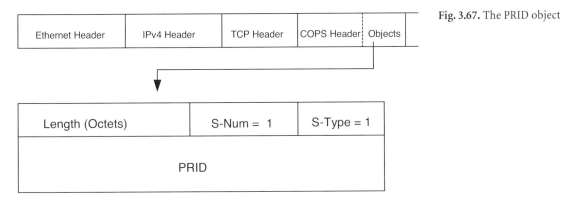

Fig. 3.67. The PRID object

3.5.5 COPS-RSVP

COPS-RSVP, otherwise known as COPS-OutSource, is defined in two RFCs, namely RFC 2749 and RFC 2750. While COPS-PR is COPS Client-Type = 2, COPS-RSVP is COPS Client-Type = 1.

COPS-RSVP suggests a new object known as POLICY_DATA; RSVP messages carry this object which includes policy information (Fig. 3.68). RFC 2205 defines an object format for RSVP which specifies that if Class-Num = 14 then the followed object will be POLICY_DATA. Although RFC 2205 left section A.13 for further study, RFC 2750 extends that object and defines it further.

Besides, Class-Num = 14 and C-Type = 1 in RSVP object format indicate the followed object is POLICY-DATA. The POLICY_DATA object includes the following:

- Data offset, a 16-bit field.
- Reserved, a 16-bit field always set to 0.
- Option list, a variable length field that includes a list of options.
- Policy element list, a variable length field for which the contents of policy elements are opaque to RSVP.

In COPS-RSVP, the policy control is performed per RSVP flow basis that is defined by TC reservation. To understand the details about RSVP please read the RSVP section of this chapter.

A PDP may consider both the Resv message and its associated state when making a policy decision.

Since RSVP flow includes one path state and one RSVP state, state association is straightforward in the common unicast case. It may be complicated in multicast case, however, as the match is many-to-many. Generally, the COPS protocol assumes that the PDP is RSVP knowledgeable and capable of determining these associations based on the contents of the client REQ message and ClientSI object.

Figure 3.69 illustrates how COPS controls a unicast RSVP flow.

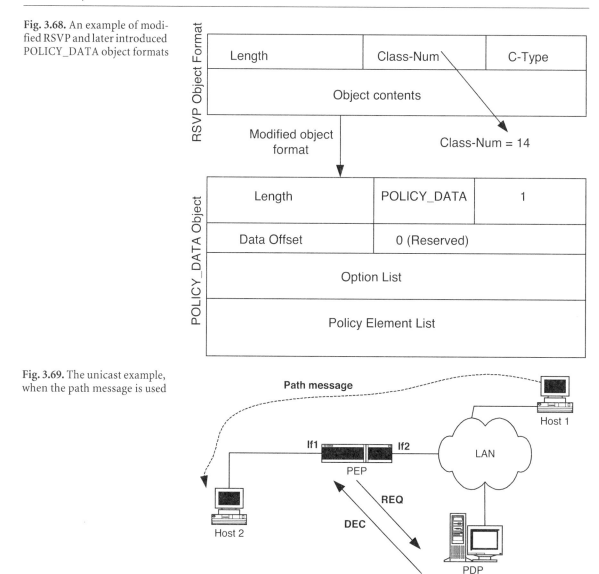

Fig. 3.68. An example of modified RSVP and later introduced POLICY_DATA object formats

Fig. 3.69. The unicast example, when the path message is used

In this figure we have two hosts negotiating RSVP flow. Host 1 sends the path message to Host 2. While this happens the PEP sends an REQ message to the PDP. The contents of the REQ are as follows:

- Handle A
- Context: in & out, path
- IN-Interface if2
- OUT-Interface if1
- ClientSI.

The PDP responds to the PEP with a DEC message that includes the following:

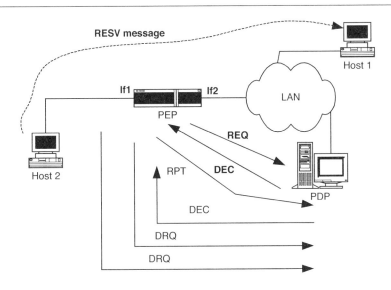

Fig. 3.70. The unicast example with the RESV message

- Handle A
- Context: in & out, path
- Decision: command, install.

Similarly when the RESV message arrives from Host 2 (Fig. 3.70), the PEP sends an REQ to the PDP with the following contents:

- Handle B
- Context: in & allocation & out, RESV
- IN-Interface if1
- OUT-Interface if 2
- ClientSI.

The PDP responds with a DEC that includes the following fields:

- Handle B
- Context: in, RESV
- Decision: command, install
- Context: allocation, RESV
- Decision: command, Install
- Decision: Stateless, Priority = 7
- Context<: out, RESV
- Decision: command, Install
- Decision: replacement, POLICY_DATA1.

The PEP then sends an RPT with the following:

- Handle B
- Report Type: commit.

Now as time passes, the PDP changes its decision with the DEC message that includes the following:

- Handle B
- Context: allocation, RESV
- Decision: command, Install
- Decision: Stateless, Priority = 3.

Since the priority is too low, the PEP preempts the flow and sends a DRQ message to the PDP with the following contents:

- Handle B
- Reason Code: Preempted.

Now as time passes, Host 1 ceases to send the path message; the PEP sends DRQ as a result with the following fields:

- Handle A
- Reason: Timeout.

3.6 PEN

In general terms policy means a rule – a rule that defines the action(s) to occur when specific condition(s) exist. Policies are simple rules, such as "If <condition(s)> then <grant access to resources>." The sample conditions can be time of day, user or group, application, SA or DA and so on. Since policies represent business goals and objectives, it is important that these goals and objectives and their realization in the network are properly defined. An example of this could be SLA (Service Level Agreements) and SLOs (Service Level Objectives). While an SLA can be written in high-level business terminology, an SLO can be more specific metrics to support SLA.

PEN is able to define and control operations according to business need using a centralized policy system. It can, for example, authenticate traffic that requests QoS and identify traffic per packet basis.

To successfully deploy PEN in line with business needs, organizations need an intelligent network infrastructure, and network systems management. Thus fortified, organizations can bind business policies to the allocation of network resources. Network administrators must provision these network resources through policies if they are to achieve an application-optimized network.

Policy management is an emerging solution set that enables business-critical applications to perform at specific levels for specific users. It implements a set of rules or policies that further an organization's business objectives (Fig. 3.71) by dictating how users, applications and organizations can access and use network resources.

The PEN strategy enables both enterprises and service providers to meet policy management's demands. It does so by offering voice and data solutions that are reliable, differentiated, scalable and secure. This section focuses on enterprise solutions but does make reference to evolving service provider solutions.

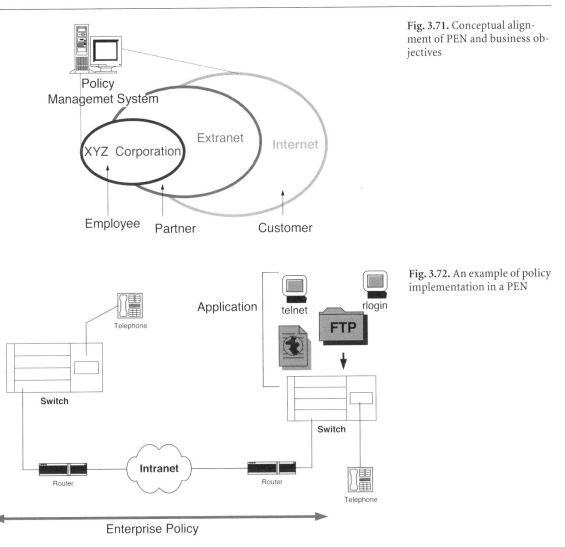

Fig. 3.71. Conceptual alignment of PEN and business objectives

Fig. 3.72. An example of policy implementation in a PEN

Policy management is one of the key aspects of a unified IP network strategy. PEN enables network operation through application of simple and consistent guidelines thus reducing the effort to manage a network and ability to define/deliver a required level of service.

As discussed earlier, the core protocol of PEN is COPS and COPS objects are used to carry defined rules to various network devices. The coordination would be done from the policy server. The complete system of policy deployment is termed the policy management system (Fig. 3.72).

The policy management enables the enforcement of a set of rules or policies that dictate access rights and use of resources based on the established profile of the application, user and group, to meet an established business objective. A comprehensive policy management solution will provide three elements: provisioning, enforcement, and verification of the policies.

Fig. 3.73. PEN service model

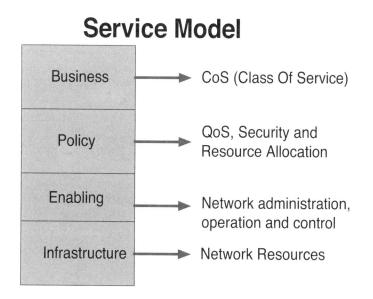

Fig. 3.73. PEN service model

Figure 3.73 shows how PEN is implemented in an enterprise. At the top of this service model, the element is business and the directive is CoS (Class of Service), which means the network service should be aligned with business need and the differentiation implied is based on defined criteria: some get better service at the expense of others. The second level in the model is policy or rule. The defined rule should be agreed throughout the network; these rules or policies include QoS, security and resource allocation. The third level is "Enabling" that includes network administration, operation and control, and the fourth is infrastructure, meaning network resources. This service model itself is nothing unless the inherited objectives are met.

While PEN is processing its decision, the network manager should consider this service model and ensure that the deployment meets all the criteria stated above.

Now, considering this service model as defined above, a network manager may want to efficiently utilize bandwidth, prioritize traffic and availability of certain services, and so on. Let's assume that video transport for the network should be available from Monday to Friday (9 a.m. to 5 p.m.) with aggregate not more than 100 Kb/s. Also, the network delay for voice should not be more than 100 ms etc.

These predefined rules (see Fig. 3.74) along with any others can be implemented throughout the network. This is done using a policy management system that resides in the policy server and downloads the profile to routers and switches that implement the PEP on them.

Such a deployment not only aligns the network resources but also ensures effective use of the service model.

One of the major difficulties a network manager always faces in PEN is to define a static QoS policy that dynamically updates the network devices. The QoS policy can simply be understood as packet classification (Fig. 3.75). For

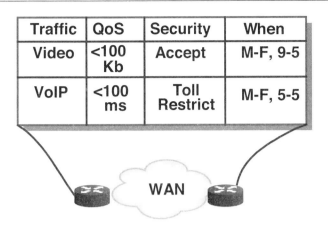

Traffic	QoS	Security	When
Video	<100 Kb	Accept	M-F, 9-5
VoIP	<100 ms	Toll Restrict	M-F, 5-5

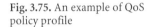

Fig. 3.74. Network resource alignment in PEN

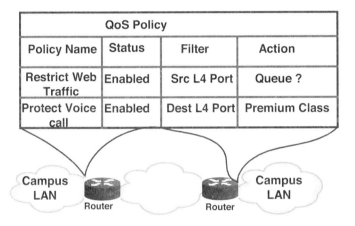

QoS Policy			
Policy Name	Status	Filter	Action
Restrict Web Traffic	Enabled	Src L4 Port	Queue ?
Protect Voice call	Enabled	Dest L4 Port	Premium Class

Fig. 3.75. An example of QoS policy profile

example, if voice is important traffic in the network, bandwidth should be reserved for it by marking incoming packets as EF class. Now in order to ensure that voice packets are treated properly, the associated UDP ports should be marked; for example, a UDP port could be assigned a 28,000 range as a criterion for special treatment.

These can now be treated as rules; a profile can be made for a particular network device in the policy server and these rules input to it. Once a device with a built-in PEP agent boots up, it will download these rules and ensure they define behavior for the transport.

PEN deployment would be most successful if network managers were very much conversant with traffic behavior, underlying protocols and business needs.

4 Voice over IP

4.1 Introduction

There is no question that Voice over IP (VoIP) is one of the hottest topics in the telecom industry today. The equipment to packetize voice calls is available, and, for service providers, the economics of VoIP can be very compelling.

The converged IP network (voice, video and data) means that multiservice traffic is carried through IP encapsulated packets. In this chapter we are not going to discuss video over IP, rather the VoIP services that are the core component of unified IP will be examined and explored.

Some equipment (i.e., routers) is capable of VoIP communication over LANs and WANs (Wide Area Networks) . In such a transport procedure, a router (those that deploy VoIP support) acts as the gateway complying with H.323 ITU-T (International Telecommunications Union) recommendations for gateway operation or may provide both gateway and gatekeeper functions. VoIP implementation in routers may vary: some may implement only a portion of the data and some may implement both data and PSTN (Public Switched Telephone Network). Some of the routers that I have worked with have both PSTN and data internetworking capabilities built in, such as Nortel Network's BCM (Business Communication Manager). This equipment may implement private branch exchange (PBX) services along with core routing functions. As such, a customer is capable of using existing PSTN along with the VoIP capability of an IP network. If the VoIP network is out of resources, this deployment allows PSTN fallback, which means a new VoIP call can use PSTN if the IP network is busy. One important consideration here is that these products provide the flexibility for traditional PSTN customers to gradually rely on unified internetworking for voice transport.

In this chapter, we will explore VoIP deployment based on ITU-T recommendations and examine the most commonly used VoIP products, test tools and techniques to isolate issues with such a network.

It must be remembered that VoIP deployment requires proper implementation of IP QoS, which is described in Chap. 3. Therefore, our final approach to VoIP deployment will demand the acquired knowledge of Chap. 3.

We will start first with voice, identifying its characteristics, defining the network requirements and understanding the key criteria of the VoIP network. Later, we will explore in depth the realm of unified IP internetworking by examining the most commonly used techniques of VoIP deployment. This chapter is practical in nature and a thorough understanding of the topics will be very helpful for deploying, testing and isolating VoIP network issues.

4.2 Wave Phenomenon

What I am about to tell you is not hypothesis but scientific fact. Everything we perceive and "listen to" can be described as having a wave-like structure – waves of sound and light enfold us. These waves are referred to as analog, meaning that they travel in continuous unbroken curves that are absolutely smooth. Another way of saying this is that an analog wave has potentially an infinite number of positions between any two points on its length. In other words, an analog signal is one that is continuous and has a range of values (Fig. 4.1). An example of an analog signal is your voice.

Waves are often referred to as "signals" when they carry information – television and radio sets receive these analog signals – and until recently they could in turn be recorded on an analog medium, such as magnetic tape or film. But computers are changing this, if they have not done so already, because it is just as likely that the sounds you listen to or the broadcasts you watch are in some way enhanced, filtered or transmitted using digital technology.

Computers communicate and process information in zeros and ones, so any information we pass to a computer must be in this form – that is, digital. We must convert the analog information of, say, a picture or a sound to a digital form that the computer will understand; this conversion process is called sampling and uses an analog-to-digital converter (ADC).

Fig. 4.1. Analog signal (sine wave form)

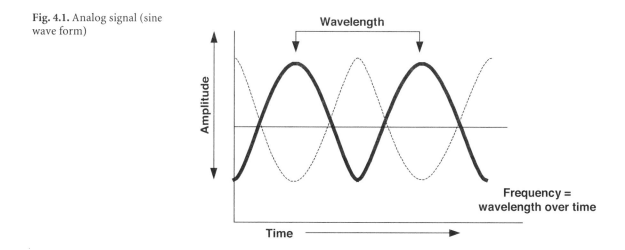

The conversion of analog to digital (A/D) is the process of converting an analog signal (waveform) into a digital format. The analog waveform may represent speech, television or music. The A/D process involves three discrete steps:

1. Sampling.
2. Quantizing.
3. Coding.

Sampling is the process of reducing a very complex waveform to a manageable numerical form – a string of ones and zeros – without losing the vibrancies and gradations of the waveform. In other words, a sample is a snapshot of the analog signal that is changed into binary symbols when converted into digital information. Key to this process is a mathematical proposition, developed by Bell Labs engineer Harry Nyquist[1] in the 1930s. The Nyquist sampling theorem is a fundamental concept and the foundation of all digital communications. The theorem suggests that any complex waveform can be reconstructed from a limited number of discrete samples.

Sampling involves taking instantaneous measurements of the waveform, especially amplitude. The more samples are taken, the more faithfully the original waveform can be reconstructed. In fact, the Nyquist theorem states that all the information contained in the waveform can be recaptured when precisely twice as many samples are taken as the highest frequency of the waveform. If, for example, the highest frequency in a human voice is 4000 cycles per second (4 kHz), then 8000 samples must be taken each second. The objective is to measure the amplitude (height) of the waveform at set time intervals (Fig. 4.2).

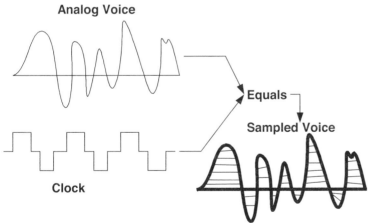

Analog Voice

Clock

Equals

Sampled Voice

Fig. 4.2. An example of analog voice sampling

---

1 Harry Nyquist was an American physicist, electrical engineer and prolific inventor who made fundamental theoretical and practical contributions to telecommunications. He earned a BS (1914) and an MS (1915) in Electrical Engineering from the University of North Dakota. He joined AT&T in 1917 after receiving his PhD in Physics from Yale University. He is known to be credited with 138 patents relating to telecommunications.

Once the waveform has been sampled, it is quantized. Quantizing is the process of mathematically assigning a value to each of the discrete samples. The basic concept is that of "rounding" values, much as all numbers on a scale of one to ten could be rounded to the closest integer.

What we actually see and hear will always be in an analog form; this is because we ourselves are analog in nature and there would be no point in listening to a CD's raw data, for a series of zeros and ones would have very little meaning to us. The use of a digital-to-analog converter (DAC), the reverse of an ADC, enables us to listen or see the results generated by the computer.

There are a number of properties that are common to all signal types, whether analog or digital. These are frequency, wavelength, amplitude and phase, all of which vary over time. And special consideration must be taken of these properties when converting an analog signal to a digital signal, if we do not want to lose or corrupt information during the sampling process (please read Nyquist's sampling theorem).

The advantage of digital signals over analog signals is that they can be processed by a computer: cutting, pasting and filtering blocks of sound, text or images can be performed within an application or program. What would have taken days to achieve using analog media can be simulated in seconds by a computer processor. Even though computer memory chips and processing speeds are always becoming cheaper and more abundant, they are finite. The disadvantages of using digital technology are found in the trade-offs between file size, speed of access and reproduction quality.

4.2.1 Modulation

So far we have looked at the wave frequencies and how they are converted from their natural form (analog) to digital form. In this regard, it is also important to understand modulation and how a particular modulation is used for voice waves. Modulation is the process by which voice, music and other "intelligence" is added to the radio waves produced by a transmitter or where a radio frequency or a light wave's amplitude, frequency or phase is changed in order to transmit intelligence. The different methods of modulating a radio signal are called modes. The characteristics of the carrier wave are instantaneously varied by another "modulating" waveform. An unmodulated radio signal is known as a carrier. When you hear "dead air" between songs or announcements on a radio station, you are "hearing" the carrier. While a carrier contains no intelligence, you can tell it is being transmitted because of the way it quietens the background noise on your radio.

There are number of ways a signal can be modulated, as follows:

* Amplitude modulation
* Frequency modulation
* Phase modulation
* Pulse modulation.

Amplitude modulation: Amplitude modulation (AM) occurs when a voice signal's varying voltage is applied to a carrier frequency. The carrier frequency's amplitude changes in accordance with the modulated voice signal, while the carrier's frequency does not change.

When combined the resultant amplitude-modulated signal consists of the carrier frequency, plus UPPER and LOWER sidebands. This is known as double sideband – amplitude modulation (DSB-AM), or more commonly referred to as plain AM.

The carrier frequency may be suppressed or transmitted at a relatively low level. This requires that the carrier frequency be generated, or otherwise derived, at the receiving site for demultiplexing. This type of transmission is known as double sideband – suppressed carrier (DSB-SC).

It is also possible to transmit a SINGLE sideband for a slight sacrifice in low-frequency response (it is difficult to suppress the carrier and the unwanted sideband, without some low-frequency filtering as well). The advantage is a reduction in analog bandwidth needed to transmit the signal. This type of modulation, known as single sideband – suppressed carrier (SSB-SC), is ideal for frequency division multiplexing (FDM).

Another type of analog modulation is known as vestigial sideband. Vestigial sideband modulation is a lot like single sideband, except that the carrier frequency is preserved and one of the sidebands is eliminated through filtering. Analog bandwidth requirements are a little more than single sideband, however.

Vestigial sideband transmission is usually found in television broadcasting. Such broadcast channels require 6 MHz of ANALOG bandwidth, in which an amplitude-modulated PICTURE carrier is transmitted along with a frequency-modulated SOUND carrier.

Frequency modulation: Frequency modulation (FM)occurs when a carrier's CENTER frequency is changed based upon the input signal's amplitude. Unlike AM, the carrier signal's amplitude is UNCHANGED. This makes FM more immune to noise than AM and improves the overall signal-to-noise ratio of the communications system. Power output is also constant, differing from the varying power output of AM.

The amount of analog bandwidth necessary to transmit a frequency-modulated signal is greater than the amount necessary for AM, a limiting constraint for some systems.

Phase modulation: Phase modulation is similar to FM. Instead of the frequency of the carrier wave changing, the PHASE of the carrier changes.

As you might imagine, this type of modulation is easily adaptable to data modulation applications.

Pulse modulation: With pulse modulation, a "snapshot" (sample) of the waveform is taken at regular intervals.

There are a variety of pulse modulation schemes:

- Pulse amplitude modulation
- Pulse code modulation
- Pulse frequency modulation
- Pulse position modulation
- Pulse width modulation.

Pulse amplitude modulation (PAM): In PAM, a pulse is generated with an amplitude corresponding to that of the modulating waveform. Like AM, it is very sensitive to noise.

While PAM was deployed in early AT&T Dimension PBXs, there are no practical implementations in use today. However, PAM is an important first step in a modulation scheme known as pulse code modulation.

Pulse code modulation (PCM): In PCM, PAM samples (collected at regular intervals) are quantized. That is to say, the amplitude of the PAM pulse is assigned a digital value (number). This number is transmitted to a receiver that decodes the digital value and outputs the appropriate analog pulse.

The fidelity of this modulation scheme depends upon the number of bits used to represent the amplitude. The frequency range that can be represented through PCM depends upon the sample rate. To prevent a condition known as "aliasing", the sample rate MUST BE AT LEAST twice that of the highest supported frequency. For typical voice channels (4 kHz frequency range), the sample rate is 8 kHz.

Where is PCM today? The primary standard for voice digitization is PCM. According to the Nyquist theorem, the 0–4000 Hz telephone voice signal amplitude is sampled at twice its highest frequency (8000 samples/s) and each sample value is assigned an 8-bit binary value. At the receiver, the samples are read and converted back to analog voice signals. A PCM signal comprises 8000×8 (bit) = 64 Kb/s. A method of digitizing audio (turning it into those ones and zeros that computers love so much) is known as PCM which periodically (8000 times a second for telephone systems, 44,100 times a second per right and left channel for audio CDs) samples the input and produces (for example) an 8-bit (for telephone systems) or 16-bit (for audio CDs) value representing the amplitude of the audio input at that instant in time.

Pulse frequency modulation (PFM): With PFM, pulses of equal amplitude are generated at a rate modulated by the signal's frequency. The random arrival rate of pulses makes this unsuitable for transmission through time division multiplexing (TDM) systems.

Pulse position modulation (PPM): Also known as pulse time modulation, PPM is a scheme where the pulses of equal amplitude are generated at a rate controlled by the modulating signal's amplitude. Again, the random arrival rate of pulses makes this unsuitable for transmission using TDM techniques.

Pulse width modulation (PWM): In PWM, pulses are generated at a regular rate. The length of the pulse is controlled by the modulating signal's amplitude. PWM is unsuitable for TDM transmission due to the varying pulse width.

4.2.2 Codec

The word codec is a contraction of coder and decoder, and means a device that digitizes voice or video signals for transmission over digital data services and undigitizes them at the other end. It is an ADC optimized for audio signals. As the name implies, codecs are used to encode and decode (or compress and decompress) various types of data, particularly those that would otherwise use up inordinate amounts of disk space, such as sound and video files. Common codecs include those for converting analog video signals into compressed video files (such as MPEG) or analog sound signals into digitized sound (such as RealAudio). Codecs can be used with either streaming (live video or audio) or file-based (AVI, WAV) content.

The two most commonly used codec categories are PCM codec and AD-PCM (Adaptive Differential Pulse Code Modulation) codec. The PCM codec is also known as the non-linear codec. Two such non-linearities are standardized:

1. The *μ-law* (pronounced "moo law" or "mew law"), used in North America, Japan, and South Korea.
2. The *A-law*, used in the rest of the world.

Converters are therefore required to interconnect these two types of PCM-digitized voice channels. The digitized audio can be carried by either ISDN (Integrated Digital Services Network) B channels or E1 or T1 channels.

On the other hand, ADPCM is a form of PCM that produces a digital signal with a lower bit rate than standard PCM. It produces this lower bit rate by recording only the difference between samples and adjusting the coding scale dynamically to accommodate large and small differences. Some applications use ADPCM to digitize a voice signal so voice and data can be transmitted simultaneously over a digital facility normally used only for one or the other.

The G.721 method uses only 32,000 bits/s per voice channel, as compared to standard telephony's 64,000 bits/s (which uses PCM). Although the use of ADPCM (rather than PCM) is imperceptible to humans, it can significantly reduce the throughput of higher speed modems and fax transmissions.

ADPCM codecs are also known as waveform codecs, which, instead of quantizing the speech signal directly, like PCM codecs, quantize the difference between the speech signal and a prediction that has been made of the speech signal. If the prediction is accurate then the difference between the real and predicted speech samples will have a lower variance than the real speech samples, and will be accurately quantized with fewer bits than would be needed to quantize the original speech samples. At the decoder the quantized difference signal is added to the predicted signal to give the reconstructed speech signal. The performance of the codec is aided by using adaptive prediction and quantization, so that the predictor and difference quantizer adapt to the changing characteristics of the speech being coded.

In the mid 1980s the CCITT standardized a 32 Kb/s ADPCM, known as G.721, which gave reconstructed speech almost as good as the 64 Kb/s PCM codecs. Later, in Recommendations G.726 and G.727, codecs operating at 40, 32, 24 and 16 Kb/s were standardized.

The currently available PCM codec chip not only implements A/D and digital-to-analog (D/A) conversions but also provides voice-band filtering, for example Texas Instruments' TCM38C17IDL. The main reasons we have to know about codecs and their architecture are for proper implementation

Fig. 4.3. An example of PCM codec deployment

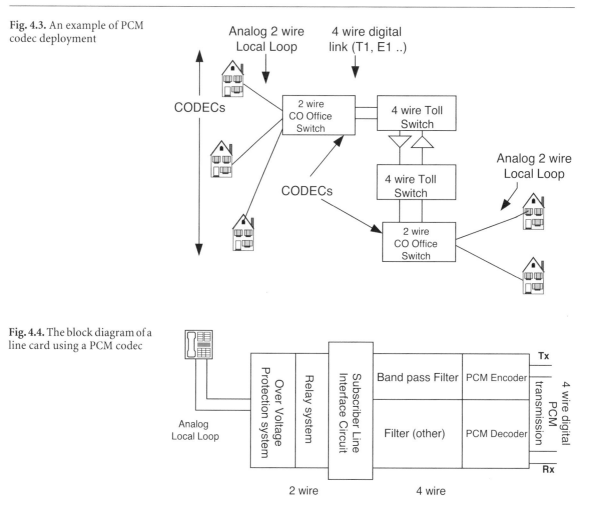

Fig. 4.4. The block diagram of a line card using a PCM codec

of VoIP and to make the testing of the functional components of a complex VoIP gateway that much easier. Examining datasheets from various codec chip manufacturers will greatly improve your understanding of this technology. However, I will try to describe here some common implementations and the typical architecture of a PCM codec. The main aspect of the voice-band PCM codec is telephony applications such as modem, CO (Central Office) line card, PBX and voice-band audio processors (Fig. 4.3).

In the CO deployment the codec is found on a line card (Fig. 4.4). For every subscriber telephone line there is an associated line card at the CO. These line cards implement PCM codecs along with a voice-band filter that provides all the function required to interface a two-wire analog telephone circuit with a TDM system (Fig. 4.5).

The codec compresses and expands the digitized data using either an *A*-law or μ-law logarithmic function. While North American and Japanese systems use the μ-law algorithm, European systems use the *A*-law.

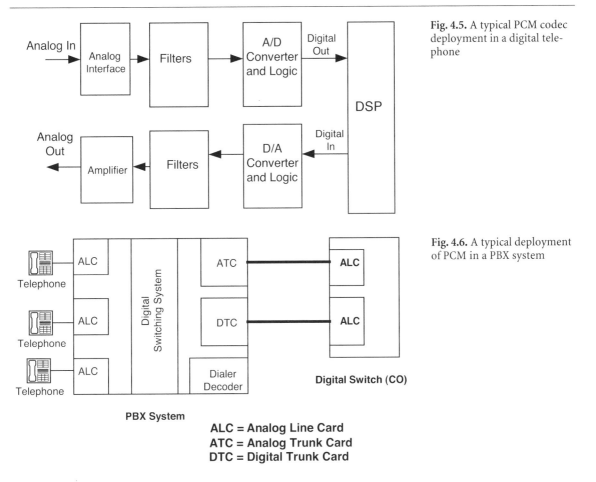

Fig. 4.5. A typical PCM codec deployment in a digital telephone

Fig. 4.6. A typical deployment of PCM in a PBX system

The implementation of the PCM codec in a system like PBX provides the filtering and frame sync timing required for a standard voice channel. Figure 4.6 shows a typical PCM codec deployment in a PBX.

4.2.2.1 Codec G.711

ITU-T Recommendation G.711 is the international standard for encoding telephone audio on a 64 Kb/s channel. It is a PCM scheme operating at an 8 kHz sample rate, with 8 bits per sample. According to the Nyquist theorem, which states that a signal must be sampled at twice its highest frequency component, G.711 can encode frequencies between 0 and 4 kHz. Telecom companies can select between two different variants of G.711: the A-law and μ-law. The A-law is the standard for international circuits.

Each of these encoding schemes is designed in a roughly logarithmic fashion. Lower signal values are encoded using more bits, higher signal values require fewer bits. This ensures that low-amplitude signals will be well represented, while maintaining enough range to encode high amplitudes.

The actual encoding does not use logarithmic functions, however. The input range is broken into segments, each segment using a different interval between decision values. Most segments contain 16 intervals, and the interval size doubles from segment to segment.

Both encodings are symmetrical around zero. The μ-law uses eight segments of 16 intervals each in each of the positive and negative directions, starting with a interval size of 2 in segment 1, and increasing to an interval size of 256 in segment 8. The A-law uses seven segments. The smallest segment, using an interval of 2, is twice the size of the others (32 intervals). The remaining six segments are "normal", with 16 intervals each, increasing up to an interval size of 128 in segment 7. Thus, the A-law is skewed towards representing smaller signals with greater fidelity.

4.2.2.2 Codec G.723

ITU-T Recommendation G.723.1 defines the requirement for a low-speed (5.3 and 6.3 Kb/s) codec. The specification is also known as " Dual Rate Speech Coder for Multimedia Communications Transmitting". As defined in G.723.1, this type of codec can support two different bit rates of 5.3 and 6.3 Kb/s. The latter provides greater quality for speech coding. The G.723 codec encodes speech or other audio signal in 30 ms frames and introduces a total algorithmic delay of 37.5 ms. It is designed to operate with a digital signal which is obtained as a result by telephone bandwidth filtering of analog input defined in ITU-T Recommendation G.712. G.723 is not well suited to music or sound effects and has a lower quality than many other codecs at similar data rates. Table 4.1 lists typical parameters for G.723.

4.2.2.3 Silence compression

Both G.723.1 and G.729, Annex B, support silence compression.

One of the key techniques for optimized VoIP deployment in business applications is reducing the use of WAN bandwidth where possible. Beyond speech compression, the best bandwidth reducing technology is silence compression, also known as silence suppression. Silence compression technology identifies the periods of silence in a conversation, and stops sending IP speech packets during those periods. In a typical telephone conversation, only about 36–40% of a full-duplex conversation is active. When one person talks, the other listens (known as half-duplex). And there are important periods of silence during speaker pauses between words and phrases.

By applying silence compression, full-duplex bandwidth use is reduced by the same amount, releasing bandwidth for other voice/fax or data communications.

Silence compression allows two conversations to fit in the bandwidth otherwise used by one. This 50% bandwidth reduction develops over a 20–30 second period as the conversation switches from one direction to another.

Table 4.1. The G.723 codec parameters

Source	Voice at 8 kHz
Compression ratio/ data rates	5.3 and/or 6.3 Kb/s (0.7–0.8 kbytes/s), depending on implementation
Compression time	Real time

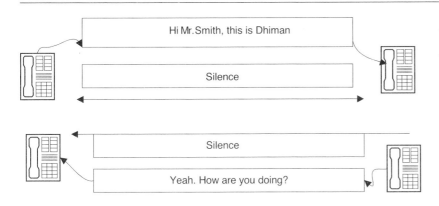

With silence suppression, the transport efficiency can be optimized by allowing two conversations to use same the bandwidth which otherwise would be used by one conversation (Fig. 4.7).

Furthermore, to provide a more natural sound, comfort noise can be added at the destination H.323 gateway during the silent periods to calls where silence compression is active. But it must be remembered that silence compression can cause a sensed degradation in audio quality. If the silence compression disabled, the bandwidth use of the LAN/ WAN approximately multiplies by 2.

Another factor which must be observed is that if an H.323 gateway works as a tandem switch in a network where circuit-switched trunk facilities have a large amount of low audio level, enabling silence compression degrades the quality of service, causing broken speech. Under tandem switching conditions, with a large amount of low audio level, the silence compression can be disabled using the IP telephony interface.

Silence compression cannot be used in cases where G.711 is deployed.

4.3 POTS

The Plain Old Telephone Service (POTS) is the most commonly known telephony service of past decades and still available in many countries. The term "Plain" is almost obsolete since today's telephony system uses some of the most sophisticated switching and transmission technology. The word "Old" implies familiarity and ease of use, which is the major reason for the sustained popularity of the telephony service. The word "Telephone" refers to the transport means of the nuances of human speech. "Service" refers to a means of responsiveness to the public, which is not often attainable from a telephone company. This dimension of the acronym is threatened due to competition and the "less service more profit policy" attitude of the service provider. The telegraph was the earlier means of communication before the invention of telephones. The method of communication was by Morse code and it was transported over wires. Morse code simply consists of dots (.) and

Fig. 4.8. The basic concept of telegraph communication

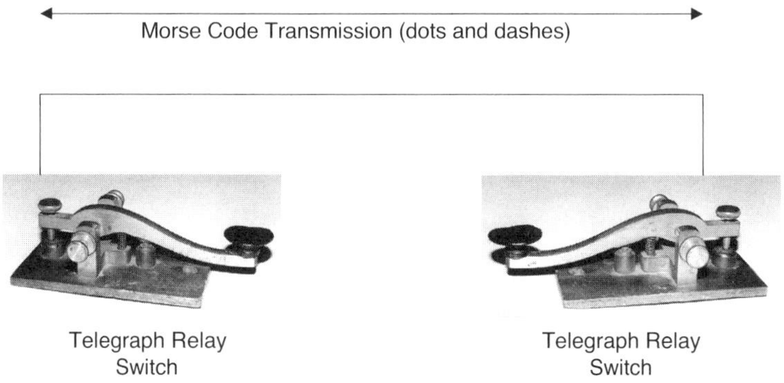

Morse Code Transmission (dots and dashes)

Telegraph Relay
Switch

Telegraph Relay
Switch

Fig. 4.9. The early telephone (Bell's liquid transmitter)

Bell Telephone Laboratories

dashes (–) and a relay switch generates tones that are transported over the wires to other relay switches. An operator hears the tones and writes down the meaning of the dots and dashes. This is a simple description of the earlier telegraph system (Fig. 4.8).

One of the disadvantage of such communication is that the operator at the receiving end has to listen carefully to the tones and wait for receipt of the complete transmission before sending back a reply. Above all, it is not appropriate for the general public. This disadvantage prompted Alexander Graham Bell to think differently about two-way communication using human speech. Although he and his assistant Thomas A. Watson demonstrated the first working model of the telephone on March 10, 1876, which was filed for patent on February 14, 1876, it was known that Elisha Grey had filed a patent for the telephone on the same day but the US Supreme Court accepted Bell's invention for the patent. One of Alexander Graham Bell's early "telephones" was the liquid transmitter. It was fashioned much in the manner of the liquid transmitter from Elisha Grey's patent caveat. It was on March 10 that the famous first words "Mr. Watson – come here – I want to see you" were spoke over a "telephone". Those words were spoken into a liquid transmitter (Fig. 4.9).

4.3.1 Telephony

The telephone network was initially designed to handle human voice signals that allow it to work within a narrow range or bandwidth. For gainful voice communications it has been identified that humans can communicate at frequencies between 300 and 3500 Hz (Fig. 4.10). Though we can hear and speak at higher and lower frequencies, voice communications between 300 and 3500 Hz are clear and efficient for the telephone network to transmit and receive. A voice channel goes from 0 to 4000 Hz and was developed to avoid any overlapping with other, adjacent voice channels.

The telephony system is a PSTN capable of transporting the human voice from one telephone to any other telephone on Earth. The switched network also supports fax, cellular phones, computers, etc., that are connected to the network. The telephones in the home are connected through a pair of copper wires to a single point known as the "protector block" (Fig. 4.11). This apparatus provides simple protection to the network from voltage overload.

The pair of copper wires connects the protector block to the CO. A bundle of twisted pair wires that connect end-users and the CO is carried inside a ca-

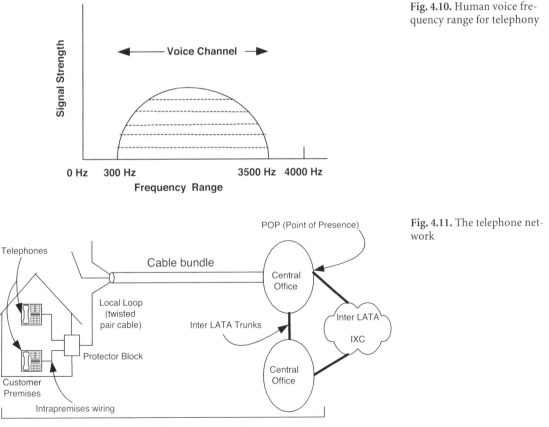

Fig. 4.10. Human voice frequency range for telephony

Fig. 4.11. The telephone network

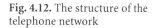

Fig. 4.12. The structure of the telephone network

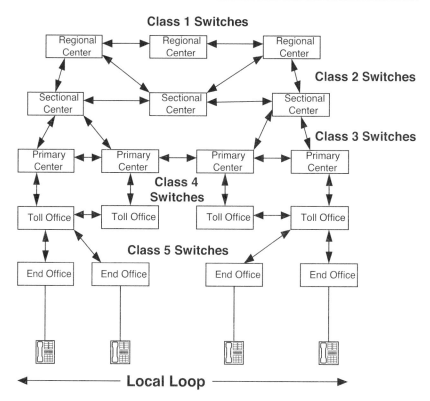

ble shield buried underground or placed in conduits or strung between telephone poles. The twisted pair cable that connects protector block and CO is known as the local loop. A call originating from a telephone in the local loop experiences the first stage of switching in the adjoining CO. From there it may be forwarded to other COs or carried over interoffice trunks. For long-distance calls, the "call setup" may traverse a long-distance network operated by a number of IXCs (Inter-eXchange Carriers) such as AT&T, MCI, Sprint, etc. The point where the connection is made between the local CO and the IXC is known as POP (Point Of Presence).

The structure of a telephone network as in North America may consist of various switches from Class 1 to Class 5 (Fig. 4.12).

The North American Numbering Plan (NANP) uses a 10-digit number assigned to the end-user to indicate the area (first three digits), the end office or service exchange (the next three digits) and the end-user or extension (last four digits) (Fig. 4.13).

The end office that uses the Class 5 switch is responsible for maintaining the local loop and giving the user voice services like call waiting or conference calling. The toll office which uses the Class 4 switch serves two functions: as a toll switch it is the user's link to long distance and as a tandem switch it allows end offices to communicate.

In the USA, there are 22 Bell Operating Companies (BOCs) that are organized into seven regional BOCs or RBOCs. These make up the majority of end

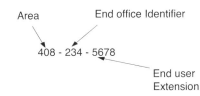

Fig. 4.13. An example of NANP

offices. The service areas of these end offices are subdivided into Local Access and Transport Areas (LATAs). There are other LATAs served by ITCs (Independent Telephone Companies) such as GTE or Cincinnati Bell.

4.3.2 The Telephone

Most of the early telephone sets were black and rotary and had limited functionality. On the contrary today's telephones are manufactured in many colors, sizes and offer push button dialing with numerous intelligent features. Although these telephones differ significantly from early telephones in how they look and function, the basic functions of the apparatus (Fig. 4.14) have not changed.

When the telephony service is required, the receiver establishes a connection with the CO by sending signals. This is done on lifting the handset, which draws a DC voltage from the CO by closing contacts within the switch hook. The switching device at the CO senses the flow of DC and thus identifies that customer desires service. Common battery apparatus at the CO has an EMF (Electro Motive Force) of 48 V and the receiver draws at least 20 mA of current over the local loop. The total resistance within the local loop must not exceed 1300 Ω.

In order to place a call the user needs to state the telephone number of the called party. This is done by means of dialing. In older telephones this is accomplished by turning a rotary dial that interrupts the DC flow with 10 dial pulses per second. Today's telephone very commonly uses push buttons and touch-tone dialing (Fig. 4.15).

Once a particular button (digit) is pushed, a unique combination of two sinusoidal tones is transmitted to the CO. For example, if the button "7" is pressed by the user, a combination of 852 Hz and 1209 Hz sine waves would be generated. The CO uses a special filter to detect the frequency and retrieve dial digit information from it. The touch-tone is known as DTMF (Dual-Tone Multi-Frequency).

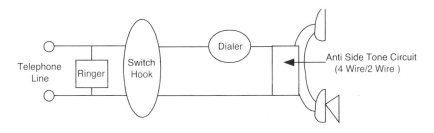

Fig. 4.14. Basic functional blocks of the telephone apparatus

Fig. 4.15. The touch-tone or push button telephone

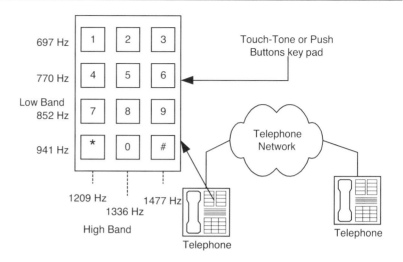

Fig. 4.15. The touch-tone or push button telephone

4.3.3 Transmission

Varieties of transmission media are used for the transport of voice in the traditional telephony system, which includes copper wire pairs for the local loop and fiber optics for CO-to-CO connectivity. For transcontinental or global telephone calls, satellite communication means are used and these satellites are located in geosynchronous orbits 22,300 miles (35,700 km) above the Earth's surface. We will talk about satellite telephony in the following section but before that let's examine the basics of traditional voice transmission.

One of the most important techniques used in traditional voice transmission is "multiplexing", which combines a number of communication signals to share a single communication medium. If analog multiplexing is used, the signals are combined by FDM, otherwise for digital multiplexing they are combined using TDM.

In FDM, the bandwidth of the transmission path serves as the frame of reference for all of the information being transmitted. The total bandwidth is divided into subchannels consisting of smaller segments of available bandwidth. Each of these subchannels is capable of carrying a separate signal (Fig. 4.16).

Although in FDM signals are transmitted simultaneously, each channel is assigned a different frequency and separated into 4000 Hz wide channels. Thus different channels are stacked together and transported over a single medium. Historically FDM has been extensively used for signal multiplexing in analog telephony (Fig. 4.17), although it has now been superseded by TDM digital signals.

On the other hand, in TDM, a number of low-rate channels are fed into a multiplexer, usually D-Bank, which combines them into a high-rate digital signal (Fig. 4.18).

Each voice frequency (VF) channel of 64 Kb/s (DS0) is assigned a specific time slot and transmitted sequentially. The common path for the digital car-

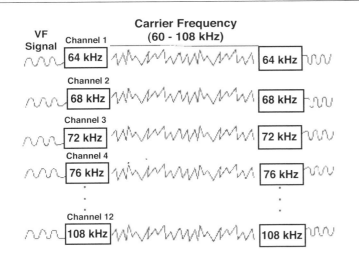

Fig. 4.16. FDM example

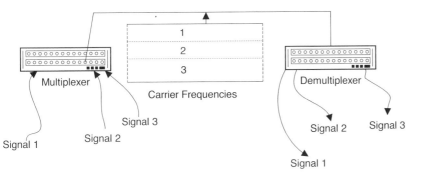

Fig. 4.17. FDM operation

Time Division Multiplexing

Fig. 4.18. TDM example

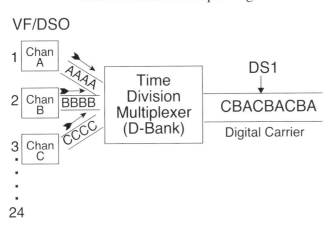

rier system operates at DS1 rate (1.544 Mb/s) which includes 24 basic voice channels. Four DS1 signals form a DS2, seven DS2 signals forms a DS3 and six DS3 signals form a DS4 signal.

In the late 1980s, AT&T replaced its entire analog multiplexing with digital multiplexing. This suite was followed by MCI in the early 1990s. Thus in the USA, analog multiplexing can be considered as obsolete.

A single digital telephone transmission at 64 Kb/s is known as DS0; a DS4 signal is 4032 DS0 signals giving it a rate of 274 Mb/s.

4.3.4 Satellite Telephony

A typical satellite network for telephony consists of a central hub, multiple PSTN gateways, satellite channels and remote terminals (Fig. 4.19) known as VSATs (Very Small Aperture Terminals). The VSAT is sometimes also known as an earth station, which is used to receive satellite transmissions (Fig. 4.20).

The VSAT dish antenna is approximately 3 to 6 feet (1 to 2 m) in diameter, which can be mounted on a wall or roof. This antenna consists of an LNB (Low Noise Blocker) which receives satellite signals and the transmitter that sends signals. The second part of the VSAT earth station is a desktop box or PC that includes a receiver/transmitter board and an interface that can communicate with existing user setups such as LAN, TVs, etc. (Fig. 4.21). The indoor unit is connected to the outdoor unit through a pair of cables.

Fig. 4.19. An example of typical telephony through the use of satellite communications that are common today: ODU, Outdoor Unit; IDU, Indoor Unit; HVP, Hub Voice Processor; HPP , Hub Protocol Processor

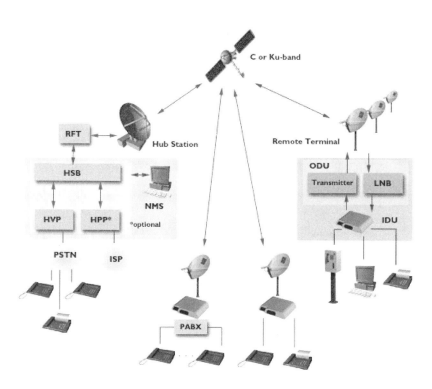

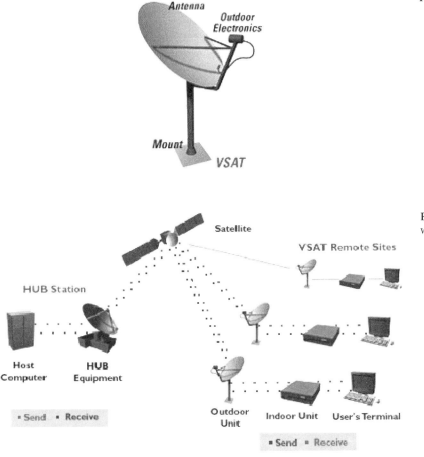

Fig. 4.20. A picture of a VSAT

Fig. 4.21. A VSAT network with satellite communication

4.3.5 Signaling

Varieties of signals are transported over the telephone network to control its operation. Normally three terms are associated with POTS: signaling supervision, signaling and call processing. Signal supervision provides simple on-hook or off-hook indications. Signaling, on the other hand, provides either dial pulses or dial tones to send call information. And call processing provides the means to communicate the status of the call. This status covers call origination, acceptance, acknowledgement and completion (Fig. 4.22).

Signal supervision: This occurs during the initiation of a call. Once a caller decides to dial another person, he/she lifts the handset off the telephone and thus seizes the line. This alerts the switching device at the CO that someone wants to place a call. The switch acknowledges the request and sends a dial tone to notify the caller to proceed with the call. At the end of the conversation, either the calling or called party hangs up, signaling the switching device at the CO to release the equipment used for the call.

Fig. 4.22. The diagram depicts signaling information to and from a telephone

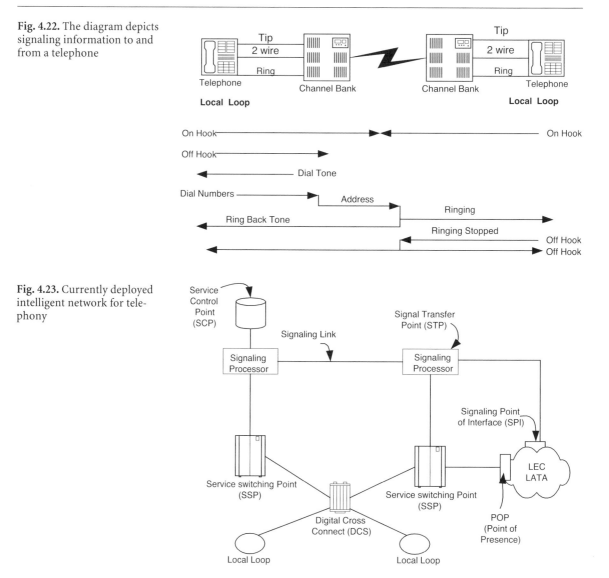

Fig. 4.23. Currently deployed intelligent network for telephony

Signaling: Signaling with dial pulses is just an extension of signal supervision. Once signaling supervision establishes a circuit connection, it is in an off-hook state. Toggling a string of on-hooks and off-hooks (dial pulse dialing) is the same as sending pulses and no pulses. Using tones to signal is the most common method, known as touch-tone phone. This method uses DTMFs from the telephone handset.

Call processing: This indicates the status of the switched message circuit. At one time it belonged only in telephone company switches. Now, with the advent of ISDN, it is also available at the end-user's location.

Modern telecommunication techniques such as IN (Fig. 4.23) integrate all means of signaling described here through the implementation of a central-

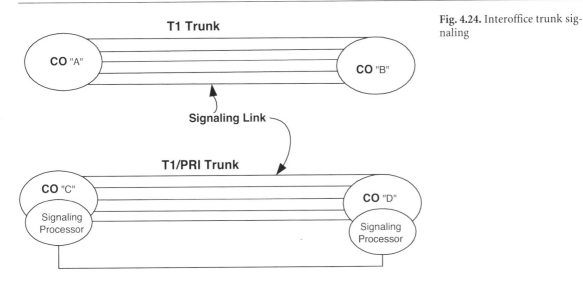

Fig. 4.24. Interoffice trunk signaling

ized database known as the service control point (SCP). The SCP contains information needed to translate 800 numbers to its location, among other features.

"Local loop signaling" occurs when the calling party goes off-hook and a current loop is completed between the switching office and the subscriber's telephone.

Once the call information is received at the CO, it is forwarded to the signaling network. When the call arrives at the destination end the telephone is either on-hook (idle) or off-hook (busy). If it is on-hook, a ringing voltage is sent to the receiving end and a signal is sent back to the calling party; otherwise, if the phone is off-hook, then the calling party receives a busy tone.

Interoffice trunk signaling (Fig. 4.24) uses per trunk signaling in which it adds one trunk at a time, starting at the CO that served the calling customer and progressing toward the CO of the called station.

4.4 VoIP Overview

In the past few years, Internet telephony has generated a great deal of excitement in industry about the ability to use an IP network to carry traditional telephone traffic. Internet telephony was originally developed to provide a means of voice communication from one computer-based telephony system (for example) to other through the Internet. In this service, users at one end may able to talk to other users in any part of the world as long they are connected via the Internet. Of course, such voice communication was not crystal clear for end-users but was good enough to exchange information.

The benefit to industry was the ability of Internet telephony to eliminate long-distance toll charges incurred when calling through PSTNs. More and

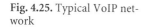
Fig. 4.25. Typical VoIP network

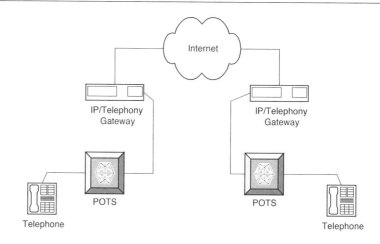

more users became attracted to the benefits of such products as simultaneous voice and data transfer, cost savings and less administration incurred
due to the service provided. Gradually, the development of the IP telephony
gateway has overcome the earlier limitations of the computer-based telephony system. Now an ordinary telephony system can be used to talk over an IP
network to any part of the world. Such IP telephony is unreliable and non-
deterministic like voice transmission over a PSTN. It is also fettered since
very few Internet telephony products implement defined standards.

Today's solutions, so to speak, are kludges and the technology is still being
developed. Therefore, a number of organizations took the initiative to standardize VoIP technology to prevent a plethora of proprietary solutions from
vendors. In fact today's VoIP is a new application of existing technology that
utilizes IP packets to carry voice calls. The voice signal is first digitized and
sliced into an IP packet and can be transmitted along with other packets such
as data. At the receiving end, the packets are reassembled and normal voice
sounds are retrieved. VoIP provides a means for integrating some voice and
data capabilities so that they can both carried through the same IP network.
This ensures end-to-end voice transmission possibilities in the network (Fig.
4.25).

Recently the International Multimedia Teleconferencing Consortium
(IMTC) initiated a VoIP forum through which it hopes to provide interoperability solutions for different vendors. The responsibility of the forum is to
define and establish a set of guidelines for implementation of VoIP and to ensure seamless product interoperability with high QoS.

4.4.1 Layered Architecture

VoIP is a four-layered architecture as defined by various organizations in
their respective standards that identifies the interfaces that exist between
each layer. The four layers are service aspect layer, session layer, transport
layer and network layer (Fig. 4.26) :

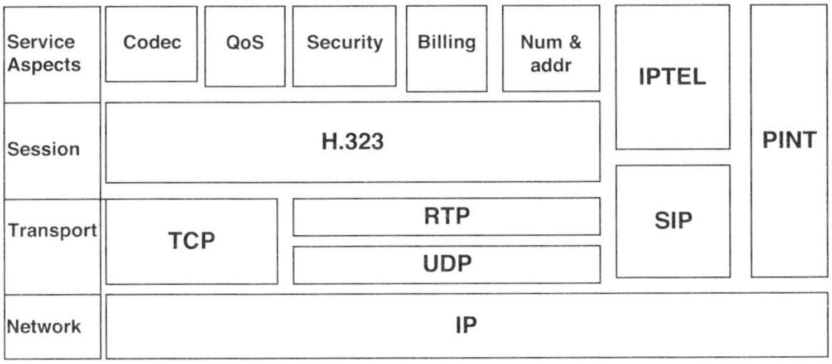

Fig. 4.26. The VoIP layered architecture

Service aspect layer: The responsibility of this layer is all aspects of VoIP service, which includes billing security and coding speech into digital packets.

Session layer: This layer helps VoIP to establish a call and perform registration when the terminal is first connected to the network.

Transport layer: This layer is responsible for end-to-end message delivery.

Network layer: This is the layer where routing services are carried out, for example IP packet transfer.

A number of standard organizations took the initiative to define various attributes of the VoIP layered architecture. These attributes are known as the "domain" of the VoIP layered concept. The ITU is responsible for the H.323 suite of specifications. Although the scope of its work includes security and codec domains, its perspective on VoIP is narrowed by omitting much of the service aspect layer. The second organization involved in VoIP standardization is IETF. It provides the specification for IP networks carrying VoIP as well as application-type protocols. The scope of work also includes PINT, SIP and IPTEL of the VoIP layered architecture (see below). The next very important contributing organization to VoIP standards is IMTC. It has introduced a working group into the VoIP forum to define a specification for interoperability among different vendor VoIP products. Currently IMTC is working on the H.323 domain of VoIP.

4.4.1.1 PINT (PSTN–Internet Interworking)

The primary object of the PINT Protocol is to address the need of connection arrangement through which Internet applications can request and enrich PSTN services. The IETF PINT working group also ensures that PINT profile 1.0 will provide optimal performance for IP-based telephony over the Internet. PINT is a protocol which invokes certain telephone services from an IP network. These services include placing calls, sending and receiving faxes, and receiving content over the telephone. The aim of this protocol is to invoke certain telephone services that if successful will allow an IP client to perform a call transaction over the IP network. In this configuration, an IP host will send a request to a server in the IP network which in turn will relay it to the telephone network. The PSTN will then perform the requested call service

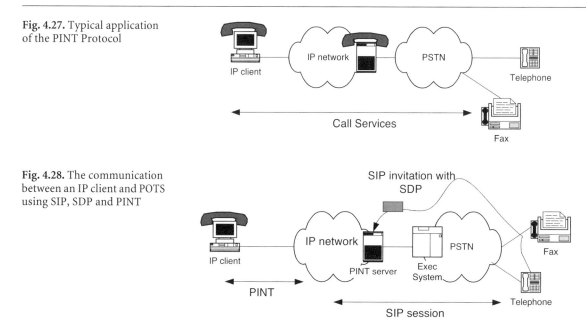

Fig. 4.27. Typical application of the PINT Protocol

Fig. 4.28. The communication between an IP client and POTS using SIP, SDP and PINT

toward a successful transaction (Fig. 4.27). PINT is still a draft with IETF but soon will become an RFC. The draft is "draft-ietf-pint-profile-00.txt" and can be obtained from: http://www.ietf.org/proceedings/98aug/I-D/draft-ietf-pint-profile-00.txt.

The term "PINT service" can be used to describe such a successful transaction from an IP client to a PSTN or vice versa. In the Internet conferencing architecture, PINT depends on SIP (Session Initiation Protocol) and SDP (Session Description Protocol). SIP is used to establish the association between participants within the call, whereas SDP is used to describe the media to be exchanged. In this model, a telephony system uses SIP to invite a remote server in the heterogeneous network into a session by imparting to it a media description through SDP. This then conveys the media description of the destination to which the telephony system wants to establish a call. The PINT server (gateway) responds to the request in order to establish a session (Fig. 4.28). Since there is no guarantee that the transmission will not fail, it is important that the network provides the requester with a status or warning message identifying the failure, if any.

4.4.1.1.1 PINT Architecture

PINT uses SIP to route the request over an IP network to the correct PINT server in a secure and reliable manner and to communicate the status. Although proxy and redirect servers can be used in a PINT system the network still has to relay the request and receive the acknowledgement. A special server is used for this purpose and known as the PINT gateway. This gateway must have a true telephone interface (i.e., an analog, PRI or SS7 interface to support DMTF, Q.signaling or ISUP) (ISDN User Part) or might be connected via an API or other protocol to an "executive system" (Fig. 4.29).

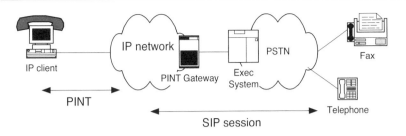

Fig. 4.29. The functional components of PINT

The executive system, if used, is capable of invoking call service within a PSTN. It is not necessary to have a PINT server and executive system deployed since a single server (currently available on the market) is capable doing both of these tasks.

4.4.1.2 SIP (Session Initiation Protocol)

SIP is a lightweight signaling protocol that is the part of the IETF conferencing control architecture. The application layer control protocol is used for creating, modifying and terminating sessions with one or more participants, which includes multimedia distribution and Internet conferencing. Some of the SIP application features are as follows:

- Provides call control features such as hold, forward, transfer, media changes. etc.
- Supports Web infrastructure, for example security, cookies, etc.
- Is Web oriented and network-protocol independent.
- Can provide event notification and "buddy lists".

SIP allows user mobility by proxying and redirecting requests to the user's current location. Users of this protocol are capable of communicating with each other via multicast or unicast, or a combination of both. The Internet draft of IETF MMUSIC (Multiparty Multimedia Session Control) describes this protocol in detail. It is described in the draft as being independent of the lower layer transport protocol in that it does not have ties to any conference control protocol and can be extended with additional capabilities if required.

SIP does not prescribe how a conference is to be managed; rather it uses a central server to manage conference and participant state and distribute that state via multicast. It can invite users to conferences by conveying the information required. Such an invitation can be done via multicast protocols, for example SAP (Systems, Applications and Products in data processing), email, news group, Web pages or directories (e.g. LDAP (Lightweight Directory Access Protocol)). It should be noted that SIP does not allocate multicast addresses; this is done by a multicast protocol such as SAP.

4.4.1.2.1 SIP operation

The operation of SIP is simple and follows eight basic steps:

1. First it uses a directory service such as LDAP to map name to user@host (SIP addressing).

2. Once this is done the protocol locates SIP servers using DNS SRV, MX, CNAME or a numeric network address.
3. The called server may also map name to the user@host addressing scheme.
4. The "callee" may accept or reject or forward the call to a new address.
5. If the protocol mechanism decides the address is new it will try to locate the SIP server again.
6. Now if the call is accepted, the caller confirms it.
7. And the conversation can start.
8. Finally, the caller or callee sends BYE to end the call.

To understand the basic operation of SIP, we should explore the following operational elements of SIP:

- **SIP addressing:** An SIP URL is used by the protocol to identify the user in the SIP addressing scheme. The SIP URL is very similar to a Telnet URL (i.e. user@host). In this form of URL, the user is the name of the user or a telephone number. On the other hand, the host part is the domain name having a DNS, SRV, CNAME or an IP address.
- **Locating a SIP server:** Like HTTP, an SIP client wishing to transmit a request may do so by sending it either to a proxy SIP server or directly to the IPaddress. Anyway, for transmission of such a request an SIP transaction allows the client to use either TCP or UDP. The SIP message format and operation are independent of the transport protocol.
- **SIP invitation:** An SIP invitation has two requests, INVITE followed by ACK. The INVITE method indicates the SIP invitation to a user or service to join in a session. The INVITE message body consists of a session description to which a callee is invited. In a two-party call the caller indicates the media it is in and its willingness for any other media to receive and send messages. The successful response must indicate the intention of the callee regarding the media. ACK is the request confirmation of the invitation, which indicates a final response to an INVITE request. ACK is used only with INVITE requests. Therefore, an INVITE request asks the callee to join a particular conference or establish a two-party conference. If the callee agrees, it will send an ACK request to confirm it. On the other hand, if the callee no longer wants to participate in the call, it will send a BYE request.

In Fig. 4.30, an INVITE request is initiated by test@ste-w.nortelnetworks.com to dhiman@iit.ernet.in to join in a session. The proxy server at iit.ernet.in contacts the location service to find the address. The location service in turn imparts to the proxy server the whereabouts of "dhiman" by indicating this address: dhm@play. Now the proxy server sends out an INVITE request to dhm@play. The agent in dhm@play alerts the user and returns a success indication. The proxy server conveys this back to the originator as success indication. The success indication is identified in the figure using dotted lines. The caller now sends out ACK through the proxy server to dhm@play to establish the session.

- **Locating a user:** Since the SIP operation supports user mobility, the location should be dynamically registered with the SIP server. The location

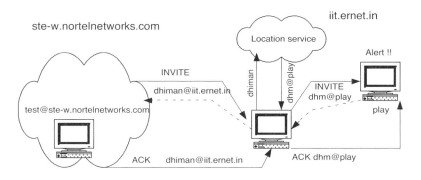

Fig. 4.30. SIP operation using a proxy server

server may use protocols such as finger (RFC 1288), rwhois (RFC2167), LDAP (RFC1777) and multicast protocols to identify user location. If the user logged in at several hosts, a location server may return several locations which may be temporarily inaccurate. The SIP server combines the outcome and yields the location or list of locations.

- **Changing an existing session:** Probably in some situations the parameters of an existing session may change. This is done by using another INVITE request with the same caller ID although the message body may be new or different from the previous message.
- **Registration services:** The REGISTER request allows a client to impart its whereabouts to the proxy or redirect the SIP server. A client my also use it to install call handling features at the server.

4.4.1.3 IPTEL (IP Telephony)

IPTEL was developed to address the need of a number of underlying protocols for successful telephony services. These include signaling and capabilities exchange and a number of "peripheral" protocols. The IETF charter for IPTEL (http://www.ietf.org/html.charters/iptel-charter.html) is actively working to provide the following supportive protocols and framework documents:

1. Call processing syntax: To establish a call, the signaling generally passes through several servers such as an H.323 gatekeeper. These servers are responsible for forwarding, redirecting or proxying the signaling messages. If the callee is busy, the responsible server may forward the call to a server closer to the user or may drop the call completely. Therefore, it is important that the callee provides input to this process and guidance to the server on how to act. Such techniques can be expressed in a call processing syntax. One draft which specifies such preference is readily available and known as "Call Processing Language Requirements" (ietf-iptel-cpl-requirements-00.txt).
2. Since a call between two endpoints (an IP host and a PSTN user) may pass through some sort of gateway (a telephony gateway, for example), the selection of such a gateway can be based on many criteria including client's preference, ISP preference, availability of gateway and telephone numbering. More likely a gateway will be implemented outside of a host's admin-

istrative domain. Therefore, a protocol is required to allow gateways in remote domains to distribute their attributes. Such a protocol must allow scalable, bandwidth-efficient and very secure transmission of gateway attributes. The IETF IPTEL working group has specified some drafts to address those needs such as "A Framework for a Peer Gatekeeper Routing Protocol" (draft-ietf-iptel-pgrp-framework-00.txt).

In the following paragraphs we will analyze those requirements and protocols.

Call processing language requirements (CPL-R): Currently, a number of protocols such as SIP and H.323 allow a call to be made over IP networks. The emerging standards provide a broad and dramatic decentralization of telephone provisioning services allowed within the user's control. Such services can be implemented within an end system. However, some attributes such as call distribution, behavior-on-busy and the like can be identified as follows:

- **Call forward on busy/no answer:** A new call if generated should ring the user's desk phone. If the user is unavailable it should be forwarded to his/ her voicemail box except in the case of a supervisor it should be forwarded to the cellular phone.
- **Administrative screening – firewall:** In some cases, an outgoing call should be rejected if the organization does not want it going to certain destinations, otherwise it should be forwarded to the appropriate destination if the call is accepted. Such calls may also need to be screened if required.
- **Central phone server:** In certain scenarios, the call should be forwarded to the people proxying for the user or it may be forwarded to a certain location where the user may be available, otherwise a recorded message should tell the caller when to call back.
- **Intelligent user location:** A call may be forwarded to a user's current location if the user is mobile, otherwise it should be forwarded to all locations where the user is registered.
- **Intelligent user location with media knowledge:** The incoming call may be forwarded to a station whose media best match the call request.
- **Intelligent user location with mixer (home phone):** The incoming call should ring every station where the user is registered and the media should be transparently mixed together and sent to the caller.
- **Third-party registration control:** The registration should be authenticated to discourage illegal usage by third parties.
- **Client billing allocation – lawyer's office:** In order to bill a client, an organization may want the time, duration and caller's identity to be logged.
- **End system busy:** For the incoming call, if the user is on another line, a call waiting tone should be generated, or if "Do not disturb" is set the caller should get a busy signal.
- **Phone bank (call distribution/queuing):** An organization may require the call to be distributed to the support engineers (for example) equally.

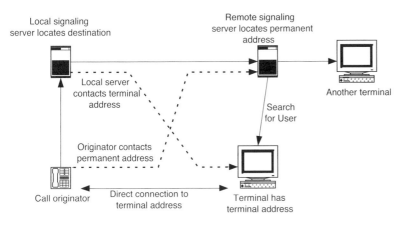

Fig. 4.31. Call signaling messages

Local signaling
server locates destination

Remote signaling
server locates permanent
address

Another terminal

Local server
contacts terminal
address

Search
for User

Originator contacts
permanent address

Call originator

Direct connection to
terminal address

Terminal has
terminal address

4.4.1.3.1 *CPL-R Architecture*

The CPL-R architecture describes two types of components that are required for Internet telephony: the end system or receive media and the network system. The end system is either a user or agent, or may be an automated system. The network system that relays signaling information can be either SIP proxy/redirect servers or H.323 gatekeepers.

The proxy server in a CPL-R architecture receives and forwards the call whereas a redirect server tells the originator of the call an alternate location to try. Registrars, on the other hand, track the user's current locations and function similar to proxy or redirect server. The Internet telephony address can be of two types: terminal address and permanent address (Fig. 4.31). The terminal address is like an IP address, which does not change. The permanent address refers to a more abstract-level user address that may change. The main purpose of CPL-R is to allow the user to modify the way the IP telephony system handles call events. The most common modification is incoming call setup, for example. In CPL-R the user creates call processing language scripts and transmits them to the network system. The script exists in the network system unless deleted or given an expiration timer. Therefore, network device should have a stable storage system.

4.5 H.323 Protocol

The ITU-T Recommendation H.323 specifies terminals and other elements that provide packet-based multimedia communication systems. This recommendation does not guarantee QoS. The H.323 elements support audio, video and data; while audio is mandatory, video and data are optional. H.323 also addresses call control, multimedia management and bandwidth management, as well as interfaces between LANs and other networks. The network through which H.323 elements communicate may be a point-to-point, point-to-multipoint or a multiple segment with complex topologies. H.323

sets multimedia standards for the existing infrastructure (i.e., IP-based networks). Designed to compensate for the effect of highly variable LAN latency, H.323 allows customers to use multimedia applications without changing their network infrastructure. IP LANs are becoming more powerful. Ethernet is moving from 100 Mb/s to 1000 Mb/s, and a mixed environment is becoming common where Gigabit Ethernet (1000 Mb/s) is used for interswitch links in a Fast Ethernet (100 Mb/s) network.

As described in the ITU-T recommendation, the H.323 entities may also interwork with H.310 terminals on B-ISDN, H.320 terminals on N-ISDN, H.321 terminals on B-ISDN, H.322 terminals on guaranteed QoS LANs, H.324 terminals on GSTN (General Switched Telephone Network) and wireless networks, V.70 terminals on GSTN, and voice terminals on GSTN or ISDN by implementing gateways.

The H.323 Recommendation covers the technical requirements for audio and video communications services in LANs that do not provide a guaranteed QoS. H.323 references the T.120 specification for data conferencing and enables conferences which include a data capability. The scope of H.323 does not include the LAN itself or the transport layer that may be used to connect various LANs. Only elements needed for interaction with the switched circuit network (SCN) are within the scope of H.323. Figure 4.32 outlines an H.323 system and its components. The H.323 Protocol is part of a series of communications standards that enable videoconferencing across a range of networks. Known as H.32X, this series includes H.320 and H.324, which address ISDN and PSTN communications, respectively. This primer provides an overview of the H.323 standard, its benefits, architecture and applications.

Here is a list of various standards that apply to H.323:

Fig. 4.32. Interworking of H.323 entities in various network configurations

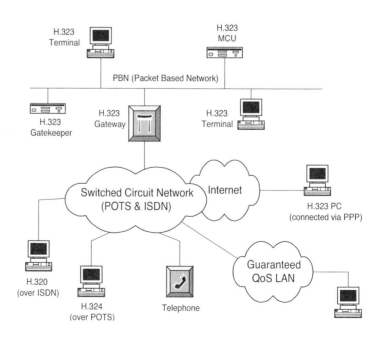

- H.320: The original ISDN videoconferencing standard.
- H.323: An extension of H.320 for videoconferencing over LANs. Composed of the following standards:
  - H.225: call control protocol
  - H.245: media control protocol
  - H.261: video codec for 64 Kb/s or higher
  - H.263: video codec for less than 64 Kb/s
  - G.711: PCM audio codec 56/64 Kb/s
  - G.722: audio codec for 7 kHz at 48/56/64 Kb/s
  - G.723: speech codec for 5.3 and 6.4 Kb/s
  - G.728: speech codec for 16 Kb/s
  - G.729: speech codec for 8/13 Kb/s.
- H.324: An extension of H.320 for videoconferencing over PSTN lines.
- Q.931: Digital subscriber signaling.
- T.120: Real-time data conferencing protocol.

The H.323 standard provides a foundation for audio, video, and data communications across IP-based networks, including the Internet. H.323-compliant multimedia products and applications from multiple vendors can interoperate allowing users to communicate without concern for compatibility. H.323 will be the cornerstone for LAN-based products for consumer, business, entertainment and professional applications.

It is an umbrella recommendation from the ITU that sets standards for multimedia communications over LANs that do not provide a guaranteed QoS. These networks dominate today's corporate desktops and include packet-switched TCP/IP and IPX over Ethernet, Fast Ethernet and Token Ring network technologies. Therefore, the H.323 standards are important building blocks for a broad new range of collaborative, LAN-based applications for multimedia communications.

H.323 defines four major components for a network-based communications system: terminals, gateways, gatekeepers, and multipoint control units.

4.5.1 Terminals

The terminals are the endpoints on the LAN that provide real-time two-way communications. They must support voice communications and can optionally support video or data communications. The most common H.323 terminals today are applications, such as Microsoft's NetMeeting, running on a PC.

An H.323 terminal includes a system control unit, H.225 layer, network interface, an audio codec Unit and two optional elements, namely a video codec unit and user data applications (Fig. 4.33).

4.5.2 Gateways

H.323 gateways provide services to H.323 clients so that they can communicate with non-H.323 entities. The most common type of H.323 gateway allows communications between H.323 terminals and telephones on the

Fig. 4.33. H.323 terminal equipment as described in ITU-T Rec. H.323 figure 4

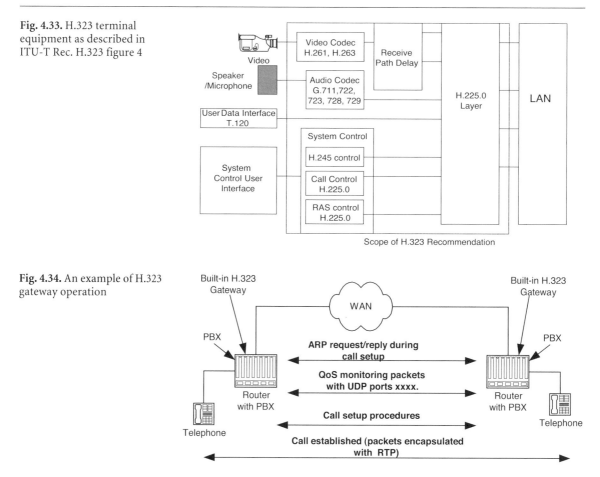

Fig. 4.34. An example of H.323 gateway operation

circuit-switched network. The gateway must provide translations between different transmission formats, communications procedures and audio codecs. ITU-T Recommendation H.246 defines the translation procedures of the H.323 gateway. The gateway also performs call setup. For example, let's consider a network which has two branch offices, both connected via T1 point-to-point link. Assuming that such a product exists, like, for example, Nortel Network's BCM, we consider all our WAN, routing, gateway and PBX services are integrated in one system as shown in Fig. 4.34. Here, a call is made from one branch office to the other. The phones are connected to the interface module of the PBX that is integrated in our imaginary system. Now, in order for the call to be routed to the other branch office, the system first needs to send ARP request and ensure that ARP reply is received. The initiation of ARP request is the primary phase here. The next phase is for the H.323 gateways to ensure that both are maintaining the same IP QoS mechanism or filtering scheme. Such a scheme can be established by defining a rule in the router for IP packets with certain UDP ports having priority treatment over other traffic. We will term it QoS monitoring; this will ensure that VoIP packets are treated with appropriate care and the gateways are ready to do so.

Once the QoS assurance is established the gateways will initiate call setup procedures. In the next phase, the call that is originated from a telephone connected to the PBX part of our imaginary system will be converted into VoIP packets and transmitted over the WAN link to the other system where it will be decapsulated and the call information will be directed to the destination telephone.

4.5.3 Gatekeepers

Gatekeepers provide call control services for H.323 endpoints, such as address translation and bandwidth management. Gatekeepers in H.323 networks are optional. If they are present in a network, however, endpoints must use their services. The H.323 standards define mandatory services that the gatekeeper must provide and specifies other optional functionality that it can provide. The gatekeeper's primary job is to provide call control services for registered H.323 endpoints.

The H.323 standards define several mandatory services that the gatekeeper must provide and specify other optional functionality that it can provide. While the standards define how communication with a gatekeeper occurs, via the Registration/Admission/Status (RAS) Protocol, they do not specify how the gatekeeper should provide its service.

A gatekeeper is capable of providing following services:

- Address translation: It performs alias address to transport address translation.
- Admission control: It authorizes network access by means of ARQ, ACF and ARJ messages (ITU-T H.225.0), which is based on call authorization, bandwidth or some other criteria that are vendor independent.
- Bandwidth control: It also supports BRQ/BRJ/BCF messages, which may be based on bandwidth management.
- Zone management: It provides the above-mentioned service for terminals and gateways which have registered with it.

Also, the following optional services are available from an H.323 gatekeeper (see, for example, Fig. 4.35) :

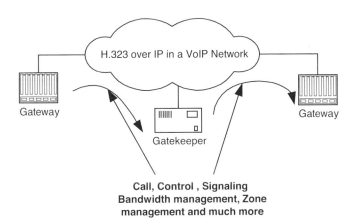

Fig. 4.35. An example of H.323 gatekeeper operation

- Call control signaling: In this optional operation, the H.323 gatekeeper may complete the call signaling procedure with an H.323 endpoint or, alternatively, can redirect the call signaling channel to each of the other endpoints.
- Call authorization: In this operation the gatekeeper may choose to reject calls from a terminal due to authorization failure.
- Call management: The gatekeeper may choose to list all the ongoing H.323 calls, which will indicate that a terminal is busy and can be useful for bandwidth management purposes.
- Bandwidth management: The H.323 gatekeeper uses this function to control the number of simultaneous connections in the network. It may reject a terminal from further access to the network due to bandwidth limitation or grant a terminal access to network if bandwidth is available.

4.5.3.1 Gatekeeper Operation

We mentioned earlier that an H.323 gatekeeper can optionally participate in call signaling. Call signaling is the procedures and messages that are used to establish a call, request bandwidth changes of the call, acquiring the status of the endpoints in a call, and call disconnect. The call signaling messages are described in ITU-T Recommendation H.225.0.

The procedure of call signaling includes the following:

- Call setup – phase 1.
- Initial communication and capability exchange – phase 2.
- Establishment of audio-visual communication – phase 3.
- Call services – phase 4.
- Call termination – phase 5.

4.5.3.1.1 Call Setup

The call setup uses call control messages specified in H.225.0. Although H.225.0 includes a description of the call control messages, those are a part of the ITU-T Q.931 messages. At the earliest possible stage a request for bandwidth reservation is performed (Fig. 4.36). We described QoS monitor-

Fig. 4.36. An example of bandwidth reservation procedures

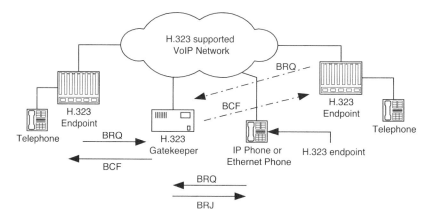

ing earlier, but that concerns IP Diffserv-specific services and should not be confused with those specified in H.225.0. The gatekeeper provides appropriate bandwidth allocation when it receives a BRQ (Bandwidth Request) from the endpoint. The gatekeeper may grant such a request through the use of BCF (Bandwidth Confirm) or reject the request through the use of BRJ (Bandwidth Reject).

The BRQ messages includes the following:

- **requestSeqNum:** This tediously increasing number is unique to the sender. The receiver for any associated message must return it.
- **endpointIdentifier:** This endpoint identifier was earlier assigned by the RCF (Registration Confirm). We will describe RCF later.
- **conferenceID:** This specifies the ID of the call that needs the bandwidth allocation.
- **callReferenceValue:** This is obtained from Q.931 and assigned by the originating interface side of the call. The gatekeeper uses this value to associate BRQ with a particular call.
- **callType:** The gatekeeper attempts to determine the "real" bandwidth usage by using this value.
- **bandwidth:** This is the number of 100-bit increments requested for the call. This absolute value includes only audio and video bitstreams and excludes headers and overhead.
- **nonstandardData:** This field specifies the data of proprietary information.
- **callIdentifier:** This is a globally unique call identifier usually assigned to the originating endpoint.
- **gatekeeperIdentifier:** This identifies the gatekeeper uniquely to the endpoints; a backup gatekeeper may exist in the network.
- **tokens:** These are sometimes required to allow operation and consist of some data.
- **cryptoTokens:** This includes encrypted tokens.
- **integrityCheckValue:** This is used for a data integrity check and is computed by the sender.
- **answeredCall:** This is set to "True" if the party was the original destination to answer the call.

The BCF message includes the following:

- **requestSeqNum:** This value is the same as included in the BRQ.
- **bandwidth:** Increments of 100 bits, the maximum allowed at this time.
- **nonstandardData:** Carries proprietary information.
- **tokens:** These are inserted in the message and carry some data.
- **cryptoTokens:** Encrypted tokens.
- **integrityCheckValue:** This is a data integrity check value computed by the sender applying an integrity algorithm and secret key upon the entire message.

The BRJ message includes the following:

- **requestSeqNum:** As described earlier.
- **rejectReason:** Specifies the reason for rejection by the gatekeeper.

- **allowedBandwidth:** The maximum allowed in this time at increments of 100 bits including current amount allowed.
- **nonstandardData:** The proprietary information.
- **altGKInfo:** Information about alternative gatekeepers. This is optional.
- **tokens:** As described earlier.
- **cryptotokens:** As described earlier.
- **integrityCheckValue:** As described earlier.

During call setup, if both the alias address and transport address are specified, the alias address will get preference. The alias address is associated with the endpoint. An endpoint may have one or more alias addresses. It is generally E.164 or partyNumber (network access number, telephone number, etc.) addresses. A gatekeeper, MC (Multipoint Controller) or MP (Multipoint Processor) should not have an alias address. There is no synchronization during the call setup. This means that both endpoints can send a setup message at the same time. It is up to the application to determine if one call is required and thus imply the appropriate action.

The action may be for the endpoint to indicate it is busy or capable of processing simultaneous calls. The endpoint is capable of sending the alerting message, which imparts that there is an incoming call. If a gateway is used, that gateway must send this message when it receives a ring indication. If an endpoint capable of responding to a setup message with connect, call proceeding, or release within 4 seconds, it is not required to send the alerting message. To understand the call setup further, we can consider several scenarios for call setup procedures which are described below.

The first consideration is that the endpoints are not registered with the gatekeeper. It should be remembered that endpoints are capable of communicating directly (Fig. 4.37).

In this case, endpoint 1 sends a setup message to the well-known call signaling channel TSAP (Telephone Service Access Point) identifier of endpoint

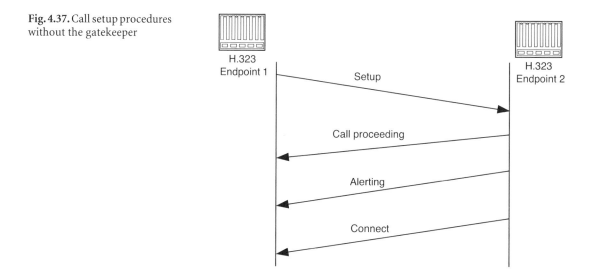

Fig. 4.37. Call setup procedures without the gatekeeper

2. To understand TSAP identifier we should know something about the network address first, which uniquely identifies an H.323 entity in the network. A group of such entities may share a network address. An endpoint may use different network addresses for different channels within the same call. Remember that for each network address, an H.323 entity may use several TSAP identifiers. These identifiers allow multiplexing of several channels sharing the same network address. Endpoints have one well-known TSAP identifier defined that is also known as the "Call Signaling Channel TSAP Identifier". The gatekeeper also has one well-known TSAP identifier, which is known as the "RAS Channel TSAP Identifier". The multicast address also has one well-known TSAP identifier known as the "Discover Multicast Address".

Now, as endpoint 2 receives the setup message it responds with a connect that contains an H.245 control channel transport address (refer to H.245 for further details on this).

Let's now assume that endpoints are registered with the same gatekeeper, and the gatekeeper has chosen direct call signaling. In this scenario, endpoint 1 initiates an ARQ (Admission Request) message, to which the gatekeeper responds with ACF.

The ARQ includes the following fields:

- **requestSeqNum:** This is a tediously incrementing number unique to the sender.
- **callType:** The gatekeeper uses this value to determine the "real" bandwidth usage. The default value is point-to-point for all calls.
- **callModel:** We mentioned earlier that endpoints are capable of handling the direct call model. If the call is routed by the gatekeeper, the endpoint will request the gatekeeper-mediated model. The gatekeeper may not comply with such a request. We will describe gatekeeper-routed calls later in this section.
- **endpointIdentifier:** This endpoint identifier is assigned by the RCF (Registration Confirm).
- **destinationInfo:** Alias addresses for the destination, namely E.164 or H.323 IDs.
- **destCallSignalAddress:** This is the transport address used at the destination for call signaling.
- **destExtraCallInfo:** Includes external addresses for multiple calls.
- **srcInfo:** This is a sequence of alias addresses for the source endpoint. It indicates the originator of the call.
- **srcCallSignalAddress:** This is the transport address used at source for call signaling.
- **bandwidth:** The number of 100 bits requested for a bidirectional call. For example, a 128 Kb/s call will be signaled at 256 Kb/s.
- **callReferenceValue:** As described earlier.
- **nonstandardData:** Proprietary data information.
- **callServices:** This field provides information regarding optional Q-series protocol support to the gatekeeper and to the terminal.
- **conferenceID:** Unique conference identifier.

- **activeMC:** If set this indicates that the calling party has an active MC, otherwise false.
- **answerCall:** This is used to indicate to a gatekeeper an incoming call.
- **canMapAlias:** When set to "True", this indicates if the ACF includes destinationInfo, destExtraCallInfo and/or remoteExtension fields; then the endpoint may copy this information to the destinationAddress, destExtraCallInfo and remoteExtensionAddress fields of the setup message.
- **callIdentifier:** This is a globally unique identifier.
- **srcAlternatives:** Prioritized sequence of source endpoint alternatives for srcInfo, srcCallSignalAddress or rasAddress.
- **destAlternatives:** Similar to srcAlternatives, this is a sequence of prioritized destination endpoint alternatives for destinationInfo or destCallSignalAddress.
- **gatekeeperIdentifier:** This identifies a gatekeeper uniquely.
- **tokens:** As described earlier.
- **cryptoTokens:** Encrypted tokens.
- **integrityCheckValue:** As described earlier.
- **transportQoS:** While used this indicates the capability of the endpoint to reserve transport resources.
- **willSupplyUUIEs:** In case the gatekeeper requests Q.931 information in IRR (Information Request Response) messages by setting this field to "True", so the endpoint will supply it.
- **endpointControlled:** The endpoint applies its own reservation mechanism.
- **gatekeeperControlled:** The gatekeeper is doing resource reservation on behalf of the endpoint.
- **noControl:** No resource reservation required.

The ACF includes the following fields:

- **requestSeqNum:** Same value as passed by the ARQ message.
- **bandWidth:** This may be less than the requested bandwidth but shows maximum bandwidth allowed for this call.
- **callModel:** This indicates whether the call is direct or gatekeeper routed.
- **destCallSignalAddress:** This is the transport address to which the Q.931 call signaling is sent.
- **irrFrequency:** This measures the frequency in seconds that an endpoint will send IRRs to the gatekeeper while on a call.
- **nonstandardData:** The proprietary information.
- **destinationInfo:** When called through a gatekeeper this is the address of the initial channel.
- **destExtraCallInfo:** The additional channel needed for a call.
- **destinationType:** This specifies the type of destination endpoint.
- **remoteExtensionAddress:** If this is required to traverse multiple gateways, it includes the alias address of a called endpoint.
- **alternateEndpoints:** The prioritized sequence of endpoint alternatives for destinationCallSignalAddress or destinationInfo.
- **tokens:** As described earlier.

- **cryptoTokens:** As described earlier.
- **integrityCheckValue:** As described earlier.
- **transportQoS:** A resource reservation request; if a gatekeeper receives this request in ARQ it returns TransportQoS in ACF.
- **willRespondToIRR:** If true the gatekeeper will send an IACK or INAK message.
- **uuiesRequested:** This indicates the set of H.225.0 call signaling messages which the endpoint notifies to the gatekeeper.

Now that we have talked about ARQ and ACF, ARJ (Admission Reject) may occur if the admission request is rejected. The ARJ includes the following fields:

- **requestSeqNum:** The same value as passed by ARQ.
- **rejectReason:** The reason for which the admission is denied.
- **nonstandardData:** Proprietary data.
- **altGKInfo:** This is optional information regarding alternative gatekeepers.
- **tokens:** As described earlier.
- **cryptoTokens:** As described earlier.
- **callSignalAddress:** The gatekeeper's call signaling address returned when the reject reason routes a call to the gatekeeper.
- **integrityCheckValue:** As described earlier.

We now know about the ARQ, ACF and ARJ messages and their message fields. Now, going to back to our original discussion about a situation when both endpoints are registered with the same gatekeeper, in this case, as shown in Fig. 4.38, the gatekeeper responds to an ARQ message of endpoint 1 with ACF, in which the gatekeeper includes the call signaling channel transport address of itself. Endpoint 1 now sends a setup message using that transport address. As a result, the gatekeeper forwards it to endpoint 2. If the

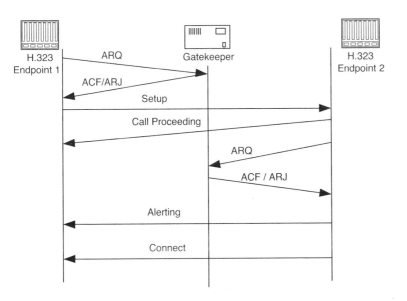

Fig. 4.38. An example of call setup procedures with gatekeeper registration

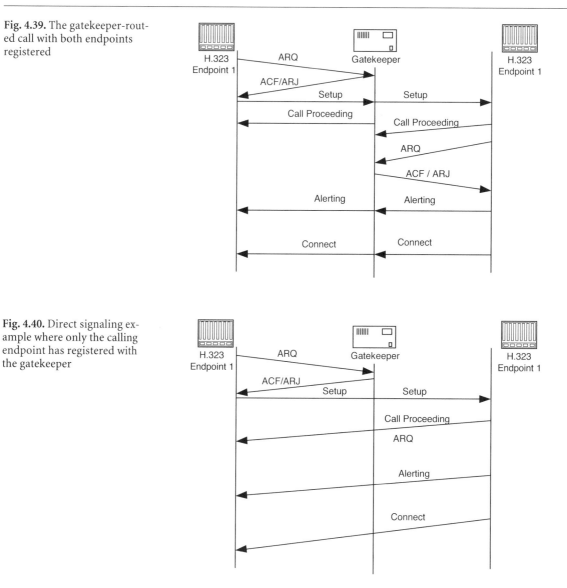

Fig. 4.39. The gatekeeper-routed call with both endpoints registered

Fig. 4.40. Direct signaling example where only the calling endpoint has registered with the gatekeeper

endpoint accepts the call it initiates the ARQ/ACF exchanges with the gatekeeper. It is also possible that an ARJ is received by endpoint 2 and, if so, it sends "Release Complete" to the gatekeeper. Alternatively, if the admission is granted through ACF, endpoint 2 then sends a connect message (Fig. 4.39).

Let's consider another scenario where only the calling endpoint has the gatekeeper. In this case, after the ARQ/ACF exchange, endpoint 1 sends a setup message to endpoint 2 using the well-known call signaling channel transport address (Fig. 4.40).

If endpoint 2 accepts the call, it responds with a connect message that includes an H.245 control channel transport address in H.245 signaling.

4.5.3.1.2 Initial Communication and Capability Exchange

After the exchanges of the call setup message in phase 1, the endpoint may use H.245 and establish the H.245 control channel. The procedures are described in ITU-T Recommendation H.245. This control channel is a part of the H.245 control function and used for carrying end-to-end control messages subject to the operations of an H.323 entity. This includes capability exchange, opening and closing of logical channels, mode preference requests, flow control messages, and general commands and indications.

The H.245 signaling occurs between two endpoints: an endpoint and a gatekeeper or an endpoint and an MC (we will discuss MC later). The endpoint establishes only one H.245 control channel per call and the channel uses the procedures and messages defined in H.245. The syntax of H.245 control messages is defined using ASN.1.

The H.245 protocol entities are as follows:

- Master/slave determination
- Capability exchange
- Logical channel signaling
- Bidirectional logical channel signaling
- Close logical channel signaling
- Mode request
- Round-trip delay determination
- Maintenance loop signaling.

Master/slave determination: It is obvious that conflict may arise between two terminals in a call when similar events occurs simultaneously. To resolve such conflicts H.245 states that one terminal should become the master and the other should assume the role of slave. This determination procedures includes a set of messages as follows:

- **Master slave determination:** This message is sent from an MSDSE (Master Slave Determination Signaling Entity) to the peer MSDSE. In this part, "terminalType" identifies the type of terminal such as terminals, MCUs (Multipoint Control Units) and gateways. The "statusDetermination-Number" in this message is a random number in the range 0 to $2^{24} - 1$.
- **Master slave determination acknowledge:** This is used to confirm the earlier message. When the decision type is the master, the terminal receiving this message is the master and if the decision type is slave, the terminal is slave.
- **Master slave determination reject:** A rejection may happen if the random numbers are equal and the terminal types are same.
- **Master slave determination release:** In case of timeout, this message is sent.

To understand this procedure further, let's imagine that there is one instance of the MSDSE in each terminal involved in a call.

In Fig. 4.41, the internal functions of an H.323 terminal are exposed with its relationship to the master slave determination procedure. Here, we have to consider one H.323 terminal's MSDSE component. The procedure we are about to describe may happen at both terminals, but for simplicity we con-

Fig. 4.41. The functional description of the MSDSE procedure for master slave determination

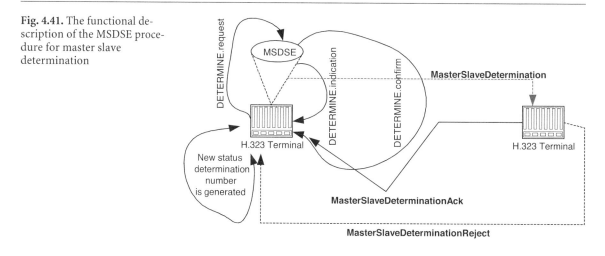

Fig. 4.42. H.245 capability exchange

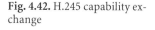

sider just one MSDSE. The master slave determination is initiated by issuing DETERMINE.request primitives to its MSDSE. At this point the MasterSlave-Determination message is sent to the peer MSDSE and timer T106 is started. If a MasterSlaveAck message is received back at the originating terminal, the T106 timer is then stopped. The DETERMINATION.confirm primitives inform the control process of the terminal that the master slave determination was successful. If for any reason MasterSlaveDeterminationReject is received instead, then a new status determination number is generated and timer T106 restarted. If timer T106 has expired then a REJECT.indication primitive will be issued by the MSDSE.

Capability exchange: This is the procedure intended to ensure the receive and transmit capabilities as well as a terminal's operative criterion. The receive capabilities describe the terminal's ability to receive and process incoming information. The transmit capabilities describe the terminal's ability to transmit information streams. As shown in Fig. 4.42, a set of terminal capability messages is exchanged during the capability exchange procedure.

The transmitting terminal assigns a number to each individual mode the terminal is capable of operating and that is set in a "Capability Table"; that is, G.723.1 audio and G.728 audio will be assigned with separate numbers for each. These capability numbers are occasionally grouped together as "Alternative Capability Set" structures. Each of these structures indicates that the terminal is capable of operating in one mode listed on the set. For example, an "Alternative Capability Set" listing [G.711, G.723.1, G.728] means that the terminal is capable of operating at any of these mode but only one at a time.

The "Simultaneous Capability Set" [{H.261}, {H.263}, {G.711, G.723.1, G.728}] means that the terminal is capable of operating two video channels and one audio channel simultaneously.

The "Terminal Capability Set" messages include information about the terminal's capability to transmit and receive. They also identify the version of H.245 in use. An instance of terminal capability set is identified with a sequence number field. The protocol identifier field is used to indicate the version of H.245 in use. The multiplex capability field identifies the capability related to multiplexing and network adaptation. A terminal should include this in the first "Terminal Capability Set" sent to its peer.

The "Capability Table" includes numbered capability lists which the terminal is capable of performing. A "Terminal Capability Set" may include 0 or more "Capability Table Entries". A new "Capability Table Entry" replaces the old one with the same "Capability Table Entry Number".

The "Capability Descriptor " indicates the capability of a terminal to transmit and receive. It also provides an independent statement of the terminal. A "Capability Descriptor" is numbered with "Capability Descriptor Number".

Logical channel signaling: The set of messages in this criterion is used both for unidirectional and bidirectional signaling. However, some parameters are different. A logical channel carries information from the transmitter to one or more receivers. The logical channels are open or closed using "openLogicalChannel" and "closeLogicalChannel" messages. The procedures for such message exchanges are defined in ITU-T Recommendation H.245.

The "openLogicalChannel" is used to open a unidirectional logical channel connection between an outgoing LCSE (Logical Channel Signaling Entity) and a peer of incoming LCSE. It is also used to open a bidirectional logical channel connection between an outgoing B-LCSE (Bidirectional Logical Channel Signaling Entity) and a peer of incoming B-LCSE.

To provide reliable opening and closing of unidirectional logical channels acknowledged procedures are identified as LCSE Protocol by H.245. The procedures are defined in terms of primitives. There are two kinds of LCSE, outgoing and incoming. At each of the outgoing and incoming sides there is one instance of the LCSE for each unidirectional logical channel. Also, there is no connection between an incoming LCSE and an outgoing LCSE at each given side, other than via primitives to and from the LCSE user. If there is an error condition at LCSE it is reported. Data transport should happen through a logical channel only at the ESTABLISHED state. The data is discarded if re-

Fig. 4.43. An example of LCSE procedures

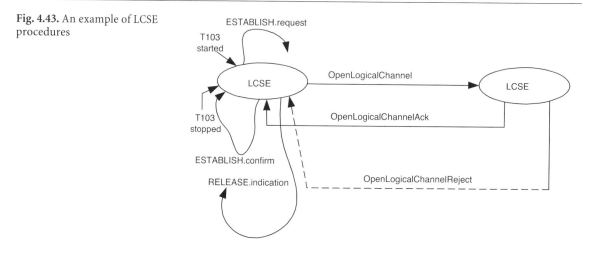

ceived through a logical channel that is not in the ESTABLISHED state; this behavior should not be considered as a fault that has occurred.

If an endpoint is not capable of processing the signals on a logical channel, the endpoint may choose to close the logical channel and transmit the relevant capability information to the remote terminal.

The user at the outgoing LCSE issues an ESTABLISH.request primitive to initiate the opening of the logical channel (Fig. 4.43). The OpenLogicalChannel message includes "forwardLogicalChannelParameters" which is sent to the peer incoming LCSE, and the timer T103 is started. The timer is stopped once an OpenLogicalChannelAck message is received in response to the OpenLogicalChannel message and the user is informed with the ESTABLISH.confirm primitive that the logical channel has been successfully opened. This ensures that the logical channel is ready to be used for the transport of user information. Now, if in response to an earlier OpenLogicalChannel message, for any reason, the system receives an OpenLogicalChannelReject message, then timer T103 is stopped and the user is informed via the RELEASE.indication primitive that the peer LCSE user has refused establishment of the logical channel.

The "Logical Channel" generally uses the following procedure (Fig. 4.44). The initiating endpoint opens an OpenLogicalChannel message as defined in ITU-T Recommendation H.245. If it is required to carry media types using RTP (Real-Time Transport Protocol), the OpenLogicalChannelAck message must contain mediaControlChannel parameters; the included transport address should be for the forward RTCP (RTP Control Protocol) channel. Media types that do not use RTP/RTCP should omit the mediaControlChannel parameters.

Bidirectional logical channel signaling: Similar to the unidirectional logical signaling procedure, bidirectional logical channel signaling (B-LCS) uses a protocol procedure known as B-LCSE. The procedures are described here in terms of primitives in the interface between B-LCSE and the B-LCSE user. There are two kinds of B-LCSE, incoming and outgoing.

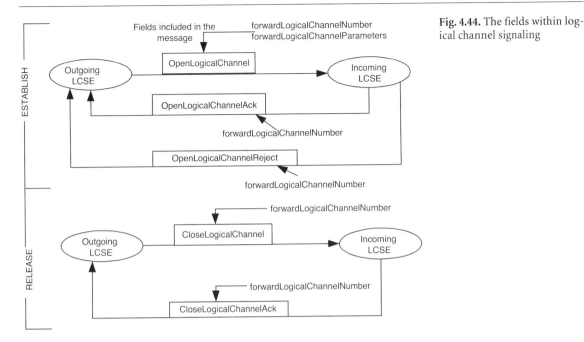

Fig. 4.44. The fields within logical channel signaling

A bidirectional channel includes a pair of unidirectional channels: "forward" (outgoing side) and "reverse" (incoming side). The "forward" channel is used to refer to transmission in the direction from the endpoint making the request for a bidirectional logical channel to the other endpoint. The "reverse" channel is used to refer to the opposite direction of transmission. During the "ESTABLISHED" state data is sent on a bidirectional channel. Nevertheless, data can be received on the forward channel if the incoming B-LCSE is in the AWAITING CONFIRMATION state. The data will be discarded if received in any state other than the ESTABLISHED state and the AWAITING CONFIRMATION state will be discarded and no fault shall be considered to have occurred. An endpoint may choose to reject a request to open a bidirectional logical channel due to its inability to support the requested reverse channel parameters. If this happens, the endpoint will reject the request identifying the cause with unsuitableReverseParameters.

Once the ESTABLISH.request is issued by the user at the outgoing B-LCSE, the opening of a logical channel is initiated (Fig. 4.45). Then, immediately after, an OpenLogicalChannel message that includes both forward and reverse logical channel parameters is sent to the peer incoming B-LCSE, and the timer T103 is started. The timer is stopped once an OpenLogicalChannelAck message is received in response to the OpenLogicalChannel message. If this happens, an OpenLogicalChannelConfirm message is sent to the peer incoming B-LCSE, and the ESTABLISH.confirm primitive informs the user that the logical channel has been successfully opened.

In response to the OpenLogicalChannel message, if for any reason an OpenLogicalChannelReject message is received then timer T103 is stopped and the user is informed with the RELEASE.indication primitive that the peer

Fig. 4.45. The B-LCS procedures

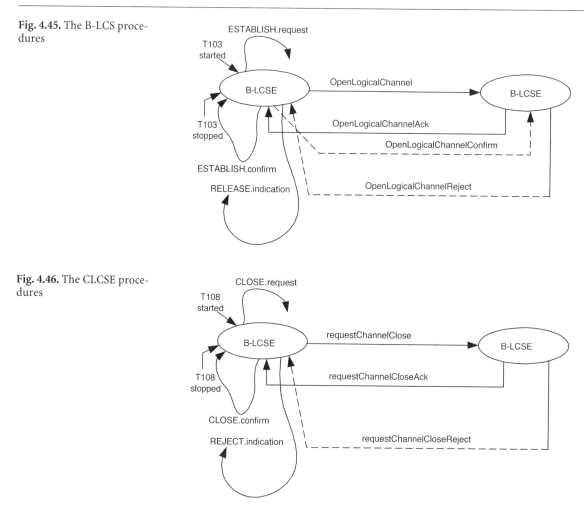

Fig. 4.46. The CLCSE procedures

B-LCSE user has refused establishment of the logical channel. The RE-
LEASE.indication primitive, and a CloseLogicalChannel message, are sent to
the peer incoming B-LCSE to inform the user if timer T103 has expired in this
period.

Close logical channel signaling: This is used by the outgoing LCSE or B-
LCSE to close the logical channel connection between peer LCSEs or B-LCS-
Es. The forwardLogicalChannelNumber identifies the logical channel
number of the forward channel of the logical channel that is to be closed. The
CLCS (Close Logical Channel Signaling) includes the CLCSE (Close Logical
Channel Signaling Entity). The messages in the CLCSE procedures are close-
LogicalChannelAck, requestChannelClose, requestChannelCloseAck, re-
questChannelCloseReject and requestChannelCloseRelease.

The CLCSE procedures (Fig. 4.46) are described in terms of primitives in
section C.6 of ITU-T Recommendation H.245. Like LCSE, the CLCSE also has
an outgoing CLCSE and an incoming CLCSE. The CLCS procedure starts

Fig. 4.47. The MRSE procedures

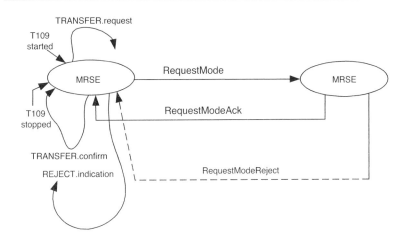

once the CLOSE.request primitive is issued by the user at the outgoing CLCSE. A requestChannelClose message is then sent to the peer incoming CLCSE, and timer T108 is started.

If, for any reason, a requestChannelCloseReject message is received then timer T108 is stopped and the REJECT.indication primitive informs the user that the peer CLCSE user has refused to close the logical channel.

Mode request: The mode request is used to request particular modes of transmission from the transmit terminal or endpoint. It is actually a list of modes that the endpoint prefers to receive. The message includes ModeDescription, Mode Element, H223ModeParameters and H2250ModeParameters. The entity that is responsible for the operation of this procedure is known as the MRSE (Mode Request Signaling Entity). The procedures for MRSE are described in terms of primitives in ITU-T Recommendation H.245 section C.9. Like other entities described earlier, the MRSE also has an outgoing MRSE and an incoming MRSE. There is an instance of MRSE per call at each of the outgoing and incoming ends.

A terminal or endpoint issues TRANSFER.response to answer a mode request positively (Fig. 4.47). It does so by initiating the logical channel signaling procedures to establish the appropriate mode of transmission as soon as possible.

Once the TRANSFER.request is issued a RequestMode message is sent to the incoming MRSE and the timer T109 is started. If a RequestModeAck is received as a result, the timer is stopped and the user is informed through the TRANSFER.confirm primitive. However, if for any reason a RequestMode-Reject is received in response to a RequestMode message then the timer T109 is stopped and the user is informed through the use of REJECT.indication. Conversely, if the timer expires then the outgoing MRSE user is informed with the REJECT.indication primitive and a RequestModeRelease message is sent.

Round-trip delay determination: It is useful to know the RTD (Round-Trip Delay) between transmit endpoint and receive endpoint. A mechanism is provided in H.245 for measuring the RTD. A set of messages is used by a

Fig. 4.48. The RTDSE procedures

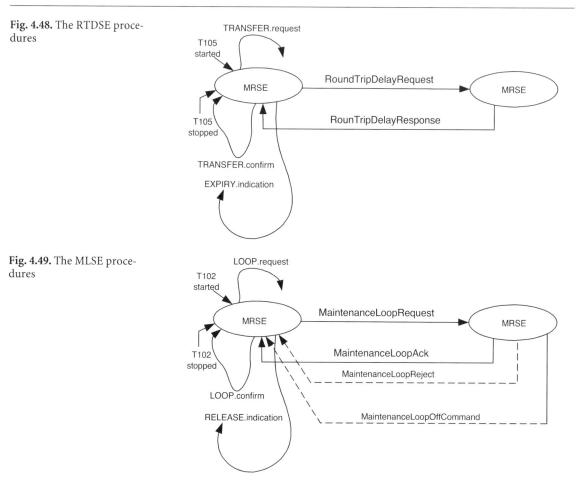

Fig. 4.49. The MLSE procedures

terminal or endpoint to determine the RTD between two communicating terminals. It also ensures an H.245 user can determine whether the peer H.245
protocol entity is alive. The RTD procedures include RoundTripDelayRe-
quest and RoundTripDelayResponse as the RTD message. The procedures
describe an entity known as RTDSE (Round-Trip Delay Signaling Entity)
(Fig. 4.48). The RTDSE is described in terms of primitives in section C.10 of
ITU-T Recommendation H.245.

Once the TRANSFER.request is initiated by the RTDSE user, a RoundTrip-
DelayRequest message is sent to the peer RTDSE, and timer T105 is started.
If the RoundTripDelayResponse message is received as a response, the timer
is stopped and the user is informed with the TRANSFER.confirm primitive of
the RTD that is the value of timer T105. Conversely, if the timer expires then
the EXPIRY.indication primitive informs the RTDSE user.

Maintenance loop signaling: Like any other entity the maintenance loop
signaling entity (MLSE) is described in terms of primitives at the interface
between the MLSE and the MLSE user, and MLSE states. It has an outgoing
MLSE and an incoming MLSE (Fig. 4.49). The terminal or endpoint with the

incoming MLSE only loops the appropriate data during the LOOPED state, not at any other time. Once the LOOP.request primitive is issued by the user at the outgoing MLSE, it is considered that the establishment of a maintenance loop is initiated.

4.5.3.1.3 *Audio-visual Communication Establishment*

After the capability exchange and master slave determination procedures, the H.245 Protocol then sets up an open logical channel for various information stream exchanges. The audio and video streams are transported over dynamic TSAP identifier through the use of unreliable protocols. The exchanged messages are openLogicalChannelAck, reverseLogicalChannelParameters, etc. Once the opening of logical channels for audio and video is done, an h2250MaximumSkewIndication message will be sent by the transmitter for each associated audio and video pair.

The following are some functional modes of operations in phase C:

- Mode changes
- Exchange of video by mutual agreement
- Media stream address distribution
- Correlation of media streams in multipoint conferences
- Communication mode command procedures.

Mode changes: ITU-T Recommendation H.245 Appendix V describes the procedure for changing channel structure, capability, receive mode and so on; the suggestion will minimize disruption of the audio. Because the opening and closing of H.245 logical channels are not synchronized with media content, it is possible that media dropout occurs between closing a logical channel and opening its replacement. Therefore, the suggested replacementFor parameter (V/H.245) allows the avoidance of such media dropout. For further details, please see the guidelines given in Appendix V of H.245.

Exchange of video by mutual agreement: H.245 also defines this procedure through the use of the optional parameter videoIndicateReadyToActive. Once this parameter is used the communication occurs as follows.

Considering two endpoints 1 and 2, endpoint 1 will not transmit video until and unless endpoint 2 has indicated its readiness to transmit video. During the communication, endpoint 1 will send the indication through videoIndicateReadyToActive once the initial capability exchange is completed. But endpoint 1 will not transmit any video signal until it receives either videoIndicateReadyToActive or incoming video from endpoint 2.

Media stream address distribution: During the unicast, endpoints open logical channels with each other. The addresses are therefore passed through the openLogicalChannel and openLogicalChannelAck. For multicast, those addresses are assigned by the MCU and transported through communicationModeCommand to the endpoints.

Correlation of media streams in multipoint conferences: To associate a logical channel with an RTP stream, the source endpoint sends an openLogicalChannel message to MC. If the source likes to specify a destination for the openLogicalChannel, it inserts the terminalLabel of the destination in the destination field of the h2250LogicalChannelParameters. The source endpoint also inserts its own terminalLAbel in the source field of h2250LogicalChannelParameters.

Communication mode command procedures: This procedure is initiated by an MCU through the use of the H.245 communicationModeCommand to indicate the communication mode for each media type: unicast or multicast. This command may enforce the closing of all logical channels and the opening of new ones.

4.5.3.1.4 Call Services
During this phase of communication, the following operations may occur:

- Bandwidth changes
- Status
- *Ad hoc* conference expansion
- Supplementary services
- Multipoint cascading
- Third-party-initiated pause and rerouting

Bandwidth changes: During admissions exchange the call bandwidth is established and approved by the gatekeeper. Every endpoint must ensure that the aggregated audio and video channels are within the approved bandwidth. This estimate excludes network headers, RTP payload and other overheads. The bandwidth can be increased or decreased at any time during conference, once requested by a gatekeeper or endpoint. The bandwidth changes are conveyed through BRQ and BCF accordingly. We described BRQ/BCF messages earlier in the call setup section; please refer to that section and Fig. 4.50.

Status: To understand whether or not the endpoint is alive or turned off, the gatekeeper uses IRQ (Information Request) and IRR (Information Re-

Fig. 4.50. An example of bandwidth change message exchange

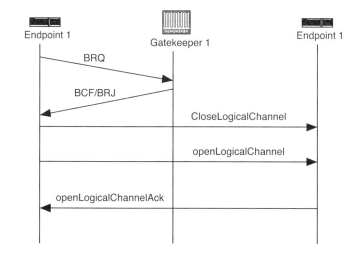

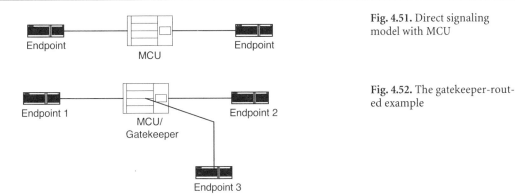

Fig. 4.51. Direct signaling model with MCU

Fig. 4.52. The gatekeeper-routed example

quest Response) message sequences, which poll the endpoints at a manufacturer's defined interval. This interval is generally greater than 10 s.

Ad hoc **conference expansion:** The *ad hoc* conference may be done by either direct call signaling or using the gatekeeper-routed call signaling model. Figures 4.51 and 4.52 show both of the configurations but in either case the MC must be present.

Supplementary services: This is optional for the H.323 gateway. The H.450 series of recommendations describes this supplementary service for the H.323 network.

Multipoint cascading: This is a method to cascade MCs. ITU-T H.323 section 8.4.5 defines multipoint cascading techniques.

Third-party-initiated pause and rerouting: In order to allow gatekeepers to reroute connections from endpoints that do not support supplementary services, endpoints respond to the reception of an empty capability set as in H.323 section 8.4.6. This feature allows "network" elements such as PBXs, call centers, and IVR (Interactive Voice Response) systems to reroute connections independently of supplementary services and facilitates preconnect announcements. It is also used to delay H.245 media establishment when features such as gatekeeper-based user locations are being used.

4.5.3.1.5 Call Termination

Either end is responsible for terminating a call. Call termination uses the procedures that are given here as follows:

- Call termination will discontinue transmission after complete transfer and all logical channels will then be closed whether they are for data or video.
- It should discontinue transmission of audio and then close all logical channels for audio.
- It should transmit the H.245 endSessionCommand message in the H.245 control channel, indicating to the far end that it wishes to disconnect the call and then discontinue H.245 message transmission.
- It should then wait to receive the endSessionCommand message from the other endpoint and then close the H.245 control channel.

- If the call signaling channel is open, a ReleaseComplete message should be sent and the channel closed.

4.5.4 Multipoint Control Units (MCUs)

MCUs provide support for conferences of three or more endpoints. An MCU manages conference resources, negotiations between endpoints for the purposes of determining the audio or video codec to use, and may or may not handle the media stream. The MCU is an endpoint on the network, which provides the capability for three or more terminals and gateways to participate in a multipoint conference. It may also connect two terminals in a point-to-point conference, which may later develop into a multipoint conference. The MCU generally operates in the fashion of an H.231 MCU; however, an audio processor is not mandatory. The MCU consists of two parts: a mandatory MC and optional MPs. In the simplest case, an MCU may consist only of an MC with no MPs. An MCU may also be brought into a conference by the gatekeeper without being explicitly called by one of the endpoints.

4.6 RTP (Real-Time Transport Protocol)

One of the important protocols used in the VoIP layered architecture is RTP. One of the questions that many readers may ask is whether or not it is really a transport layer protocol. Well, RTP is certainly not a protocol like TCP. It does not provide any form of reliability and congestion control that exists in TCP. However, RTP uses required craftiness for adding some flow control as well as application-specific reliability. Although the name suggests it is a real-time delivery mechanism, it is not an end-to-end protocol. It should be noted that RTP by itself does not provide any kind of QoS or timely delivery of data. It always requires the support of a lower layer protocol that actually has control over resources of switches and routers. IETF has specified a definition of this protocol in RFC 1889. As stated in the RFC, RTP provides an end-to-end, in-time delivery mechanism for real-time data such as audio and video. RTP usually runs on the top of UDP (Fig. 4.53) .

In some areas TCP may be more appropriate than UDP to use with RTP. So, why not use TCP for reliable delivery of real-time data? There are a number of reasons why TCP or other reliable transport protocols such as XTP (Xpress Transport Protocol) are inappropriate:

1. Let's consider we have used TCP for audio and video transmission. Due to the phenomenon of the network, some packets may lose or miss reaching the destination. When the receiver discovers the missing packets and re-transmits them, one round-trip or more time has elapsed. Therefore, the receiver has to wait either for the retransmission or defeat the TCP mechanism by discarding the retransmitted packets. In general, TCP will force the receiver application to wait. This behavior of TCP will induce in-

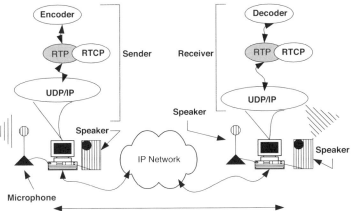

Fig. 4.53. A typical real-time data transmission example

Voice transmission between two end users using RTP in a IP network

creased delay for every packet lost in the network and ultimately this delay would be drastic.

2. TCP does not support multicast.
3. Above all, the TCP congestion control mechanism uses a slow start procedure, that is to say it reduces a congestion window when a packet loss is detected. On the other hand, it is not possible to decrease the transmission rates of audio and video without starving the receiver. For example, PCM audio requires 64 Kb/s plus any header overhead and usually cannot be delivered in less than that.
4. The TCP header is much larger than that of UDP. It is 40 bytes whereas the UDP header is only 8 bytes. For audio and video transmission in LANs, TCP does not provide much advantage since the LAN offers sufficient bandwidth and minimal packet loss.

As we have described earlier, RTP is an end-to-end protocol but it does not have any notion of connection. It can be either connection oriented or connectionless. It has no dependencies on particular address formats and only requires that framing and segmentation are taken care of by lower layer protocols.

Therefore, to summarize the benefits of RTP, the following statements are appropriate:

- RTP provides end-to-end delivery services for real-time audio and video multiparty conferencing.
- No special system enhancements required.
- Easily tailored for additional functions.
- Does not guarantee delivery or prevent out-of-order delivery, but rather relies on RTCP for control functions

RTP uses RTCP (RTP Control Protocol) to monitor QoS and to convey information in an ongoing session. In general, RTP has two parts: one is data and the other is control functionality (Fig. 5.54).

Fig. 4.54. A network implementation overview

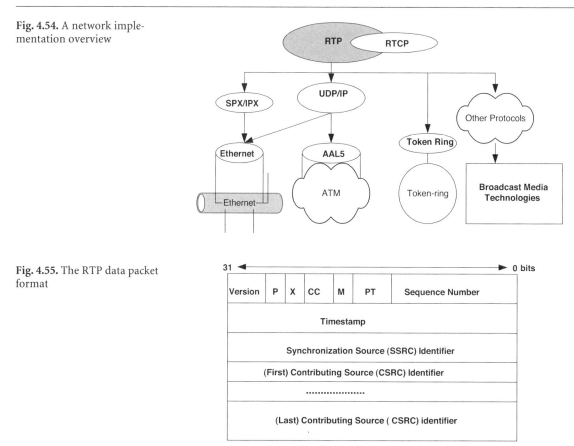

Fig. 4.55. The RTP data packet format

The data part of the RTP consists of a 12-byte header followed by the payload (Fig. 4.55).

The first 2 bits of the RTP data part is the version field, which identifies the version of RTP. According to the RTP specification, the value of this field is 2. The next field after version is a 1-bit padding (P) field. If the padding bit is set, the packet should have one or more additional paddings at the end of the payload. Some encryption algorithm may require the padding.

The CC field is known as "Contributing Source (CSRC) Count". This is a 4-bit field, which contains the number of CSRC identifiers. Next to the CC field is a 1-bit marker (M) field. The interpretation of a marker bit depends on the payload type. For video, it marks the end of a frame; for audio, the beginning of a talkspurt.

The next field after the marker (M) bit is the 7-bit payload type (PT) field. It identifies the RTP payload format and interprets by application.

Next is the 16-bit sequence number field. The receiver uses this field to detect packet loss and restore the packet sequence. During RTP packet transmission the sequence number is increased for each packet sent. The sequence number uses a random or unpredictable sequence, which is difficult to break using plain text attacks on encryption. As for the sequence number, the initial value of the timestamp is also randomized. Several RTP packets may have equal timestamps; if so they are generated at once. For example, those consecutive RTP packets are part of the same video frame.

The next field is the SSRC (Synchronization Source) identifier, a 32-bit field. It identifies the synchronization source. It is chosen randomly so that two synchronization sources within the same RTP session will not have the same SSRC identifier. If a transmission source changes its transport address, it must also choose a new SSRC identifier. Otherwise, the source would be identified as a looped source. The field next to the SSRC identifier is the CSRC (Contributing Source) identifier. It has 0–15 items and each of the item is 32 bits long. The CSRC identifier is also known as the CSRC list. This list identifies the contributing sources for a payload. The CC field determines the number identifier existing in the CSRC list. It can only identify 15 contributing sources at a time.

RFC 1889 specifies a header extension for RTP. This extended header allows a user to experiment with a new payload, which may require additional information to be carried on the header. This header extension is done after examining the value of the X field in the RTP header. If the value of X is one, a variable length header extension is inserted into the RTP header after the CSRC list. The extension contains a 16-bit length field, which can count the number of 32-bit code words in the extension.

The "control functionality" of the RTP is known as RTCP, defined above, which provides control functionality for real-time applications and ensures send, receive and interpretation reports for these applications. An RTCP message consists of a number of "stackable" packets, each with its own type code and length indication. Their formats are fairly similar to data packets; in particular, the type indication is at the same location. RTCP packets are multicast periodically to the same multicast group as data packets. Thus, they also serve as a liveness indicator of session members, even in the absence of transmitting media data.

The functionality of RTCP is described briefly below:

- **QoS monitoring and congestion control:** RTCP packets contain the necessary information for QoS monitoring. Since they are multicast, all session members can survey how the other participants are faring. Applications that have recently sent audio or video data generate a sender report. It contains information useful for intermedia synchronization (see below) as well as cumulative counters for packets and bytes sent. These allow receivers to estimate the actual data rate. Session members issue receiver reports for all video or audio sources they have heard from recently. They contain information on the highest sequence number received, the number of packets lost, a measure of the interarrival jitter, and timestamps needed to compute an estimate of the RTD between the sender and the receiver issuing the report.
- **Intermedia synchronization:** The RTCP sender reports contain an indication of real time (wallclock time) and a corresponding RTP timestamp. These two values allow the synchronization of different media, for example lip-syncing of audio and video.

- **Identification**: RTP data packets identify their origin only through a randomly generated 32-bit identifier. For conferencing applications, a little more context is often desirable. RTCP messages contain a source description (SDES) packet, in turn containing a number of pieces of information, usually textual. One such piece of information is the so-called canonical name, a globally unique identifier of the session participant. Other possible SDES items include the user's name, email address, telephone number, application information and alert messages.
- **Session size estimation and scaling**: RTCP packets are sent periodically by each session member. The desire for up-to-date control information has to be balanced against the desire to limit control traffic to a small percentage of data traffic even with sessions consisting of several hundred members. The control traffic load is scaled with the data traffic load so that it makes up a certain percentage of the nominal data rate (5%).

4.7 VoIP Operational Environment

Although we have learnt about the protocol stack of the VoIP architecture, to implement such a service requires the interaction and interoperability of different vendors' products. Unless this is done creating an end-to-end VoIP network is quite difficult. Therefore, to provide a successful implementation of various standards in a VoIP infrastructure, the IMTC VoIP forum has specified an Interoperability Agreement (IA) as "VoIP IA1.0".

This IA can be only used as a clarification over the existing H.323 series of recommendations and is not intended to take precedence over it. The IA describes the VoIP operational environment (Fig. 4.56). The primary intention of such an environment is to packetize voice encapsulated with IP and then route those packets over an IP network between two or more VoIP-capable devices. The VoIP operational environmental model describes various physical network elements such as PSTN, LAN, ADSL, etc., and call setup through such networks.

The IA also describes the interaction of various layers in a VoIP protocol stack (Fig. 4.57).

Fig. 4.56. The VoIP operational environment

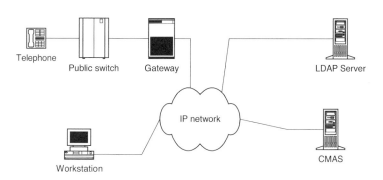

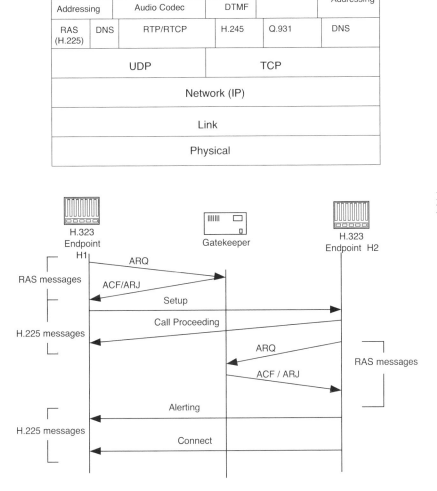

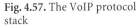

Fig. 4.57. The VoIP protocol stack

Fig. 4.58. The H.323 call establishment

4.7.1 ITU-T Message Exchange

We have so far discussed the VoIP network and ITU-T messages to set up a call for such a network. Let's now consider all the ITU-T message exchanges during a call setup to further understand the operation of a VoIP network. We will describe the steps involved in creating an H.323 call, establishing media communication and releasing the call. In this imaginary network we have two H.323 endpoints, H1 and H2 connected through a gatekeeper. The method of message exchange is direct signaling and RTP is used for media stream encapsulation.

In Fig. 4.58, H1 (H.323 endpoint) sends an RAS ARQ message on the RAS channel to the gatekeeper for registration. The gatekeeper confirms the admission of H1 by sending an ACF message to H1. The gatekeeper may indicate in the ACF that H1 can use direct call signaling. Immediately after, H1 sends an H.225 call signaling setup message to H2 requesting a connection.

The H2 endpoint responds with an H.225 call proceeding message to H1. Now H2 must register with the gatekeeper. Therefore, it sends an RAS ARQ message on the RAS channel to the gatekeeper which confirms the H2 RAS request by sending an RAS ACF message.

H2 alerts H1 of connection establishment by sending an H.225 alerting message. H2 then confirms the connection establishment by sending a connect message to H1 and the call is established.

```
- - - - - - - - - - - - - - - - - - - Frame 5 - - - - - - - - - - - - - - - - -
Frame   Source Address    Dest. Address      Size
5       JACKSON           KAMBI              50
Rel. Time      Delta Time    Abs. Time              Summary
0:00:01.768    0.001.792     09/27/2000 12:14:11 AM DLC: DCE->DTE Length=50
          FRELAY: DLCI=16
          IP:   D=[192.168.169.1] S=[192.168.169.2] LEN=24 ID=4874
      TCP: D=1720 S=1169 SYN SEQ=1283875 LEN=0 WIN=8192
DLC: ----- DLC Header -----
     DLC:
     DLC:
     DLC: Frame 5 arrived at  00:14:11.7682; frame size is 50 (0032 hex) bytes.
     DLC: Destination = DTE
     DLC: Source = DCE
     DLC:
FRELAY: ----- Frame Relay -----
     FRELAY:
     FRELAY: Address word = 0401
     FRELAY:  0000 01..  0000 .... = DLCI 16
     FRELAY:  .... ..0.  .... .... = Response
     FRELAY:  .... ....  .... 0... = No forward congestion
     FRELAY:  .... ....  .... .0.. = No backward congestion
     FRELAY:  .... ....  .... ..0. = Not eligible for discard
     FRELAY:  .... ....  .... ...1 = Not extended address
     FRELAY:
FRELAY: ----- Multiprotocol over Frame Relay -----
     FRELAY:
     FRELAY: Control  pad(s) = 03
     FRELAY: NLPID = 0xCC (Internet IP)
     FRELAY:
IP: ----- IP Header -----
     IP:
     IP: Version = 4  header length = 20 bytes
     IP: Type of service = B8
     IP:       101. ....  = CRITIC/ECP
     IP:       ...1 ....  = low delay
     IP:       .... 1...  = high throughput
     IP:       .... .0..  = normal reliability
     IP:       .... ..0.  = ECT bit - transport protocol will ignore the CE bit
     IP:       .... ...0  = CE bit - no congestion
     IP: Total length      = 44 bytes
     IP: Identification    = 4874
     IP: Flags             = 4X
```

```
      IP:         .1.. .... = don't fragment
      IP:         ..0. .... = last fragment
      IP: Fragment offset   = 0 bytes
      IP: Time to live       = 128 seconds/hops
      IP: Protocol           = 6 (TCP)
      IP: Header checksum = 13B5 (correct)
      IP: Source address       = [192.168.169.2]   JACKSON
      IP: Destination address = [192.168.169.1]    KAMBI
      IP: No options
      IP:
TCP: ----- TCP header -----
      TCP:
      TCP: Source port         = 1169
      TCP: Destination port     = 1720 (H225 Call Signaling)
      TCP: Initial sequence number = 1283875
      TCP: Next expected Seq number= 1283876
      TCP: Data offset         = 24 bytes
      TCP: Flags               = 02
      TCP:                ..0. .... = (No urgent pointer)
      TCP:                ...0 .... = (No acknowledgment)
      TCP:                .... 0... = (No push)
      TCP:                .... .0.. = (No reset)
      TCP:                .... ..1. = SYN
      TCP:                .... ...0 = (No FIN)
      TCP: Window              = 8192
      TCP: Checksum            = 0548 (correct)
      TCP:
      TCP: Options follow
      TCP: Maximum segment size = 702
      TCP:
ADDR  HEX                                          ASCII
0000: 04 01 03 cc 45 b8 00 2c 13 0a 40 00 80 06 13 b5 | ....E.. ..@.?...
0010: c0 a8 a9 02 c0 a8 a9 01 04 91 06 b8 00 13 97 23 | ...............#
0020: 00 00 00 00 60 02 20 00 05 48 00 00 02 04 02 be | ....`. ..H......
0030: 6a dc                                           | j.


- - - - - - - - - - - - - - - - - - - - - Frame 6 - - - - - - - - - - - - - - - -
Frame  Source Address     Dest. Address      Size
6      KAMBI              JACKSON            50
Rel. Time     Delta Time     Abs. Time      Summary
0:00:01.770   0.001.952      09/27/2000 12:14:11 AM DLC: DTE->DCE Length=50
  FRELAY: DLCI=16
IP: D=[192.168.169.2] S=[192.168.169.1] LEN=24 ID=1027
  TCP: D=1169 S=1720 SYN ACK=1283876 SEQ=315526 LEN=0 WIN=8424
DLC: ----- DLC Header -----
      DLC:
      DLC:
      DLC: Frame 6 arrived at  00:14:11.7702; frame size is 50 (0032 hex) bytes.
      DLC: Destination = DCE
      DLC: Source = DTE
      DLC:
FRELAY: ----- Frame Relay -----
      FRELAY:
      FRELAY: Address word = 0401
      FRELAY:  0000 01.. 0000 .... = DLCI 16
```

```
      FRELAY:  .... ..0.  .... .... = Response
      FRELAY:  .... ....  .... 0... = No forward congestion
      FRELAY:  .... ....  .... .0.. = No backward congestion
      FRELAY:  .... ....  .... ..0. = Not eligible for discard
      FRELAY:  .... ....  .... ...1 = Not extended address
      FRELAY:
FRELAY: ----- Multiprotocol over Frame Relay -----
      FRELAY:
      FRELAY: Control  pad(s) = 03
      FRELAY: NLPID = 0xCC (Internet IP)
      FRELAY:
IP: ----- IP Header -----
      IP:
      IP: Version = 4  header length = 20 bytes
      IP: Type of service = B8
      IP:        101. ....   = CRITIC/ECP
      IP:        ...1 ....   = low delay
      IP:        .... 1...   = high throughput
      IP:        .... .0..   = normal reliability
      IP:        .... ..0.   = ECT bit - transport protocol will ignore the CE bit
      IP:        .... ...0   = CE bit - no congestion
      IP: Total length    = 44 bytes
      IP: Identification  = 1027
      IP: Flags           = 4X
      IP:        .1.. ....   = don't fragment
      IP:        ..0. ....   = last fragment
      IP: Fragment offset = 0 bytes
      IP: Time to live    = 128 seconds/hops
      IP: Protocol        = 6 (TCP)
      IP: Header checksum = 22BC (correct)
      IP: Source address      = [192.168.169.1]  KAMBI
      IP: Destination address = [192.168.169.2]  JACKSON
      IP: No options
      IP:
TCP: ----- TCP header -----
      TCP:
      TCP: Source port           = 1720 (H225 Call Signaling)
      TCP: Destination port      = 1169
      TCP: Initial sequence number = 315526
      TCP: Next expected Seq number= 315527
      TCP: Acknowledgment number  = 1283876
      TCP: Data offset           = 24 bytes
      TCP: Flags                 = 12
      TCP:              ..0. .... = (No urgent pointer)
      TCP:              ...1 .... = Acknowledgment
      TCP:              .... 0... = (No push)
      TCP:              .... .0.. = (No reset)
      TCP:              .... ..1. = SYN
      TCP:              .... ...0 = (No FIN)
      TCP: Window                = 8424
      TCP: Checksum              = 33C4 (correct)
      TCP:
      TCP: Options follow
      TCP: Maximum segment size = 702
      TCP:
```

```
ADDR  HEX                                                ASCII
0000: 04 01 03 cc 45 b8 00 2c 04 03 40 00 80 06 22 bc | ....E.. ..@.?.".
0010: c0 a8 a9 01 c0 a8 a9 02 06 b8 04 91 00 04 d0 86 | ................
0020: 00 13 97 24 60 12 20 e8 33 c4 00 00 02 04 02 be | ...$`. .3.......
0030: 30 ee                                           | 0î
```

```
- - - - - - - - - - - - - - - - - - - Frame 7 - - - - - - - - - - - - - - - - -
Frame  Source Address    Dest. Address      Size
7      JACKSON           KAMBI              46
Rel. Time    Delta Time    Abs. Time           Summary
0:00:01.771  0.001.696     09/27/2000 12:14:11 AM DLC: DCE->DTE Length=46
FRELAY: DLCI=16
  IP:  D=[192.168.169.1] S=[192.168.169.2] LEN=20 ID=5130
  TCP: D=1720 S=1169     ACK=315527 WIN=8424
DLC: ----- DLC Header -----
     DLC:
     DLC:
     DLC: Frame 7 arrived at  00:14:11.7719; frame size is 46 (002E hex) bytes.
     DLC: Destination = DTE
     DLC: Source = DCE
     DLC:
FRELAY: ----- Frame Relay -----
     FRELAY:
     FRELAY: Address word = 0401
     FRELAY:  0000 01.. 0000 .... = DLCI 16
     FRELAY:  .... ..0. .... .... = Response
     FRELAY:  .... .... .... 0... = No forward congestion
     FRELAY:  .... .... .... .0.. = No backward congestion
     FRELAY:  .... .... .... ..0. = Not eligible for discard
     FRELAY:  .... .... .... ...1 = Not extended address
     FRELAY:
FRELAY: ----- Multiprotocol over Frame Relay -----
     FRELAY:
     FRELAY: Control  pad(s) = 03
     FRELAY: NLPID = 0xCC (Internet IP)
     FRELAY:
IP: ----- IP Header -----
     IP:
     IP: Version = 4  header length = 20 bytes
     IP: Type of service = B8
     IP:      101. ....   = CRITIC/ECP
     IP:      ...1 ....   = low delay
     IP:      .... 1...   = high throughput
     IP:      .... .0..   = normal reliability
     IP:      .... ..0.   = ECT bit - transport protocol will ignore the CE bit
     IP:      .... ...0   = CE bit - no congestion
     IP: Total length  = 40 bytes
     IP: Identification  = 5130
     IP: Flags         = 4X
     IP:      .1.. ....   = don't fragment
     IP:      ..0. ....   = last fragment
     IP: Fragment offset = 0 bytes
     IP: Time to live  = 128 seconds/hops
     IP: Protocol      = 6 (TCP)
     IP: Header checksum = 12B9 (correct)
```

```
          TCP: No TCP options
          TCP:
ADDR  HEX                                               ASCII
0000: 04 01 03 cc 45 b8 00 28 14 0a 40 00 80 06 12 b9 | ....E..(..@.?...
0010: c0 a8 a9 02 c0 a8 a9 01 04 91 06 b8 00 13 97 24 | ...............$
0020: 00 04 d0 87 50 10 20 e8 48 8b 00 00 34 c8        | ....P. .H<..4.
```

```
- - - - - - - - - - - - - - - - - - - Frame 8 - - - - - - - - - - - - - -
Frame Source Address    Dest. Address      Size
8    JACKSON            KAMBI              563
Rel. Time      Delta Time    Abs. Time   Summary
0:00:01.803    0.031.424     09/27/2000 12:14:11 AM DLC: DCE->DTE Length=563
    FRELAY: DLCI=16
    IP:  D=[192.168.169.1] S=[192.168.169.2] LEN=537 ID=5386
    TCP: D=1720 S=1169      ACK=315527 SEQ=1283876 LEN=517 WIN=8424
    H225: Setup
    H225: type=Setup userid=126 length=489
DLC: ----- DLC Header -----
    DLC:
    DLC:
    DLC: Frame 8 arrived at  00:14:11.8033; frame size is 563 (0233 hex) bytes.
    DLC: Destination = DTE
    DLC: Source = DCE
    DLC:
FRELAY: ----- Frame Relay -----
    FRELAY:
    FRELAY: Address word = 0401
    FRELAY: 0000 01.. 0000 .... = DLCI 16
    FRELAY: .... ..0. .... .... = Response
    FRELAY: .... .... .... 0... = No forward congestion
    FRELAY: .... .... .... .0.. = No backward congestion
    FRELAY: .... .... .... ..0. = Not eligible for discard
    FRELAY: .... .... .... ...1 = Not extended address
    FRELAY:
FRELAY: ----- Multiprotocol over Frame Relay -----
    FRELAY:
    FRELAY: Control  pad(s) = 03
    FRELAY: NLPID = 0xCC (Internet IP)
    FRELAY:
IP: ----- IP Header -----
    IP:
    IP: Version = 4  header length = 20 bytes
    IP: Type of service = B8
    IP:      101. ....  = CRITIC/ECP
    IP:      ...1 .... = low delay
    IP:      .... 1... = high throughput
    IP:      .... .0.. = normal reliability
    IP:      .... ..0. = ECT bit - transport protocol will ignore the CE bit
    IP:      .... ...0 = CE bit - no congestion
    IP: Total length    = 557 bytes
    IP: Identification  = 5386
    IP: Flags           = 4X
    IP:      .1.. .... = don't fragment
    IP:      ..0. .... = last fragment
    IP: Fragment offset = 0 bytes
    IP: Time to live    = 128 seconds/hops
```

```
      IP: Protocol         = 6 (TCP)
      IP: Header checksum = 0FB4 (correct)
      IP: Source address      = [192.168.169.2]  JACKSON
      IP: Destination address = [192.168.169.1]  KAMBI
      IP: No options
      IP:
TCP: ----- TCP header -----
      TCP:
      TCP: Source port          = 1169
      TCP: Destination port     = 1720 (H225 Call Signaling)
      TCP: Sequence number      = 1283876
      TCP: Next expected Seq number= 1284393
      TCP: Acknowledgment number = 315527
      TCP: Data offset          = 20 bytes
      TCP: Flags               = 18
      TCP:              ..0. .... = (No urgent pointer)
      TCP:              ...1 .... = Acknowledgment
      TCP:              .... 1... = Push
      TCP:              .... .0.. = (No reset)
      TCP:              .... ..0. = (No SYN)
      TCP:              .... ...0 = (No FIN)
      TCP: Window              = 8424
      TCP: Checksum            = 79E4 (correct)
      TCP: No TCP options
      TCP: [517 Bytes of data]
      TCP:
H225: ----- H.225 Call Signaling -----
      H225:
      H225: Protocol discriminator  = 8
      H225: Length of call reference = 2
      H225: Call reference field = 6661
      H225:  0... ....  .... .... = Message from originator
      H225:  .110 0110  0110 0001 = Call reference value = 26209
      H225: Message type = 5 (Setup)
      H225:
      H225: Sending Complete Information
      H225: ID flag = A1
      H225: 1... .... = Expected extension bit
      H225: .010 0001 = Information element ID = 33
      H225:
      H225: Bearer Capacity
      H225: Information element identifier = 4
      H225: Length of bearer capacity = 3
      H225: Coding and capability flags = 88
      H225:              1... .... = Expected extension bit
      H225:              .00. .... = Coding standard = 0
                                    (CCITT standardized coding)
      H225:              ...0 1000 = Information transfer capability = 8
                                    (Unrestricted digital information)
      H225: Mode and rate flags = 90
      H225:         1... .... = Expected extension bit
      H225:         .00. .... = Transfer mode = 0 (Circuit mode)
      H225:         ...1 0000 = Information transfer rate = 16 (64 kbit/s)
      H225: Layer 1 protocol flag = A5
      H225:          1... .... = Expected extension bit
      H225:          .01. .... = Layer 1 identification = 1
      H225:          ...0 0101 = Layer 1 protocol = 5 (H.221 and H.242)
      H225:
```

```
H225:
       H225: ----User-User Information----
       H225:
       H225: Information element identifier = 126 (User-User)
       H225: Length        = 489
       H225: Discriminator = 5 (X.208/X.209 (ASN.1))
       H225:
       H225: Flags       = 20
       H225: 0... .... = No extension values present in H323-UserInformation
       H225: .0.. .... = user-data is not present
       H225: ..1. .... = Extension values present in h323-uu-pdu
       H225: ...0 .... = nonStandardData is not present
       H225: .... 0... = No extension values present in h323-message-body
       H225: h323-message = 0 (Setup)
       H225:
       H225: Flags       = 98
       H225: 1... .... = Extension value(s) present in Setup
       H225: .0.. .... = h245Address is not present
       H225: ..0. .... = sourceAddress is not present
       H225: ...1 .... = destinationAddress is present
       H225: .... 1... = destCallSignalAddress is present
       H225: .... .0.. = destExtraCallInfo is not present
       H225: .... ..0. = destExtraCRV is not present
       H225: .... ...0 = callServices is not present
       H225:
       H225: Protocol id = {0.0.8.2250.0.2}
       H225:
       H225: Flags       = 2A
       H225: 0... .... = No extension value(s) present in sourceInfo
       H225: .0.. .... = nonStandardData is not present
       H225: ..1. .... = Vendor is present
       H225: ...0 .... = Gatekeeper is not present
       H225: .... 1... = Gateway is present
       H225: .... .0.. = MCU is not present
       H225: .... ..1. = Terminal is present
       H225:
       H225: .... ...0 = No extension value(s) present in vendor
       H225: Flags       = C0
       H225: 1... .... = Product ID is present
       H225: .1.. .... = Version ID is present
       H225:
       H225: ..0. .... = No extension value(s) present in vendor
       H225: T.35 country code = 0x20 (Canada)
       H225: T.35 extension    = 0
       H225: Manufacture code = 0x  FF (?)
       H225: Product Id = Nortel Networks Enterprise Edge VoIP Gateway
       H225: Version Id = 2.0.1.8
       H225:
       H225: Flags       = 00
       H225: 0... .... = No extension value(s) present in gateway
       H225: .0.. .... = protocol is not present
       H225: ..0. .... = nonStandardData is not present
       H225:
       H225: ...0 .... = No extension value(s) present in terminal
       H225: .... 0... = nonStandardData is not present
       H225: .... .0.. = MC = 0
       H225: .... ..0. = Undefined node = 0
       H225:
```

```
H225: Number of destinationAddress = 1
H225:
H225: Flags        = 03
H225: 0... .... = No extension value(s) present in destinationAddress
H225: destinationAddress = 0 (E164)
H225: Length of e164 = 7
H225: E.164 = 99995B
H225:
H225: destCallSignalAddress
H225:
H225: Flags        = 80
H225: 1... .... = Extension value(s) present in destCallSignalAddress
H225: destCallSignalAddress = 0 (IP address)
H225: IP    = 192.168.169.1
H225: Port = 1720
H225:
H225: Flags        = 00
H225: 0... .... = Active MC = 0
H225: Conference id = 5634343434EF0D002111F7B5771828B9
H225: Flags        = 00
H225: 0... .... = No extension value(s) present in conferenceGoal
H225: Conference goal = 0 (Create)
H225:
H225: callType
H225: ...0 .... = No extension value(s) present in callType
H225: callType = 0 (Point to point)
H225:
H225: .... ..0. = Extension length determinant
H225: Number of extension = 9
H225: .... .1.. = sourceCallSignalAddress is present
H225: .... ..0. = remoteExtensionAddress is not present
H225: .... ...1 = callIdentifier is present
H225: Flags        = 1C
H225: 0... .... = h245SecurityCapability is not present
H225: .0.. .... = tokens is not present
H225: ..0. .... = cryptoTokens is not present
H225: ...1 .... = fastStart is present
```

```
ADDR  HEX                                                ASCII
0000: 04 01 03 cc 45 b8 02 2d 15 0a 40 00 80 06 0f b4 | ....E..-..@.?...
0010: c0 a8 a9 02 c0 a8 a9 01 04 91 06 b8 00 13 97 24 | ...............$
0020: 00 04 d0 87 50 18 20 e8 79 e4 00 00 03 00 02 05 | ....P. .y.......
0030: 08 02 66 61 05 a1 04 03 88 90 a5 70 08 a1 36 36 | ..fa......¥p..66
0040: 36 36 32 38 35 7e 01 e9 05 20 98 06 00 08 91 4a | 66285~... .....J
0050: 00 02 2a c0 20 00 00 ff 2b 4e 6f 72 74 65 6c 20 | ..*. ...+Nortel
0060: 4e 65 74 77 6f 72 6b 73 20 45 6e 74 65 72 70 72 | Networks Enterpr
0070: 69 73 65 20 45 64 67 65 20 56 6f 49 50 20 47 61 | ise Edge VoIP Ga
0080: 74 65 77 61 79 06 32 2e 30 2e 31 2e 38 00 01 03 | teway.2.0.1.8...
0090: 00 99 99 5b 80 c0 a8 a9 01 06 b8 00 56 34 34 34 | .™™[?.......V444
00a0: 34 ef 0d 00 21 11 f7 b5 77 18 28 b9 00 45 1c 07 | 4...!...w.(..E..
00b0: 00 c0 a8 a9 02 04 91 11 00 56 34 34 34 34 ef 0c | .........V4444..
00c0: 00 21 11 f7 b5 77 18 28 b9 81 5e 0e 13 00 00 00 | .!...w.(._^.....
00d0: 0e 04 01 02 80 0a 04 00 01 00 c0 a8 a9 02 6d 99 | ....?.........m™
00e0: 13 00 00 01 0e 00 01 02 80 0a 04 00 01 00 c0 a8 | ........?.......
00f0: a9 02 6d 9b 12 00 00 02 0d 60 02 80 0a 04 00 01 | ..m......`.?....
0100: 00 c0 a8 a9 02 6d 9d 12 00 00 03 0d 40 02 80 0a | .....m......@.?.
0110: 04 00 01 00 c0 a8 a9 02 6d 9f 13 00 00 04 0d 00 | ........m.......
0120: 00 c0 00 0a 04 00 01 00 c0 a8 a9 02 6d a1 12 00 | ............m...
0130: 00 05 0c 60 1d 80 0a 04 00 01 00 c0 a8 a9 02 6d | ...`.?.........m
```

```
0140: a3 12 00 00 06 0c 20 1d 80 0a 04 00 01 00 c0 a8 | ...... .?.......
0150: a9 02 6d a5 1e 40 12 99 06 04 01 00 4e 04 01 02 | ..m¥.@.™....N...
0160: 80 11 14 00 01 00 c0 a8 a9 02 6d 98 00 c0 a8 a9 | ?.........m.....
0170: 02 6d 99 1e 40 12 99 06 04 01 00 4e 00 01 02 80 | .m™.@.™....N...?
0180: 11 14 00 01 00 c0 a8 a9 02 6d 9a 00 c0 a8 a9 02 | .........m_.....
0190: 6d 9b 1d 40 12 99 06 04 01 00 4d 60 02 80 11 14 | m..@.™....M`.?..
01a0: 00 01 00 c0 a8 a9 02 6d 9c 00 c0 a8 a9 02 6d 9d | .......m......m.
01b0: 1d 40 12 99 06 04 01 00 4d 40 02 80 11 14 00 01 | .@.™....M@.?....
01c0: 00 c0 a8 a9 02 6d 9e 00 c0 a8 a9 02 6d 9f 1e 40 | .....m......m..@
01d0: 12 99 06 04 01 00 4d 00 00 c0 00 11 14 00 01 00 | .™....M.........
01e0: c0 a8 a9 02 6d a0 00 c0 a8 a9 02 6d a1 1d 40 12 | ....m......m..@.
01f0: 99 06 04 01 00 4c 60 1d 80 11 14 00 01 00 c0 a8 | ™....L`.?.......
0200: a9 02 6d a2 00 c0 a8 a9 02 6d a3 1d 40 12 99 06 | ..m......m..@.™.
0210: 04 01 00 4c 20 1d 80 11 14 00 01 00 c0 a8 a9 02 | ...L .?.........
0220: 6d a4 00 c0 a8 a9 02 6d a5 01 00 01 00 06 80 01 | m......m¥.....?.
0230: 00 ae fb                                        | ...
```

```
- - - - - - - - - - - - - - - - - - Frame 9 - - - - - - - - - - - - - - -
Frame Source Address    Dest. Address     Size
9     KAMBI             JACKSON           46
Rel. Time      Delta Time    Abs. Time              Summary
0:00:01.925   0.122.240     09/27/2000 12:14:11 AM DLC: DTE->DCE Length=46
 FRELAY: DLCI=16
    IP:  D=[192.168.169.2] S=[192.168.169.1] LEN=20 ID=1283
    TCP: D=1169 S=1720     ACK=1284393 WIN=7907
DLC: ----- DLC Header -----
     DLC:
     DLC:
     DLC: Frame 9 arrived at  00:14:11.9255; frame size is 46 (002E hex) bytes.
     DLC: Destination = DCE
     DLC: Source = DTE
     DLC:
FRELAY: ----- Frame Relay -----
     FRELAY:
     FRELAY: Address word = 0401
     FRELAY:  0000 01..  0000 .... = DLCI 16
     FRELAY:  .... ..0.  .... .... = Response
     FRELAY:  .... ....  .... 0... = No forward congestion
     FRELAY:  .... ....  .... .0.. = No backward congestion
     FRELAY:  .... ....  .... ..0. = Not eligible for discard
     FRELAY:  .... ....  .... ...1 = Not extended address
     FRELAY:
FRELAY: ----- Multiprotocol over Frame Relay -----
     FRELAY:
     FRELAY: Control  pad(s) = 03
     FRELAY: NLPID = 0xCC (Internet IP)
     FRELAY:
IP: ----- IP Header -----
     IP:
     IP: Version = 4  header length = 20 bytes
     IP: Type of service = B8
     IP:        101. ....   = CRITIC/ECP
     IP:        ...1 ....   = low delay
     IP:        .... 1...   = high throughput
     IP:        .... .0..   = normal reliability
     IP:        .... ..0. = ECT bit - transport protocol will ignore the CE bit
```

```
    IP:         .... ...0 = CE bit - no congestion
    IP: Total length    = 40 bytes
    IP: Identification  = 1283
    IP: Flags           = 4X
    IP:         .1.. .... = don't fragment
    IP:         ..0. .... = last fragment
    IP: Fragment offset = 0 bytes
    IP: Time to live    = 128 seconds/hops
    IP: Protocol        = 6 (TCP)
    IP: Header checksum = 21C0 (correct)
    IP: Source address      = [192.168.169.1]  KAMBI
    IP: Destination address = [192.168.169.2]  JACKSON
    IP: No options
    IP:
TCP: ----- TCP header -----
    TCP:
    TCP: Source port            = 1720 (H225 Call Signaling)
    TCP: Destination port       = 1169
    TCP: Sequence number        = 315527
    TCP: Next expected Seq number= 315527
    TCP: Acknowledgment number  = 1284393
    TCP: Data offset            = 20 bytes
    TCP: Flags             '    = 10
    TCP:               ..0. .... = (No urgent pointer)
    TCP:               ...1 .... = Acknowledgment
    TCP:               .... 0... = (No push)
    TCP:               .... .0.. = (No reset)
    TCP:               .... ..0. = (No SYN)
    TCP:               .... ...0 = (No FIN)
    TCP: Window                 = 7907
    TCP: Checksum               = 488B (correct)
    TCP: No TCP options
    TCP:
ADDR  HEX                                            ASCII
0000: 04 01 03 cc 45 b8 00 28 05 03 40 00 80 06 21 c0 | ....E..(..@.?.!.
0010: c0 a8 a9 01 c0 a8 a9 02 06 b8 04 91 00 04 d0 87 | ................
0020: 00 13 99 29 50 10 1e e3 48 8b 00 00 66 9d        | ..™)P...H<..f.
```

```
- - - - - - - - - - - - - - - - - - Frame 10 - - - - - - - - - - - - - -
Frame Source Address    Dest. Address     Size
10    KAMBI             JACKSON           205
Rel. Time      Delta Time      Abs. Time            Summary
0:00:02.430    0.505.056     09/27/2000 12:14:12 AM DLC: DTE->DCE Length=205
FRELAY: DLCI=16
  IP:  D=[192.168.169.2] S=[192.168.169.1] LEN=179 ID=1539
   TCP: D=1169 S=1720      ACK=1284393 SEQ=315527 LEN=159 WIN=7907
H225: Call Proceeding
   H225: type=Call proceeding userid=126 length=147
DLC: ----- DLC Header -----
    DLC:
    DLC:
    DLC: Frame 10 arrived at  00:14:12.4306; frame size is 205 (00CD hex) bytes.
    DLC: Destination = DCE
    DLC: Source = DTE
    DLC:
FRELAY: ----- Frame Relay -----
```

```
      FRELAY:
      FRELAY: Address word = 0401
      FRELAY:  0000 01..  0000 .... = DLCI 16
      FRELAY:  .... ..0.  .... .... = Response
      FRELAY:  .... ....  .... 0... = No forward congestion
      FRELAY:  .... ....  .... .0.. = No backward congestion
      FRELAY:  .... ....  .... ..0. = Not eligible for discard
      FRELAY:  .... ....  .... ...1 = Not extended address
      FRELAY:
FRELAY: ----- Multiprotocol over Frame Relay -----
      FRELAY:
      FRELAY: Control  pad(s) = 03
      FRELAY: NLPID = 0xCC (Internet IP)
      FRELAY:
IP: ----- IP Header -----
      IP:
      IP: Version = 4  header length = 20 bytes
      IP: Type of service = B8
      IP:       101. ....   = CRITIC/ECP
      IP:       ...1 ....  = low delay
      IP:       .... 1...  = high throughput
      IP:       .... .0..  = normal reliability
      IP:       .... ..0.  = ECT bit - transport protocol will ignore the CE bit
      IP:       .... ...0  = CE bit - no congestion
      IP: Total length   = 199 bytes
      IP: Identification = 1539
      IP: Flags          = 4X
      IP:       .1.. ....  = don't fragment
      IP:       ..0. ....  = last fragment
      IP: Fragment offset = 0 bytes
      IP: Time to live    = 128 seconds/hops
      IP: Protocol        = 6 (TCP)
      IP: Header checksum = 2021 (correct)
      IP: Source address      = [192.168.169.1]  KAMBI
      IP: Destination address = [192.168.169.2]  JACKSON
      IP: No options
      IP:
TCP: ----- TCP header -----
      TCP:
      TCP: Source port          = 1720 (H225 Call Signaling)
      TCP: Destination port     = 1169
      TCP: Sequence number      = 315527
      TCP: Next expected Seq number= 315686
      TCP: Acknowledgment number = 1284393
      TCP: Data offset          = 20 bytes
      TCP: Flags                = 18
      TCP:              ..0. ....  = (No urgent pointer)
      TCP:              ...1 ....  = Acknowledgment
      TCP:              .... 1...  = Push
      TCP:              .... .0..  = (No reset)
      TCP:              .... ..0.  = (No SYN)
      TCP:              .... ...0  = (No FIN)
      TCP: Window           = 7907
      TCP: Checksum         = 4339 (correct)
      TCP: No TCP options
      TCP: [159 Bytes of data]
      TCP:
```

```
H225: ----- H.225 Call Signaling -----
      H225:
      H225: Protocol discriminator   = 8
      H225: Length of call reference = 2
      H225: Call reference field = E661
      H225:  1... ....  .... .... = Message to originator
      H225:  .110 0110  0110 0001 = Call reference value = 26209
      H225: Message type = 2 (Call Proceeding)
      H225:
      H225:
H225:
      H225: ----User-User Information----
      H225:
      H225: Information element identifier = 126 (User-User)
      H225: Length        = 147
      H225: Discriminator = 5 (X.208/X.209 (ASN.1))
      H225:
      H225: Flags     = 21
      H225: 0... .... = No extension values present in H323-UserInformation
      H225: .0.. .... = user-data is not present
      H225: ..1. .... = Extension values present in h323-uu-pdu
      H225: ...0 .... = nonStandardData is not present
      H225: .... 0... = No extension values present in h323-message-body
      H225: h323-message = 1 (Call proceeding)
      H225: Flags     = 80
      H225: 1... .... = Extension values present in CallProceeding-UUIE
      H225: .0.. .... = h245Address is not present
      H225: Protocol Id = {0.0.8.2250.0.2}
      H225:
      H225: Destination information
      H225: Flags     = 2A
      H225: 0... .... = No extension value(s) present in destinationInfo
      H225: .0.. .... = nonStandardData is not present
      H225: ..1. .... = Vendor is present
      H225: ...0 .... = Gatekeeper is not present
      H225: .... 1... = Gateway is present
      H225: .... .0.. = MCU is not present
      H225: .... ..1. = Terminal is present
      H225:
      H225: .... ...0 = No extension value(s) present in vendor
      H225: Flags     = C0
      H225: 1... .... = Product ID is present
      H225: .1.. .... = Version ID is present
      H225:
      H225: ..0. .... = No extension value(s) present in vendor
      H225: T.35 country code = 0x20 (Canada)
      H225: T.35 extension    = 0
      H225: Manufacture code = 0x  FF (?)
      H225: Product Id = Nortel Networks Enterprise Edge VoIP Gateway
      H225: Version Id = 2.0.1.8
      H225:
      H225: Flags     = 00
      H225: 0... .... = No extension value(s) present in gateway
      H225: .0.. .... = protocol is not present
      H225: ..0. .... = nonStandardData is not present
      H225:
      H225: ...0 .... = No extension value(s) present in terminal
```

```
H225: .... 0... = nonStandardData is not present
H225: .... .0.. = MC = 0
H225: .... ..0. = Undefined node = 0
H225:
H225: .... ...0 = Extension length determinant
H225: Number of extension = 5
H225: .... ..1. = callIdentifier is present
H225: .... ...0 = h245SecurityMode is not present
H225: Flags      = 20
H225: 0... .... = tokens is not present
H225: .0.. .... = cryptoTokens is not present
H225: ..1. .... = fastStart is present
H225: Length of callIdentifier = 17
H225:
H225: Flags      = 00
H225: 0... .... = No extension value(s) present in callIdentifier
H225: Guid = V4444<EF0C00>!<11F7B5>w<18>(<B9>
H225: Number of fastStart = 2
H225: Length of fastStart = 26
H225: Fast start = <0000000E040102801114000100C0A8A901>m`<00C0A8A901>ma
H225: Length of fastStart = 23
H225: Fast start = @<000006040100>N<040102800A04000100C0A8A901>ma
H225:
H225: Flags      = 06
H225: 0... .... = Extension length determinant
H225: Number of extension = 4
H225: .... ...0 = h4501SupplementaryService is not present
H225: Flags      = 80
H225: 1... .... = h245Tunneling is present
H225: .0.. .... = h245Control is not present
H225: ..0. .... = nonStandardControl is not present
H225: Flags      = 00
H225: 0... .... = H245 tunneling = 0
H225:
ADDR   HEX                                                  ASCII
0000: 04 01 03 cc 45 b8 00 c7 06 03 40 00 80 06 20 21  | ....E..Ç..@.?. !
0010: c0 a8 a9 01 c0 a8 a9 02 06 b8 04 91 00 04 d0 87  | ...............
0020: 00 13 99 29 50 18 1e e3 43 39 00 00 03 00 00 9f  | ..™)P...C9......
0030: 08 02 e6 61 02 7e 00 93 05 21 80 06 00 08 91 4a  | ...a.~...!?....J
0040: 00 02 2a c0 20 00 00 ff 2b 4e 6f 72 74 65 6c 20  | ..*. ...+Nortel
0050: 4e 65 74 77 6f 72 6b 73 20 45 6e 74 65 72 70 72  | Networks Enterpr
0060: 69 73 65 20 45 64 67 65 20 56 6f 49 50 20 47 61  | ise Edge VoIP Ga
0070: 74 65 77 61 79 06 32 2e 30 2e 31 2e 38 00 12 20  | teway.2.0.1.8..
0080: 11 00 56 34 34 34 34 ef 0c 00 21 11 f7 b5 77 18  | ..V4444...!...w.
0090: 28 b9 34 02 1a 00 00 00 0e 04 01 02 80 11 14 00  | (.4.........?...
00a0: 01 00 c0 a8 a9 01 6d 60 00 c0 a8 a9 01 6d 61 17  | ......m`.....ma.
00b0: 40 00 00 06 04 01 00 4e 04 01 02 80 0a 04 00 01  | @......N...?....
00c0: 00 c0 a8 a9 01 6d 61 06 80 01 00 b1 f3           | .....ma.?....
```

```
- - - - - - - - - - - - - - - - - - - Frame 11 - - - - - - - - - - - - - - - -
Frame Source Address    Dest. Address    Size
11    KAMBI             JACKSON          205
Rel. Time      Delta Time    Abs. Time            Summary
0:00:02.437    0.006.496     09/27/2000 12:14:12 AM DLC: DTE->DCE Length=205
FRELAY: DLCI=16
IP:   D=[192.168.169.2] S=[192.168.169.1] LEN=179 ID=1795
```

```
   TCP: D=1169 S=1720      ACK=1284393 SEQ=315686 LEN=159 WIN=7907
 H225: Alerting
 H225: type=Alerting userid=126 length=147
 DLC: ----- DLC Header -----
       DLC:
       DLC:
       DLC: Frame 11 arrived at  00:14:12.4371; frame size is 205 (00CD hex) bytes.
       DLC: Destination = DCE
       DLC: Source = DTE
       DLC:
 FRELAY: ----- Frame Relay -----
       FRELAY:
       FRELAY: Address word = 0401
       FRELAY:  0000 01..  0000 .... = DLCI 16
       FRELAY:  .... ..0.  .... .... = Response
       FRELAY:  .... ....  .... 0... = No forward congestion
       FRELAY:  .... ....  .... .0.. = No backward congestion
       FRELAY:  .... ....  .... ..0. = Not eligible for discard
       FRELAY:  .... ....  .... ...1 = Not extended address
       FRELAY:
 FRELAY: ----- Multiprotocol over Frame Relay -----
       FRELAY:
       FRELAY: Control  pad(s) = 03
       FRELAY: NLPID = 0xCC (Internet IP)
       FRELAY:
 IP: ----- IP Header -----
       IP:
       IP: Version = 4  header length = 20 bytes
       IP: Type of service = B8
       IP:       101. .... = CRITIC/ECP
       IP:       ...1 .... = low delay
       IP:       .... 1... = high throughput
       IP:       .... .0.. = normal reliability
       IP:       .... ..0. = ECT bit - transport protocol will ignore the CE bit
       IP:       .... ...0 = CE bit - no congestion
       IP: Total length    = 199 bytes
       IP: Identification  = 1795
       IP: Flags           = 4X
       IP:       .1.. .... = don't fragment
       IP:       ..0. .... = last fragment
       IP: Fragment offset = 0 bytes
       IP: Time to live    = 128 seconds/hops
       IP: Protocol        = 6 (TCP)
       IP: Header checksum = 1F21 (correct)
       IP: Source address     = [192.168.169.1]  KAMBI
       IP: Destination address = [192.168.169.2]  JACKSON
       IP: No options
       IP:
 TCP: ----- TCP header -----
       TCP:
       TCP: Source port          = 1720 (H225 Call Signaling)
       TCP: Destination port     = 1169
       TCP: Sequence number      = 315686
       TCP: Next expected Seq number= 315845
       TCP: Acknowledgment number  = 1284393
       TCP: Data offset          = 20 bytes
       TCP: Flags                = 18
       TCP:          ..0. .... = (No urgent pointer)
```

```
TCP:                    ...1 .... = Acknowledgment
TCP:                    .... 1... = Push
TCP:                    .... .0.. = (No reset)
TCP:                    .... ..0. = (No SYN)
TCP:                    .... ...0 = (No FIN)
TCP: Window             = 7907
TCP: Checksum           = 4398 (correct)
TCP: No TCP options
TCP: [159 Bytes of data]
TCP:
H225: ----- H.225 Call Signaling -----
      H225:
      H225: Protocol discriminator  = 8
      H225: Length of call reference = 2
      H225: Call reference field = E661
      H225:  1... .... .... .... = Message to originator
      H225:  .110 0110  0110 0001 = Call reference value = 26209
      H225: Message type = 1 (Alerting)
      H225:
      H225:
H225:
      H225: ----User-User Information----
      H225:
      H225: Information element identifier = 126 (User-User)
      H225: Length        = 147
      H225: Discriminator = 5 (X.208/X.209 (ASN.1))
      H225:
      H225: Flags      = 23
      H225: 0... .... = No extension values present in H323-UserInformation
      H225: .0.. .... = user-data is not present
      H225: ..1. .... = Extension values present in h323-uu-pdu
      H225: ...0 .... = nonStandardData is not present
      H225: .... 0... = No extension values present in h323-message-body
      H225: h323-message = 3 (Alerting)
      H225: Flags      = 80
      H225: 1... .... = Extension values present in Alerting-UUIE
      H225: .0.. .... = h245Address is not present
      H225: Protocol Id = {0.0.8.2250.0.2}
      H225:
      H225: Destination information
      H225: Flags      = 2A
      H225: 0... .... = No extension value(s) present in destinationInfo
      H225: .0.. .... = nonStandardData is not present
      H225: ..1. .... = Vendor is present
      H225: ...0 .... = Gatekeeper is not present
      H225: .... 1... = Gateway is present
      H225: .... .0.. = MCU is not present
      H225: .... ..1. = Terminal is present
      H225:
      H225: .... ...0 = No extension value(s) present in vendor
      H225: Flags      = C0
      H225: 1... .... = Product ID is present
      H225: .1.. .... = Version ID is present
      H225:
      H225: ..0. .... = No extension value(s) present in vendor
      H225: T.35 country code = 0x20 (Canada)
      H225: T.35 extension    = 0
```

```
H225: Manufacture code = 0x  FF (?)
H225: Product Id = Nortel Networks Enterprise Edge VoIP Gateway
H225: Version Id = 2.0.1.8
H225:
H225: Flags      = 00
H225: 0... .... = No extension value(s) present in gateway
H225: .0.. .... = protocol is not present
H225: ..0. .... = nonStandardData is not present
H225:
H225: ...0 .... = No extension value(s) present in terminal
H225: .... 0... = nonStandardData is not present
H225: .... .0.. = MC = 0
H225: .... ..0. = Undefined node = 0
H225:
H225: .... ...0 = Extension length determinant
H225: Number of extension = 5
H225: .... ..1. = callIdentifier is present
H225: .... ...0 = h245SecurityMode is not present
H225: Flags      = 20
H225: 0... .... = tokens is not present
H225: .0.. .... = cryptoTokens is not present
H225: ..1. .... = fastStart is present
H225: Length of callIdentifier = 17
H225:
H225: Flags      = 00
H225: 0... .... = No extension value(s) present in callIdentifier
H225: Guid = V4444<EF0C00>!<11F7B5>w<18>(<B9>
H225: Number of fastStart = 2
H225: Length of fastStart = 26
H225: Fast start  = <0000000E040102801114000100C0A8A901>m`<00C0A8A901>ma
H225: Length of fastStart = 23
H225: Fast start  = @<000006040100>N<040102800A04000100C0A8A901>ma
H225:
H225: Flags      = 06
H225: 0... .... = Extension length determinant
H225: Number of extension = 4
H225: .... ...0 = h4501SupplementaryService is not present
H225: Flags      = 80
H225: 1... .... = h245Tunneling is present
H225: .0.. .... = h245Control is not present
H225: ..0. .... = nonStandardControl is not present
H225: Flags      = 00
H225: 0... .... = H245 tunneling = 0
H225:
ADDR  HEX                                               ASCII
0000: 04 01 03 cc 45 b8 00 c7 07 03 40 00 80 06 1f 21 | ....E..Ç..@.?..!
0010: c0 a8 a9 01 c0 a8 a9 02 06 b8 04 91 00 04 d1 26 | ...............&
0020: 00 13 99 29 50 18 1e e3 43 98 00 00 03 00 00 9f | ..™)P...C.......
0030: 08 02 e6 61 01 7e 00 93 05 23 80 06 00 08 91 4a | ...a.~...#?....J
0040: 00 02 2a c0 20 00 00 ff 2b 4e 6f 72 74 65 6c 20 | ..*. ...+Nortel
0050: 4e 65 74 77 6f 72 6b 73 20 45 6e 74 65 72 70 72 | Networks Enterpr
0060: 69 73 65 20 45 64 67 65 20 56 6f 49 50 20 47 61 | ise Edge VoIP Ga
0070: 74 65 77 61 79 06 32 2e 30 2e 31 2e 38 00 12 20 | teway.2.0.1.8..
0080: 11 00 56 34 34 34 34 ef 0c 00 21 11 f7 b5 77 18 | ..V4444...!...w.
0090: 28 b9 34 02 1a 00 00 00 0e 04 01 02 80 11 14 00 | (.4.........?...
00a0: 01 00 c0 a8 a9 01 6d 60 00 c0 a8 a9 01 6d 61 17 | ......m`.....ma.
00b0: 40 00 00 06 04 01 00 4e 04 01 02 80 0a 04 00 01 | @......N...?....
00c0: 00 c0 a8 a9 01 6d 61 06 80 01 00 84 df           | .....ma.?...ß
```

```
- - - - - - - - - - - - - - - - - - - - Frame 12 - - - - - - - - - - - - - - -
Frame Status Source Address   Dest. Address      Size
12           JACKSON          KAMBI              46
Rel. Time     Delta Time    Abs. Time      Summary
0:00:02.439   0.002.240     09/27/2000 12:14:12 AM DLC: DCE->DTE Length=46
   FRELAY: DLCI=16
    IP:  D=[192.168.169.1] S=[192.168.169.2] LEN=20 ID=8714
   TCP: D=1720 S=1169     ACK=315845 WIN=8106
DLC: ----- DLC Header -----
     DLC:
     DLC:
     DLC: Frame 12 arrived at  00:14:12.4393; frame size is 46 (002E hex) bytes.
     DLC: Destination = DTE
     DLC: Source = DCE
     DLC:
FRELAY: ----- Frame Relay -----
     FRELAY:
     FRELAY: Address word = 0401
     FRELAY:  0000 01..  0000 .... = DLCI 16
     FRELAY:  .... ..0.  .... .... = Response
     FRELAY:  .... ....  .... 0... = No forward congestion
     FRELAY:  .... ....  .... .0.. = No backward congestion
     FRELAY:  .... ....  .... ..0. = Not eligible for discard
     FRELAY:  .... ....  .... ...1 = Not extended address
     FRELAY:         .
FRELAY: ----- Multiprotocol over Frame Relay -----
     FRELAY:
     FRELAY: Control  pad(s) = 03
     FRELAY: NLPID = 0xCC (Internet IP)
     FRELAY:
IP: ----- IP Header -----
     IP:
     IP: Version = 4  header length = 20 bytes
     IP: Type of service = B8
     IP:      101. ....   = CRITIC/ECP
     IP:      ...1 .... = low delay
     IP:      .... 1... = high throughput
     IP:      .... .0.. = normal reliability
     IP:      .... ..0. = ECT bit - transport protocol will ignore the CE bit
     IP:      .... ...0 = CE bit - no congestion
     IP: Total length   = 40 bytes
     IP: Identification = 8714
     IP: Flags          = 4X
     IP:      .1.. .... = don't fragment
     IP:      ..0. .... = last fragment
     IP: Fragment offset = 0 bytes
     IP: Time to live   = 128 seconds/hops
     IP: Protocol       = 6 (TCP)
     IP: Header checksum = 04B9 (correct)
     IP: Source address     = [192.168.169.2]  JACKSON
     IP: Destination address = [192.168.169.1]  KAMBI
     IP: No options
     IP:
TCP: ----- TCP header -----
     TCP:
     TCP: Source port          = 1169
     TCP: Destination port     = 1720 (H225 Call Signaling)
```

```
TCP: Sequence number          = 1284393
TCP: Next expected Seq number= 1284393
TCP: Acknowledgment number    = 315845
TCP: Data offset              = 20 bytes
TCP: Flags                    = 10
TCP:                 ..0. .... = (No urgent pointer)
TCP:                 ...1 .... = Acknowledgment
TCP:                 .... 0... = (No push)
TCP:                 .... .0.. = (No reset)
TCP:                 .... ..0. = (No SYN)
TCP:                 .... ...0 = (No FIN)
TCP: Window                   = 8106
TCP: Checksum                 = 4686 (correct)
TCP: No TCP options
TCP:
ADDR  HEX                                                ASCII
0000: 04 01 03 cc 45 b8 00 28 22 0a 40 00 80 06 04 b9 | ....E..(".@.?...
0010: c0 a8 a9 02 c0 a8 a9 01 04 91 06 b8 00 13 99 29 | .............™)
0020: 00 04 d1 c5 50 10 1f aa 46 86 00 00 6d a2        | ....P...F...m.
```

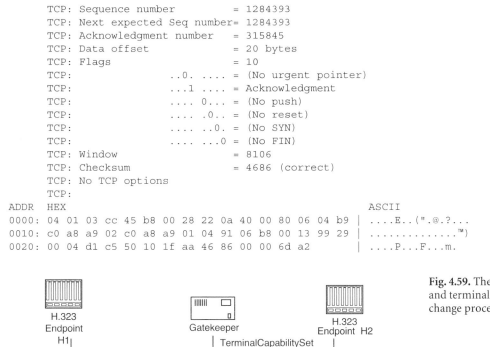

Fig. 4.59. The H.245 messages and terminal capability exchange procedures

Once the call is established the endpoints start their H.245 capability exchanges as shown in Fig. 4.59.

At first an H.245 control channel is established between H1 and H2. H1 sends an H.245 TerminalCapabilitySet message to H2 for the exchange of terminal capabilities. H2 acknowledges H1's capability by sending a Terminal-CapabilitySetAck message. Then H2 exchanges its capability by sending an H.245 TerminalCapabilitySet message to H1.

H1 acknowledges H2's capability by sending an H.245 TerminalCapabilitySetAck message to H2. Now H1 opens a media channel to H2 by sending an H.245 OpenLogicalChannel message. The transport address of the RTCP channel is also included in the message.

Fig. 4.60. The H.323 media stream and media control messages

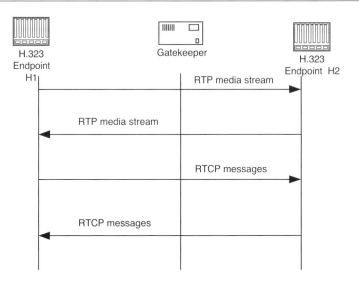

H2 acknowledges the establishment of a unidirectional logical channel from H1 to H2 by sending an H.245 OpenLogicalChannelAck message. Included in the message are the RTP transport address allocated by H2 to be used by H1 for sending the RTP media stream and the RTCP address received from H1 earlier.

Then, H2 opens a media channel with H1 by sending an H.245 OpenLogicalChannel

message. The message also includes the transport address of the RTCP channel. H1 acknowledges the message by sending an H.245 OpenLogical-ChannelAck and confirms the establishment of bidirectional media stream communication.

Now H1 sends an RTP-encapsulated media stream to H2 as shown in Fig. 4.60. H2 also sends the RTP-encapsulated media stream to H1. As a response H1 sends the RTCP message to H2. As the sequence of messages, H2 sends the RTCP message to H1.

Once the media stream is done the information (i.e., voice) is transported from one endpoint to the other. The H.323 call needs to be released. This is done through the exchange of a sequence of messages. H2 initiates the call release by sending an H.245 EndSessionCommand message to H1 (Fig. 4.61).

H1 releases the call endpoint and confirms the release by sending the End-SessionCommand to H2. In turn, H2 completes the call release by sending an H.225 Release Complete message to H1. Both of the endpoints then disengage with the gatekeeper by sending an RAS DRQ message to the gatekeeper. The gatekeeper in turn disengages H1 and H2 and confirms by sending DCF messages to both of the endpoints.

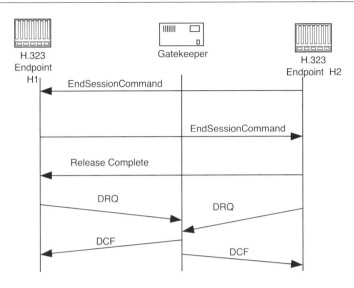

Fig. 4.61. H.323 Call release messages

4.7.2 Voice Quality

Traditional PSTNs have long since addressed the voice quality problem by optimizing their circuits for the dynamic range of the human voice and the rhythms of human conversation. The PSTN is optimized to provide best service for the time-sensitive voice applications that require low delay, low jitter, and constant but low bandwidth. Although these networks do not produce perfect quality, users have become accustomed to PSTN levels of voice quality (VQ), and comparisons are often made in this context. In other words, the PSTN VQ is relatively the standard and predictable. On the other hand, IP networks were built to support non-real-time applications such as file transfer or email. Although these applications are bursty in their characteristics and sometimes demand high bandwidth, they are not sensitive to delay or delay variation. With the recent trend of converged IP internetworking, the unified IP network must provide mechanisms that ensure the QoS required in transporting the voice. The current implementation of VoIP is striving to provide a comparable service quality to PSTN. The VoIP technologies have made maintaining VQ more complex by adding non-linear compression and the need for timely packet delivery to networks not originally set up for these conditions. Transmission conditions that pose little threat to non-real-time data traffic can introduce severe problems to real-time packetized voice traffic. A number of the VQ issues that must be considered for data networks are as follows:

1. Real-time transport: As mentioned earlier, the data network is not designed for the real-time bandwidth requirements of speech. Although data network design does not need to rely on packets arriving at their destination within narrow time windows, with the advent of unified IP internetworking techniques this issue is somewhat addressed. But VQ can still

suffer if implied methods are not deployed properly. Although bandwidth requirements for voice are reasonably low, the voice transport needs a constant available bandwidth for linear codecs or directly available bandwidth for low-bit-rate codecs. It is often seen that non-linear compression techniques can be a cause of reduced VQ.

2. Gateway processes: The VoIP networks often rely on the network processes that are built into the gateways. This may cause some VQ issues: for example, silence compression that is used to prevent packets not being created and transported during quite periods of spoken phrases; and echo cancellers that are needed to eliminate the echo introduced when delay occurs. Both of these situations may cause degraded VQ.

3. Packet loss: It is obvious that there may be some packet loss; the data network compensates for this through the use of TCP retransmission. Since the VoIP network uses UDP, there is no guarantee of packet delivery. Therefore, packet loss mean lost voice information. It is assumed that if any word is not heard it can be requested. If TCP were to introduce the retransmission of voice packets that would cause unnecessary delay and streams of packets.

4. Delay: The delay is the main factor for voice transmission. ITU-T Recommendation G.114 suggests that a "one-way transmission delay" of up to 400 ms is acceptable. The standard explains such a delay requirement as follows:

   (a) 0 to 150 ms is acceptable for most applications.
   (b) 150 to 400 ms is acceptable provided that the network designer is well aware of its impact on some user applications.
   (c) 400 ms or above is unacceptable.

G.114 has defined delay considerations for various media and listed them in table A.1/G.114. For the sake of understanding, we are listing them as follows:

- Coaxial cable or radio transmission: 4 µS/km.
- Fiber optic cable: 5 µS/km.
- Coaxial cable undersea: 6 µS/km.
- Fiber optic cable undersea: 13 ms at transmit end and 10 ms at receive end.
- Satellite system: 12 ms at 1400 km altitude, 110 ms at 14,000 km altitude and 260 ms at 36,000 km altitude.
- G.712 (PCM coder/decoder): 0.75 ms.
- G.721, G.726 and G.727 codecs (ADPCM): 0.25 ms.
- Public land mobile system: 80 to 110 ms.
- H.260 series video coder and decoder: not yet defined.
- ATM (AAL1): 6.0 ms.

To get a complete list of such defined delay requirements and further explanation, please refer to G.114.

Considering the above-mentioned delay requirements, the computation of a one-way delay for some networks can be as follows:

(a) Analog networks (analog PSTN): The delay should be calculated as 12 + (0.004 _ transmission distance in km) ms. For example, 12 ms is the compensation for network equipments and 0.004 ms is the delay per km for coaxial cable.

(b) Mixed analog and digital networks: The calculation is the same as given for analog networks.

(c) Digital networks: The transmission time between local exchanges should not exceed 3 + (0.004 _ distance in km) ms. The 3 ms is the constant term that compensates for the PCM coder/decoder and five digital switches. If fiber optics are used as the transmission media 0.004 ms can be replaced with 0.005 ms.

5. Non-linear codecs: One of the important reasons to measure VQ is the continued development and use of non-linear codecs. The voice compression technique used in the non-linear perceptual codec, although preserving how the voice sounds, does not preserve frequency information.

4.7.2.1 VQ Measurement

PSQM (Perceptual Speech Quality Measurement) is one of the techniques for measuring VQ. It is defined by ITU-T Recommendation P.861. The procedures used in PSQM are defined as objective measurement procedures, which implies that PSQM is the objective measurement of speech quality. The procedures are clearly depicted in the Fig. 4.62.

Although PSQM was originally developed to test codecs, it has found wide acceptance as the *de facto* standard for testing VoIP systems. The algorithm functions by comparing the signal after it has passed through the coder and decoder process with the original signal.

If the input and output are identical, the algorithm is designed to produce a perfect score. Similarly, the objective is that if the input and output have inaudible differences the score should not be degraded. Although PSQM does not have a direct correlation to MOS, the subjective quality is inferred from the objective quality. That is, if a person listens to a speech sample that has a PSQM value of 2, that person would think the quality was worse than a speech sample that had a PSQM value of 1. Some equipment translates a PSQM value

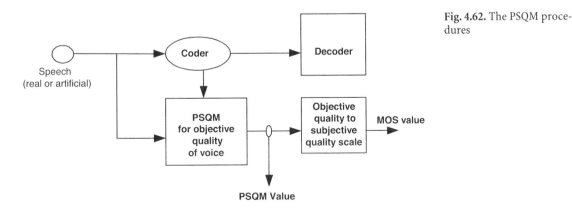

Fig. 4.62. The PSQM procedures

of 0 (good) to a mean opinion score (MOS) of 5, and a PSQM value of 6.5 (bad) to an MOS value of 1. In 1998, the ITU added another algorithm to Recommendation P.861-MNB (Measuring Normalized Blocks). This is constructed using a multiscale spectrogram-based comparison, and does not give as good results as PSQM. BT (British Telecom) has developed another standard that is known as PAMS (Perceptual Analysis Measurement System). This is not an international standard and BT licenses the algorithm. BT claims its performance is superior to PSQM. PSQM+ is not yet an ITU-T recommendation. It was proposed by the original developers of PSQM (KPN, the Netherlands) in December 1997. The algorithm takes the PSQM value and does some postprocessing on it based on PSQM and signal power. It accounts for different perceptions of volume or loud distortions and speech that has dropouts. The major problem with PSQM is the alignment of the output signal with the input signal. The delay through the network is unknown, and for an IP network it could be between 30 and 300 ms. The PSQM and PSQM+ algorithms operate by comparing the two signals. If they are not properly aligned the output will be invalid. Abacus uses a proprietary method for aligning these signals. If there is variation in the delay, this will affect the speech quality. Such a variation may occur because of the load on the network and packets are lost or delayed. The manufacturers of VoIP equipment try to minimize the variation in delay by optimizing the buffer size at the receiver. The variation in delay is called jitter. The optimization of buffer size generally results in little or no jitter during a spoken word. Instead, there may be changes to the gaps between words. These changes to the gaps are less annoying to a listener than are changes to the rate at which a spoken word is received. Regardless of the buffer size on the receiver, the VoIP network can still lose packets during a spoken word. Such losses are annoying to the listener. These losses are what PSQM+ is designed to measure. That is, the algorithm weighs the effect of these dropouts as they might be perceived by a listener. The algorithm is not "more tolerant" of these dropouts. In PSQM+, the correlation and synchronization are unchanged, but the algorithm improves the mapping from PSQM to MOS. On Abacus, you can select whether Abacus should report the PSQM value or the PSQM+ value. The source can be real or artificial speech. Speech or speech-like test signals are required because the system is designed to transmit only speech. Artificial speech has advantages in reduced redundancy and talker independence. It reproduces time and spectral characteristics of long-term average spectrum, short-term average spectrum, instantaneous amplitude distortion, and voiced and unvoiced structure of speech waveform. This sample is short in duration, about 2 s, and with no pauses. Thus it is suitable for use as a continuously spoken phrase. If you record your own speech, you should ensure that the speech sample has low ambient noise and short meaningful sentences. The reference power should be about –6 dBm, and recorded directly as PCM 64 Kb/s. You should use speech from different talkers (male, female and children), and use different languages. This will allow you to obtain the most objective results. You can use Abacus to test your network for the effect of talkers with high ambient noise, or poor digitization, but the results of the PSQM analysis (cf.

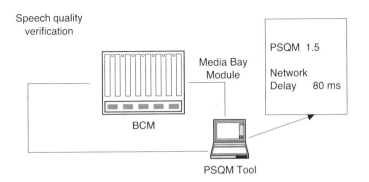

Speech quality
verification

Media Bay
Module

PSQM 1.5

Network
Delay   80 ms

BCM

PSQM Tool

Fig. 4.63. An example of PSQM verification in standalone mode; it should be ideal over an IP network

Fig. 4.63) will not give you realistic values for the quality of the network under test.

4.7.2.2 MOS

Subjective testing is essential for achieving high-quality voice services. This is especially true for IP networks, which use speech compression codecs, noise reduction algorithms, and other digital signal processing (DSP) techniques. These techniques introduce changes to the sound quality of the speech and delays in transmission. Subjective testing can reveal the effects of the changes on user satisfaction.

The results of subjective testing on the quality of speech signals are used to:

- Define performance targets.
- Guide network planning.
- Define national and international standards.

ITU-T defines subjective testing methods in Recommendation P.800. This recommendation includes methods such as the mean opinion score (MOS), degradation MOS (DMOS), and comparison MOS (CMOS). Each of these methods uses statistical techniques to quantify subjective responses from a group of users. MOS is used to determine the overall speech quality by asking listeners to rate the quality of a speech sample. DMOS require that subjects rate the magnitude of any perceived degradation, whereas CMOS can capture quality improvements as well as degradations.

In this section, I am going to discusses what is involved in performing a subjective audio quality experiment using MOS techniques. The section attempts to clarify common misconceptions concerning MOS.

4.7.2.2.1 Experimental Methods

There are three types of experimental methods used to determine speech quality: controlled listening tests, listening tests, and conversation tests. Controlled listening tests involve one or two expert listeners who assess defined test cases. Controlled tests can be completed quickly and cost effectively, but the results are not as reliable as those from listening or conversation tests. Codec designers often use controlled listening tests during the design phase to assess the effects of algorithmic changes on speech quality.

Listening tests consist of prerecorded samples that are played to subjects during a testing session. Subjects provide their quality ratings using pencil and paper or response keys connected to a computer. This allows a large number of test cases to be played relatively quickly. Subjects can provide quality ratings for about one hour so, depending on the length of the samples, up to 300 trials may be tested in one session.

The speech samples consist of two to four sentences and are 2–8 s in duration. Usually, the samples are recorded from four or more male and female speakers to ensure that a range of voices is heard during a study. Unfamiliar and unrelated sentences are used so subjects can attend to the speech quality rather than meaning. The sentences are also constructed to contain a good representation of speech sounds. Examples of these sentences include:

- What time of the year are parsnips planted?
- A tusk is used to make costly gifts.
- The Frenchman was gone when the sun rose.

In a typical experiment, speech samples are processed using different encoding algorithms. Modifications are introduced into some samples in order to mimic what occurs during normal use in a network environment. Subjects hear samples over a headset, handset or loudspeaker, depending on the purpose of the test, and record their ratings. The standard rating categories for MOS tests are defined as:

1 = bad   2 = poor   3 = fair   4 = good   5 = excellent

Conversation tests are used to assess the interactive aspects of a voice connection. A conversation test may be conducted in the laboratory or in the field. Laboratory tests can use simulated network connections to evaluate speech compression codecs, noise reduction algorithms, echo cancellers and other devices. Field tests are more difficult to control and tend to produce more variable results than lab tests, but they are important when assessing real-world performance.

Subjects in conversation tests are presented with randomly ordered test connections and are asked to perform a task. The conversations can be as short as 30 s or as long at 2 min depending on the feature or issue being evaluated. In conversation tests, only 20–30 connections can be evaluated during a session because of the time needed to complete each task.

For all the subjective tests, the randomization of the trials is usually constrained in order to get accurate results. For example, it is important to ensure that a particular sample does not always follow a sample that is considerably higher or lower in quality. This will cause the subject to rate the sample extremely, which will make it difficult to distinguish among small differences in quality. Also, subjects are given warm-up trials at the beginning of a test session to gain experience with the task, learn the rating scale, and to ask questions. This ensures that subjects feel confident about the procedure before continuing with the main test.

When preparing an experiment it is important to consider the number of subjects that are needed in order to get accurate results. In the case of listening tests, 40–60 subjects are necessary, and 30–40 subjects are ideal for conversation tests. This number of subjects produces standard deviations that are in an acceptable range and ensures the results can be statistically meaningful.

The subjects that are invited to an experiment are drawn from a pool that represents the general user population. They are generally people with no hearing problems and are unfamiliar with telephone and network technologies and DSP. Subjects are screened for hearing sensitivity and are not offered information about the research questions or specific comparisons in the experiment. This allows the subjects to participate in other experiments and become reliable when following instructions and concentrating on the task during the session. Some experiments do require subjects who have experience with certain technologies, such as cellular phones or overseas calls, and other special studies may require subjects with hearing limitations or other special requirements.

Analysis and interpretation of results: I have conducted some experiments in order to show you how to analyze MOS variations in different codecs. Therefore I have included standard cases and called reference cases in the experiment in order to assist in the interpretation of the results. These reference cases have known qualities or some known relationship with the test cases. For example, a current codec could be a reference case in an experiment that evaluates the quality of a new codec. Alternatively, a reference case may be a sample treated with a modulated noise reference unit (MNRU). MNRU is an ITU recommendation that describes a calibrated degradation added to a clean speech signal. MNRU cases can be used to ensure that listeners are responding as expected during a session and can provide reference scores based on a known degradation scale. The MNRU samples are randomly inserted in the experiment and then evaluated with the other samples during the analysis.

A statistical analysis of the subjective tests includes the calculation of means, standard deviations and confidence intervals. These statistics are used to determine the consistency of the data and to check for statistically reliable differences. Where differences are statistically reliable, conclusions are drawn concerning the differences observed.

The data in Fig. 4.64 shows sample MOS ratings for different codecs collected in four experiments. G.711 is a standard codec that provides a high-quality speech signal at the expense of a high bit-rate. G.711 is commonly used in telephone networks and often used as a reference case for subjective experiments. Reduced bit-rate codecs, such as G.726, G.729 and G.723.1, allow more calls in a system but they tend to have lower speech quality ratings.

The figure shows an important feature of MOS testing: there is a relatively large difference between the MOS scores in Experiments 1 and 4 for the G.729 codec. This is due to the context set by the other samples in each test, and to normal variability between experiments. The variability in scores illustrates that one MOS test cannot be used to define the quality of any codec. Nevertheless, in all four experiments, the pattern of results is the same and G.711 is always rated higher than the rest.

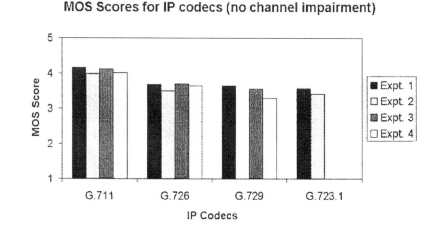

Considerations on the interpretation of MOS: There are two important constraints on the interpretation of MOS. First, MOS is not a fixed number. This is because it is derived from a study depending on the context in which it is gathered. In general, conclusions are drawn by examining and interpreting differences or patterns among the test cases in a study, rather than from the absolute number obtained for any particular case. For example, consider G.711, which generally receives an MOS rating in the range of 4 to 4.5: if the same G.711 samples are tested with wideband audio samples they will receive a rating around 2.

Second, because of the way the test cases are prepared, the results of actual listening tests may indicate the potential speech quality of each system, rather than the in-service quality. For example, end-to-end speech quality over IP networks depends on many factors that are difficult to examine in one experiment including:

- Intranet or internet systems
- Number of hops in the path
- Synchronization ("jitter") buffer size
- Acoustic and audio performance of terminal equipment
- Overall system traffic
- Packet loss
- Delay
- Type of codec used.

Subjective testing is the only method that can directly measure perceived quality. With careful design and preparation of experiments and test samples, subjective techniques are powerful measurement tools for examining the quality of voice services. A subjective assessment of speech quality using MOS lets developers and service providers understand factors that contribute to user satisfaction. However, caution must be exercised when referring to absolute MOS numbers and results that are drawn from different studies.

Customer opinion: Customer opinion, as a function of loudness loss, can vary with the test group and the particular test design. The opinion results presented in Fig. 4.64 are representative of laboratory conversation test results for telephone connections in which other characteristics such as circuit noise are contributing little impairment. These results indicate the importance of loudness loss control.

4.7.2.3 VoIP Engineering Guidelines

The following factors must be considered for deployment of a VoIP network:

Echo cancellation: When a two-wire telephone cable connects to a four-wire PBX interface or a CO interface, the system uses hybrid circuits to convert between two wires and four wires. Although hybrid circuits are very efficient in their conversion ability, a small percentage of telephony energy is not converted but instead is reflected back to the user. This is called echo.

If the user is near the PBX or CO switch, the echo comes back so quickly it cannot be detected. However, if the delay is more than about 10 ms, the user can hear an echo. To prevent this occurrence, gateway vendors include a special code in the DSPs that listens for the echo signal and subtracts it from the listener's audio signal.

Echo cancellation is important for gateway vendors because the IP network delay can be 40–50 ms, so the echo from the far-end hybrid can be important at the near end. Far-end echo cancellation removes this. Echo cancellation can cause broken speech in conversations in a low audio conversation. Although echo cancellation can be disabled, it is not recommended.

Non-linear processing: Non-linear processing (NLP) is part of echo cancellation. It improves echo cancellation by reducing remaining echo. NLP mutes background noise during periods of far-end silence and prevents additional comfort noise from occurring. Some listeners find muted background noise a problem. NLP can be disabled to prevent this, but with the trade-off of increased heard echo.

Jitter buffer: A major cause of reduced VQ is IP network packet delay and network jitter. Network delay represents the average length of time for a packet to move across a network. Network jitter represents the differences in arrival time of a packet. Both are important in determining VQ: delay is like the average, jitter is like the standard deviation.

To allow for differences in arrival time of a packet and continue to produce a steady outgoing stream of speech, the far-end gateway does not play out the speech when the first packet arrives. Instead, it holds it for some time in part of its memory called the jitter buffer, and then plays it out. The amount of this hold time is the measure of the jitter buffer; for example, a 50 ms hold time indicates a 50 ms jitter buffer.

As the network delay (total time, including codec processing time) exceeds about 200 ms, the two speakers increasingly use a half-duplex communications mode, where one speaks, the other listens and pauses to make sure the speaker is done. If the pauses are ill-timed, they end up "stepping" on each other's speech. This is the problem that occurs when two persons speak over a satellite telephony connection. The result is a reduction in VQ.

When a voice packet is delayed and does not arrive at the far end in time to fit into the voice stream going out of the far-end gateway, it is discarded, and the previous packet is replayed. If the scenario occurs often, or twice in a row, the listener hears reduced VQ.

The jitter buffer hold time adds to the delay, so if the network has high jitter, the effect is a long delay in the voice stream. For example, a network can have an average delay of 50 ms and a variability of 5 ms. The network is said to have 5 ms of jitter, a low figure. The jitter buffer hold time is only 5 ms, so the network total delay is 55 ms.

If a network has a low average delay of 15 ms, but 10% of the time the delay goes out to 100 ms, while 90% of the time the delay is a brief 4 ms, the jitter buffer is 100 ms and the total network delay is 115 ms, a long delay. Network jitter can be more important than average delay in many VoIP gateway applications.

VoIP gateway voice calls use an adaptive jitter buffer that changes the hold time over the duration of the call. The installer or administrator configures the maximum hold time.

VoIP gateway fax calls use a fixed jitter buffer that does not change the hold time over the duration of the call. Fax calls are more prone to packet loss. In conditions of high jitter, increased delay (through the use of a deeper jitter buffer) is preferred.

To adapt, VoIP gateway provides a separate jitter buffer setting for fax calls. The voice jitter buffer parameters directly affect the end-to-end delay and audio quality. IP telephony dynamically adjusts the size of the jitter buffer to adjust for jitter in the network. The installer or administrator sets the starting point for the jitter buffer.

Fax calls: Most of the readily available H.323 gateway system supports fax calls which automatically use the G.711 codec and require the associated bandwidth.

As the gateway does not know in advance that a call carries a fax transmission, it first establishes a voice channel. The voice channel can use G.729 or G.723.1 audio compression. When detecting the answering fax machine's called station identification (CED) tone, the terminating gateway performs the following operations:

- Starts the procedure to revert the speech path to a G.711, 64 Kb/s clear channel.
- Disables the adaptive jitter buffer feature.
- Sets the hold time for the jitter buffer to the value indicated in the local gateway settings to improve late IP packet tolerance.

The answering fax machine must produce its CED tone within 15 s of connection. The terminating gateway turns off CED tone detection after 15 s to prevent false tone detection during a voice call. This method sets the following restrictions:

- Interoperability with other IP gateways. A terminating gateway must support CED fax tone detection, and start the procedure as described in the previous paragraphs. An originating gateway must support the H.323 request mode procedure, but does not need to detect fax tones. The originating gateway must additionally be capable of supporting the large G.711 packets used for fax transmission.
- In order for the gateways to revert to a G.711 clear channel, the terminating fax machine must issue a CED tone when answering the call. Manually started fax transmissions, where the user at the terminating end first talks with the originating user before setting the terminating fax to receive the document, are not supported.
- Fax machines allow a maximum RTD of 1200 ms. Media processing in the two gateways introduces an RTD of approximately 300 ms, and the delay caused by the jitter buffer. If a 250 ms jitter buffer is used, IP latency must never exceed $1200 - [300 + (2 \times 250)] = 400$ ms RTD, or approximately 200 ms one way.

Fallback threshold: When choosing a VoIP gateway, it is better to choose a product that implements PBX and data transport in the same box. If such a product is available, more likely it will provide PSTN fallback capability. With PSTN fallback capability a new VoIP call can be redirected to the PSTN network if the data network condition is poor. The decision to understand when a fallback can be implied is guided through "fallback threshold parameters". There are two fallback threshold parameters: the receive fallback threshold (Rx) and the transmit fallback threshold (Tx), set on a per site pair basis.

For the fallback threshold to operate accurately it is important to verify the QoS values, measure them and then initiate the fallback.

The network manager must understand the deployment of QoS parameters for a network and the measurement of intranet QoS. The users of the enterprise voice and data services expect these services to meet a level of QoS which in turn affects the network design (Fig. 4.65). The purpose is to design and allocate enough resources in the network to meet user needs. QoS metrics or parameters help in meeting the needs required by the user of the service.

There are two interfaces that the installer needs to consider:

1. IP telephony interfaces with the end-users; voice services made available need to meet user QoS objectives.
2. The gateway's interface with the intranet; the service provided by the intranet is "best-effort delivery of IP packets", not guaranteed QoS for real-time voice transport. IP telephony translates the QoS objectives set by the end-users into IP-adjusted QoS objectives. The guidelines call these objectives the intranet QoS objectives.

In the process to determine the appropriate QoS level for operating the voice network, site pairs can have very different QoS measurements, either because some traffic flows are local, or because other traffic flows are inter-

Fig. 4.65. QoS considerations in a VoIP network

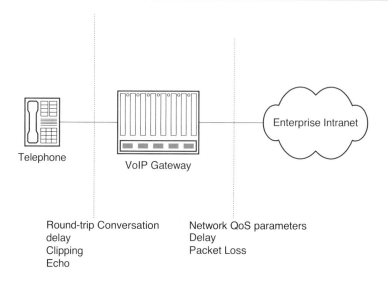

continental. The network administrator may consider setting a higher QoS level for the local sites compared to the international sites, keeping costs down for international WAN links.

Normally, the fallback threshold is set in both directions to the same QoS level. In site pairs where the applications are such that one direction of flow is more important, the installer or administrator can set up asymmetric QoS levels.

Enterprise edge uses routes to determine which outgoing facilities to use. A given destination code can have an alternate route configured. The alternate route is used if the main route is not available to process calls. For example, calls use the alternate route if all lines in the line pool are busy.

IP trunks can use this capability. Unique to IP trunks is the ability to take advantage of the QoS monitoring capability that is part of IP telephony. If fallback functionality is enabled, any QoS damage in the intranet, which causes any monitored remote gateway to exceed its threshold, results in the configuration of an alternate route (if configured). Until the QoS improves, IP trunks are all considered busy.

4.7.2.3.1 VoIP Network Analysis

This section describes possible actions to examine the sources of delay and error in the intranet. Several methods are useful for reducing one-way delay and packet loss. The key methods are:

- Reduce link delay.
- Reduce hop count.
- Adjust the jitter buffer size.
- Set IP telephony QoS objectives.

Reduce link delay: In this and the next few subsections, the guidelines examine different ways of reducing one-way delay and packet loss in the network.

The time taken for a voice packet to queue on the transmission buffer of a link until received at the next hop router is the link delay. Methods to reduce link delays are:

- Upgrade link capacity to reduce the serialization delay of the packet, but more so, to reduce the utilization of the link, reducing the queuing delay. Before upgrading a link, the installer or administrator must check both routers connected to the link for the upgrade and ensure correct router configuration guidelines.
- Change the link from satellite to terrestrial to reduce the link delay by an order of 100 to 300 ms.
- Put into operation a priority queuing rule.
- Identify the links with the highest use and the slowest traffic. Estimate the link delay of these links using the Traceroute program. The service provider should provide help with improving your QoS.

Reducing hop count: Reducing end-to-end delay can reduce hop count, especially on hops that move across WAN links. Some of the ways to reduce hop count include:

- Improve meshing. Add links to help improve meshing, adding a link from R1 to R4 instead of having the call routed from R1 to R2 to R3 to R4 reducing the hop count by two.
- Router reduction. Join colocated gateways on one larger and more powerful router.

Adjust the jitter buffer size: The parameters for the voice jitter buffer directly affect the end-to-end delay and audio quality. IP telephony dynamically adjusts the size of the jitter buffer to adjust for jitter in the network. The installer or administrator sets the starting point for the jitter buffer.

The jitter buffer can be lowered to decrease one-way delay and provide less waiting time for late packets. Late packets that are lost are replaced with silence. Quality decreases with lost packets. The size of the jitter buffer can be increased to improve quality when jitter is high.

IP telephony fax calls use a fixed jitter buffer that does not change the hold time over the duration of the call. Fax calls are more prone to packet loss. In conditions of high jitter, the delay can be increased (through the use of a deeper jitter buffer). To allow for this increase, IP telephony provides a separate jitter buffer setting for fax calls.

Reduce packet errors: Packet errors in intranets correlate to congestion in the network. Packet errors are high because the packets are dropped if they arrive faster than the link can transmit.

Identifying which links are the most used to upgrade removes a source of packet errors on a distinct flow. A reduction in hop count provides for less occurrences for routers and links to drop packets.

Other causes of packet errors not related to delay are as follows:

- Bad link quality
- Overloaded CPU

- Saturation
- LAN saturation
- Limited size of jitter buffer.

If the underlying circuit has transmission problems, high line error rates, outages, or other problems, the link quality is bad. Other services such as X.25, frame relay or ATM can affect the link. The service provider should be checked for more information.

The router's threshold CPU utilization level should be found, and checked to see if the router conforms to the threshold. If a router is overloaded, the router is continuously processing intensive tasks. Process-intensive tasks prevent the router from forwarding packets, and it should be reconfigured or upgraded.

Routers can be overloaded when there are too many high-capacity and high-traffic links configured on it. Routers must be configured to vendor guidelines.

Saturation refers to too many packets on the intranet. Packets can be dropped on improperly planned or damaged LAN segments.

Packets that arrive late at the destination are not placed in the jitter buffer and are lost packets.

Routing issues: Routing problems cause unnecessary delay. Some routes are better than other routes. The Traceroute program allows the user to detect routing anomalies and to correct these problems.

Possible high delay differences causes are:

- routing instability
- wrong load splitting
- frequent changes to the intranet
- asymmetrical routing.

Components of delay: End-to-end delay is the result of many delay components. The major components of delay are as follows:

- Propagation delay: This is the result of the mileage and the medium of links moved across. Within a country, the one-way propagation delay over terrestrial lines is under 18 ms. Within the USA, the propagation delay from coast to coast is under 40 ms. To estimate the propagation delay of long-haul and transoceanic circuits, a rule of thumb of 1 ms per 100 terrestrial miles (160 km) can be used . If a circuit goes through a satellite system, estimating each hop between earth stations adds 260 ms to the propagation delay.
- Serialization delay: This is the time it takes to transmit the voice packet 1 bit at a time over a WAN link. The serialization delay depends on the voice packet size and the link bandwidth, and is the result of the formula in Fig. 4.66.
- Queuing delay: This is the time it takes for a packet to wait in the transmission queue of the link before it is serialized. On a link where packets are processed in a first-come, first-served order, the average queuing time in ms is the result of the formula in Fig. 4.67.

$$\text{queuing time in ms} = p \times p \times \frac{\text{average packet size in bytes}}{(1-p)(\text{link speed in kbit/s})}$$

Fig. 4.66. Serialization delay estimating formula

Where p is the link utilization level.

$$\text{Serialization delay in ms} = 8 \times \frac{\text{IP packet size in bytes}}{\text{link bandwidth in kb/s}}$$

Fig. 4.67. The queuing delay formula

The average size of intranet packets carried over WAN links generally is between 250 and 500 bytes. Queuing delays can be important for links with bandwidth under 512 Kb/s, while with higher speed links they can allow higher utilization levels.

Routing and hop count: Each site pair takes different routes over the intranet. The route taken determines the number and type of delay components that add to end-to-end delay. Sound routing in the network depends on correct network design.

Bibliography

Books

AMD. Ethernet/IEEE 802.3 Family: 1994 World Network Data Book/Handbook. AMD, 1994.

Roger L. Freeman. *Practical Data Communications.* New York: John Wiley & Sons, 1995.

Jerry D. Gibson. *The Communication Handbook.* Boca Raton, FL: CRC/IEEE Press, 1997.

Gilbert Held. *Ethernet Networks.* New York: John Wiley & Sons, 1996.

Christian Huitema. *IPv6: The New Internet Protocol.* Englewood Cliffs, NJ: Prentice Hall PTR, 1996.

Kalevi Kilkki. *Differentiated Service for the Internet.* Indianapolis: Macmillan Technical Publishing, 1999.

Andrew S. Tanenbaum. *Computer Networks (third edition).* Englewood Cliffs, NJ: Prentice Hall PTR, 1994.

Thomas M. Thomas II. *OSPF Network Design Solutions.* Indianapolis: Cisco Press/Macmillan Technical Publishing, 1998.

Internet Drafts

Loa Andersson, Paul Doolan, Nancy Feldman, Andre Fredette, Bob Thomas. *LDP Specification* (draft-ietf-mpls-ldp-11.txt). August 2000.

Christophe Boscher, Pierrick Cheval, Liwen Wu, Eric Gray. *LDP State Machine* (draft-ietf-mpls-ldp-state-03.txt). January 2000.

J. Boyle, R. Cohen, D. Durham, S. Herzog, R. Rajan, A. Sastry. *The COPS Protocol* (draft-ietf-rap-cops-08.txt). February 2000.

R. Callon, P. Doolan, N. Feldman, A. Fredette, G. Swallow, A. Viswanathan. *A Framework for Multiprotocol Label Switching* (draft-ietf-mpls-framework-05.txt). September 1999.

M. Fine, K. McCloghrie, J. Seligson, K. Chan, S. Hahn, A. Smith, Francis Reichmeyer. *Framework Policy Information Base* (draft-ietf-rap-framework-pib-00.txt). March 2000.

S. Herzog. *RSVP Extensions for Policy Control* (draft-ietf-rap-rsvp-ext-06.txt). July 2000.

Kwok Ho Chan, David Durham, Silvano Gai, Shai Herzog, Keith McCloghrie, Francis Reichmeyer, John Seligson, Andrew Smith, Raj Yavatkar. *COPS Usage for Policy Provisioning* (draft-ietf-rap-pr-02.txt). October 2000.

Francois Le Faucheur, Liwen Wu, Bruce Davie, Shahram Davari, Pasi Vaananen, Ram Krishnan, Pierrick Cheval, Juha Heinanen. *MPLS Support of Differentiated Services* (draft-ietf-mpls-diff-ext-07.txt). August 2000.

J. Lennox, H. Schulzrinne. *CPL: A Language for User Control of Internet Telephony Services* (draft-ietf-iptel-cpl-01.txt). November 2000.

J. Lennox, H. Schulzrinne. *Call Processing Language Framework and Requirements* (draft-ietf-iptel-cpl-framework-02.txt). November 2000.

D. Moore, E. Ellesson, J. Strassner. *Policy Framework Core Information Model* (draft-ietf-policy-core-info-model-02.txt). October 1999.

K. Nichols, Brian Carpenter. *Definition of Differentiated Services Behavior Aggregates and Rules for their Specification* (draft-ietf-diffserv-ba-def-01.txt). February 2000.

Eric C. Rosen, Arun Viswanathan, Ross Callon. *Multiprotocol Label Switching Architecture* (draft-ietf-mpls-arch-07.txt). July 2000.

Eric C. Rosen, Yakov Rekhter, Daniel Tappan, Guy Fedorkow, Dino Farinacci, Tony Li, Alex Conta. *MPLS Label Stack Encoding* (draft-ietf-mpls-label-encaps-08.txt). July 2000.

J.Rosenberg, H.Schulzrinne. *A Framework for Telephony Routing over IP* (draft-ietf-iptel-gwloc-framework-06.txt). June 2000.

A. Smith, D. Partain, J. Seligson. *Definitions of Managed Objects for Common Open Policy Service (COPS) Protocol Clients* (draft-ietf-rap-cops-client-mib-02.txt). March 2000.

R. Yavatkar, D. Pendarakis, R. Guerin. *A Framework for Policy-based Admission Control* (http://www.ietf.org/internet-drafts/draft-ietf-rap-framework-03.txt). February 2000.

RFCs

J. Postel. *ASSIGNED NUMBERS* (RFC 790). September 1981.

Information Sciences Institute, University of Southern California prepared for Defense Advanced Research Projects Agency. *INTERNET PROTOCOL DARPA INTERNET PROGRAM PROTOCOL SPECIFICATION* (RFC 791). September 1981.

R. Braden. Requirements for Internet Hosts – Communication Layers (RFC 1122). October 1989.

J. Moy. *OSPF protocol analysis* (RFC 1245). July 1991.

Y. Rekhter, T. Li. *A Border Gateway Protocol 4* (RFC 1771). March 1995.

Y. Rekhter, P. Gross. *Application of the Border Gateway Protocol in the Internet* (RFC 1772). March 1995.

H. Schulzrinne, S. Casner, R. Frederick, V. Jacobson. *RTP: A Transport Protocol for Real-Time Applications* (RFC 1889). January 1996.

J. Halpern, S. Bradner. *RIPv1 Applicability Statement for Historic Status* (RFC 1923). March 1996.

S. Sherry, G. Meyer. *Protocol Analysis for Triggered RIP* (RFC 2092). January 1997.

R. Braden, L. Zhang, S. Berson, S. Herzog, S. Jamin. *Resource ReSerVation Protocol (RSVP) – Version 1 Functional Specification* (RFC 2205). September 1997.

J. Wroclawski. *Specification of the Controlled-Load Network Element Service* (RFC 2211). September 1997.

S. Shenker, C. Partridge, R. Guerin. *Specification of Guaranteed Quality of Service* (RFC 2212). September 1997.

S. Shenker, J. Wroclawski. *General Characterization Parameters for Integrated Service Network Elements* (RFC 2215). September 1997.

S. Shenker, J. Wroclawski. *Network Element Service Specification Template* (RFC 2216). September 1997.

J. Moy. *OSPF Version 2* (RFC 2328). April 1998.

S. Deering, R. Hinden. *Internet Protocol, Version 6 (IPv6) Specification* (RFC 2460). December 1998.

K. Nichols, S. Blake, F. Baker, D. Black. *Definition of the Differentiated Services Field (DS Field) in the IPv4 and IPv6 Headers* (RFC 2474). December 1998.

S. Blake, D. Black, M. Carlson, E. Davies, Z. Wang, W. Weiss. *An Architecture for Differentiated Services* (RFC 2475). December 1998.

J. Boyle, R. Cohen, D. Durham, S. Herzog, R. Rajan, A. Sastry. *COPS usage for RSVP* (RFC 2479). January 2000.

J. Heinanen, F. Baker, W. Weiss, J. Wroclawski. *Assured Forwarding PHB Group* (RFC 2597). June 1999.

V. Jacobson, K. Nichols, K. Poduri. *An Expedited Forwarding PHB* (RFC 2598). June 1999.

J. Boyle, R. Cohen, D. Durham, S. Herzog, R. Rajan, A. Sastry. *The COPS (Common Open Policy Service) Protocol* (RFC 2748). January 2000.

S. Herzog. *RSVP Extensions for Policy Control* (RFC 2750). January 2000.

R. Yavatkar, D. Pendarakis, R. Guerin. *A Framework for Policy-based Admission Control* (RFC 2753). January 2000.

IEEE Standards

802-1990 IEEE Standards for Local and Metropolitan Area Networks: *Overview and Architecture.*

802.1Q-1998 IEEE Standard for Local and Metropolitan Area Networks: *Virtual Bridge Local Area Networks.*

802.3-1998 Edition Information technology–*Telecommunications and information exchange between systems–Local and metropolitan area networks–Specific requirements–Part 3: Carrier sense multiple access with collision detection (CSMA/CD) access method and physical layer specifications.*

802.3ab-1999 Supplement to IEEE Std 802.3, 1998 Edition: *Physical Layer Parameters and Specifications for 1000 Mb/s Operation over 4-Pair of Category 5 Balanced Copper Cabling, Type 1000BASE-T.*

802.5c-1991 (R1997) Supplement to IEEE Std 802.5–1989: *Recommended Practice for Dual Ring Operation with Wrapback Reconfiguration.*

802.5t-2000 Supplement to IEEE Standard for Information technology: *Telecommunications and information exchange between systems–Local and metropolitan area networks–Specific requirements–Part 5: Token ring access method and physical layer specifications: 100 Mbit/s Dedicated Token Ring Operation Over 2-Pair Cabling.*

802.11a-1999 Supplement to Information technology: *Telecommunications and information exchange between systems–Local and metropolitan area networks–Specific requirements–Part 11: Wireless LAN Medium Access Control (MAC) and Physical Layer (PHY) Specifications: High Speed Physical Layer (PHY) in the 5 GHz Band.*

802.11b-1999 Supplement to Information technology: *Telecommunications and information exchange between systems–Local and metropolitan area networks–Specific requirements–Part 11: Wireless LAN Medium Access Control (MAC) and Physical Layer (PHY) Specifications Higher Speed Physical Layer (PHY) Extension in the 2.4 GHz band.*

8802-2: 1998 (ISO/IEC) [ANSI/IEEE 802.2, 1998 Edition]: *Information technology–Telecommunications and information exchange between systems–Local and Metropolitan area networks–Specific requirements–Part 2: Logical link control.*

8802-3: 1996 (ISO/IEC) [ANSI/IEEE Std 802.3, 1996 Edition]: Information technology–*Telecommunications and information exchange between systems–Local and metropolitan area networks–Specific requirements–Part 3: Carrier sense multiple access with collision detection (CSMA/CD) access method and physical layer specifications.*

8802-5: 1998 (ISO/IEC) [ANSI/IEEE 802.5, 1998 Edition]: *Information technology–Telecommunications and information exchange between systems–Local and metropolitan area networks–Specific requirements–Part 5: Token ring access method and physical layer specifications.*

8802-5: 1998/Amd. 1: 1998 (ISO/IEC) [ANSI/IEEE 802.5j and 802.5r, 1998 Editions]: *Information technology–Telecommunications and information exchange between systems–Local and metropolitan area networks–Specific requirements–Part 5: Token ring access method and physical layer specifications– Amendment 1: Dedicated token ring operation and fibre optic media.*

8802-11: 1999 (ISOIEC) (IEEE Std 802.11, 1999 Edition): *Information technology–Telecommunications and information exchange between systems–Local and metropolitan area networks–Specific requirements–Part 11: Wireless LAN Medium Access Control (MAC) and Physical Layer (PHY) Specifications.*

P802.3ad, D3.1 Supplement to IEEE Std 802.3, 1998 Edition: *Link Aggrega-tion.*

15802-2 : 1995 (ISO/IEC) [ANSI/IEEE Std 802.1B, 1995 Edition]: *Information technology-Telecommunications and information exchange between sys-tems-Local and metropolitan area networks-Common specifications-Part 2: LAN/MAN management.*

15802-3: 1998 (ISO/IEC) [ANSI/IEEE Std 802.1D, 1998 Edition]: *Information technology-Telecommunications and information exchange between sys-tems-Local and metropolitan area networks-Common specifications-Me-dia access control (MAC) bridges.*

15802-4: 1994 (ISO/IEC) [ANSI/IEEE Std 802.1 E, 1994 Edition]: *Information technology-Telecommunications and information exchange between sys-tems-Local and metropolitan area networks-Common specifications-Part 4: System load protocol.*

15802-5 : 1998 (ISO/IEC) [ANSI/IEEE Std 802.1G, 1998 Edition]: *Information technology-Telecommunications and information exchange between sys-tems-Local and metropolitan area networks-Common specifications-Part 5: Remote Media Access Control (MAC) Bridging.*

Index